The Early Church in Wales and the West

Recent work in Early Christian Archaeology, History and Place-Names

Edited by

Nancy Edwards and Alan Lane

Oxbow Monograph 16
1992

Published by
Oxbow Books, Park End Place, Oxford OX1 1HN

© The individual authors 1992

ISBN 0 946897 37 9

This book is available direct from
Oxbow Books, Park End Place, Oxford, OX1 1HN
(Phone: 0-865-241249; Fax: 0-865-794449)

and

The David Brown Book Company
PO Box 5605, Bloomington, IN 47407, USA
(Phone: 812-331-0266; Fax: 812-331-0277)

Printed in Great Britain by
The Short Run Press, Exeter

Contents

List of Contributors

Elizabeth Alcock, 29 Hamilton Dr, Glasgow G12 8DW, Scotland

Diane Brook, 7 Werfa St, Cardiff CF2 5EW, Wales

Dr Ken Dark, Department of Anglo-Saxon, Norse, and Celtic, 9 West Rd, Cambridge CB3 9DP, England

Professor Wendy Davies, Department of History, University College, London WCIE 6BT, England

Dr Nancy Edwards, School of History and Welsh History (Archaeology), University College of North Wales, Bangor LL57 2DG, Wales

Canon J. Wyn Evans, Trinity College, Carmarthen SA31 3EP, Wales

Dr Ann Hamlin, Historic Monuments and Buildings, 5–33 Hill St, Belfast BT1 2LA, Northern Ireland

Heather James, Dyfed Archaeological Trust, The Old Palace, Abergwili, Carmarthen SA31 2JG, Wales

Terrence James, formerly of Dyfed Archaeological Trust, and now of RCAHMW, Plas Crug, Aberystwyth, Wales

Jeremy Knight, Cadw, Brunel House, 2 Fitzalan Rd, Cardiff CF2 1UY, Wales

Dr Alan Lane, School of History and Archaeology, University of Wales College of Cardiff, Cardiff CF1 3XU, Wales

Elizabeth O'Brien, Corpus Christi College, Oxford OX1 4JF, England

Ann Preston-Jones, Goonbell Chapel, St Agnes, Cornwall, England

Dr Huw Pryce, School of History and Welsh History, University College of North Wales, Bangor LL57 2DG, Wales

Tomos Roberts, Department of Manuscripts, University College of North Wales, Bangor LL57 2DG, Wales

Professor Charles Thomas, Lambessow, St Clement, Truro, Cornwall TR1 1TB, England

List of Figures

Preface

THE MAIN AIM of this book is to bring together the results of recent archaeological work on the early Welsh church. However, the archaeological evidence cannot be viewed in isolation, either from the documentary sources or the place-names. Complementary work outside Wales, from the English borderland, Cornwall, Ireland and Scotland has also been included, with the particular aims of, first, demonstrating methodologies which might be applicable to the Welsh material and, second, highlighting parallels and contrasts with it.

This book has grown out of a conference held at the University of Wales College of Cardiff in April 1989. Much of the work presented there was still in progress but, in view of the new evidence and interpretations which emerged during the conference, publication of the papers seemed a high priority. With the exception of Eric Cambridge's study of the Anglo-Saxon church, which he had already agreed to publish elsewhere (1989), and Ken Dark's new classification of the Class I monuments, which is also to be published elsewhere, all the original papers are included, though some are in a substantially revised form. In addition, there are two contributions on Ireland. Ann Hamlin's article on the problems of identifying the location and function of early Irish church sites was not given at the conference owing to illness. Elizabeth O'Brien's paper was commissioned subsequently because the relevance of her work on Irish burial became increasingly obvious as the conference progressed. Charles Thomas' 'Concluding remarks', which here appear in a slightly abridged form, were given as the original conclusion to the conference. They provide a glimpse of what aroused particular interest at the time and suggest some avenues for future research. His comments on the papers not published here have been omitted.

Our hope is that the publication of these papers will stimulate further work and open new avenues for research on the early Welsh church. We also hope that the important results of current work in Wales will be brought to a larger audience and in turn play their part in wider debates about early Christianity in Britain and Ireland.

Acknowledgements

EACH PAPER CARRIES its own acknowledgements but the editors would also like to express their thanks to the following institutions and individuals for their help with the organization of the original conference: the Board of Celtic Studies of the University of Wales; the staff of the Department of Extra-mural Studies, University of Wales College of Cardiff (UWCC) and in particular Peter Webster; the School of History and Archaeology (UWCC); Leslie Alcock; David Crouch; Richard Gem; Elizabeth O'Brien and Deirdre O'Sullivan. For help in the preparation of the subsequent publication we would like to thank Ewan Campbell; Viola Dias; June Hughes; John Illsley; Terry James; Alec McSkimming; Huw Pryce; and Cathy Rees.

The Archaeology of the Early Church in Wales: An Introduction

Nancy Edwards and Alan Lane

The archaeology of the early Welsh church has received little attention compared with that of many other parts of Britain and Ireland. This is partly to do with the meagreness of the documentary sources (Davies, W. 1982a, 198–216): for example, there is nothing to parallel Adomnán's early description of Iona (Anderson, A.O. and Anderson, M.O. 1961) or Bede's of Monkwearmouth, Jarrow and other Northumbrian monasteries (Plummer 1896) which have provided the crucial inspiration for and impetus behind rewarding excavations (Cramp 1969; 1976; Daniels 1988). But more important is the very scantiness of the upstanding remains (see Pryce below). There is nothing to compare with the round towers of Ireland (Edwards, N. 1990, 127–8) or the stone churches of Anglo-Saxon England (Taylor, H.M. and Taylor, J. 1965; 1978). Even the considerable quantity of sculpture — early inscribed memorials, cross-marked stones and carved crosses (Nash-Williams 1950) — has been overshadowed by the more elaborate and often better executed monuments of Ireland, Scotland and Anglo-Saxon England (Edwards, N. 1990, 161–71; Allen and Anderson 1903; Cramp 1984; Bailey and Cramp 1988). The problems of the historical and archaeological evidence have also been exacerbated because of the limited number of people involved in research on early medieval Wales.

It was the early Christian sculpture which first attracted antiquarian attention to the archaeological evidence for the early Welsh church. For example, in Gibson's revised and enlarged edition of Camden's *Britannia* with additions by Edward Lhuyd (1722), many inscribed stones were described and illustrated, as were some carved crosses, such as Maen Achwyfan (Flints.) and those at Llantwit Major (Glamorgan). The discovery of long-cist graves was also sometimes reported as, for example, at Mathry churchyard (Pembs.) (Fenton 1810, 28, note r) and near Pentrefoelas (Denbigh.), during the construction of Telford's road, when 40 long-cist graves were uncovered in a field called Dôl Trebeddau (Anon. 1819–20). One of these graves was covered by an inscribed stone (Nash-Williams 1950, no. 183) which was found face-downwards, clearly in a reused position. Possibly the earliest recorded archaeological excavation of an ecclesiastical site in Wales was conducted in 1846 by W.O. Stanley at Tywyn-y-Capel (*Llansanffraid*, Anglesey). On this sand-dune site, now largely destroyed by sea erosion, Stanley uncovered 60–70 long-cist graves and the drystone foundations of a chapel which had stood until comparatively recent times (Stanley 1846).

The foundation of the Cambrian Archaeological Association in the same year heralded a great upsurge in the report and study of all aspects of Welsh archaeology, including the church. This was also the period when many medieval churches in Wales were either heavily restored or completely demolished to make way for new buildings (A.E. 1846). The need to prevent such mass destruction heightened antiquarian interest in medieval church architecture and new discoveries of earlier remains were also made. For example, at Merthyr Mawr (Glamorgan) an inscribed stone was found during church restoration (Knight 1984b, 374; see below) while at Llangaffo (*Merthyr Caffo*, Anglesey) cross-marked stones were revealed during the destruction of the fifteenth-century church (RCAHMW 1937, 88–9). Because of new discoveries such as these it is also possible to detect a deepening understanding of the inscribed stones and other sculpture which were first catalogued by T.J. Westwood (1876–9). The late nineteenth century also saw major advances in the study of Celtic philology in the course of which John Rhŷs considered the language of the inscribed stones (eg. Rhŷs 1877a, 272–328, 379–415; 1877b), while Romilly Allen made a study of the Insular ornament on the crosses (eg. Allen 1899; 1989).

Excavation of ecclesiastical sites was, however, rare, no doubt because of the continuing use of the majority for burial and worship. One exception was at Clynnog Fawr (Caerns.), where

Basil Stallybrass (1914) excavated the floor of St Beuno's Chapel (which had formerly housed the saint's relics) adjoining the main church and uncovered an earlier chapel together with burials, including at least one long-cist. The long-abandoned hermitage site on Ynys Seiriol (Anglesey) also attracted archaeological attention (Hughes, H. 1901) as did the ruinous Chapel of St Justinian near St David's (Pembs.) (Boake 1926). In retrospect early excavations at the Roman town of Caerwent (Monmouth.) can also be seen as important for the light they shed on both the origins of Christianity in Wales and continuing Christian activity long after the Roman withdrawal (see below).

Apart from excavations such as these, continued reports of the discovery of long-cists, and brief descriptions of many ecclesiastical sites in the Royal Commission volumes, most research continued to concentrate on the sculpture. R.A.S. Macalister's *Corpus Inscriptionum Insularum Celticarum* (1945; 1949), which catalogued inscriptions throughout the Celtic West, was unfortunately marred by inaccuracies. However, V.E. Nash-Williams' *Early Christian Monuments of Wales* (1950) provided not just an illustrated catalogue of the Welsh sculpture, but also set out to classify and date it as well as consider its origins and affinities. Though some of the views expressed are now being called into question (see Knight and Dark below), the work remains of continuing importance (a new edition is in preparation) as does Kenneth Jackson's discussion of the language of the inscribed stones (1953) though this, also, is now in need of some revision.

A new departure can be detected in the work of the historical geographer E.G. Bowen (1954; 1977). On the one hand he sought to trace the origins, growth and spheres of contact of the early Welsh church by studying the distribution of dedications to particular 'Celtic' saints. On the other he made a study of the locations of church sites with Celtic dedications and the forms of any associated settlements. Aspects of his work, especially his adoption of the concept of a pan-Celtic monastic church (see Davies below for the problems of this approach) and his rather uncritical use of dedications and suspect historical sources to write an account of the peregrinations of the early saints and their supposed foundation of early church sites, have proved particularly misleading, though such views continue to be espoused in some more popular accounts of the early Welsh church (e.g. Victory 1977). On the other hand his ideas on the location of church sites and the potential value of dedications to local and other 'Celtic' saints as a tool for identifying early church sites continue to provide inspiration for modern scholars (see below).

Over the last 25 years there has been an increasing interest in all aspects of the archaeological study of the early church in Britain and Ireland. But work in Wales has often been overshadowed by more dramatic discoveries elsewhere and there has sometimes been the tendency to assume that the archaeology of the Welsh church must be more-or-less identical with that in the other Celtic countries, especially Ireland. In a series of conference papers on *Christianity in Britain 300–700* W.H. Davies, reviewing the evidence for the early Welsh church, recognized the archaeological potential but remarked, 'With one important exception [the sculpture] virtually nothing of any direct importance can be discerned for the contemporary ecclesiastical scene' (1968, 131). Some years later in a similar conference on *The Early Church in Western Britain and Ireland* (Pearce 1982), Wales is not represented. Elsewhere the Welsh archaeological evidence sometimes appears on the sidelines (e.g. Thomas, C. 1971; 1981a) but seldom takes centre stage. Where the Welsh church is a major subject under consideration, results have been mixed. Archaeology plays a minor role in Siân Victory's *The Celtic Church in Wales* (1977), a book which testifies to the problems of explaining the subject to the general reader with the type of evidence available, especially when it is compared with its companion volume on the Irish church (Hughes and Hamlin 1977) where the wealth of information makes the task undoubtedly easier. But archaeology is used much more successfully as an adjunct to the historical evidence in both Wendy Davies' *Wales in the Early Middle Ages* (1982a) and Jeremy Knight's study of Glamorgan in the period AD 400–1100 (Knight 1984a; 1984b).

The volume of archaeological excavation in Wales has greatly increased since the late 1960s and especially since the inception of the four Welsh Archaeological Trusts in 1974–5. The emphasis has naturally been on rescue work, but this has led to the investigation of a number of minor ecclesiastical sites and cemeteries (see H. James below) which might not otherwise have attracted attention, often with interesting results. Many of the sites excavated have yet to reach final publication and one of the aims of this volume is to place them in a broader context and make them known to a wider audience. Survey work, particularly air photography (see T. James below), together with topographical studies (see Brook below) (though patchy in coverage and underfunded in execution) are also proving of immense importance in our bid to gain a better understanding of the archaeology of the Welsh church.

Evidence for the Early Medieval Church in Wales

In order to extend our knowledge of the early Welsh church from its origins up to the coming of the Normans, and to identify ecclesiastical sites and their functions, it is important to make use of *all* types of evidence: historical, onomastic, topographical and archaeological. The worth of this approach has been proven for both the Irish and the Cornish material (see Preston-Jones and Hamlin below). It is equally valuable for Wales, where the overall scantiness of the evidence means that it is often only possible to recognize an early site by putting together various small pieces of information culled from widely differing sources which together suggest its antiquity (e.g. Brook, D.L. 1985–8). It is like having a few jig-saw pieces, some of which may join, but the majority remain missing, many irretrievably.

The pre-twelfth-century historical sources for the early Welsh church have, for the most part, been exhaustively studied and go some way towards illuminating the broader issues of church organization and institutions, spirituality and ecclesiastical wealth (Davies, W. 1982a, 141–93, 198–216; see Pryce below). Yet there is still no comprehensive study of the early church in Wales which integrates the results of modern scholarship (Wormald 1978, 198–200). However, Michael Lapidge has given us a foretaste of what might be won from a close study of the textual evidence. The possibility that aspects of Latin learning were preserved in a direct and remarkably conservative succession, from the fifth or sixth century to the later pre-Norman period (Lapidge 1986) has important implications for our view of the early Welsh church as has the recognition that an education in late classical rhetoric lies behind the language of Gildas (Lapidge 1984).

But the importance of the early church in Wales in the development of Christianity in Britain and Ireland as a whole has not been fully explored in recent work. Olson's research on early monasteries in Cornwall points to South Wales as a major source of spiritual leadership

which, to judge by the career of St Samson, also extended to Brittany (1989, 9–20, 48–50). Ann Preston-Jones likewise identifies South Wales as a key area (see below). There is certainly also British influence on the early Irish church in the sixth century, some of which must have come from what was to become Wales (Sharpe 1984c, 200–1). In contrast after the sixth century Irish influence on the Welsh church is much better attested than vice versa (Chadwick 1958; Ó Riain 1981; Lapidge 1986). In the case of Anglo-Saxon England the career of Asser at Alfred's court and the presence of Welsh ecclesiastical manuscripts in English churches in the late ninth and tenth centuries implies a debt to Welsh learning in Wessex (Hughes, K. 1970, 58–9; David Dumville, unpublished O'Donnell lectures 1978 'England and the Celtic world in the ninth and tenth century').

Some aspects of the organization of the early medieval Welsh church and the pastoral care it gave to the lay population are becoming clearer. Huw Pryce (forthcoming) has noted that 'The cumulative impression conveyed by the evidence ... is that the key component of the ecclesiastical structure in Wales from the sixth century onwards were communities to which a monastic vocabulary was applied, but which also contained ordinary clergy who could have performed pastoral work'. The difficulty is what term should be given to these communities? Pryce suggests *monasterium* rather than *clas*. In the past the latter has often been applied, frequently in a rather sloppy fashion, sometimes with the implication that such communities were degenerate. In fact the term *clas* is not used unequivocally to apply to an ecclesiastical community in Wales until the twelfth century and even thereafter its meaning is not entirely clear. Sources of the twelfth and thirteenth centuries do, however, show that communities, sometimes referred to as *clasau*, headed by abbots, existed in areas of the country which remained in native hands (see Evans below). Although by this stage the abbot might be a layman and the community might consist of both clerical and/or lay portioners, it probably also contained an ordained priest. Sources for this period also indicate a pattern of mother and daughter churches. These major ecclesiastical communities or mother churches are frequently traceable back to the pre-Norman period. Their number may have been comparatively small since they seem to have had large *parochiae* coterminous with the secular administrative division of *cantref* or *commote*. Many of the daughter churches, which would have served the local population, may have been founded only from the eleventh century onwards, especially in the sparsely settled upland areas. In lowland parts, especially south-east Wales, there is more evidence of local churches at an earlier date. Elsewhere in the lowlands archaeological evidence and the known existence of local cult sites combine to suggest their existence.

For the archaeologist the pre-twelfth-century historical sources for the early Welsh church are of the most immediate value for identifying particular sites and sometimes indicating their function and status (see below). However this is not always as straightforward as it might first appear and some of the problems of trying to identify different types of ecclesiastical sites from the historical and archaeological record are demonstrated for northern Ireland by Ann Hamlin (see below). There can be little doubt that in the past there has been a tendency for archaeologists to focus on the term 'monastery', and in the case of Wales *clas*, because of the dominant 'Age of the Saints' view of the Welsh church when, in reality, things were much more complex. Indeed, the distinction between a monastic and a secular church is probably only made clear with the arrival of the Normans in the late eleventh century (Cowley 1977, 1–39) and sites described in the sources using a monastic vocabulary were much more diverse than communities simply sharing a monastic rule.

It is also important to make use of the more plentiful twelfth-century and later documentary sources for the light they may be able to shed on the existence of ecclesiastical sites at an earlier date because of the survival of archaic institutions and practices. This is amply demonstrated in Wyn Evan's paper on the *clas* in twelfth- and thirteenth-century Wales (see below).

Place-names are also important in our bid to identify early church sites and the worth of such onomastic studies can also be demonstrated for both Ireland and Cornwall (see Preston-Jones and Hamlin below). In this volume Tomos Roberts, building on the work of Melville Richards, has identified a number of place-name elements denoting ecclesiastical sites. Elements borrowed from Latin include *basaleg* from *basilica*, meaning an early church containing major relics; *merthyr* from *martyrium* meaning, in Charles Thomas' words, 'a place possessing the physical remains of a martyr which acquired the sense of a church' (1971, 89); *ecclesia*, 'church';

and *myfyr* from *memoria*, one of the meanings of which is a 'grave'. Welsh place-name elements include *tŷ*, a 'house', the equivalent of the Irish *teg* or *tech*, and *llan*, meaning an enclosure. More work also needs to be done on Celtic saints' dedications in Wales (Yates 1973; Wade-Evans 1910). Some, such as Teilo, are common within a particular locality (Bowen 1954, 56–8), probably indicating the sphere of influence of a particular ecclesiastical community, while others, such as Caffo are only found once, at Llangaffo (*Merthyr Caffo*) (Anglesey), and would appear to indicate a local cult site.

The archaeological and topographical evidence is varied but often difficult, if not impossible, to date. However the location of ecclesiastical sites, when coupled with other factors, may give an indication of their antiquity. E.G. Bowen noted that in Wales sites with Celtic dedications were located 'in lowlying parts of the country, on the lower valley-slopes and on the valley-floors, and especially in close proximity to the sea and to tidal waters' (1954, 116). Following Bowen's lead Vincent Hurley found that in south-west Ireland 'the most favoured location of church sites appears to have been on the shoulder of a low hill or ridge, often overlooking a river or stream. Other situations which were favoured include the sides of hills, coastal headlands, islands, either off the coast or in lakes, and occasionally hilltops' (Hurley 1982, 310). In this volume Ann Preston-Jones demonstrates the significance of the predominantly coastal and estuarine distribution of *lann* sites in Cornwall which leads her to suggest that Christianity was brought in from outside by waterborne contact (see Preston-Jones below). However in Wales little work has been done since Bowen on the general topography of ecclesiastical sites. It is a subject which might well repay further attention.

Secondly, the shape and size of ecclesiastical enclosures are thought to be significant. Charles Thomas first pointed out the likely antiquity of curvilinear churchyard enclosures, though he also indicated that some known early ecclesiastical sites, such as Iona, were surrounded by rectangular earthworks. The role of such enclosures seems to have been to divide the sacred from the secular and to mark out an area of sanctuary. He also suggested that the size of ecclesiastical enclosures might be informative: the greater the area enclosed, the more important the site. More controversially, he hinted that the concept of circular enclosures might be inherited from the pagan past; indeed, some ecclesiastical sites and burial grounds are known to have made use of earlier curvilinear enclosures (Thomas 1971, 38–43, 51–3).

These hypotheses have now been tested by several more detailed studies (e.g. Hurley 1982; Swan 1985; O'Sullivan 1980) and the data accumulated is persuasive. Sometimes churchyard enclosures have survived unchanged for centuries, but often it is necessary to trace the changing shape backwards through time using old maps (see Brook and Preston-Jones below). Alternatively, air photography can prove invaluable for indicating ancient enclosure lines and can also suggest complexities of layout, such as multiple concentric enclosures, which are otherwise invisible (see T. James below). The difficulty is that without excavation it is impossible to determine the date of a specific enclosure, and, if excavation does take place, it is only possible to calculate the date of construction in the broadest of terms. In Wales only two examples of churchyard enclosures have been excavated. At Capel Maelog (Radnor.) a radiocarbon date provided a *terminus post quem* of cal. AD 766–1020 for its construction (Britnell 1990; and see H. James below) but the temporal relationship between the enclosure and the majority of graves is impossible to determine, though the church is later than the enclosure. At Burry Holms (Glamorgan), a likely hermitage site situated on a tidal islet, excavation revealed at least two phases of the enclosure; the earlier predated the construction of the twelfth-century church (Hague 1973, 29–33; RCAHMW 1976, 14–5).

Thirdly, the presence of early medieval inscribed stones and/or other Christian sculpture (Nash-Williams 1950) is rightly used as a major indicator of the antiquity of a church site. However, it is important to determine, especially with the inscribed stones, whether they were brought to the church for safe-keeping, usually during the last century. At Penmachno (Caerns.), for example, one of the inscribed stones came to light during the demolition of the church in 1857, another was found immediately adjacent near the Eagles Hotel and there was a third cross-marked stone in the churchyard (Nash-Williams 1950, nos 102, 104, 104a). These attest to the antiquity of the site, probably stretching back to the fifth or sixth centuries. But two other inscribed stones were brought onto the site, one (Nash-Williams 1950, no. 101) from further up the valley beside the Roman road and one (Nash-Williams 1950, no. 103) from a site called *Beddau Gwŷr Ardudwy* ('The graves of the men of Ardudwy') near Ffestiniog approximately

8km (5 miles) to the south-west. Recent (unpublished) excavations at *Beddau Gwŷr Ardudwy* (Gwynedd Archaeological Trust 1990), from where another inscribed stone has been recorded (Nash-Williams 1950, no. 277, now lost), have failed to locate the site, but in some instances, such as Arfryn (Anglesey) (White, R.B. 1971–2), inscribed stones are known to come from cemeteries unassociated with modern church sites.

The inscribed stones remain a major source of information for the earliest Christian centuries in Wales but much remains opaque about their origins, significance and date. Jeremy Knight's paper (see below) suggests 'that the Latin memorial formulae were introduced into western Britain from western France in the mid to late fifth century and were grafted onto a separate tradition of Irish origin ... using ogam script and the filiation so important to Irish society'. But what are the chronological and religious implications of the use of ogam? Are the inscribed stones necessarily Christian if they have no explicit Christian symbol or reference? Are they normally associated with burial and what is their precise connection with routeways and boundaries? Here a systematic programme of survey, both surface and geophysical, with the subsequent excavation of inscribed stones thought to remain *in situ* is required. Cyril Fox's excavation of Maen Madoc (Brecs.) (1940a), though inconclusive, and Aileen Fox's topographical study of other inscribed stones on the Glamorgan uplands (1939) have yet to be superseded. We also need to re-examine what dating can be wrested from the epigraphy of the inscribed stones. In this volume Kenneth Dark offers a critique of their current dating (see below) with the promise of a new, but probably controversial analysis, in a future publication. The language of the inscribed stones likewise awaits a new synthesis to replace Kenneth Jackson's magisterial pronouncements (1953), though enough has already been published at a specialist level (Gratwick 1982; Russell 1985) to suggest that fresh insight may well be gained from this source.

More work is also needed on the free-standing stone crosses, cross-inscribed stones and other sculpture in order better to understand their origins, dating and affinities. With a few notable exceptions (Lewis, J.M. 1976; RCAHMW 1976; Clarke, J. 1981) there has been remarkably little research on these monuments since Nash-Williams' corpus (1950). The new edition of *The early Christian monuments of Wales* by John Lewis and Gwyn Thomas (forthcoming) will update the corpus but is not expected to offer any radical revision or major new synthesis of the material.

Fourthly, the possession of ornamental metalwork or occasionally illuminated manuscripts, whether still extant or mentioned in some documentary reference, can suggest the antiquity of a particular site (see Pryce below). For example, the only evidence for an early ecclesiastical site at Llanrhyddlad (Anglesey), apart from four long-cist graves, is a bronze hand-bell of Celtic type (Baynes 1935, 189; RCAHMW 1937, 109, Pl. 57; Bourke 1980) and the discovery of a fragmentary ringed pin (location now unknown) during grave-digging in the churchyard at Llanfairpwll (Anglesey) also hints at the antiquity of this site (Fox, C. 1940b).

As we have seen, the discovery of long-cists has been reported since the beginning of the nineteenth century. As they were usually oriented and almost always findless they came to be regarded as the graves of the early Christian Welsh and were compared with similar long-cists elsewhere in northern and western Britain and Ireland. However, over the last 25 years excavations have revealed a great deal about early medieval burials and cemeteries, not just in Wales (see H. James below), but also in Scotland (see Alcock below) and Ireland (see O'Brien below). The picture which is beginning to emerge is complex and, although some elements now stand out clearly, many of the ramifications remain difficult to unravel.

To begin with dating is still a major problem, since without grave-goods we are dependent upon radiocarbon samples which are only available where bone or some other organic substance, such as a decayed wooden coffin, survive. We do not know, for example, when long-cists came into fashion, though it is often assumed to have been during the fourth century (Green 1982, 67). Nor do we know how long the vogue lasted; some later medieval examples of cist burial have been suggested (Reece 1981, 104).

The lack of close dating goes hand-in-hand with other problems. How can we understand more fully the changes in burial practice which took place during the first millennium AD, or even attribute burials to approximately the Christian centuries without close dating? Indeed, how are we to distinguish Christian burials from pagan ones since it is now recognized that east/west orientation is not exclusively Christian (Rahtz 1978; Kendall 1982; Black 1986)? Unless we can assume (in contrast with Scotland and Ireland) that all burials after the fourth century

in Wales are Christian on the grounds that the documentary sources are silent about continuing paganism (Davies, W. 1982a, 169–71), we cannot be sure that any of our burials are Christian unless they are directly associated with an ecclesiastical structure. What we need is independent dating for as many cemeteries and types of graves as possible. With a tighter chronology we may be able to identify cultural, social, religious and chronological variation throughout northern and western Britain and Ireland.

During the early middle ages in Wales and elsewhere we are dealing, not just with long-cist graves, but with a diversity of inhumation burials. (In Ireland cremation also continued into the early medieval period.) Firstly there are simple dug graves but in the acidic soils so common in Wales the bones in these will often have completely disappeared. Where bones do survive there is sometimes evidence for shrouds. Secondly, traces of timber features have also occasionally been recorded in the form of wooden coffins and covers. There is also one example of a lead coffin (Nash-Williams 1950, no. 27). Finally, the term 'long-cist' embraces a variety of stone-lined and lintel-covered graves (see Alcock and O'Brien below). In addition some graves may be marked out with special features, most likely indicative of status. In Wales both square timber structures and square-ditched enclosures were used for this purpose and there is also some evidence for burial under cairns or barrows (Davies, W. 1982a, 186–8).

We now know that many early medieval Welsh cemeteries (as elsewhere) had their roots in the prehistoric past. Early medieval graves have been found associated with a variety of Bronze Age burials and ritual monuments. They have also been found associated with Iron Age burials and enclosures (as well as Roman cemeteries). There is clearly an element of continuity here but the nature of this continuity is extremely difficult to determine. In some instances there seems to be the reuse of an earlier site; in others some continuity of burial over the centuries seems possible. We may be witnessing the continuing use or reuse of tribal, kin or family cemeteries, though Richard Bradley (1987) has argued that the reuse of older burial sites in the post-Roman period is part of a wider phenomenon where the past is used to legitimate current social elites rather than evidence of any actual meaningful continuity. But how should we view such sites in terms of religion? Indeed, do they represent the period of conversion from paganism to

Christianity, or, as now seems the case, their continuing use for some centuries after the conversion until burial on explicitly ecclesiastical sites became the norm? Some early cemeteries, such as Caer, Bayvil (Pembs.), never attained full ecclesiastical status. Others, such as Capel Eithin (Anglesey) did only to be abandoned at a later date. In the case of long-cist graves found in or adjacent to modern churchyards, such as Llanychlwydog (Pembs.) (Murphy 1987) and Llechcynfarwy (Anglesey) (Baynes 1935), it is unclear whether an early cemetery later acquired a church building, in other words becoming, in Thomas' phraseology (1971, 51), a 'developed cemetery', or whether the foundation of an ecclesiastical site led to burial in the surrounding churchyard.

Almost nothing can be said about pre-twelfth-century church buildings in Wales since, with the possible exception of an Anglo-Saxon church at Presteigne (Radnor.) (Taylor, H.M. and Taylor, J. 1965, ii, 497–9), none survives. Although the existence of early stone churches certainly cannot be ruled out, especially on some of the more important ecclesiastical sites, wooden churches are likely to have been the norm, though the only excavated example is the tiny structure on Burry Holms (Glamorgan) (RCAHMW 1976, 14–5; see Pryce below). The earliest stone churches which are known to survive are Romanesque. In many cases, for example Tywyn (Merioneth) and Llantwit Major (Glamorgan), other evidence, particularly sculpture, together with the known status of the sites, suggests these replaced earlier buildings; but at Capel Maelog, the only totally excavated ecclesiastical site to date, this was clearly not the case (Britnell 1990; and see H. James below). The absence of surviving stone buildings is very striking when comparison is made with Anglo-Saxon England, and, although stone churches in Ireland do not appear to have become common until the eleventh and twelfth centuries, they certainly existed from the late seventh century onwards (Edwards, N. 1990, 124). Are we witnessing material poverty, piety, later destruction, or some aspect of Welsh social structure or attitudes which strongly militated against pre-Romanesque stone churches? In view of the strength of English contacts with Wales in the pre-Norman centuries, it seems unlikely that some major churches were not in stone even if, as Huw Pryce suggests, the acquisition and disposal of wealth did not aid investment in the church. During the twelfth century stone churches became common in both Anglo-Norman and Welsh areas. Yet there is no evidence that

Wales became more prosperous at this time though the introduction of coinage and urban markets may have made the concentration of wealth easier. Only excavation coupled with the intensive analysis of standing structures will resolve this and we must encourage the investigation of the Welsh equivalents of the Old Minster Winchester (Biddle and Biddle forthcoming), Wells Cathedral (Rodwell, 1981) and Deerhurst (Rahtz 1976) as well as taking the opportunity for exploration of minor sites, such as Pennant Melangell (Montgomery.) (see below), offered by rescue archaeology.

Other hints can be gleaned from standing buildings and records of earlier churches which have now disappeared. For example, the existence of multiple churches on the sites of Meifod (Montgomery.) in the twelfth century and Penmachno (Caerns.) in the early modern period suggests a much earlier arrangement (Davies, W. 1982a, 26; RCAHMW 1956, 168–9). In other parts of Britain and Ireland important ecclesiastical sites, for example Jarrow (Tyne and Wear) and Clonmacnoise (Co Offaly), are known to have had multiple churches in the early middle ages, some of which still stand today. Multiple churches were each required to fulfil a different function: perhaps a large church for lay congregations, a smaller church for members of the ecclesiastical community or a tiny chapel to house the relics of the founding saint (Edwards, N. 1990, 112). Good evidence for the last of these survives in the form of *capeli y bedd* ('chapels of the grave'), small late medieval chapels which stand either adjoining the church or elsewhere within the churchyard. As already mentioned excavations beneath the floor of the standing *capel y bedd* at Clynnog Fawr (Caerns.) revealed the foundations of an earlier stone chapel, sealed by a layer of clay containing a coin of Edward I or II, and a considerable number of oriented inhumations including at least one cist-and-lintel grave (Stallybrass 1914). Are the present chapels at Llaneilian (Anglesey) (RCAHMW 1937, 59–61) and Caer Gybi (Anglesey) (see below) also on top of earlier structures and, if so, what are their dates? Again, excavation is essential to clarify the sequence of development.

Francis Jones (1954) has charted the prehistoric pagan origins of holy wells in Wales, their likely adoption by early Christians, the continuing prosperity of well cults in the later middle ages and their revival during the eighteenth and nineteenth centuries. He recorded nearly 200 examples associated with ecclesiastical sites and many of them are dedicated to Celtic saints. The presence of a well is usually regarded as evidence for the antiquity of the site but the antiquity of the well itself is extremely difficult to prove. The famous well of *Gwenfrewi* (Winifred) at Holywell (Flint.) only emerges into history in 1093 when it was given to the monastery of St Werburg in Chester (Jones, F. 1954, 49). In this instance the well chapel is a splendid example of Perpendicular architecture probably dating to the very early sixteenth century (Hubbard 1986, 371–3). But small masonry superstructures sometimes with outbuildings are more characteristic as exemplified by Llangybi (Caerns.) which is datable to the eighteenth century (RCAHMW 1960, 205–6). Many wells are, however, simply holes in the ground: there is a fine example in the churchyard at Cerrig Ceinwen (Anglesey).

There has been little archaeological investigation of holy wells. *Ffynnon Degla*, Llandegla (Denbigh.) was excavated in 1935 revealing two layers under the present paving. The upper contained eighteenth- and ninteenth-century coins, the lower many pieces of white quartz and calcite, but there was no indication of date (Rees, A.D. 1935). In 1981 a small excavation in the forecourt of the holy well at Penmon (Anglesey) produced nothing of antiquity (Edwards, N. 1986, 26–7). Unfortunately holy wells are a feature of the Welsh landscape which are fast disappearing. Even some associated with churchyards, for example Cwm (Flint.) (Edwards, N. forthcoming) are now largely forgotten and the physical remains of those which are left should be recorded before it is too late.

Some Examples of Early Church Sites

In order to see how the various types of evidence can be used in conjunction with each other to identify early ecclesiastical sites and perhaps indicate the nature of the activity on them, five different examples will be examined in more detail. It should be emphasized, however, that these are sites for which the evidence is relatively plentiful and indicates that they were of considerable importance. For most Welsh ecclesiastical sites there is no mention in the documentary record which testifies to or hints at their antiquity. Only intensive survey or excavation, as at Capel Maelog (Britnell 1990), for example, can reveal the sequence of development at the many more modest sites about which the documentary sources are silent.

The only indications of Christianity in Roman Wales come from the south-east (Thomas, C. 1981a, Fig. 16) and the only archaeological evidence is from the *civitas* capital of Caerwent (*Venta Silurum,* Monmouth.). It comes in the form of a fragmentary pewter bowl with a roughly scratched chi-rho monogram. It was found in 1906 in a house opposite the north-east corner of the forum-basilica, but the graffito was only noted in 1961 (Boon 1962). The bowl was found with late fourth century pottery and other objects in a sealed pottery urn set into the floor and it has been suggested that the group could be part of an *agape* set (Knight 1984a, 357, note 3). (It should, however, be noted that the 'church' identified by Nash-Williams is in fact a post-medieval cottage (Thomas, C. 1981a, 166–8).) But evidence for Christianity in Caerwent does not terminate with the end of the Roman period. Burial continued outside the east gate of the town. Over 118 burials including some long-cists have been found in this partially explored cemetery — some cut into the ruins of a house and some into the Roman road. Here we are faced with the problem of whether or when this became a Christian cemetery. There was a second cemetery inside the town near the present church of St Tatheus; again there were some long-cists and some of the burials were cut into the main east/west street and into adjacent buildings. Radiocarbon dates from the Eastgate cemetery together span the mid-fourth to the mid-tenth century while those from the intra-mural cemetery span the mid-fourth to the mid-eighth (Edwards and Lane 1988, 35–7, 137). The Life of St Tatheus (c. 1200) claims that an Irish monastery was founded within the town in the fifth or sixth centuries (Knight 1970–1) but the earliest definite reference to a monastery in Caerwent is not until the mid-tenth century when it is mentioned in a Llandaff charter (Davies, W. 1979a, 136, 180 no. 218). It may also be the place called *Wintonia* mentioned in Asser's *Life of Alfred* (Keynes and Lapidge 1983, 261).

Like Caerwent, the church at Caer Gybi (Anglesey) is located within a former Roman site, this time a fourth-century fortified landing place in the north-east corner of Holy Island (also known as Ynys Cybi) (RCAHMW 1937, 28–31). According to the Life of St Cybi (c. 1200) the fort was donated to St Cybi by King Maelgwn and this was where he was buried (Wade-Evans 1944, 234–51). But the only reliable early documentary reference is to the Viking raid on Caer Gybi in 961 (Jones, T. 1955, 14–5) which testifies to the importance of the site by that date. Fragments of twelfth-century masonry survive (Hughes, H.

1923, 67) but the earliest part of the present church of St Cybi is of the thirteenth century. In the south-west corner of the churchyard is a second building, the *Eglwys y Bedd* (also known as *Llan-y-Gwyddel*). It is datable to the fourteenth century and may have housed the relics of St Cybi. There is a reference to an Irish raid on these in the fifteenth century. Curiously, there is no early medieval sculpture from this important site. Though *ffon Cybi* (Cybi's staff) carved with 'leaves and ripe nuts' is mentioned by the fifteenth-century bard Dafydd Llwyd ap Llywelyn (Baring-Gould and Fisher 1911, ii, 212), the description of the ornament possibly indicates a later medieval date. The only early medieval archaeological evidence consists of long-cist graves reported from within the fort (Lhwyd 1833, 205) and the discovery of an Anglo-Saxon penny of Edward the Martyr (975–8) close to the inside face of the fort wall a short distance from the north-west angle. It may have been an offering to the church (Dolley and Knight 1970, 80–1) or it may be indicative of an ecclesiastically-controlled market. There was formerly a holy well dedicated to St Cybi situated outside the fort to the north-east at the junction of St Cybi Street and Cybi Place (Williams, R.T. 1877, 93–6). It was much frequented in the early eighteenth century and was still extant a century later (Jones, F. 1954, 142; UCNW MS 3/140).

Merthyr Mawr (Glamorgan) is located beside the Ogmore river but no indications of the ancient topography survive. In contrast to Caer Gybi, the main evidence for the antiquity of the site is the large collection of early medieval sculpture, some of which was found in the churchyard, and the rest in the immediate vicinity. It comprises a fragmentary inscribed stone commemorating Paulus or Paulinus (datable to the fifth or sixth centuries?), which seems to have had carving added at a later date on the opposite face, two 'parallel-cross' slabs and two slab crosses (all of which are approximately datable to the eleventh century), a square slab with interlace and pellet ornament, seven other cross-carved stones and a socketed base (Nash-Williams 1950, nos 238–43, 245–7; RCAHMW 1976, nos 847, 917–8, 927–8, 952, 964–70, 987). The inscription on one of the slab crosses seems to be recording a transfer of land to the church (Davies, W. 1982b, 268, 270 note 41). The only early documentary reference is also a land grant. One of the Llandaff charters, which has been dated to c. 862 (Davies, W. 1979a, no. 212), records the donation of *Merthir Miuor* by

King Hywel to Bishop Cerennyr. The *merthyr* place-name is also worthy of note (see Roberts below) and indicates that the original dedication may have been to Myfor or Mofor, rather than to Teilo as at present (RCAHMW 1976, 16) and may suggest that at some point the site became subject to a Teilo church before, eventually, coming under the sway of Llandaff.

Today Gwytherin is a small and remote village on the Denbighshire moors centred round the nineteenth-century church which has only recently been reprieved from redundancy. However there are various clues which together suggest that this was an early medieval ecclesiastical site of some importance. Indeed, the documentary evidence hints that it might have been a double monastery catering for both men and women (Evans, J.W. 1986, 66). The church is dedicated to *Gwenfrewi* (Winifred) and a reference in the twelfth-century *Life of Wenefred* by Robert, Prior of Shrewsbury (Acta Sanctorum 1887, 708–31) indicates that Gwytherin was the site of her grave but that her relics had recently been translated to the Benedictine Abbey of Shrewsbury. Later *The Survey of the Honour of Denbigh* (1334) states that there were *abbates* ('abbots') at Gwytherin who were supported by bond under-tenants, again suggesting the presence of an earlier ecclesiastical community (Vinogradoff and Morgan 1914, 187–92; Jones, G.R.J. 1960–3, 127; Evans, J.W. 1986, 68). The churchyard at Gwytherin is situated on a small but pronounced promontory with steep slopes to south, east and north. Wyn Evans (Evans, J.W. 1986, 67) has indicated that the church may have been founded within an ?Iron Age promontory fort but there is no archaeological evidence to support this. The site is, however, likely to date back to at least the fifth or sixth centuries AD since to the north of the church there is an inscribed stone commemorating Vinnemaglus, son of Senemaglus (Nash-Williams 1950, no. 177). It is the most westerly in a line of four stones (the other three are uncarved) and, while it cannot be proven to be *in situ*, there is no indication that it has been brought onto the site. It is likely that the churchyard was originally considerably larger than today. A glance at the six-inch Ordnance Survey map shows that to the north modern buildings may have been built within the original ecclesiastical enclosure since the road beyond follows a pronounced curve. To the south a churchyard extension is marked together with the site of 'Penbryn Chapel'. In fact this appears to be the location of '*Kappel Gwenfrewi*' which was still standing at the end of the seventeenth century, when it was reported to Edward Lhuyd, and seems to have been functioning as a *capel y bedd*. It was demolished some time in the early eighteenth century. Lhuyd also gives a remarkable illustration of the shrine of Gwenfrewi which may have survived at Gwytherin as late as the mid-nineteenth century (Evans, J.W. 1986, 66–7). The ornament suggests that it is of early medieval date (Butler and Graham-Campbell forthcoming).

Pennant Melangell (Montgomery) is also unusual in that it is dedicated to a female saint: Melangell (Monacella). Again, there are no early documentary references; her Life, *Historia Divae Monacellae*, survives only in the form of two variants of post-Reformation date, perhaps with a late medieval core (Radford and Hemp 1959,

81–2). But the Life mentions both a female community founded by Melangell and 'freeholding abbots of thy [Melangell's] sanctuary' (*liberi tenentes dict' abbates tui sanctuarii*) (Williams, R. 1848, 141) which may, like Gwytherin, hint at a double community. By the thirteenth century, however, it was simply a parish church (Radford and Hemp 1959, 85). The site is located in a deep cwm near the head of the Tanat valley, a spot so remote as to suggest that it may have, at least initially, functioned as a hermitage. The churchyard is large and curvilinear. The earliest phase of the present church is twelfth century and the only earlier evidence is for burial. Unusually the church had an eastern apse which has recently been re-excavated. This opened off the church via an off-centre archway. On the south side of the apse

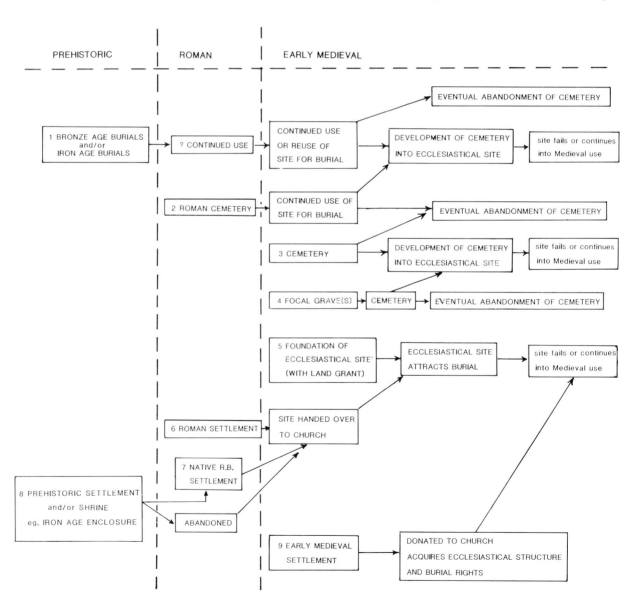

Fig. 1.1 *Nine models for the origin and initial development of early medieval ecclesiastical sites in Wales*

a grave covered by a large slab and edged with stones was relocated and a second slab-covered grave was found beneath the wall of the apse. In 1959 the former was interpreted as the grave of St Melangell. This is unprovable but the opening into the apse does appear to respect the grave. It has been suggested that the apse was built as a *cell-y-bedd* to house the impressive Romanesque stone shrine of St Melangell, which was reconstructed in the 1950s from many fragments incorporated into the fabric of the church and lychgate. Recent excavations outside the north wall at the western end of the church also revealed earlier graves under the twelfth-century foundations, several of which were capped with large numbers of quartz pebbles (Radford and Hemp 1959; Britnell and Jones 1989).

These examples illustrate the kinds of information which can at present be gleaned about specific early Welsh ecclesiastical sites. Indeed, the comparative increase in the archaeological evidence for Welsh ecclesiastical sites and cemeteries over the last 25 years now enables various models of development to be suggested (Fig. 1.1). This diagram shows nine possible origins for ecclesiastical sites and cemeteries, some with either prehistoric and/or Roman-period prior activity or *de novo* foundation in the early medieval period. Some of these sequences of development will be familiar; others less so.

Conclusion

In the future it is archaeology, where the body of evidence is constantly growing, which offers the greatest potential for the identification of new sites and, when used in conjunction with historical and other sources such as place-names, for improving our understanding of their development, functions and status. In his concluding remarks at the conference for which these papers were prepared, Professor Charles Thomas drew particular attention to the need for further survey work both on the ground and from the air and for the need for proper funding of this work. The exploration and recording of both the ecclesiastical and secular landscape is clearly of great urgency in areas threatened by both urban and rural development and by agricultural change. Ann Preston-Jones has demonstrated just how far Wales lags behind Cornwall (and, indeed, other parts of England) in the synthesis of its ecclesiastical landscape. But once we have the sites on the map further exploration is necessary. The complex outer enclosures emerging from aerial photography cry out for geophysical survey and excavation. Likewise the meaning of the inscribed stones can only be explicated by excavation of *in situ* examples. Indeed, selective but intensive excavation will be required on a variety of ecclesiastical and cemetery sites in order to understand their sequential history on the ground and to tease out their dates and functions; it is only then that the more general patterns of development may begin to emerge more clearly.

In the past there has, with a few honourable exceptions, been little interest in the ecclesiastical archaeology of Wales and a consequent failure to apply resources to a major aspect of the cultural and intellectual heritage of Wales. We hope this volume and the conference which gave rise to it will help focus attention on what has been done, what is currently underway, and what should be done in the future.

The Myth of the Celtic Church

Wendy Davies

Despite a considerable volume of scholarly comment to the contrary, notably that of Kathleen Hughes and Jane Stevenson in recent years (1981; 1987), we still quite frequently encounter the belief that there was such a thing as a Celtic Church in the early middle ages. It comes at all levels: serious books bear titles like *The Celtic Church in Britain* or *Wales* or *Somerset* (Hardinge 1972; Victory 1977; Porter 1971); undergraduate essays invoke the Celtic Church when they seek to explain the conversion of seventh-century England; respectable radio and television presenters assume it necessary background to give context to this or that place (usually in Ireland); while every tourist who visits a religious site in a Celtic country will be presented with snippets of generalized waffle around the subject, usually heavily larded with anecdotes from the less credible Saints' Lives. It is a very persistent and a very powerful notion.

It is, however, a misleading one. For the third time, therefore, I want to demonstrate its limitations and point the way to some more fruitful approaches. Although I am glad to say that I have modified my views on some aspects of the relevant material since I first wrote about them, I remain committed to the view that there was no such thing as a Celtic Church; the concept is unhelpful, if not positively harmful (Davies, W. 1974–5; Davies and Wormald 1980). That I have modified my views at all is tribute to the excellent work that has been done in the past 15 years and I have therefore tried to cite the best of it in this paper; Kathleen Hughes's work on the early Irish church, however, remains absolutely fundamental to any assessment (1966).

I have said that the Celtic Church idea is unhelpful. More than that, it could be considered positively harmful: if we assume similarities in Celtic countries, we ignore differences and fail to investigate them; we also lack an appreciation of such similarities as did exist in Britain, Ireland and the continent; and we tend to classify the continent as one standardized norm, run from Rome. This certainly was not the case in the earlier middle ages: practice could vary quite significantly in different parts of continental Europe in the sixth or seventh or eighth century,

and – like that of the Spanish church – might be openly hostile to that of Rome; it took many centuries for the church of Rome to establish itself at the pinnacle of a western hierarchy (cf. Mayr-Harting 1972, 174–82). Hence, a fixation with the Celtic Church makes it very difficult to assess the place of Celtic countries in the religious history of Europe as a whole. By insisting on the category, instead of making a statement about the historical past, we say nothing and we lose such opportunities as there are for investigating the dynamic of change.

The Image and its Origins

When people talk or write about a Celtic Church they usually have several images in mind nowadays. They imagine that there were common beliefs, common religious practices, and common religious institutions in Celtic countries, and that these were distinct from beliefs, practice and institutions in England and on the continent. They also imagine that the church in Celtic countries was distinctively saintly and monastic; moreover, it was individual, unorganized and the very opposite of Roman.

Hence we can observe some totally inappropriate associations of the Celtic Church with the Protestant mentality and with the Anglican Settlement of the early modern period. We read of Irish monks as 'the Christian leaven in a rude society, able to implant and preserve Christian culture like a cultivated garden amid a wilderness of disorder' (McNeill 1974, 86). More than this, proponents of the Celtic Church idea are often unclear about period: some suppose it characteristic of the entire pre-Norman early middle ages, from the fifth to the eleventh or twelfth century; others prefer to focus on the earlier centuries, fifth, sixth, seventh and eighth especially. Most lack an interest in the niceties of chronological change: the Celtic Church is focussed in place rather than in time and inhabits a type of religious Otherworld; here the normal rules for handling primary source material lapse, as a word from one source and a sentence from another are taken to apply to all areas and all centuries; we find material from eleventh-century Saints' Lives used to illuminate sixth-century developments, Irish texts appropriated to apply to Wales or Brittany, and Bede's eighth-century views of seventh-century Celts in Northumbria used to typify all Celts in all centuries (*Hist. Ecc.*, Colgrave and Mynors 1969).

In fact we do have very serious source problems. There is far more from and about Ireland than from other Celtic areas; hence the temptation to make Irish material fit all regions. Material relating to Scotland is exceptionally thin after the eighth century and that relating to Brittany almost non-existent before the ninth; for Wales there are moderate amounts for the south-east but very little for other areas; and Cornwall and the Isle of Man have even thinner coverage. It is not only a problem of unevenness: much of the existing material is difficult to handle and a very high proportion is unprovenanced. Although we might have a generalized idea of its area of production (Ireland, or Brittany, say), we have no idea where precisely and in what context it was produced. Many texts are undated too, and although dates can be suggested, sometimes on strong grounds, this is not the same as working with texts that are clearly located in time and space.

We may ask why this Celtic Church idea is so persistent. It is partly, of course, because those studying seventh-century England are unduly influenced by Bede's preoccupation with the problems arising when different groups of Christians could not agree on the correct day for the celebration of Easter. Although Bede himself is careful to note a range of deviations, and to distinguish between Irish and British (cf. Charles-Edwards 1983), his setpiece conflict at Whitby in 664 has too often been transmitted by English historians as a conflict between 'Celts' and 'Romans'. But this is only part of an answer. More fundamentally, we have to recognize that the Celtic Church is a marketable idea. Denizens of our industrialized world like to believe in the saintly hero and choose to patronize this escape route. It is as suitable a subject for nostalgia about a (non-existent) byegone age as elves and pixies; it complements the twee, folksy, whimsical. This is not so curious as might at first appear. Belief in the Celtic Church has come to be one aspect of the wider belief in the Celt as an 'abnormal visionary being whose mind is fixed ... on the spiritual, the occult, the ideal'; and in the Celtic peoples as 'spiritual, impractical, rural, natural and poetic'. I quote Patrick Sims-Williams, whose Edinburgh O'Donnell lecture is an elegant study of this 'Visionary Celt' and of the origins of the 'ethnic preconception', which finds its full formulation in the mid-nineteenth century; his analysis of the factors contributing to its formulation is compelling – a complex of the mass psychology of invaders and defenders, of defence strategies, of the pseudo-historical substance behind the German Romantic vision 'preoccupied with an idealized past' (Sims-Williams 1986). Thoughts of a Celtic Church have an earlier origin than this fully developed vision, although they slot nicely into it; they were essentially formulated in the sixteenth and seventeenth centuries in justification of the Anglican Settlement; Celtic Christians of the early middle ages were deemed the natural ancestors of the true Protestants of the early modern period, championing simplicity and independence against the tyranny of Rome; in the late eighteenth and nineteenth century it was widely held that Archbishop Ussher (in his paper of 1631) had proved 'that the religion of the Columbans [i.e. the Iona family of monasteries] was for substance the same which the Protestants now profess' (Hay 1927, 76).[1] As such the Celtic Church idea holds a place in the history of *mentalités*: its proper historical context is the complex of religious and intellectual attitudes surrounding the Anglican Settlement. That it has been sustained in an age which, with regional exceptions, is much less concerned about religious affiliations, is very much a consequence of the appeal of the 'Visionary Celt'.

Character

Why should we not speak of a Celtic Church in the early middle ages? No-one who has read the seventh-century or later Lives of St Patrick, or the eleventh-century Life of St Cadog, could sustain the notion of a characteristic withdrawn saintliness; the malevolent power that these saints could and did use, especially through cursing, prohibits it: men were dashed to pieces, the earth swallowed them up, they were consumed by fire, all for thwarting the saints. No-one who has considered the monastic history of eighth- and ninth-century Ireland, with its large, wealthy, powerful communities, with its open warfare between abbots and monasteries, could suppose these men either withdrawn or insistently individual (Hughes, K. 1966, 169–72). No-one who has noted the power of bishops in tenth- and eleventh-century Wales to command the attendance of local clergy and to require lay adherence to their rulings could imagine that all

Celtic churches were unorganized (Davies, W. 1978a, 148–9). No-one who has considered the mission sent to Rome for advice by Irish clerics in the 630s, or noted the characteristic classification of one Irish group as 'Romani' in the seventh- and eighth-century Irish canons, can imagine that all Celtic churches were entirely un-Roman (Hughes, K. 1966, 106–7). Certainly there were *saints*, that is ascetic, withdrawn, holy people; certainly at times there were parties who chose to follow a non-Roman line; certainly there were monks and monasteries. But to suppose these were distinctive and exclusive characteristics is to ignore a good proportion of the clear evidence which does exist and ignore the fact that one could easily find the same characteristics in England and on the continent too. Even a cursory reading of the available evidence is sufficient to dispose of the romantic image.

Institutions

We can be more positive than this. Firstly, it is patently obvious that there was no single institutional structure encompassing the churches of all, or most, Celtic countries at any point in the early middle ages. There was no head of this church; there was no general council; there was no policy-making body regulating church affairs; there was no ruler who might be thought to guarantee orthodoxy, as late Roman and then Byzantine emperors tried to do. Indeed, by contrast, it is perfectly clear that there were *regional* synods within Celtic areas, when bishops met together and made decisions for their regions, or failed to do so. Thus the bishops of eastern Brittany met with the bishops of north-west France, in the province of Tours and elsewhere, during the fifth and sixth and occasionally the seventh centuries (*Conc. Gall.*, A.511, 549, 567, 614, 647–53, de Clercq 1963); the (seven) bishops of the 'neighbouring British province' (wherever that may have been) met Augustine of Canterbury in 603, and failed to agree with him (*Hist. Ecc.*, ii. 2, Colgrave and Mynors 1969); the leaders of the Irish church deliberated together in the 630s, and the southern Irish made an independent decision (*Hist. Ecc.*, iii. 3, Colgrave and Mynors 1969); the leaders of the Welsh church (perhaps the north Welsh church only, since the bishop who effected the change was later localized to Gwynedd) made decisions in 768 for (north ?) Wales (*Ann. Camb.*, Williams ab Ithel 1860). Although some may feel that the Easter problem itself has been

somewhat overrated, there is nothing more telling — and nothing more damaging to the idea of a single Celtic church — than the fact that different regions chose to respond in different ways at different times to the Roman call for standardization of Easter computations: Brittany does not appear to have been deviant in any case and may well have followed the decision of the Frankish Council of Orléans in 541 (La Borderie 1898, 264); southern Ireland had conformed by 640; some British in Britain (we do not know where) had done so by 703, although many had still not done so in 731 (*Hist. Ecc.*, v. 15, 23, Colgrave and Mynors 1969); the whole of Ireland had done so by 704, quite probably following the synod of Birr in 697 (*Hist. Ecc.*, v. 15, Colgrave and Mynors 1969; Harrison 1982, 309); Iona, off the west coast of Scotland, and its dependencies (probably in Scotland) did so in 716 as did Pictland (*Hist. Ecc.*, v. 22, 21, Colgrave and Mynors 1969); Wales (or north Wales only) did so in 768 (*Ann. Camb.*, Williams ab Ithel 1860). We have no information about practice in Cornwall or the Isle of Man.

Secondly, far from there being a single church with a single institutional structure, there were institutional differences within and between Celtic regions. Although Celtic churches are churches largely without archbishops and without metropolitan provinces, there are areas in which at times — infrequently and sporadically — there is evidence of honorific *archiepiscopi*; in other words, notable individuals were honoured with a superior title, as a mark of respect without any implication of jurisdiction or hierarchical authority. This happened twice in ninth-century Wales — of Gwynedd and St David's respectively — and several times in relation to St Andrews (*ardepscop*) in tenth- and eleventh-century Scotland; it may also be implied of Dunkeld in 865 (*primepscop*) (Davies, W. 1982a, 160; Donaldson 1952–3, 110–11). By contrast prominent bishops and their communities at times behaved as if they sought substantial archiepiscopal authority. This is most striking in the case of Armagh in the later seventh century, for a series of documents is witness to claims of appellate jurisdiction throughout Ireland as well as of control of many northern Irish churches; Kildare was in competition with Armagh for control of churches and (following Cogitosus) it looks as if her bishop was prepared to settle for dominance of the southern half of Ireland; however, these attempts were not sustained much beyond 700 (Sharpe 1984a). Similar claims were made in the ninth century for Dol to serve as metropolitan see for Brittany, with local political backing, although we know little of any powers consistently exercised (Smith, J.M.H. 1982, 67). All three cases arise from particular, local, political and politico-religious circumstances.

Although there were archiepiscopal pretensions in early Ireland and claims in ninth-century and later Brittany, authority in most areas lay with bishops and abbots. Which of the two predominated is a question that has attracted considerable discussion and there is a large literature on Irish aspects of the issue. In some areas powerful abbots acquired the managerial powers which the early Christian church had entrusted to bishops, that is the management of finances and of religious personnel, and they were exempt from episcopal visitation and inspection, whether regular or irregular; bishops performed sacramental functions only.[2] This was clearly so in the Iona zone of influence (especially in western Scotland) in the late seventh and early eighth century, and was developing in some parts of Ireland during the course of the eighth century (*Hist. Ecc.*, iii. 4, Colgrave and Mynors 1969; Hughes, K. 1966, 68–9). However, this was never the only pattern of authority in Ireland. Moreover, it was demonstrably not the case in Wales, throughout the early middle ages, for bishops clearly retained administrative powers, and powers of visitation, and many exercised them within discrete territories (Davies, W. 1978a, 149–59; Hughes, K. 1981; Davies, W. 1982a, 158–64). Nor was it the case in eastern Brittany in the ninth century, where a clear framework of dioceses allowed for episcopal visitation from time to time (Davies, W. 1988, 25; Guillotel 1979, 255–6). We also know of bishops in the Isle of Man and in Cornwall; although we know rather less about them, at least the Cornish bishop Kenstec, at his 'episcopal seat' in the monastery of *Dinnurrin, c.* 850, and the restoration of the lands of the bishopric of St Germans to Bishop Conan in 936, look focal to the structure of local religious authority (Haddan and Stubbs 1869–71, i, 674; Padel 1978, 26). In Scotland we know of early bishops in the south west and of other bishops in the east and west intermittently throughout the pre-Norman period, with some suggestions of competition between Dunkeld and St Andrews for a type of primacy and some possibility that St Andrews inherited an earlier Abernethy tradition of authority (Donaldson 1952–3). Although evidence is fragmentary, modern scholars argue that most of the twelfth-century bishoprics were

of ancient origin (Duncan 1975, 257–9); the 'ancient' Scottish bishoprics of the twelfth century had connections with widely scattered and intermingled churches and this may perhaps point to yet another pattern of organization in which (at least in central Scotland) episcopal authority was not exercised in discrete territories (Watt 1969; 1975).

As for the complication of monastic bishoprics, it is certainly true that there were many in Celtic areas – bishops whose episcopal households are referred to as monasteries, who themselves were monks and who ruled the 'monastery' as well as their own proper area of jurisdiction: Welsh Llandeilo Fawr in the early ninth century, Cornish *Dinnurrin* in the ninth century, Scottish Dunkeld in 865, perhaps Breton Dol until the ninth century, and Irish Armagh until the eighth century, for after 793 there was a tendency for the offices of abbot and bishop to be separate (Davies, W. 1978a, 148, 149–50; Haddan and Stubbs 1869–71, i, 674; Donaldson 1952–3, 109; Gougaud 1922, 100–1; Guillotel 1977; Hughes, K. 1966, 68–9). However, these monastic bishops were hardly distinctive in early Christian history; we find them outside Celtic areas: we can remember St Augustine of Hippo or Pope Gregory the Great, as well as the cathedral monasteries of late Saxon England, for example. Nor were monastic bishops invariably the rule in Celtic areas; monastic and episcopal office were commonly separated in Ireland from the ninth century, often with a lay abbot or coarb distinct from the bishop. Again this underlines the fact that there was a range of possible arrangements.

The monastic federation has also often been seen as characteristic of and distinctive to Celtic churches – associations of monastic houses, sometimes widely scattered, and all more or less subject to the abbot of the mother house or *matrix ecclesiae*. It is true that there were some large federations of monasteries and many small ones: the Iona 'family' of monasteries is the best (and earliest) evidenced but there are others like, for example, the smaller association of monastic houses (and churches) affiliated to Llancarfan in south Wales (Davies, W. 1978a, 141–2). However, there is little that is distinctive about this: we can find associations of monastic houses in many parts of the continent, where, from the tenth century, the large and scattered federation becomes much more characteristic than it had ever been of Celtic areas. Further, as Richard Sharpe has recently pointed out, the connection between the members of a Celtic federation was often extremely loose and the powers exercised by the mother abbot often limited or negligible (Sharpe 1984b, 246–7. So too there were varieties of monastic order and different patterns of monastic authority in eleventh- and twelfth-century Europe, where freedom from episcopal interference was highly prized by groupings such as that associated with the monastery of Cluny in Burgundy. Heritability of office and of monastic property was just as common to Europe as to Britain and Ireland: certainly both monastic and non-monastic offices were often heritable in Celtic areas, from the priestships of Breton villages in the ninth century to the stewards of tenth-century monasteries in south Wales to the lay abbots of pre-Conquest Ireland (Davies, W. 1983; Davies, W. 1978a, 128–30; Ó Corráin 1981a, 328–31). But these are features as familiar in eighth-century England or in tenth-century France or Germany as in the Celtic West. There is nothing particularly Celtic about them, although Anglo-Norman reformers of the later eleventh and twelfth centuries sometimes behaved as if there was, since much of the rest of western Europe had already been caught up in the movement for reform of lay and hereditary interests, and of marriage of the clergy; change came later in Celtic areas and there, and there alone, lies the difference.

Practice

We can be as emphatic about differences in practice within Celtic areas as we can about institutional differences. It is true, however, that assessment and classification of the liturgy is difficult, for there is very little useful early evidence from Celtic areas. However, we should remember that there was some diversity in liturgical usage on the continent, at the least between the Roman and the several versions of the Gallican liturgy (Stevenson, J. 1987, xv-xx); while it seems likely that more than one Gallican version of the mass circulated in Ireland (Stevenson, J. 1987, lxvii). If Michael Lapidge is right in suggesting that some Welsh were still using a pre-Gregorian liturgy in the ninth century — and his argument is a strong one — then they clearly clung to a very archaic usage (1986, 93). This serves to emphasize the difference between Welsh and Irish (or at least between some Welsh and some Irish), a distinction of which some Irish were conscious: Irish canons of the early eighth century present the British mass as unacceptably deviant

(Stevenson, J. 1987, lix; *Coll. Can. Hib.*, lii. 6, Wasserschleben 1885).

The evidence about baptism and the consecration of bishops is somewhat similar. Both Bede and the seventh-century penitential of Archbishop Theodore suggest that the British form of baptism was deviant, though not the Irish; we do not know what the deviation was, or indeed if Theodore and Bede really knew that the rite was different, but in any case diversity was common in Europe until the Carolingian pressure for standardization began in the later eighth century (*Hist. Ecc.*, ii. 2, Colgrave and Mynors 1969; Haddan and Stubbs 1869–71, iii, 197; cf. Stevenson, J. 1987, liii-iv). Theodore chose to reconsecrate Bishop Chad because he had originally been consecrated by British bishops; again, we do not know that the rite itself was deviant; Eddius Stephanus commented that Chad had been consecrated by Quartodecimans – those who celebrated Easter on the fourteenth of the Paschal month — and the objection may well have been to the consecrators rather than to the rite of consecration used (*Hist. Ecc.*, iv. 2, Colgrave and Mynors 1969; *Vit. Wilf.*, xiv, Colgrave 1927).[3]

As for private penance, I will only say that I find it difficult to see any evidence that this habit was characteristic of Celtic churches and transmitted thence (largely by the Irish) to continental Europe, as is commonly supposed. Certainly we have many penitentials of British and of Irish origin; and there is considerable Insular influence in the script of manuscripts of Frankish penitentials of the eighth and ninth century (cf. Pierce, R. 1975, 35); but the penitential texts are not in themselves evidence for private or public performance of the penance. Moreover, it is quite evident that penance was done publicly until the eighth century, at least in Ireland and western Scotland: one seventh- or eighth-century Irish canon makes explicit reference to the public nature of confession — *confessionem peccatorum coram sacerdote et plebe* (Bieler 1963, 164; cf. Bieler 1963, 56: 'come with witnesses on completion of penance'); and Adomnán details the arrangements made for a penitent who came to Iona and confessed to Columba 'before all' and another (a priest) who did so in Meath (*Vita. Columb.*, i. 30, 40, Anderson, A.O. and Anderson, M.O. 1961). The very fact that Irish monasteries had (group) facilities for penitents underlines the public nature of penance undertaken at this period (*Vita Columb.*, i. 30, Anderson, A.O. and Anderson, M.O. 1961; Warren 1881, 148–9). We have no evidence here of any distinctive Celtic practice, and we must acknowledge that the habit of private confession and penance developed in Britain and Ireland, as on the continent, by some means that remains obscure.

Problems relating to the tonsure are similar to those of baptism and consecration, although we have more specific information to assist our assessment. When Abbot Ceolfrid of Jarrow wrote to King Nechtan of the Picts in the early eighth century, apart from commenting that deviation was not a very serious matter, he pointed out that several types of tonsure had been used in the past and several types were currently in use; however, he thought the crown-like tonsure of Simon Peter was the best (*Hist. Ecc.*, v. 21, Colgrave and Mynors 1969). Tuda from southern Ireland seems to have adopted this most acceptable of tonsures before 664, probably in contrast to British practice for *c*. 700 some Irish canons noted that the British had the unacceptable tonsure of Simon Magus 'from ear to ear'; other British, according to Bede, had no tonsure at all (*Hist. Ecc.*, iii. 26, Colgrave and Mynors 1969; *Coll. Can. Hib.*, lii. 6, cf. xx. 6, Wasserschleben 1885; *Hist. Ecc.*, v. 22, Colgrave and Mynors 1969; cf. Aldhelm, in Haddan and Stubbs 1869–71, iii, 270). Other Irish, like Colman, seem to have preferred one of the less acceptable tonsures, for he left England in 664 rather than conform; the Iona community — like Nechtan and the Picts — did not move to the crown-like tonsure until the early eighth century (*Hist. Ecc.*, iii. 26, Colgrave and Mynors 1969). For all the complexities of this issue, it is clear that diversity was normal in Europe in the seventh and eighth centuries, and that diversity within Celtic areas is perfectly well evidenced: the British were often seen as deviant, but not all Irish followed the same practice anyway (see James, E. 1984).[4]

It is the trouble over the calculation of Easter dates that has attracted most attention from modern scholars. It was a matter which also often attracted attention in western Europe in the fifth, sixth, seventh and eighth centuries since practice was so varied and could result in embarrassing differences. The problem arose because Easter was determined in relation to the lunar year, which is shorter than the solar year; to overcome the discrepancy, several months were intercalated over a period of years (as we now intercalate one day every four years on 29 February); there were several methods of calculating the intercalation, most of which had some element of inaccuracy. The issues which concerned Christians included the correct calculation of the vernal equinox, the appropriate point to begin the day (evening or morning), and the appropriate point to begin Easter week (on the 14th or 15th or 16th of the month) as well as the choice of the correct tables for making the annual calculation (Jones, C.W. 1943). Tables based on an 84-year cycle for intercalation were favoured by St Columbanus in the late sixth/early seventh century, a method that had been very common in Europe in the fourth century, and was probably taken to Ireland by British missionaries in the late fourth or fifth century. This was an archaic common standard; with such, it is certainly possible that in the late fourth century and through the fifth century, British and Irish practice was essentially the same. However, although Columbanus stuck to this 84-year cycle — on the grounds that more recent cycles were inaccurate — it is clear that the chronology of the 'Chronicle of Ireland' (the set of annals upon which the early parts of the Annals of Ulster are ultimately based) was partly determined by a 19-year cycle (that of Victorius of Aquitaine) from about 550, and that the superior 19-year tables of Dionysius were used as the foundation of the 'Chronicle' by 606; the Dionysian system was known at Bangor (even if not always used) by 600 (Harrison 1977–8; 1982, 316, 319; 1984). The southern Irish church undoubtedly changed to use a 19-year cycle in the 630s, as separate regions did subsequently seriatim (*Hist. Ecc.*, iii. 26, Colgrave and Mynors 1969; see above); although the Welsh decision to change to the system of Dionysius did not come until 768, some British clerics were using a 19-year Victorian cursus when compiling the *Historia Brittonum* in the late eighth or very early ninth century. This seems to have spanned the fifth and some of the sixth centuries and may have been of Irish origin. That it was used *c*. 800 is interesting; but there must be a possibility that it was also used in Wales before this (Dumville 1974).

Although much has been made of the polemical comment by Columbanus (*S Columb. Op.*: Ep., ii. 5, Walker 1957) that everyone in the entire western church used the 84-year cycle, and some have supposed that this must have included Bretons as well as Insular Christians, it is patently obvious that 19-year cycles were known and used in some parts of Britain and Ireland in the sixth century. Again, there was diversity. Hence, although it may be reasonable to suppose that British and Irish practice was the same in the fifth and early sixth centuries (when it was also the same as that in use in parts of the continent), there was clearly increasing diversity of practice in the second half of the sixth century, a diversity which culminated in the open conflicts of the seventh century. It was as a direct consequence of these differences that Tómméne of Armagh launched a mission to Rome in 631 to discover 'the truth'.

We can see, then, that in matters of religious practice not only was there diversity within Celtic churches but a constant tendency for the Welsh to be the most conservative and for a party of the Irish (often southern Irish) to be most closely influenced by Roman practice. Between those two extremes the northern Irish, Iona and western Scotland, and Pictland lagged at various rates behind the southern Irish; what we know of Brittany suggests that it was a curious mixture of conservatism and compliance with Gallic practice as it changed over the early middle ages, although regional differences within Brittany are probably concealed by the very fragmentary pre-ninth-century evidence. In all this we should remember that continental practice was not one standardized whole.

Belief

Just as there is no evidence of one single Celtic practice, neither can we find evidence of any single Celtic doctrine although Bede's History might be thought to suggest that there was an identifiable 'Scottish' doctrine in which Oswald was instructed (*Hist. Ecc.*, iii. 1, Colgrave and Mynors 1969). This *doctrina* means presumably no more than 'teaching' and is far too slight to substantiate any suggestion that Irish doctrine was distinct and amounted to unorthodoxy. Notably, when Columbanus was accused of unorthodoxy in respect of the Easter question, he objected violently and maintained that his belief and teaching were entirely orthodox (*S Columb. Op.*: Ep. ii. 7, 9; Ep. v. 3, Walker 1957). Leslie Hardinge has made a serious attempt to determine what the Irish believed, by analysing the large corpus of seventh- and eighth-century glosses; interesting as this is, it merely serves to emphasize that the Irish approach to faith was overwhelmingly influenced by the Bible and the fathers (1972, 53–73). On the other hand, there is some reason to argue that the heresy of Pelagianism had a particular and long-lasting influence in parts of Britain and Ireland. Pelagian ideas seem to have been strongly supported in Britain in the fifth century, when Pope Celestine sent Bishop Germanus from Auxerre to deal with them (Wood 1984, 7–14); in the mid-seventh century Pope John thought Pelagian ideas were reviving sufficiently in Ireland to cause concern, although it has been suggested that he was mistaken (*Hist. Ecc.*, ii. 19, Colgrave and Mynors 1969). In any case, Pelagian approaches can be identified in eighth-century Irish glosses on biblical texts, particularly those in the Würzburg Epistles, and in the Prefaces to the Pauline Epistles in the early ninth-century Book of Armagh; Pelagius is sometimes cited by name — like Patrick and Gildas — as an authority in the Irish canons (*Coll. Can. Hib.*, xxvii. 13; xlii. 4, Wasserschleben 1885); and a Pelagian commentary was copied in Wales in the late seventh or early eighth century (Dumville 1985b). I do not think we should see this Pelagian influence as consistent or standard or overwhelming (Bede, who loathed Pelagianism, did not usually regard the Irish as heretics); however, the ideas had a long life, on *both* sides of the Irish Sea.[5]

Some Similarities

It is not difficult, therefore, to find material that demonstrates regional differences between Celtic areas in religious affairs in the early middle ages, such that any notion of a single Celtic Church is easily disposed of. These points are obvious; they are not controversial; they do not need defending; they simply need noting by a wider readership than the relatively small company of scholars that knows them well.

There clearly was no single Church, as such. However, if we reformulate the question to ask when, where and in what circumstances were Celtic churches similar, then there are some interesting things to say. I have already pointed out the interest in Pelagian ideas manifest on both sides of the Irish sea in the seventh and eighth centuries. This is but one indication of the fact that there was in many respects a shared Latin culture for several centuries in Wales, Cornwall, Ireland and to some extent Brittany: clerics and monks were studying the same Latin works, using the same terms, thinking within the same conceptual framework, and using similar biblical texts, related to the older *Vetus Latina* rather than the Vulgate (Lapidge 1986, 91–2, 98, 102; Stevenson, J. 1987, lxxv-vi). They studied within the framework of a learning that was biblical and patristic rather than classical, a learning sometimes strongly influenced by the late classical grammatical tradition (James, E. 1982; 1984; Contreni 1986). Their approach to ecclesiastical status and to the place of the church in politics and society was heavily influenced by the Old Testament and by Mosaic Law in particular (Fournier 1909; Ó Corráin, Breatnach and Breen 1984, 394; cf. Hardinge 1972, 49–50). This is much better evidenced in Ireland than in other areas but the sporadic occurrence of distinctive terms in Welsh and Cornish texts shows how widespread was the approach (Enright 1985, 94). For example, we find the word *princeps*, 'prince, ruler', used to mean 'abbot' in Ireland, Scotland, Wales and perhaps Cornwall; this is not just an unusual word, but one which emphasizes the abbot's powers of control – he who holds the *principatus* (Davies, W. 1982c, 83–5; Dumville 1985a, 71–4). We find the word *refugium* used for sanctuary, in its territorially expanded western sense of a specially protected zone where special penalties applied for infringements, taken from Leviticus 'civitates refugii'; this is an Old Testament usage, but a usage not taken up on the continent, although immunities as such were common enough (Pryce 1984, 2). Huw Pryce can therefore postulate that there was a text of the Irish collection of canons available at an ecclesiastical centre in Wales in the early middle ages, a text which came to influence the much later material of the secular Welsh law tracts (Pryce 1986, 122–7). The evidence for Brittany in this respect is not quite so strong, but there are characteristically 'hisperic' stylistic touches in the Breton Saints' Lives (cf. Wood 1988, 382); grammatical texts and Gospels were copied in the ninth century (Dumville's valuable Oxford O'Donnell Lectures 1978, as yet unpublished; Guillotel 1985); and many Irish manuscripts were copied in the latter part of that century.

The Latin culture of Celtic areas for a time also influenced the record-making tradition of most parts in respect of property transactions: western charter forms are odd, although a derivative of late Roman forms, and do not change over time in the way that continental charter forms do. We find the distinctive western form in Wales and western Brittany especially, up to the eleventh century; in Cornwall in the tenth century; sufficient traces in Scotland to imply the same from seventh to twelfth century; few in Ireland, but enough seventh-century fragments and quotations in Saints' Lives to indicate that the forms were received, tried, had a limited influence, but did not attract wide usage (Davies, W. 1982b). More generally successful was the Insular system of scripts; again late Roman in origin, if we follow Julian

Brown's analysis, it was transmitted to Ireland and thence back to Britain and England (Brown 1984). There were regional variations, of course, but Insular scripts were normal in Insular countries and Brittany until the latter – the first to abandon them – moved to caroline minuscule in the early ninth century (Guillotel 1985, 17, 36; cf. Dumville, O'Donnell Lectures 1978).[6] Despite the overweighting of the Irish evidence, we cannot ignore the fact that we find common material in the written traditions (as also in the tradition of writing) again and again in Ireland, Wales, Brittany and Cornwall. This does not make for a Celtic Church, but it does argue for a common pool of literary tradition and some sustained contact as it developed. In this Scotland is a problem; after Adomnán in the early eighth century we have so few sustained texts that we simply do not know about the literary culture, Latin or vernacular, of the area (cf. Hughes, K. 1980).

I would raise another possible similarity, an institutional one, to consider. There seem to me to be some indications – rather tenuous – that in Ireland, Wales, Cornwall, Brittany and possibly Scotland (again the subject is bedevilled by the paucity of Scottish material) institutions for the pastoral care of the laity were more developed than in many other parts of Europe before the tenth century. A case for the existence of a rural proto-parochial structure can be made at an unusually early date for some Celtic areas. Whereas in most of continental Europe it was the tenth, eleventh and twelfth centuries which was the period that saw the real implementation of the parish structure in the countryside, whatever earlier clerics and rulers may have wished, it is perfectly clear, from very good evidence, that the geographical framework of the later structure as well as the provision of priests for local village communities was solidly (and possibly anciently) established in eastern Brittany by the early ninth century (Davies, W. 1983). On the basis of much more tenuous – but extremely suggestive – evidence discovered by Lynette Olson and Oliver Padel, the same may be suggested for parts of Cornwall by the tenth century (1986). On the basis of the very large number of churches in south-east Wales by the eleventh century one might be tempted to argue the same, although we know nothing of the role of these churches in relation to their local communities (Davies, W. 1982a, 143–4); at least the early development of distinctive, small-scale, local cults suggests plenty of lay participation in religious experience (Davies, W. 1978a, 131–2). If Ann

Preston-Jones's argument for the early development of local cults in Cornwall be accepted, then the same may be said of Cornwall too (see Preston-Jones below). The several seventh- and eighth-century texts from Ireland (*Ríagail Phátraic, Córus Béscnai,* and several Latin canons) make it quite clear that some group(s) in Ireland was trying to ensure that baptism and burial services were performed for at least some of the laity, through episcopal agencies, and tithes duly collected (Ó Corráin, Breatnach and Breen 1984, 408–9; Sharpe 1984b, 252, 259–60).[7] This material is prescriptive, and is what you might expect a good bishop to attempt; as such it is comparable with the Carolingian legislation on the subject and, like the Carolingian case, there is no especial reason to suppose that the prescriptions were invariably carried out (McKitterick 1977; Lemarignier 1982). However, these prescriptions do find expression at a surprisingly early date, and there was certainly no shortage of churches in seventh-century Ireland and no shortage of local cult by 800 (Sharpe 1984b, 254; cf. Doherty 1984a, 306). There may be a contrary suggestion for Scotland before the mid-twelfth century; before that large minsters are believed to have served very large areas, with priests travelling out to the localities from a central base (cf. Duncan 1975, 297–9).[8] Scotland notwithstanding, it is worth considering and pursuing the rest. If true it would not in some senses be surprising: Christianity in Celtic countries was necessarily rural; if there was to be any provision of pastoral care at all, it had to be rural-based; rural institutions would have to have been developed *ab initio* (cf. Sharpe 1984c, 201).

Change over Time

We might in the end draw some chronological distinctions. In the fifth and early sixth centuries, when there was British missionary work in Ireland and Scotland, and quite possibly in Brittany too, institutions and practice are likely to have been very similar in all areas. There are likely to have been some bishops, plenty of priests, not so many monasteries, the use of the 84-year cycle for calculating the date of Easter, late Roman modes of property registration, the use of scripts derived from late Roman 'expert' cursives, and so on. As Plummer pointed out nearly a hundred years ago, Britain perpetuated archaic continental practice (1896, ii, 354). In the later sixth and very early seventh centuries, by contrast, we have evidence of

change within the Irish church: monasteries were founded, sometimes many; ascetic principles were adopted by many and became influential; the *peregrinationes*, long-ranging journeys to England and the continent, began (Hughes, K. 1966). In short, despite the continuing influence of British masters like Gildas and Finnian/Uinniau in the Irish church (Dumville 1984c; 1984d), and despite continuing respect for their authority, the conditions for diversity were being established, although the written Latin culture seems to have remained conservative. In the course of the seventh century, religious differences between Britain and Ireland became very clear, as did differences within Ireland too; some clerics developed a greater awareness of 'Rome', and hence of contrasts in custom and practice; some communities and their leaders developed ambitions of establishing themselves at the pinnacle of hierarchical authority; some lay families developed close relations with particular monastic communities. By the eighth century regional characteristics were obvious, and the British/Irish divide was apparent and often noticed. At various times in the next three centuries the different regions changed from these deviant patterns — Brittany began to change in the ninth century, Wales in the late tenth and eleventh, Ireland and Scotland in the mid- and later eleventh century. But by the late eleventh century, whatever the outset, and whatever the recent change, all looked deviant to the leaders of the newly reformed western church — deviant because they were only slightly touched by continental reform (just as the Anglo-Saxon church looked deviant to the Anglo-Norman historians of the early twelfth century). The notion of 'Celtic Church', therefore, is most appropriate to the fifth and early sixth century, although the church in Celtic areas was not so different from the continent at that period.[9] By contrast, the late eleventh century was a period when the otherness of the Celtic churches became a concern of many western observers.

We might also take note that our perceptions of the Celtic Church issue are confused by the tension between the shared Latin culture of many of those churches in the sixth, seventh and eighth centuries and the differing social consequences of conversion in those areas. There are times when elements of the clergy were thinking the same thoughts and doing the same things, but the local experience of Christianity varied. Thus the impact of Christianity on, for example, the status of women varied: whereas Irish women accepted the call to chastity, adopted the committed Christian life and achieved sanctity in large numbers by 800, Breton women do not appear to have done so — we find no Breton nuns nor Breton female saints in this period. So also the impact of monasticism on men varied: whereas Irish men responded to the call to ascetic principles by picking up their bags and walking, Britons and Bretons and Scots seem to have been much less mobile; this was not entirely so, but it is the Irish who developed a quite remarkable mobility. It may also be true that whereas Welsh, Cornish and Bretons harboured their slaves, Irish and Scots were more stimulated to give slaves their freedom, at least by accepting them into religious institutions and making manumission an acceptable penance in recompense for sins.

****

So, in a conference where the emphasis is on the archaeology of Welsh Christianity, do not be misled by the Celtic Church model: you are not likely to find many traces of shared Latin culture on the ground, nor — if it is appropriate — of parishes. Do not expect that everything will or should look Irish, although some things might; do not expect that everything will look monastic, and/or eremitic; do expect Welsh things to tend to be archaic; and think very carefully about burial, as yet the largest corpus of unexploited material that we have (see H. James below). We may even, in time and with a good series of dates, be able to relate this material to parochial development. If that happens, we really will have a breakthrough, as much in European as in Celtic history.[10]

June 1989

Notes
1. I am grateful to Wyn Evans for drawing this refreshingly vigorous work to my attention.
2. Sharpe argues that bishops retained responsibility for pastoral care in these cases; this is possible — and an interesting proposal — but the available evidence is not decisive (1984b, 258–61).
3. Jane Stevenson also points out that the anointing of priests was not a Roman custom, but it <u>was</u> Gallican (1987, lvi).
4. The monks of Landévennec in western Brittany still had a tonsure which the Carolingians found deviant in the early ninth century, called 'Irish' by Louis the Pious (*Vita Winwal.* ii, 13, in de La Borderie 1888). I do not think we need suppose this was necessarily Irish — it may merely have been classified as such in the flurry of 'iromania' (see James, E. 1982, 380).
5. It is possible that the Irish Romani had some different interpretation of the psalms, if a (?)Northumbrian text of *c.* 700 is to be believed (Ó Cróinín 1982, 285).
6. Cf. orthographic similarities too, although the debate on whether the distinctive practices have a British or an Irish origin still rages (Harvey 1989, and references there cited). Patrick McGurk has demonstrated that, although there was a distinctive *Irish* bookmaking tradition, there is not enough evidence to say that it was distinctively *Celtic* (1987).
7. There is a problem over the intended beneficiaries of these services; *Ríagail Phátraic* suggests that they are only intended for *manaig*, monastic tenants; Ó Corráin's reading of *Córus Béscnai*, however, clearly indicates the entire lay population, whether monastic tenants or otherwise (Ó Corráin, Breatnach and Breen 1984, 408–9; but cf. Ó Corráin 1981a, 334).
8. Charles Thomas argued that the church of Ardwall Island, off south-west Scotland, served the local population, although there is no direct evidence for this (1967c, 174); and suggested that the *kirks* of south-west Scotland represented ancient parish foci — again possible, but we lack any direct evidence (Thomas 1967c, 181).
9. Richard Sharpe would argue that the similarities were more noticeable than the differences in the late sixth century (1984c, 201–2); this may have been so, although at present I am more inclined to note the range of Easter tables in use in the late sixth century than to believe that the influence of British masters in Ireland necessarily made for homogeneity/standardization.
10. Grateful thanks are due to Patrick Wormald for his comments on the written draft of this paper.

Ecclesiastical Wealth in Early Medieval Wales

Huw Pryce

I

Wealth is not, perhaps, a word which immediately springs to mind when considering the surviving archaeological evidence from pre-Norman churches in Wales. With the possible exception of Presteigne (Taylor, H.M. and Taylor, J. 1965, 497–9), the fabric of any stone church built prior to *c.* 1100 has yet to be discovered, while none of the (admittedly substantial) corpus of stone sculpture dating from the ninth to eleventh centuries matches the finest freestanding crosses erected in Ireland in that period. The ecclesiastical metalwork surviving into this century totals seven handbells, and of the fewer than a dozen surviving manuscripts, only three are illuminated (see below). Likewise, by comparison with many other parts of early medieval Europe, the written sources available for an investigation of ecclesiastical wealth are meagre. For instance, we largely lack the insights offered by texts of canon and secular law, although some brief penitentials have been argued to derive from sixth-century Wales and an undefined amount of material in the medieval Welsh lawbooks, first compiled in their present form in the late twelfth and thirteenth centuries, may date from the pre-Norman period. With the exception of the first Life of Samson, written in Brittany possibly in the early seventh century, the earliest Lives of Welsh saints date from the late eleventh century; otherwise, the nearest we get to historical writing are Gildas's *De Excidio Britanniae*, the *Historia Brittonum*, and the *Annales Cambriae* (Davies, W. 1982a, 198–218). Moreover, none of these sources furnish detailed descriptions of ecclesiastical treasures comparable with those found in, say, the seventh-century account of Kildare in Cogitosus's Life of Brigit or in Aethelwulf's early ninth-century poem, *De Abbatibus* (Connolly and Picard 1987, 25–6; Campbell, A. 1967). Even if we turned to texts of the twelfth century and later, it would be impossible to attempt a history of art and architecture in early medieval Wales based primarily on written sources such as has been accomplished for Anglo-Saxon England (cf. Dodwell 1982, 12–23 *et passim*).

Yet the prospect is not entirely bleak. We do, after all, possess a considerable body of evidence relating to the landed wealth of churches in southern, and especially south-eastern, Wales — namely the 158 charters contained in the early twelfth-century gospel book, *Liber Landavensis* or the *Book of Llandaf*. These have been convincingly shown to derive from genuine early medieval records, and, although their mode of preservation undoubtedly poses problems of interpretation, their importance to the present inquiry can hardly be denied (Davies, W. 1973; 1979a; Sims-Williams 1982). Together with other charters and some of the hagiography they reveal an aspect of ecclesiastical wealth which would remain invisible if we were to rely on the testimony of archaeology alone. Indeed, a critical appraisal of the written evidence in general can help to modify the impression of poverty conveyed by the limited quantity and quality of the ecclesiastical structures and artefacts surviving from pre-Norman Wales.

Before going any further, though, two caveats need to be entered. First, this paper is not arguing that Wales was an ecclesiastical El Dorado, hitherto unnoticed, in early medieval Europe. Wealth is always relative. By comparison with many other areas of Europe Wales was economically underdeveloped and sparsely populated; commercial exchange and the use of coin were very limited; there were no towns (Davies, W. 1982a, 31–58, 194–5). We should not, therefore, expect Welsh churches to have matched the wealth of the greatest monasteries of (say) Ireland, England or northern France. The argument here is simply that some of those churches must have been wealthy in the specific social and economic context of early medieval Wales.

Admittedly — and here we come to the second caveat — the picture of ecclesiastical wealth which can be pieced together from the available sources is patchy and incomplete. We do not know how many churches there were in early medieval Wales, let alone the proportion of them which might be considered centres of wealth. Many early Welsh churches are extremely obscure. Their existence may be revealed by a single pre-Norman reference, or else inferred from the location of early medieval stone monuments as well as from place-names and the evidence of sources written later in the middle ages (Davies, W. 1982a, 141–8). In addition, it is worth stressing how few churches can confidently be shown to have continued in existence throughout the early medieval period (cf. Davies, W. 1978a, 123–4; 1982a, 145–6). Some early foundations may have disappeared: Bangor Is-coed is a likely case in point (see below). The fortunes of others will have waxed and waned. Thus Llandeilo Fawr, and possibly also Welsh Bicknor and Llanbadarn Fawr, lost episcopal status; in the early eleventh century Llandaff almost certainly gained it (Davies, W. 1978a, 149–59; 1982a, 158–60). The distribution of Early Christian monuments in Dyfed has been interpreted as reflecting shifts in ecclesiastical foci between the fifth and sixth centuries on the one hand and the ninth century and later on the other, with only Nevern and St Dogmaels showing evidence of continuity from the earlier period onwards (Lewis, J.M. 1976, 184–6). In general, the written sources tend to be weighted in favour of churches in south Wales which survived into the era of Norman conquest and settlement in the late eleventh and twelfth centuries.

The uneven chronological and geographical spread of the sources means, then, that (with the partial exception of Llandaff) it is impossible to provide a detailed account of the accumulation or loss of wealth by individual churches over the early medieval period. Moreover, the brevity and imprecision of much of the information provided often make it difficult to catch more than fleeting glimpses of ecclesiastical wealth. Nevertheless such glimpses can be very suggestive. Take Gildas, for example: in his *De Excidio* (cc. 66–7, 108) he denounces both sycophantic and simoniacal clergy, who neglected alms-giving while filling their own bellies, strongly implying that ecclesiastical office was regarded primarily as a source of status and profit in the recently established British kingdoms of sixth-century Britain (Winterbottom 1978, 52–4, 77–8). This church probably had its roots in the late Roman period, and was clearly part of the political establishment (Davies, W.H. 1968, 140–1, 149 n. 108; Hughes, K. 1981, 3, 10, 15; Knight 1984a, 340). Its worldliness may have been challenged by the monastic movement discernible by the sixth century (Davies, W. 1982a, 146–8), but the contrast should probably not be drawn too sharply, since even in Gildas's day it would appear that monks' definitions of what

constituted unacceptable wealth varied. The *Fragmenta* ascribed to Gildas condemn those who took asceticism to self-righteous extremes: it was not right to welcome monks fleeing from abbots merely because the latter possessed animals and vehicles, for only a superabundance of possessions amounted to luxury and riches (Winterbottom 1978, 81; cf. Sharpe 1984c, 197–9). That monasteries were not always places of ascetic self-denial is further suggested by c. 10 of Gildas's Preface on Penance, which envisaged members of a religious community being too drunk to sing the Psalms; the problem of excessive drinking is also addressed in cc. 1–4 of the (possibly sixth-century) Excerpts from a Book of David (Bieler 1963, 63, 71). In a similar vein, the Life of Samson (I. 14, 16–21) contrasts Illtud's monastery — a busy place the control of which was keenly sought by its founder's nephews — with that of Pirus, where a more rigorous monastic regime prevailed (Fawtier 1912, 113, 115–21).[1]

It seems, then, that already in the sixth century there was a diversity of ecclesiastical establishments in Wales, some of which were wealthier than others. Moreover the practice of individual poverty and asceticism need not have entailed rejection of corporate wealth. This is suggested by Bede's account of Bangor Is-coed in the early seventh century (*Historia Ecclesiastica* II. 2): the 'most noble monastery' of the Britons was said to have contained over 2,000 monks, 'all of whom used to live by the labour of their own hands' (Plummer 1896, I, 82–4). There is no means of verifying the numbers reported by Bede but the possibility that Bangor Is-coed contained a community running into hundreds should not be ruled out.[2] After all, it seems to have been a complex institution which, in addition to monks, housed bishops and 'learned men' as well as a holy anchorite. Presumably it was well endowed with land, perhaps by the monks' *defensor*, Brochfael, who may have belonged to the Cadelling dynasty of Powys (Plummer 1896, I, 82, 84; Thacker 1987, 239).

Although Bangor Is-coed may never have recovered from the massacre of its monks at the battle of Chester c. 616 (Plummer 1896, I, 84, II, 75), evidence indicative of ecclesiastical wealth does not dry up after the seventh century. Above all, that wealth is implied by the accounts of raids on churches. An inscription recorded by Edward Lhuyd at Llanddewibrefi possibly records a raid on the church as early as the first half of the seventh century (Gruffydd and Owen 1956–8); but it is only from the late ninth

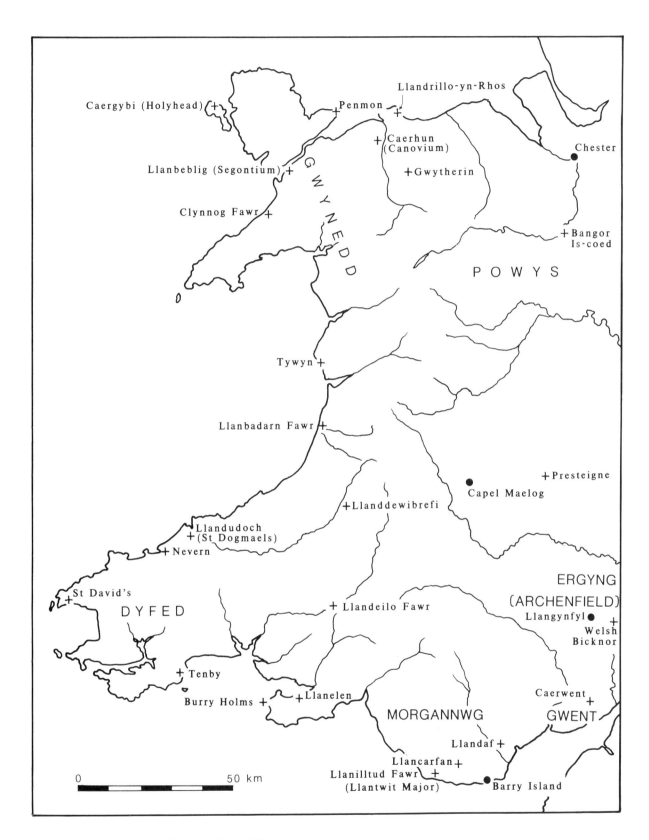

Fig. 3.1 *Map of Wales, showing places mentioned in the text*

+ churches founded before *c.*1100   ● other sites

century that references to raids by native kings on (south Welsh) churches and their possessionsmultiply (Davies, W. 1978a, 133; Keynes and Lapidge 1983, 94–6). The exact nature of the resources taken on those occasions is seldom specified, but certainly included food and drink (see below). Accounts of Viking attacks on churches are similarly imprecise. Concentrated mostly in the late tenth century, but continuing throughout the eleventh, these raids point to the continuing attraction of churches as sources of plunder, and provide a rough guide to the most important churches at that time. Recorded targets comprised Caergybi (Holyhead) (961) and Penmon (971) in Anglesey, Bangor (1073), Clynnog Fawr (978) and Tywyn (963) in Gwynedd, Llanbadarn Fawr (988), Llandudoch (St Dogmaels) (988) and St David's (11 times between 907 and 1091) in Dyfed, and Llanilltud Fawr (Llantwit Major) (988) and Llancarfan (988) in Morgannwg (Williams ab Ithel 1860, 21–3, 26–9; Jones, T. 1952, 8–13, 16–8; 1973, 15–9, 23, 29–33). In addition Bishop Cyfeilliog of Ergyng (Archenfield) was captured by the Vikings in 914 and ransomed by Edward the Elder (Whitelock 1955, 194).

It will be noticed that, apart from St David's, all the churches listed were struck only once (although Llanbadarn Fawr was also raided by Gruffudd ap Llywelyn in 1039). This may merely reflect the St David's provenance of the *Annales Cambriae* and the annals underlying the versions of the thirteenth-century Welsh chronicle, *Brut y Tywysogyon*, and may give a misleading impression of the extent of damage inflicted on the other churches (cf. Lloyd 1928; Hughes, K. 1980, 67–85). But if raids on places as far away from St David's as Penmon or Llancarfan could be recorded once, surely they could have been recorded again had they occurred? The frequency of the attacks on St David's points to considerable powers of recovery, suggesting that the church whose founding saint was famed for his asceticism possessed substantial resources — as do Asser's account of the plundering of the church and its lands by King Hyfaidd of Dyfed in the late ninth century and the relatively large amount and high standard of its ninth-to-eleventh-century sculpture (Davies, W. 1982a, 119–20; Keynes and Lapidge 1983, 94–6; Nash-Williams 1950, 207–11). We should not underestimate the short-term impact of Viking raids, though. After all, two bishops of St David's were killed as a result of them (in 999 and 1080). In addition, the Life of Caradog relates that the church had once been

deserted for almost seven years as a result of frequent Norse raids, describing how a certain priest had taken seven days to cut his way through the undergrowth to reach David's tomb (Horstmann 1901, 174), and, even if these periods of time merit scepticism, the general tenor of the account is consistent with other evidence.

If, however, the repeated plundering of St David's is testimony to its resilience, the paucity of recorded attacks on other Welsh churches may be interpreted, conversely, as evidence of their poverty — although of course churches situated at a distance from the Irish Sea, such as those of Morgannwg, stood less chance of becoming targets in the first place, since the raiders seem usually to have operated from bases in Ireland (Davies, W. 1982a, 116–7). More generally, it is striking how lightly churches in Wales fared at the hands of the Vikings by comparison with those of Ireland or eastern England, for example. This unattractiveness to the Norse in turn probably underlines the point made earlier, that we are dealing with a society which was relatively poor and economically undeveloped in European terms, and which was therefore unlikely to have sustained numerous wealthy churches.

II

Only once do we learn what the Vikings seized from the churches they raided: in 1089 the saint's shrine was stolen from the church of St David's and despoiled of its gold and silver (Williams ab Ithel 1860, 28–9). As has been mentioned, the extant and recently extant ecclesiastical metalwork from early medieval Wales amounts to seven handbells made of iron and copper alloy (Fisher 1926; Fox, A. 1946, 121–2; Knight 1984b, 370–1, 405 n. 26).[3] Written sources show, nevertheless, that early Welsh churches were adorned with more precious objects than this paltry total might suggest. Bells, croziers and enshrined gospel-books associated with saints are mentioned in the hagiography (Evans and Rhŷs 1893, 135–6, 137; Wade-Evans 1944, 110–2, 126, 228–32, 238), and their continued popularity as relics is attested at the end of the twelfth century by Gerald of Wales, who wrote that, like the Irish and Scots, the Welsh people and clergy 'have such a reverence for portable bells, staffs crooked at the top and encased in gold, silver or bronze, and other similar relics of the saints, that they are more afraid of swearing oaths upon them and then breaking their word than they are upon the Gospels' (Dimock 1868, 27). It is hard to believe that none of these relics was pre-Norman.

Post-medieval antiquarian sources point to the existence of other early medieval treasures which have since been lost. Thus Edward Lhuyd, Henry Rowlands and Richard Fenton recorded a variety of bells, and the head of St Baglan's crozier survived until the late seventeenth century (Fisher 1926, 332–3; Knight 1984b, 371). These objects cannot be proved to have been pre-Norman; but a casket at the church of Gwytherin, depicted in some detail in a drawing by Edward Lhuyd, quite clearly was.[4] This was still extant in the early nineteenth century (Evans, J.W. 1986, 66–7) and is a reminder that the loss of some pre-Norman artefacts may be fairly recent, although raids by Norse, Welsh and Normans, followed by Protestant and then Puritan desecration in the sixteenth and seventeenth centuries, must have taken their toll (cf. Thomas, L. 1930, 75–8, 102–8; Gresham 1968, 57–9; Knight 1984b, 389).

Loss and destruction almost certainly help to explain the paucity of surviving illuminated manuscripts — and indeed of manuscripts in general — from churches in early medieval Wales. That the chances of survival were small is shown by the fact that all extant Welsh manuscripts written prior to 1100 have been preserved outside Wales, principally in England (cf. Lindsay 1912). This is also true of the Lichfield Gospels, an eighth-century book of unknown provenance kept at Lichfield since at least the eleventh century, but present at the church of Llandeilo Fawr by the early ninth. The Gospels are damaged and incomplete but their decoration is of a sufficiently high standard to have prompted comparisons with the Lindisfarne Gospels and the Book of Kells (Jenkins and Owen 1983; Henderson, G. 1987, 122–9). How many other luxury Gospel Books were possessed by Welsh churches, only to be later transferred elsewhere or lost? What happened, for example, to the Gospels allegedly written by Gildas, covered with gold and silver, which Caradog of Llancarfan tells us were still in the church of Llancarfan in the 1120s or 1130s (Williams, H. 1899–1901, II, 406; cf. Brooke 1986, 42)? Of course, such books need not always have been made in Wales: the Lichfield Gospels may have been illuminated in England, although an Irish or even Welsh provenance cannot be ruled out (Jenkins and Owen 1983, 41–8; Henderson, G. 1987, 124–9). That a Welsh cleric could engage in manuscript-illumination in the eleventh century

is demonstrated by the Psalter and Martyrology of Rhigyfarch (Dublin, Trinity College MS 50 (A.4.20)), decorated by his brother Ieuan. The latter was the scribe and probably also the illuminator of Cambridge, Corpus Christi College MS 199, containing a copy of St Augustine's *De Trinitate* (Lawlor 1914, I, xix–xxi). It is also suggestive in this connection that the scribe of a mid-thirteenth-century manuscript of the Welsh laws (British Library, Cotton Caligula MS A.iii) was apparently able to draw upon an Insular gospel book for his drawings of evangelist symbols. Had such a book passed from a native Welsh church to the Cistercian monastery, possibly Valle Crucis, where the legal manuscript was almost certainly produced (Huws 1986, 123, 127–8, Pls 1–2)?

We know very little indeed about the church buildings which housed the metalwork and manuscripts (Hague 1973; Davies, W. 1982a, 25–6). It is highly likely that, as in Ireland, churches were small. The stone cathedral church of Llandaff was a mere 40 feet long (12.2m) in 1120. Its date of construction is unknown, but the account in *Liber Landavensis* implies it to have been in existence before Urban became bishop in 1107 and it was therefore almost certainly built before the twelfth century (Evans and Rhŷs 1893, 86; cf. Crouch 1989, 12–13). Nor is it impossible that other early medieval Welsh churches were built of stone. Those situated in or near the Roman forts of Caergybi (Holyhead), Llanbeblig (Segontium) and Caerhun (Canovium) and the Roman town of Caerwent could have utilized stone robbed from the adjacent ruins, although there is no clear evidence for the use of Roman building-materials in church fabrics in Wales before the twelfth century (Thomas, H.J. 1983). Early medieval stone churches may also have been obscured by later building on the same site. Welsh clergy travelling to Ireland, England or the Continent would have come across stone churches and at the end of the period the late eleventh-century Life of Cadog (cc. 35–6) could depict the saint building a stone church and bridge in Brittany and a stone monastery in Scotland (Wade-Evans 1944, 94–100). It is difficult to believe that the idea of building in stone would have been totally unfamiliar in Wales, especially by the tenth and eleventh centuries, or that it would have been wholly impracticable.

Nevertheless, until firm evidence to the contrary is forthcoming, the assumption must be that timber was the normal building-material used for churches in pre-Norman Wales. The early twelfth-century stone church on Burry Holms, off the Gower coast, was preceded by a tiny wooden structure (3.35m x 3.05m), believed by the excavator to be of the late eleventh century (Hague 1973, 29–32; RCAHMW 1976, 14–5).[5] It is clear that the twelfth century witnessed widespread church building in stone, both *ab initio* — including on early medieval cemetery sites such as Barry Island and Capel Maelog near Llandrindod Wells — and, presumably, on sites which previously had timber churches. The size of churches grew significantly in the twelfth century too, with the building of abbeys and priories and the rebuilding of cathedrals on a scale unparalleled in the pre-Norman period (Knight 1984b, 395; Britnell 1990; Davies, R.R. 1987, 184, 187–8).[6]

Early medieval churches in Wales appear, then, to have been small and usually built of timber. Such architectural simplicity is hardly indicative of ecclesiastical wealth. In itself, however, it does not necessarily allow us to go further and conclude that churches were poor. Large stone churches may not have been regarded as providing appropriate places of worship — one thinks of how Malachy's plans in 1140 to replace the timber church at Bangor, Co Down by one of stone were reportedly greeted by the local inhabitants with the hostile assertion that such an edifice would be a superfluous novelty (Lawlor 1920, 109–10). Instead, as has been suggested with regard to early medieval Ireland, resources may have been invested mainly in the construction of fine timber churches and in their embellishment with wood carving and metalwork, surrounded by imposing pieces of stone sculpture (cf. Hamlin 1984, 121–2, 126; Hare with Hamlin 1986, 135). We do, after all, have the 125 crosses and cross-slabs of ninth- to eleventh-century date listed by Nash-Williams in his Group III of monuments to demonstrate the capacity — albeit unskilful at times — to produce stone sculpture in Wales (Nash-Williams 1950, 27–47). In addition, we should not exaggerate the extent to which Wales lagged behind its Insular neighbours: although important churches had been built of stone at an early date in both Ireland and England, it was only in the eleventh and twelfth centuries that the construction of such churches became widespread in those countries (Hamlin 1984, 118–9; Gem 1988; Morris, R.K. 1988). Yet, notwithstanding the validity of these various points, the impression of poverty remains. That no Welsh church — with the possible exception of Presteigne (see above) — has as yet yielded

evidence of pre-Norman fabric is surely ultimately explicable in terms of inadequate resources.

III

Precious objects such as relics and books, together with sculpture and buildings, can all be interpreted as indices of ecclesiastical wealth. However, in Wales, as elsewhere in early medieval Europe, what sustained churches from year to year, enabling them to recover from short-term catastrophes, was land. Here the evidence is relatively full and unambiguous. The Llandaff charters demonstrate that substantial estates, most ranging between 100 acres (40ha) and 1000 acres (400ha) and almost always located on the best soils, were alienated to churches in south Wales from the late sixth or seventh to the eleventh centuries (Davies, W. 1978a, 24–42; 1978b, 6–8; cf. Sims-Williams 1982, 126); Clynnog Fawr received grants over a similar period according to the charter preserved in a fifteenth-century copy but apparently drawing on an earlier text (Ellis 1838, 257–8; Davies, W. 1982b, 271); two ninth-century grants to Llandeilo Fawr are recorded in the Lichfield Gospels (Evans and Rhŷs 1893, xlv; Jenkins and Owen 1983, 52–4, 56–7); and the Life of Cadog contains 14 charters some of which have been dated to between the seventh and ninth centuries (Wade-Evans 1944, 124–36; Davies, W. 1982b, 260 & n. 10; Knight 1984a, 348–50). Doubtless other charters once existed but no longer survive; it seems, for example, that in the sixteenth century William Salesbury and possibly also Leland saw some from St David's (Davies, W. 1982b, 261 & n. 19).

The charter evidence has been analysed in detail, above all by Wendy Davies. She has argued, principally with reference to the Llandaff material, that grants were concentrated in the eighth century, coinciding with major changes in land tenure as kings lost their monopoly of making donations and the size of grants fell, possibly reflecting the fragmentation of estates originating in the late Roman period (Davies, W. 1973; 1978a; 1978b; 1979a; 1979b). The full ramifications of this argument need not concern us now. What needs to be emphasized, however, is that churches in south Wales at least had been generously endowed with land by the late ninth century. It is perhaps not mere coincidence that it is mostly from then onwards that native Welsh rulers, their own resources presumably depleted by the generosity of their predecessors, are recorded as plundering ecclesiastical possessions (see above).

Such attacks probably supply the context for the vigorous defence of property-rights in some of the saints' Lives, especially that of Cadog, and raise the possibility that churches lost lands donated to them even before the Normans seized ecclesiastical estates in south Wales and granted them to religious houses in England and France (Davies, W. 1981). The Llandaff charters are of course only evidence for the time of the grants which they record; additional evidence is required to establish whether the lands in question remained ecclesiastical property in the twelfth century or later (Davies, W. 1978a, 25). Nevertheless it is very unlikely that any pre-Norman appropriations of church lands matched the scale and intensity of those of the late eleventh and early twelfth centuries (cf. Davies, R.R. 1987, 180–1). That churches could retain property over many centuries is, moreover, suggested by the fact that a number of pre-Norman churches in Gwent claimed as belonging to Llandaff in *Liber Landavensis* were still held by the church in the thirteenth century, when they are listed among the cathedral's prebends (Brook 1985–8, 72–4).

Likewise it is doubtful whether lay appropriation of ecclesiastical lands by native Welsh kindreds, as found at Llanbadarn Fawr in the twelfth and thirteenth centuries (Evans, below), was as common earlier in the middle ages. Gerald of Wales's assertion that laymen, originally called in as custodians or *advocati*, came eventually to exercise full rights of possession over churches' lands, leaving only spiritual revenues such as tithes to the clergy, may relate to fairly recent developments when he wrote in the early 1190s (Dimock 1868, 120).[7] Indeed such lay control, involving the division of churches and their property into portions and their transmission by partible hereditary succession, should probably be viewed in the context of more general changes in the pattern of free and aristocratic land-holding in twelfth- and thirteenth-century Wales. These cannot be explored here, but it would be unwise to overlook the likely connections between, on the one hand, the expansion of population and the segmentation of kindreds into patrilineal descent-groups (*gwelyau*, sg. *gwely*), together with their quest for additional resources (Jones, G.R.J. 1972, 320–34; Davies, R.R. 1987, 125–7, 146–58; cf. Griffiths, M. 1988–9, 201–13), and, on the other, kindreds' seizure and hereditary transmission of ecclesiastical lands (Palmer 1886;

Pryce 1988, 38–9). To return to the charters, the grants appear normally to have been of estates in working order, peopled by tenants who paid their food renders thenceforth to the church rather than to the king or other secular lord (Davies, W. 1978b, 7–8). Admittedly some sixth- and early seventh-century monasteries seem to have practised economic self-sufficiency, to judge from one of Gildas's *Fragmenta* and Bede's account of Bangor Is-coed (see above), while a section extolling the Egyptian-style monasticism of St David and his companions in cc. 21–32 of Rhigyfarch's Life of the saint suggests that such self-sufficiency could still be valued, if only as an ideal, at the end of the eleventh century (James, J.W. 1967, 12–4). But such establishments may well have been exceptional. For the charters, together with some of the hagiography and Domesday Book, indicate that, as in other early medieval societies, churches in Wales were supported by peasant surpluses. The two charters in the Lichfield Gospels and most of the Llancarfan charters specify the food renders due from the lands granted. The Llandaff charters are less explicit. Although many claim exemption from paying census to the king, these clauses have been argued to be nearly always twelfth-century interpolations (Jones, G.R.J. 1972, 305–6; Davies, W. 1978a, 47–50). Both the Llandaff and Llancarfan charters do, however, refer to the obligations of outlying estates to provide hospitality when the bishop or abbot visited (Evans and Rhŷs 1893, 185, 238, 272; Wade-Evans 1944, 128; cf. Davies, W. 1978a, 130–1). So too does the ninth- or tenth-century colloquy, *De raris fabulis*, which envisages members of a religious community visiting neighbouring settlements to receive food and clothing (Stevenson, W.H. 1929, 11).[8] These provisions were reportedly ample enough for them to be seized on occasion by lay rulers and their retainers who feasted and intoxicated themselves on them (Evans and Rhŷs 1893, 238, 272; Wade-Evans 1944, 58, 62, 196–8). By the end of the period, moreover, material incorporated in the Life of Cadog (cc. 48–9) describes what seems to be a classic manorial organization, in which the canons of Llancarfan were supported by a combination of demesne farms worked by gardeners (*hortolani*) and townships (*villae*) which provided clothing and food (Wade-Evans 1944, 120).

It is likely, though, that the organization and social structure of Welsh ecclesiastical estates were fairly complex well before the late eleventh century. Unfortunately we lack estate surveys comparable to the Carolingian polyptyques or even inventories of ecclesiastical possessions like those of late Anglo-Saxon England (cf. Campbell, J. 1986, 164–6) and, as so often, we have to make do with fragments of evidence. But enough is known to demonstrate that churches had both slaves and tenants of free origin. The colloquy speaks of the monastery's *subiecti*, also termed *servi* or *captivi*. These seem to have been slaves, based at the monastery, since when the abbot and his *familia* went to dinner with one of the local *seniores* they were accompanied by all their *subiecti* except for one cook or baker, the door-keeper and the herdsmen (Stevenson, W.H. 1929, 2). Some of the Llandaff charters record the donation of slaves to churches, and the Life of Cadog (c. 33) relates how a certain peasant was given in perpetual slavery to Cadog's monastery as punishment for perjury (Evans and Rhŷs 1893, 127, 185, 236; Wade-Evans 1944, 94–6; cf. Davies, W. 1978a, 43, 46–7).

Whether there were also servile dependents with holdings of land — bond tenants — is unclear. Indeed the origins of bondmen in Wales, including their relationship to slavery, remain obscure. Bondmen certainly existed by the late twelfth century, for the Welsh lawbooks stipulate the food renders which they owed to the king and refer explicitly to bond townships. Glanville Jones has, however, drawn attention to the resemblances between those renders and the *census* laid down in the two ninth-century charters in the Lichfield Gospels, as well as to the coincidence of bond tenures with pre-Norman ecclesiastical sites such as Gwytherin and Clynnog Fawr in later medieval surveys from north Wales, and argued that bondmen formed a majority of the Welsh population before the twelfth century (Jones, G.R.J. 1960–3, 125, 127–8; 1972, 299–302, 312–3, 334–9). There are grounds for supposing, therefore, that already in the pre-Norman period churches possessed bond tenants who paid rent for their land in the form of food renders. In addition, if, as seems probable, some of the grants recorded in the Llandaff charters had been carved out of larger units of agrarian exploitation (or, as Professor Jones has called them, multiple estates), and if within those units they had formed demesne centres containing a substantial labour-force of slaves, then it is possible that their new ecclesiastical owners may have found it more convenient to provide the slaves with holdings in return for rent (cf. Davies, W. 1978b, 11–13; Jones, G.R.J. 1979, 126–9; 1984, 32). This would

have been especially so when estates were situated at some distance from the church, making direct supervision difficult unless stewards were employed — the Life of Cadog (c. 43) refers to a steward who guarded Llancarfan's land on the Liffey in Ireland (Wade-Evans 1944, 112–4; cf. 128), and Bishop Joseph of Llandaff had a *prepositus* associated with Llangynfyl who witnessed a charter in c. 1030 (Evans and Rhŷs 1893, 264; cf. Davies, W. 1979a, 128).

Unfortunately most grants to churches make no mention of tenants, but a small number of charters record the donation of *heredes* or *hereditarii* together with the land (Evans and Rhŷs 1893, 148, 207–8, 240). These 'appear to have been either occupying or managing tenants' (Davies, W. 1978b, 10) and, since they seem to have possessed hereditary rights in the land, they presumably enjoyed free status. In other examples the *heredes* or *hereditarii* are said themselves to have made or consented to the grant, in association with a king (Evans and Rhŷs 1893, 143, 158, 179, 195, 209). In all these instances it is likely that the free tenants subjected themselves — whether voluntarily or involuntarily we cannot tell — to the church, promising to pay their surplus produce to it rather than the king. In at least five charters the donor bound his heirs to serve the church in perpetuity (Evans and Rhŷs 1893, 127, 176; Wade-Evans 1944, 126, 128, 130–2 [cc. 56, 59, 63] and cf. 128–30 [c. 61]). What we may well be seeing here is the creation of a distinct class of ecclesiastical tenants resembling the *manaig* of early medieval Ireland. The latter appear to have been free kindreds subject to the authority of the abbot, and it has been argued that their transfer was often effected by means of a solemn declaration or will (*audacht*) which 'enabled legal arrangements to persist after the death of the head of the kindred who had initiated them' (Charles-Edwards 1984, 171). One of the Llancarfan charters suggests that analogous transactions may have occurred in Wales too, since it records how the donor bequeathed (*commendavit*) the *villa* of Penacarnou to his son 'so that he and his heirs should serve the *familia* of Cadog from the produce of that land in addition to themselves' (Wade-Evans 1944, 128 [c. 59]).

One mechanism for transferring agrarian surpluses to churches for which there is virtually no evidence before the twelfth century in Wales, is tithe. None of the early medieval charters refer to the granting of tithes together with the land granted. This is particularly striking in the case of the Llandaff charters, since early twelfth-century material elsewhere in *Liber Landavensis* upholds the church's right to tithes and therefore any references to tithes in the original charters would surely have been included in the edited versions copied in the book (Evans and Rhŷs 1893, 27, 37, 70, 88, 90, 93; cf. Willis-Bund 1897, 44). The Life of Cadog (c. 51) envisages the payment of tithe, but the text is late, dating from the end of the eleventh century, and the passage does not make it clear whether payment was a regular obligation (Wade-Evans 1944, 122; cf. ibid. 276, 298). In addition, Gerald of Wales claims that the Welsh had an ancient custom, instituted by Germanus of Auxerre and Lupus of Troyes, of paying a 'great tithe' on the special occasions of marriage, pilgrimage and penance (Dimock 1868, 203). If this really was an early practice, though, it would have brought only occasional income to churches, and there is nothing to suggest that tithe was levied on a regular, territorial basis until the twelfth century (Davies, J.C. 1946–8, II, 456–7; cf. Brett 1975, 225 and, for a different view, Cowley 1977, 170). Instead, churches in the pre-Norman period seem to have depended principally on their estates for their economic support.

A church might receive an occasional windfall, however. The Lichfield Gospels were donated to Llandeilo Fawr by a certain Gelhi, who had purchased them from Cyngal for his best horse; according to Asser, churches in Wales were among the recipients of gifts by Alfred; and Gruffudd ap Llywelyn (d. 1063) is said to have made a penitential gift to Llandaff of precious metals for the benefit of widows and orphans (Evans and Rhŷs 1893, xliii, 269; Keynes and Lapidge 1983, 107; cf. Jackson 1969, 130). It is also worth noting that Gruffudd ap Cynan of Gwynedd bequeathed money to a number of churches in Wales and beyond on his death in 1137 (Evans, D.S. 1977, 31–2). In addition, 17 of the Llandaff charters allege that bishops in south-east Wales received substantial grants of land from kings in the tenth and eleventh centuries in lieu of compensation in gold or silver for wrongs committed against clergy and churches. The compensation was exacted in synods, following excommunication of the culprits. Although in most cases the narrations in these charters seem to be later interpolations, three are probably reliable (Evans and Rhŷs 1893, 218–21, 233–4, 237–9; cf. Davies, W. 1978a, 106, 133–4; 1979a, 21–4, 120, 123–4). But churches could presumably augment their resources by virtue of their temporal as well as

their spiritual authority, through the exercise of jurisdiction over their tenants and other dependents. The Life of Cadog refers to the *oppidani*, 'townspeople' of Llancarfan and the Life of Gwynllyw claims that Cadog held the government as well as abbacy (*regimen et abbaciam*) of the valley of Llancarfan (Wade-Evans 1944, 112, 178). Twelfth-century sources also imply that churches such as Tywyn and Llanddewibrefi controlled the settlements situated around them (Pryce 1986–7, 278).[9]

Nevertheless, ecclesiastical wealth in early medieval Wales derived principally from a combination of demesne exploitation and food renders, themselves the consequence of lay and especially royal generosity. It seems undeniable that, at least from the eighth and ninth centuries onwards, a small number of Welsh churches were well endowed, receiving grants over many generations – Clynnog Fawr, patronized by the kings of Gwynedd, is an important case in point, if its charter is reliable (see above). If this was so, however, the question implicitly posed at the beginning of this paper remains: namely, why is there so little physical trace today of the ecclesiastical wealth of pre-Norman Wales?

The preceding discussion points to an answer which goes something as follows. In part, our perception of ecclesiastical wealth is distorted by accidents of survival: there were clearly more artefacts and structures than now survive, and more may turn up in excavations. Yet there are limits to how far we can push this line of argument. Other areas of Europe for which there is more material evidence of ecclesiastical wealth than Wales were subject to similar factors making for destruction and loss. The balance of probability would seem to be, therefore, that the contrast, say, between Wales and Ireland with respect to the amount and quality of extant early medieval ecclesiastical metalwork reflects a real historical contrast, albeit less stark than visits to those countries' national museums might lead us to believe.

The most likely explanation for this contrast, and others like it, is economic. In short, it seems that the agrarian surpluses transferred to churches in Wales were not converted into lasting forms of wealth to the same degree as in some other parts of Europe (cf. Davies, W. 1982a, 60; Maddicott 1989, 49). This was presumably because such surpluses were smaller and less regular than those obtained in regions with higher agrarian productivity, and also because little attempt was made to exchange livestock and foodstuffs for coin. Similar factors, combined

with the costs of war, may have limited the capacity of secular rulers to bestow precious metals on churches. It is true that Gruffudd ap Llywelyn (d. 1063) was praised for his 'innumerable treasures of gold and silver and gems and purple raiment', and that both he and Gruffudd ap Cynan (d. 1137) donated silver to churches (Jones, T. 1973, 27; and above). But when Rhys ap Tewdwr reportedly disposed of 'immense treasure' in 1088, it was as payment to Irish mercenaries (Jones, T. 1973, 31), and, more generally, it is suggestive that no early medieval Welsh ruler minted coin — the Hywel Dda penny notwithstanding — and that tributes to English kings were normally paid in animals prior to the thirteenth century. Indeed, it was only thanks to the arrival in the twelfth century of profit-minded Anglo-Norman and Cistercian colonists that the commercial potential of Wales's pastoral resources began to be exploited, thereby promoting greater specialization in the agrarian economy and helping to quicken the tempo of exchange and trade (Davies, R.R. 1987, 159–62; cf. Wickham 1985).

In conclusion, then, given an economic context of minimal commercialization, what wealth churches enjoyed in early medieval Wales may more often have been displayed in feasting and alms-giving, or the support of substantial households, than in beautifying or building churches. The claims in the Lives of Cadog and Illtud that those saints maintained hundreds of people, including widows and paupers, are doubtless idealized but the ideal is itself a significant indication of attitudes to wealth (Wade-Evans 1944, 62, 208). As in parts of the Continent, the absence of easily accessible urban markets to absorb surplus foodstuffs would have left churches with little alternative to storing and distributing produce locally, thereby reinforcing structures of subordination and also ensuring that in times of famine the labour-force would not starve (cf. Leyser 1982, 2–4). Indeed, the wealth of churches may have consisted above all in their being fixed centres capable of generating a surplus and supporting concentrations of population. Unlike, however, Irish monastic sites such as Kildare and Clonmacnois, no Welsh church appears to have developed into a town by the tenth or eleventh century — although churches like Llancarfan or Caerwent may well have been more like towns than any other places in Wales at the end of the pre-Norman period (cf. Davies, W. 1982a, 58; Doherty 1985). The contrast is instructive, providing a further illustration of both the relative underdevelopment of the early Welsh economy and the constraints which this imposed on the creation of permanent and tangible expressions of ecclesiastical wealth.

Acknowledgements

I wish to thank the editors for their helpful comments on this paper as well as all those who commented on the earlier version of it given at the conference in Cardiff.

Notes

1. I have considered the problems surrounding the sources' application of monastic vocabulary to ecclesiastical communities in pre-Norman Wales in another paper (Pryce forthcoming). These problems do not, however, significantly affect the present discussion.

2. We cannot be certain of the size of any early medieval ecclesiastical community in Wales (Davies 1982a, 150). Bede says that Bangor Is-coed was held to have been divided into seven *portiones*, each of which contained at least 300 monks; about 1,200 of these were killed at the battle of Chester in *c.* 616, and only 50 escaped (Plummer 1896, I, 84). Bede was of course referring to events over a century before he wrote his *Historia Ecclesiastica* (731) and his source is unknown. It is, however, worth noting that he claims that there were almost 600 'brothers' in his own monastic community of Monkwearmouth-Jarrow when Abbot Ceolfrith left in 716 (Plummer 1896, I, 382; cf. 400). Of course, the numbers may well have included all members of the communities in question, and not just professed monks, but even so they must have been wealthy establishments. By contrast, sources of the late eleventh and early twelfth centuries speak of only 12, 24, 36 or 50 clergy serving Welsh churches (Wade-Evans 1944, 120, 210, 294; Evans and Rhŷs 1893, 88). Such figures probably give a fair impression of the situation at the end of the pre-Norman period, although their largely hagiographical context puts their accuracy in doubt (cf. Brooke 1986, 91).

3. Mention should also be made of the gold enamelled ring found on Llysfaen Common near Llandrillo-yn-Rhos which apparently belonged to Alhstan, bishop of Sherborne in the ninth century. How this came to be there is unknown: it may simply have been lost by the bishop, or it could have been given to a Welsh cleric or layman (Davies, W. 1982a, 48; Edwards, N. forthcoming).

4. This was shown in the 1989 O'Donnell Lecture in the University of Wales by James Graham-Campbell, who intends to publish Lhuyd's MS drawing of the casket in an article written jointly with Lawrence Butler.

5. Although the foundations of a rectangular stone structure uncovered beneath St Beuno's Chapel at Clynnog Fawr have been argued to belong to the saint's original (?seventh-century) chapel, this conclusion was not supported by the dating-evidence cited — namely a silver penny of Edward I or Edward II in the layer of clay above the foundations — which merely showed that the structure must have been built prior to the late thirteenth or early fourteenth century (Stallybrass 1914, 275–84). Timber churches are occasionally referred to in the written sources, including (possibly) line 31 of the ninth- or tenth-century poem in praise of Tenby, *Etmic Dinbych* (Williams, I. 1980, 164–5, 169), a late eleventh-century account of consecrating a church in Ergyng (Evans and Rhŷs 1893, 277), and c.5 of the twelfth-century Life of Gwynllyw (Wade-Evans 1944, 176). The stone church at Llanelen, Gower may also have been preceded by a timber structure (Walls 1984, cited by Davidson A.F. and J.E. *et al.* 1987, 269), but to judge by reports of the excavation the latter's dimensions and date seem to be beyond recovery. I am grateful to Andrew Davidson for procuring information held by the Glamorgan-Gwent Archaeological Trust on the Llanelen excavation, which was conducted by the Pendragon Society.

6. The first phase of the church at Capel Maelog has been dated by the excavator to the late twelfth or early thirteenth century on the basis of radiocarbon evidence, although on stylistic grounds it could be placed in the later eleventh or early twelfth century (Britnell 1990). I would like to thank Bill Britnell for allowing me to see the final draft of his final report prior to publication.

7. Unfortunately Gerald's account is chronologically imprecise: '*primo* tanquam oeconomi seu potius ecclesiarum patroni et defensores a clero constituti, *postea processu temporis* aucta cupidine totum sibi jus usurparent' (my emphasis).

8. The colloquy is extant in a manuscript of the first half of the tenth century and appears to have been written by a Cornishman; since, however, it contains Welsh words in the text and glosses the text may well be of Welsh rather than Cornish origin (Davies, W. 1982a, 213; Lapidge and Sharpe 1985, 31).

9. Compensation-payments to churches and ecclesiastical lordship are discussed by me in detail in a forthcoming book on native law and the church in medieval Wales.

The Survival of
the *Clas* as an Institution in Medieval Wales: Some Observations on Llanbadarn Fawr

J. Wyn Evans

The Calendar of the Church in Wales designates 15 April as the feast of St Padarn. It is fitting, therefore, that the observations upon which this paper is based were offered on that day, since the remarks that follow are focused on the major site associated with Padarn: Llanbadarn Fawr near Aberystwyth in Cardiganshire. The paper will concentrate on the resilience and capacity for survival of the *clas* as an institution in the native church in Wales in the face both of conquest and of the strictures of twelfth- and thirteenth-century ecclesiastical reformers.

Some commentators (for example Chadwick 1958, 131) assume that Llanbadarn possessed a *clas*, that is the kind of ecclesiastical or quasi-ecclesiastical community referred to in the Welsh laws, (for example Wiliam 1960, 23), headed by an abad ('abbot'), and thus, perhaps, of monastic origin, which was associated with the major or mother churches of the pre-conquest Welsh church. The term *clas* is thought to derive from the Latin *classis*, a band or a body of people (Lloyd 1911, 205). The origins of the *clas* are obscure; so are its precise nature and function, since many of the surviving references are ambiguous.

Llanbadarn certainly possessed features characteristic of other major Welsh pre-conquest churches. It had an abbot, albeit a lay one (Thorpe 1978, 180); it had an archpriest in Ieuan son of Bishop Sulien (Jones, T. 1952, 52); its saint was celebrated in a *Vita* to which was attached part of a cartulary (Wade-Evans 1944, 252–69); it at one time possessed an important relic, the *Cyrwen* or staff of Padarn (Bromwich 1972, 181–9); it had a *noddfa* or place of refuge (Jones, T. 1952, 92); it nurtured a tradition of scholarship as exemplified by the family of Sulien (Lapidge 1973–4, 68–106; Peden 1981, 21–46); it possesses two carved stone crosses dated to the ninth-eleventh centuries (Nash-Williams 1950, nos 111–2); and its parish was once the largest in Wales (62,550ha; Bowen 1979, 48). What it does not appear to have had is a *clas* and there does not appear to be any direct

evidence in the surviving documentary sources for the occurrence of *clas* or words compounded from it such as *claswr* (man/member of a *clas*). On the other hand, several sources include evidence which indirectly but strongly suggests the existence of such a community at Llanbadarn Fawr, as well as its survival during the twelfth and thirteenth centuries, albeit in an attenuated form.

In 1110, King Henry I granted Ceredigion to Gilbert fitzRichard de Clare, who by 1116 had bestowed Llanbadarn Fawr and its lands on the Benedictine Abbey of St Peter of Gloucester for the purpose of constructing a priory there (Hart 1863, I, 106, II, 73–4; Lloyd 1937, 45). This gift brought to an end the great days of Llanbadarn Fawr; no longer would there be a Sulien to be led away from Llanbadarn to become bishop of St David's; nor would there be a Ieuan to praise his father and his family in Latin verse; nor a Rhigyfarch to write a *Vita* of the patron saint of Wales. Indeed, for Rhigyfarch, the coming of the Normans to Ceredigion meant that 'the labours of earlier days lie despised; the people and the priest are despised by the word, heart and work of the Normans' (Lapidge 1973–4, 91). However the twelfth-century Welsh chronicle, *Brut y Tywysogyon*, retained an interest in Llanbadarn Fawr, not least in recording the obits of many members of the family of Sulien, for example Ieuan 'archpriest of Llanbadarn Fawr' in 1137 (Jones, T. 1952, 52). But by 1137 the situation had changed.

An important source for the assessment of the events relating to Llanbadarn in the twelfth and thirteenth centuries is the Ledger Book of Vale Royal (BL MS Harley 2064, ff. 294b-6a; Brownbill 1914, 164–8; see also Lewis, F.R. 1938, 25). The inclusion of Llanbadarn material in the records of this Cistercian abbey in Cheshire is itself a reflection of the changes which befell the Cardiganshire church, since Llanbadarn was granted to Vale Royal on 7 November 1360 (Lewis, F.R. 1938, 26). The Ledger Book contains records of cases relating to disputes about lands located around Llanbadarn Fawr. On 1 September 1326, a jury convened in Genau'r-glyn, the commote in which part of the parish of Llanbadarn lay, stated that on the feast of the Holy Trinity in the fourteenth year of King John (20 May 1212), A and B, and other Welshmen (unfortunately, no names are given) 'wickedly killed' C and D, monks of the abbot of St Peter's of Gloucester, who had been deputed to the custody of the church. According to the jury, until that date, the abbot and convent of Gloucester had held Llanbadarn Fawr and all its appurtenances as of right in frankalmoign peacefully since the time that Gilbert fitzRichard had given it to them. Not content with killing the two unfortunate monks, the said Welshmen occupied the church, its lands, holdings, mills, revenues and liberties until Edward I conquered Wales from Llywelyn ap Gruffydd in 1284. In addition, they had also seized and had occupied the spiritualities of the church for the same period of time. When the jury was asked whether Prince Llywelyn had appointed rectors or incumbents to the church, they replied that he had not, but that the said Welshmen had divided the spiritualities and bestowed them on clerks of their relations and kindred 'as in eight parcels'. There was, however, one major omission in the jury's evidence. Gloucester had not, as we know from the strictures of Gerald of Wales, enjoyed peaceful and undisturbed possession of the church from 1110 to 1212 (nor, for that matter, had it held Llanbadarn in unbroken succession until 1284).

It will be recalled that Gerald, on the occasion of his visit in 1188, expressed his horror that Llanbadarn possessed a lay abbot in Ednywain ap Gwaithfoed, and also pointed out that Ednywain's sons were officiating at the altar. He omitted to say that Ednywain was the son of one native lord of Ceredigion and the brother of another (Bartrum 1963–4, 99–100, 126–7), but did state that in the reign of King Henry I, 'St Peter's monastery in Gloucester administered this church in peace and tranquillity'. On the death of Henry I in 1135, 'the English were driven out and the monks expelled'. Laymen then took 'forcible possession of the church and brought in their own clergy' (Thorpe 1978, 180). This state of affairs certainly continued in the reign of Stephen (1135–54), because Gerald recounts the story of the knight from Brittany who had come to Llanbadarn Fawr on a feast day, and with others, was awaiting the arrival of the abbot so that Mass could be celebrated. What the knight then saw caused

him to abandon his travels and return home forthwith. It was no ecclesiastical procession that arrived but about 20 armed youths preceded by a man with a long spear in his hand: this was the abbot. It was, of course, during the same reign, that Ieuan ap Sulien died (1137), and the implication of the entry in the *Brut* is that he died at Llanbadarn while functioning as archpriest. Given what is known about the family of Sulien, their general demeanour seems at variance with the situation which Gerald describes, especially since he also tells us that the 'wicked generation' of 1188 held that their predecessors had murdered a bishop of Llanbadarn, and it was on these grounds that they justified the seizure of both the property of, and authority, spiritual and temporal, over Llanbadarn Fawr. What is not known is whether there was any kin relationship between the families of Sulien and Ednywain.

Gloucester does not, however, appear to have abandoned its claim to Llanbadarn after 1135 because Gerald's uncle, David fitzGerald, bishop of St David's 1148–76, issued a confirmation to the abbey of 'the church of St. Patern and its appurtenances, namely the land which is between the two waters Rediou and Clarach' (Davies, J.C. 1946, i, 282; Hart 1863, II, 76). This land was the same as that granted by Gilbert fitzRichard in 1110, and as will be seen below was a frequent bone of contention between the ecclesiastical authorities and certain families in or around Llanbadarn. Unfortunately Bishop David's confirmation is undated, and may be a forgery to bolster Gloucester's attempt to regain Llanbadarn from Vale Royal (Lewis, F.R. 1938, 17). Also, however, in the Gloucester records is a judgement by the same bishop, in favour of the abbot and monks of the abbey of the 'church of St Patern, which certain persons, in time of war, took away from them, and for a long time unjustly detained occupied' (Davies, J.C. 1946, i, 278). This is dated, on no firm evidence as far as can be seen, to 1175. The implication is that, at that time, Gloucester was not in actual possession of the church, hence the attempt to gain episcopal judgement in the favour of the abbey; and that it continued to be occupied by the Welsh. F.R. Lewis (1938, 18) believed that between 1158 and 1165 Ceredigion was lost to the Welsh; it may well be that Gloucester had succeeded in regaining possession of Llanbadarn during those years.

It can be assumed, therefore, in the light of the remarks he made about the situation he encountered in 1188, that, had he been aware of it, Gerald would have been moved to comment equally unfavourably upon that obtaining at Llanbadarn after 20 May 1212 when the two monks of St Peter's Gloucester were murdered. He was, of course, still alive in 1212, and it can be argued that news of what had happened had indeed reached him; and that he did comment unfavourably on events at Llanbadarn Fawr but in terms rather different from those he used to refer to the situation obtaining in 1188.

Among letters which he wrote at this period, preserved in *Speculum Duorum*, is one in which he makes various complaints as to the state of the diocese of St David's to Geoffrey de Henlaw, its bishop 1203–15 (Richter 1974, 262ff). He complains about the bishop's laxity, timidity, greed and rapacity, not least in: 'the matter of new institutions, and the issue of new charters to the disadvantage of old ones, as in the case of Llanbadarn Fawr last year (*anno preterito*). Again there is the matter of negligence and neglect of pastoral duties, as in the case of the sacrileges committed at that venerable and sacred spot last year (*hoc anno*), which were neither reproved by you nor put right by ecclesiastical legislation' (Richter 1974, 265). Richter argued that, although it is impossible from internal evidence to give a firm date to this letter, it must be prior to the lifting of the papal Interdict on England, so he suggested a date either late in 1213 or 1214. (1974, xlix). But there is evidence from other sources to suggest that it is Llanbadarn Fawr in Ceredigion which Gerald had in mind, and that, although Richter translates both *anno preterito* and *hoc anno* as 'last year', two separate incidents in two separate years are being condemned by Gerald; and that the letter may, thus, have been written in 1212/3.

Two other passages in the work of Gerald appear to illuminate this matter. In his *De Jure et Statu Menevensis Ecclesiae* of *c.* 1218 (Brewer, Dimock and Warner 1861–91, iii, 349), Gerald condemns Bishop Geoffrey for his greed, for example, in the unjust substitution of charters and institutions, in words almost identical to those in the passage quoted above, but without the second clause about sacrileges. The passage about substitutions does, however, have the following addition: '*sicut de clerico Falconis apud Lanpatern-Maur super ecclesie canonicos superstites instituto*' 'just as with Falco's cleric at Llanbadarn Fawr instituted against (in defiance of?) the surviving canons of the church'.

In another letter to Bishop Geoffrey, also in *Speculum Duorum*, Gerald complains about the failure of the bishop to install him into corporeal possession of the church of Tenby. Bishop Geoffrey had informed him that it was unsafe for the installation to take place because of Falco, 'who had once again taken up the bailiwick (*bailliam*) of the area' (Richter 1974, 212–3). It would appear that this Falco was Falkes de Breauté, sheriff of Pembroke, sheriff of Glamorgan and trusted officer of King John. Further, both the *Brut* and *Chronica de Wallia* state that Falkes was in Penweddig, the northern cantref of Ceredigion in 1211, building a castle at Aberystwyth for the king (Griffiths, R.A. 1977, 77). In that case, it can be argued that the intrusion by Falco of his cleric into Llanbadarn Fawr took place in 1211, and that Gerald was aware not only of this but of the murder of the Gloucester monks in 1212, and that these were the 'sacrileges' of which he complained to the bishop.

In 1246, however, Henry III presented Master Laurence of St Martin to Llanbadarn which was in his gift by right of conquest of the lands of Maelgwn ap Maelgwn (ap yr Arglwydd Rhys) (Davies, J.C. 1946, i, 372). There was no mention of Gloucester's rights to the church, although in 1242 the Crown had issued a protection without term for the church of Llanbadarn Fawr in favour of Gloucester (Lewis, F.R. 1938, 18). Another document preserved in the Gloucester archives introduces a further factor into the equation. At some time during his episcopate, Anselm le Gras, bishop of St David's from 1231 to 1247 issued an ordinance regulating the relationship between St David's and Gloucester in connection with Llanbadarn Fawr. In order to bring to an end a controversy of long standing between the cathedral and the abbey over Llanbadarn, Anselm resolved to divide the church into two equal portions, and to institute a vicarage taxed from the portions of both Gloucester and St David's. The next line is significant: 'the portions in the said church not yet vacant (*portiones in eadem ecclesia nondum vacantes*), when they shall be vacant, shall accrue to the portions of both churches by equal division' (Davies, J.C. 1946, i, 374(D.544); Hart 1863, II, 77–8). Clearly the situation regarding Llanbadarn was more complicated than the abbot of Gloucester would have had people believe, but at the same time it brings Llanbadarn into line with other former major Welsh churches. As Professor Glanmor Williams (1962, 17) noted, many of the *clas* churches of Wales survived not only as parish churches, cathedrals and collegiate churches, but also as portionary churches. In the case of North Wales, as Palmer observed (1886), a number are listed as such in the *Taxatio* of 1291. He emphasized the clan or family interest in churches of this nature. Llanbadarn is not listed as a portionary church in the *Taxatio* but, if it did conform to this type at an earlier date, as appears likely, then the confusion over the ownership of the church can be explained, as can Gerald's reference to 'surviving canons'. Whatever had happened to the members of the community in 1110 – and in one case, that of Daniel ap Sulien, it is known that he migrated to Powys, where at his death in 1127 he was archdeacon (Jones, T. 1952, 50) – on the expulsion of the Normans from Ceredigion in 1136, the old order appears to have been re-established at Llanbadarn, and to have continued in some form for a considerable period of time; hence the obits of the family of Sulien, with Ieuan as archpriest and Rhigyfarch ap Sulien as 'teacher in the church of Llanbadarn' (Jones, T. 1952, 54). It is in this context of portions that we should see the bestowal of the 'eight parcels' on the clerical members of the kindred of 'A and B and other Welshmen' in 1212, a state of affairs which the jury of 1326 believed survived until 1284; as well as the 'surviving canons' for whom Gerald took up the cudgels in his condemnation of Bishop Geoffrey in the *De Jure*.

There are, however, difficulties in this interpretation of the evidence as far as the canons are concerned, in both particular and general terms. *Canonicus* is a term of universal application in the medieval church to describe members of non-monastic communities, both capitular, collegiate and quasi-monastic. In the case of outsiders commenting on the institutions of the native Welsh church, it must be asked whether they were using terms familiar to themselves as the nearest equivalent to describe those institutions, rather than ones which the said institutions would have used to describe themselves. Thus, in the description of the canons of St Cadog of Llancarfan appended to the *Vita Cadoci*, and clearly referring to a period prior to the appropriation of Llancarfan to Gloucester shortly after 1100 (Cowley 1971, 95), it may well be that this was the term used by the compiler of the Vespasian manuscript at about 1200, within an Anglo-Norman context; it appears to be linked with both Gloucester and Monmouth (Knight 1984b, 385). Even if this is not the case, the original author of the Life of Cadog was Lifris, *magister* of Llancarfan, archdeacon of Glamorgan and son of Bishop Herewald of Llandaff. The description he gives of

the canons, their prebends and their possessions, seems anachronistic in terms of the period of Cadog, and appears to reflect a period when Norman influence had permeated the church in South Wales. This is not to say, however, that at the period to which the list of the canons and their possessions appears to belong, probably the late eleventh century, major churches like Llancarfan, which still possessed communities of clergy, did not call them canons, whatever term they may have employed earlier. This would parallel the situation in England at the time of compiling Domesday Book and other sources where certain 'superior' churches, usually former minsters, are described as possessing, or once possessing, *canonici* (Blair 1985, 106; Hase 1988, 59; Lennard 1959, 396–404).

In this connection, therefore, it is instructive to examine material relating to two Gwynedd churches, Aberdaron and Clynnog Fawr, both portionary in 1291 (Record Commission 1802, 291). In 1252 an agreement was drawn up regulating the relationship between the Augustinian canons of the abbey of Bardsey, founded *c*. 1200 (Smith, J.B. 1972, 392), and the church of Aberdaron (Ellis 1838, 252). The clergy of Aberdaron are termed *canonici seculares*, in contrast to the Augustinian canons regular of Bardsey. Given that the agreement was drawn up for Dafydd ap Gruffudd, at that time lord of Cymydmaen, presumably the term was the one which contemporaries used of the clergy of Aberdaron. In any case, the agreement of 1252 safeguarded the rights of the secular canons albeit in an attenuated form. At an earlier date, as the *Historia Gruffud vab Kenan* implies, the clergy of Aberdaron had also been termed canons, since the Welsh equivalent, *canonwyr*, is used of them (Evans, D.S. 1977, 19). Given that the *Historia* appears to have been produced for Owain Gwynedd, Dafydd ap Gruffudd's ancestor, and that it has been argued that the original was written in Latin (Evans, D.S. 1977, ccxxvii, ccxliv), it was probably the case that *canonici* was the term translated as *canonwyr*, and would have been understood in the twelfth century as the usual nomenclature for the clergy of the native community of Aberdaron.

In the case of Clynnog Fawr, the foundation of Beuno, which survived as a collegiate church into the late medieval period, there is a reference in an agreement made in 1261 between the bishop of Bangor and Prince Llywelyn ap Gruffudd (NLW Peniarth 231B, p.36; Haddan and Stubbs 1869–71, i, 489) to the misuse of the seal of the chapter (*capitulum*) of Clynnog. The judgement states that if 'by occasion of the said affixing [of the seal] he has taken anything away from the canons (*canonicis aliquid abstulit*) it ought to be restored to the same'. Since Clynnog was portionary in 1291 (rather than collegiate which it appears to have become by the fifteenth century) (Johns 1960, 19), the term 'canons' appears to be describing the clergy of the portionary church, which was certainly termed a *clas*, in a text preserved in two legal manuscripts of the mid-thirteenth century (NLW MS Peniarth 29, 42; Owen, A. 1841, i, 106). Further, a clause in Redaction B of the Latin version of the Welsh laws, (Emanuel 1967, 249): '*Nemo Menevensem episcopum sine ipso et suis canonicis audeat iudicare. Et similiter de Sancto Beuno, et Terillo, et Tydecho*' ('No one presumes to pronounce judgement upon a bishop of St David's unless he himself and his canons be present. And similarly in respect of St Beuno, Trillo and Tydecho') seems to suggest that it, together with other pre-conquest Welsh churches, was recognized as having canons at an earlier (but unknown) date. This, however, is far more speculative given the problems of dating the different strata of the Welsh laws. The question of the status of the clergy of St David's prior to Bishop Bernard's reorganization (see below), is, however, intriguing.

It is also true that the laws in both their Latin and Welsh versions use the term *canonici* and *canonwyr* in relation to the communities with which the terms *matrix ecclesia* and *mam eglwys* are associated (Emanuel 1967, 217, 337, 461; Williams, S.J. and Powell 1961, 43). But the term *presbiter* or *offeriad* is used rather than *clas*. This usage is paralleled by the *Brut*, when it describes the violation of the sanctuary of Llanddewi Brefi in 1109, when certain people had taken refuge with the priests (*effeiryeid*) of that church (Jones, T. 1941, 46). On the other hand, in the legal text known as *Hyfr y Damweiniau*, extant in manuscripts of the mid-thirteenth century and later, when the question of the distribution of the property of the *abad* after his death is discussed, it is the '*clas* and the canons' ('e clas a'r kanongwyr') who inherit it (Owen, A. 1841, ii, 10).

It would thus seem reasonable that in the case of Llanbadarn Fawr in 1212, Gerald in the *De Jure* is indeed describing members of the community of Llanbadarn, as probably reconstituted after the Welsh clergy re-established themselves in the mid and late twelfth century. There still remain problems, however, with this interpretation. In 1284, the

abbot of Wigmore petitioned King Edward I to give aid in the sustenance of two or three canons, since 'it would be to the honour of God and the King, and to the profit of the town to have there men of religion conversing'. The place he had in mind was Llanbadarn Fawr because 'at all times when Wales was in the King's peace, they were wont to have at Lanpadervaur houses and land and an oratory and canons dwelling in the faith' (Rees, W. 1975, 490). As Rees points out, the implication is that Wigmore, a house of Austin canons (Knowles and Hadcock, 1971, 144), probably gained an interest in Llanbadarn in or after 1280 when Roger Mortimer of Wigmore received a grant of Genau'r-glyn from the Crown. There is no evidence that there was a house of Austin canons at Llanbadarn at any prior date, and, in any case, the abbot may have been referring to the borough of Aberystwyth, founded in 1277, rather than to Llanbadarn itself.

Thus, if the canons of 1212 are not Austin canons, it is possible that they were the surviving members of the *clas* community of Llanbadarn Fawr, or its portionary successor. The key word is of course 'surviving' and this makes it the more likely that Gerald was referring to the native community, such as it was. It is noteworthy that there clearly appears to have been more than one canon; and that these canons appear to have had rights in the church. This would seem to be the force of the 'super': the canons had been cheated out of the expectation of appointing, or retaining the appointment, of a cleric to Llanbadarn. Such an expectation appeared to be supported by charters in their favour from the bishop or his predecessors, charters which he had set aside out of the same fear of Falco that he exhibited in the case of Tenby.

Theoretically, as we have seen, Llanbadarn was still under the jurisdiction of Gloucester and no canons, surviving or otherwise, should have exercized any authority whatsoever over any part of the church. On the other hand, Bishop Anselm's reference to 'portions not yet vacant' (see above), would seem to suggest that Gloucester may only have received a part of the church by 1110, in the expectation that as the other portions became vacant, the whole of the church would fall to them. This is unprovable; but in any case there is an inconsistency between Gerald's attitude to Llanbadarn in 1188 and his observations on the situation in 1212, especially in view of his general attitude towards the organization of the unreformed church in Wales. Gerald had certainly not graced the clergy of

Llanbadarn Fawr with the title of canons in 1188. Indeed, he was at pains to point out the irregularity of the situation. Further, it will be recalled that in his account of the episcopate of Bernard (bishop of St David's 1115–48) also contained in the *De Jure* (Brewer, Dimock and Warner 1861–91, iii, 183–4), Gerald described the organization of the church of Menevia (St David's) before Bernard reorganized it. He dismissed the native clergy the *Glaswir* (*recte Claswyr*) as those who with 'barbaric rites and without order and rule were outrageously occupying the goods of the church'. These *claswyr* were presumably the successors of 'the *clas* of the Lord Dewi (David) and that of the church of Menevia (*clas er argluyd Dewi ac un egluys Vynyu*) who had been led by Bishop Sulien down to Porth Clais to meet Gruffudd ap Cynan of Gwynedd in 1081 (Evans, D.S. 1977, 13). Bernard seems, according to this account, to have had no high view of them and in their place he instituted the canons and canonries characteristic of a contemporary secular cathedral chapter. It is unclear here, however, whether we are dealing with Bernard's attitude to the *claswyr* of Menevia or that of Gerald. In either case, however, the old and the new systems were being contrasted; and canons and canonries, at least in Gerald's view, belonged to the new, not the old order. The inconsistency between his view of Llanbadarn in 1188 and his defence of the 'surviving canons' of 1212 can be explained by the suggestion that he was speaking to different audiences. What must still be asked is whether his use of the term 'canons' is the equivalent of another native term for the members of the community of a major church: *claswr/claswyr*.

Unfortunately, it has to be stated at the outset that most of the surviving references to *claswr/claswyr* are not helpful to our present discussion. In addition to that quoted above from the *De Iure*, a number of other references survive, drawn from sources of differing date and type. The description of 'Thursday's Child' in the seventeenth-century *Llyfr Ffortun Bangor* as having *llygaid mawr gwallt tene claswyr*, although it may, indeed, preserve a folk memory of the appearance of pre-conquest ecclesiastics with 'large eyes and thin hair' perhaps because of their tonsures, does not advance our knowledge of the system to which they belonged (Williams, I. 1927, 116). Nor is Goronwy Gyrriog's description of Matthew of Englefield (bishop of Bangor 1328–57) as 'an eagle over claswyr, an ecclesiastical heir' (*eryr ar glaswyr,*

aer eglwysig) helpful in terms of the pre-Norman arrangements at Bangor Cathedral. Goronwy may either be referring to the contemporary cathedral chapter at Bangor; or he may be using *claswyr* as a general term for clerics; and he may, in any case, be constrained by the exigencies of metre, *cynghanedd* and bardic vocabulary (Anwyl 1909, 228).

Two sixteenth-century documents are valuable in revealing the presence of the term in connection with sites which were undoubtedly major churches at one time: Aberdaron and Llangurig. In the case of Llangurig, an Elizabethan inquisition of the manors of Arwystli and Cyfeiliog includes the following entry in the survey of Arwystli Uwchcoed: 'The Manor of Classe Kyrrick ... Also we doe present that within the said commode (*sic*) there is a manor called Y Classe, the freeholders there be chargeable to the court of the same Classe and the tenants there called classwyre and chargeable with the rent of assize yearly £3.0.0.'(Evans, E. 1949–50, 31). It is unclear whether the *claswyr* of 1560/1 are freeholders themselves and perhaps the descendants in blood or title of the members of an ecclesiastical community or tenants of freeholders; and whether they possess any rights which may have devolved upon them from any previous ecclesiastical system. In the case of Aberdaron, a document of 1592 (PRO Exchequer SC12/17/85) exempts a class of tenant known as *Gwir y Classe* in the hamlets of Dywros, Anhegraig and Bodernabwy in the vill of Is-sely from any dues except for relief of 12 pence. Other 'free tenants' of the Queen in the same vill paid two shillings for relief. It is unclear from the document who or what these *Gwŷr y Clas* (note that the term is not *Claswyr*) were, i.e. whether they were the descendants or inheritors of *claswyr* who had been associated with Aberdaron or whether they were descendants of former tenants. It is worth observing, however, that in the agreement of 1252, the portionaries of the church of Aberdaron, wherever they should be in the demesnes of the Abbot of Enlli, only paid 12 pence in *ebediw* and *amobr*. The amount of relief noted for *Gwŷr y Clas* in 1592 seems to echo the payments of the *porcionarii* of 1252 (Smith, J.B. 1972, 395–8; 407), so the *Gwŷr y Clas* of 1592 might well be the descendants or successors of the portionaries of 1252.

In the lengthy confirmation charter of the possessions of the Cistercian Abbey of Strata Florida, issued by Henry VI in 1426 (Williams, S.W. 1889, lvii–lxxiv), among the witnesses of the confirmation of Cynan ap Maredudd ap Owain (ap Gruffudd ap yr Arglwydd Rhys) who died in 1295 (Bartrum 1974, 781), we find the name of Cadwgan son of Griffin Glassour, who signed among the secular clergy. Cynan's confirmation seems, from the names appearing in the witness list, to date from the early 1280s. It may well be that Cadwgan's father had been, or was, a member of the native community of Llanddewi Brefi, reconstituted as a collegiate church by Thomas Bek, bishop of St David's in 1287 (Williams, Gl. 1962, 18). On the other hand, Griffin may have been a tenant of Llanddewi, and his son's clerical status nothing to do with any native major church.

Of more value is an entry in the *Calendar of Papal Letters* for the year 1402 (Bliss and Twemlow 1904, 521). In that year, Gruffudd Young, rector of Llanynys in Dyffryn Clwyd received a reply to his petition to Pope Boniface X requesting that the revenues of the church, which had been reduced over a period of time, be consolidated anew. In the petition Gruffudd had stated that they had formerly been of more than 100 marks in value and had been divided into 24 portions called *claswriaethe*, for the maintenance of 24 perpetual portionaries called *abbatathelaswyr*: i.e. *abad a chlaswyr*, presumably the *clas* community of Llanynys. A document of 1260 issued by Dafydd ap Gruffudd, in favour of a local nobleman called Madog ap Anian ap Gruffudd, refers to Madog as 'abbot over the fourth part of the right of patronage of the township of Llanynys and Gyffylliog' ('*abatem super quartam partem iuris patronatus de ville de llanenys at kyffellyauc*') (Davies, J.C. 1943–4, 29–32). It is unclear whether the abbacy had been divided into four parts or whether it represented one quarter of the right of patronage to the church of Llanynys and its dependency, Gyffylliog. What is clear is that the abbacy had been appropriated by powerful laymen, the kind of situation condemned by Gerald at Llanbadarn in 1188. There is mention neither of abbot nor *claswyr* in the *Taxatio* of 1291 but Llanynys is listed as a portionary church, with David capellanus having a share of £4:6:8 (Record Commission 1802, 291).

There is also one reference in the Welsh laws to *claswyr* (Owen, A. 1841, ii, 66). In a passage relating to the right of a church to appraise on oath the relics and furniture of a church, it is stated that the '*claswyr* and parsons' (*claswyr ar personeit*) can do so, because they are the owners of the church. This reference is ambiguous, since the distinction between *claswyr*

and parsons is not at all clear, given that we might expect *claswyr* to be the sole rectors and owners of their own church. The manuscript (F, Peniarth 34) in which the reference appears dates, however, from the fifteenth century (Owen, M.E.. 1974, 202), and therefore, should not refer to a period when the *clas* was an active force in the administration of major churches in Wales. If, however, the term *claswyr* survived as a name for the tenants of the lands of former major churches, as the instance of Llangurig noted above suggests that it did, then, the distinction makes sense. There is also another explanation that can be offered. Since the laws contain elements drawn from various periods, the clause may refer to a time when *claswyr* were indeed portionaries in a mixed community, and it may thus be describing the kind of situation which Gerald encountered at Llanbadarn Fawr in 1188. This would help to explain the distinction drawn at the end of the clause where it is observed that the *claswyr* and *personeit* may indeed swear to (*damdwng*) the relics of the church even though they were in the posssession of laymen (*lleygyon*). It is also worth observing that the parallel instance of this clause in the earlier laws text *Damweiniau Colan*, preserved in a manuscript of the mid to late thirteenth century, has 'the *clas* and the parsons' (*e clas a'r personeu*) which would tend to reinforce this conclusion (Jenkins 1973, 32–3).

On balance, however, it seems relatively clear that Gerald in 1212 was referring to the remnants of the *clas* of Llanbadarn Fawr, who were recognized by him, notwithstanding his remarks about St David's prior to Bishop Bernard's reorganization, nor his view of Llanbadarn in 1188, as being of clerical status, with rights to the church. Further, the clan interest in Llanbadarn revealed by the jury of 1326, as being the major factor in the recovery of Llanbadarn by 'A and B' and their Welsh companions is reinforced by two further entries in the Ledger Book of Vale Royal (BL MS Harley 2064, ff.294–5; Lewis, F.R. 1938, 19–20). In 1284, a certain Hywel ap Cadifor ap Heylyn was laying claim to 32 carucates between the Rheidol and the Clarach, the precise area granted by Gilbert fitzRichard to Gloucester in 1110. Hywel claimed that his ancestors had been seised of them as their lay fee. The rector of Llanbadarn, William D'Estavayer, on the other hand, maintained that they were frankalmoign belonging to the church, and thus of his right; and that Hywel's ancestors and others had occupied them in time of war. The jurors came to the conclusion that the lands were frankalmoign, but in 1322, a descendant of Hywel's, 'Mauredicus ap Ieuan Fychan', made a claim to the identical lands, again unsuccessfully as far as can be seen. That these lands lay at the core of the territorial possessions of Llanbadarn is also attested by a plea *quo warranto* of 1344, where the then rector of Llanbadarn stated that his rights of lordship dated back to the gift of Llanbadarn, not by Gilbert fitzRichard to Gloucester, but to that of Maelgwn Gwynedd to Padarn, and the *Vita* clearly indicates that it was the lands between the Rheidol and the Clarach which were meant (*Placita de Quo Warranto*, Record Commission 1818, 820; Wade-Evans 1944, 258).

Although the term *clas* itself does not occur in connection with Llanbadarn Fawr, nor does *claswr*, it seems reasonable to conclude that, not only do the 'surviving canons' of 1212 represent a community of similar type, but that the eight parcels shared out among 'clerks of their kindred' by A and B, and the portions 'not yet vacant' of

1246, reveal the kind of portionary church into which so many Welsh major churches developed, and which Archbishop Pecham condemned in his visitation of 1284 (Haddan and Stubbs 1869–71, i, 564). The *Taxatio* reveals that in north Wales, Pecham's strictures were ignored; indeed some churches, such as Llandinam, retained their portionaries well into the sixteenth century. Nor was it only the clerical interest of the *clas* that survived. The territorial aspects of lordship and tenancy as revealed by the freeholders of *Clas Curig* in the sixteenth century are paralleled by the efforts of Hywel ap Cadifor and Meurig ap Ieuan Fychan to secure the patrimony of Padarn in the thirteenth and fourteenth centuries; indeed, they may have been both descendants in blood as well as in title to the members of an older native community. Clerical and lay, they all represent the persistent and stubborn survival, albeit in an attenuated form, of a once powerful and influential institution in the native church in Wales: the *clas* and its *claswyr* or canons.

Welsh Ecclesiastical Place-Names and Archaeology

Tomos Roberts

Welsh place-names can be used as evidence by archaeologists and historians of all periods. They can provide testimony about prehistoric monuments, early Christian sites, medieval settlements, transport and communications, industrial history, social developments and even belief in the supernatural. In the case of early Christian history they are less dependable because of the problem of documentation. Unlike other countries and other regions in Britain the documentation of many Welsh place-names is quite late. Apart from a few names documentation begins in the twelfth century. In North Wales many church and parish names are not attested before 1200. A few are not recorded before 1535 when they appear in *Valor Ecclesiasticus* (The Commissioners of the Public Records of the Kingdom 1810–34).

There are techniques, however, which can be employed to prove the antiquity of a place-name. It could, for instance, contain a personal name. By now, thanks to the works of P.C. Bartrum we have a very good guide to the currency of Welsh personal names (1966). If a name is not recorded in Bartrum's genealogies after 915 then the place-name which contains that personal name must be earlier. It is also important to look at place-name elements as common nouns. If an element is not recorded as a common noun in *Geiriadur Prifysgol Cymru* (Thomas, R.J., then Bevan, G.A. 1950–) during the medieval period then it had already disappeared from the language and any place-name containing it must therefore be old.

Welsh ecclesiastical place-names, properly documented or subjected to the rough dating methods mentioned above can be of value to the archaeologist and could point to previously unknown and early sites. A number of place-name elements are of importance and these will now be discussed. Some are native Welsh words; others have been borrowed from Latin and English. Most of these elements have been discussed by Melville Richards (1968; 1971). However 20 years have lapsed since their publication and important works on cognate elements, Latin loanwords and early Christian history have in the meantime been published (Doherty 1984a; Padel 1985; Thomas, C. 1981a) and these throw a new light on Welsh place-names. The elements to be discussed have been divided into three classes — Latin loanwords, native Welsh words, and one English loanword.

Latin Loanwords

The first Latin loanword occurs just once as a place-name element. It is not to be found as a common noun in Welsh. The ecclesiastical parish of Basaleg lies in the civil parish of Graig in Monmouthshire (Gwent). For almost a hundred years the name has been held to be a borrowing from the Latin *basilica*. This attribution has been made by such eminent men as Dr Hugh Williams (1899–1901, i 28–9), Dr Kuno Meyer (Stokes and Meyer 1900, 240), Sir J.E. Lloyd (1911, i, 278) and Sir Ifor Williams. The last named published a note on the name in 1934 (Williams, I. 1933–5, 277) and, as far as I know, this has not been challenged. The earliest form of the name, *Basselec* belongs to the year 1102 (Clark 1910, i, 38). By 1330 there seems to have been a vowel change for the form by then is *Bassaleg* (Deputy Keeper 1891, 507–8). At that time Basaleg was the home of Ifor Hael the patron of the poet Dafydd ap Gwilym, and the seventeenth- and eighteenth-century copyists of Dafydd's work gradually changed the name to *Maesaleg*. Whether there were other vowel changes before 1102 one cannot say.

Now, however, there is further supporting evidence. Charles Doherty has shown that the Irish place-name *Baislec* is almost certainly a borrowing from Latin *basilica* and that the name refers to an early church that contained major relics (Doherty 1984a). It has also been shown that the Scottish place-name *Paisley* comes from Irish *baslec* 'church' (Nicolaisen 1970, 149). Basaleg lies in Gwynllwg in south-east Wales, an area often described as the cradle of Christianity in Wales. If there were to be a very early church in Wales containing important relics then Basaleg is in the right position. William Coxe has described a small building (now demolished) standing near Basaleg parish church in this way: 'A small gothic edifice, now a school-room, stands a few paces from the south side of the church and was probably an ancient chapel' (Coxe 1904, 74). I think that this should be investigated.

It is important to differentiate between the common noun **merthyr** 'martyr' and the place-name element *merthyr*. Both words are borrowings from Latin, but they are separate borrowings; **merthyr** 'martyr' is a borrowing from *martyrem* the accusative case of *martyr-is*; *merthyr* is a borrowing from *martyrium* 'grave of a martyr, shrine'. Many attempts have been made to suggest a meaning for the place-name element, *merthyr*. I prefer Charles Thomas' interpretation: 'a place possessing the physical remains of a martyr which acquired the sense of a church, a cemetery, holding the physical remains of a named saint or martyr' (Thomas, C. 1971, 89). He then suggests that churches named *Merthyr-* were developed cemeteries.

I think that the significance of a *Merthyr-* place-name to archaeologists is that it is a strong indication of burials — probably early Christian burials. The fact that the majority of the *Merthyr-* names in Wales contain a personal name suggests that they are the places which did possess the remains of 'a named saint or martyr'. Many of the persons named such as Cynog, Dyfan and Tydfil are connected with tales of martyrdom, but the tales should be treated warily and I suggest that you should read Gwynedd Pierce's note on the name *Merthyr Dyfan* (Pierce 1968, 133–5). Melville Richards has shown that, in several cases *merthyr* was replaced as a place-name element by *llan* 'church', *eglwys* 'church' and *capel* 'chapel' (Richards 1968, 11). This suggests that *merthyr* lost its specialized meaning and came to be regarded as merely meaning 'church'.

Two *Merthyr-* church sites in Anglesey are, I think, worthy of excavation. In both cases the place-name element *merthyr* has been replaced by *llan*. The first, Llangaffo, was originally called *Merthyr Caffo* (Richards 1968, 11). Here a new church was built within the churchyard in 1846 and the old church was subsequently demolished (RCAHMW 1937, 88; Prichard 1898). A number of early gravestones have been found on and around the site which is undisturbed apart from some nineteenth-century burials. The second site is Llanfeirian, a chapel in the parish of Llangadwaladr. The original form of the name was *Merthyr Meirion* (Richards 1968, 11). The chapel had become ruinous by the second half of the eighteenth century (Llwyd 1833, 196–7), but

the site is still undisturbed although it is heavily wooded.

The Welsh word *eglwys* is a borrowing from the Latin *ecclesia* 'church'. It occurs as a place-name element and is recorded as a common noun from the twelfth century. Kenneth Cameron has put forward the view that the English place-name element *eccles* denoted 'a British Church' (Cameron 1968, 87). That view has not been accepted by everyone and a balanced account of all the current opinions on the matter has been given by Charles Thomas (1981a, 262–3). In my view Welsh place-names containing the element *elgwys* do not follow the pattern suggested by Cameron. Some names containing *eglwys* may relate to very old Christian centres. The element is not a very common one and I have noticed that there is never more than one *Eglwys-* name in a commote. This may be a pointer to antiquity. There are certainly more *Eglwys-* names in the eastern parts of Wales than in the west. The element *eglwys* has been dislodged by the element *llan* in some names such as *Eglwys Cain*, now Llan-gain (Richards 1968, 11). The element *eglwys* has also been used by antiquarians to denote ruined or suspected ecclesiastical sites, such as Eglwys y Beili, Aberffraw (Morris, L. 1878, 31). The element is often followed by a personal name such as *Cyffig* or *Nunnid*. It rarely occurs as a simplex.

There are three place-names known to me containing the element *eglwys* which are quite unusual and could be of interest to the archaeologist: *Eglwys rhos*; *Eglwys Ail* (Langadwaladr) and *Heneglwys*.

Eglwys-rhos in the commote of Creuddyn and cantref of Rhos, Clwyd, stands near the important centre of Degannwy. The present church building was extensively restored twice during the nineteenth century (RCAHMW 1956, 91). Quite often a *Llan-* name containing a personal name is followed by a township name as a qualifier. Here, very unusually, the qualifier is a cantref name. Was this perhaps the only church in the whole cantref at one time?

Eglwys Ail is the former name of Llangadwaladr, Anglesey. The form *Eglwys Ail* is first recorded in 1254 (Lunt 1926, 193). The form *Llangadwaladr* does not occur until 1508 (Sotheby 79). It then gradually supersedes the form *Eglwys Ail*. The second element of this name, *ail*, means 'wattled'. Here then we may have a reference to an early wooden church, again near a centre of power in Gwynedd — Aberffraw. The former name of Llangynidr (Breconshire) is Eglwys Iail. Here the second element *Iail* is a stream name.

The name *Heneglwys*, Anglesey is first recorded in a poem in *The Black Book of Carmarthen*, the earliest Welsh poetical manuscript, written about 1250. The church is also called *mynw[ent] Corbre* 'Corbre's graveyard' in the same poem (Evans, J.G. 1888, 32). Subsequent evidence also shows that the church was originally dedicated to the Irish saint, Cairbre (Evans, J.G. 1898, 978). By 1352 the church was dedicated to the saints, Faustinus and Bacellinus (Baron Hill 6714, 30). It has been shown that when the adjective *hen* precedes a noun or place-name element, then the meaning is not 'old' but 'former' (Ford 1970). Here then we have an old, abandoned church site built upon again and re-dedicated by 1352. The church was demolished and rebuilt in 1845 (RCAHMW 1937, 22).

The Welsh word *myfyr* is a borrowing from Latin *memoria*. One of the meanings of the Welsh word is 'grave'. An early Welsh poem mentions *glas fyfyr* 'green graves' (Williams, I. 1935, 39, 216). *Myfyr* also occurs as a place-name element. The place-name *Myfyr* in Tudweiliog, Llŷn is recorded from 1720 (Baron Hill 3260), but it does not seem to have an ecclesiastical context. However, the chapel at Llaneilian church, Anglesey, formerly standing apart from the church itself (RCAHMW 1937, 60–1) has been known as *Myfyr Llaneilian* or *Myfyr Eilian* at least since 1696 (Jones, B.L. 1973, 185). I wonder if the chapel can be connected with the *cella memoria*, the surround of a martyrial tomb which later had a church or chapel built over it (Thomas, C. 1971, 140–4). If so the chapel may well have been built over the grave of Eilian himself.

Capel is a late borrowing from Latin *capella* 'chapel'. It is a common place-name element and the lateness of the borrowing is reflected in the chronology of the place-name forms. The earliest *Capel-* name that I have seen is *Capel Curig* which is recorded from 1536–9 (Smith, L.T. 1906, 81). However, it should be noted that *capel* is often followed by an early personal name such as *Aeddan, Beuno* or *Cynog. Capel-* names should be treated with care as there are many different kinds including the names of hundreds of nonconformist chapels. *Capel* has also been used by antiquarians to name or re-name ruined churches or chapels. I include some examples taken from a list of Anglesey chapels published in 1920 (Baynes 1920). I have placed the original names of the buildings in brackets: *Capel Llanfeirian* (*Llanfeirian / Merthyr Meirion*); *Capel Dygwel* (*LLanddygwel*); *Capel Machwda* (*Betws*

Mwchwdw); *Capel Mynwent y Llwyn* (*Llwyn Tygái*).

Mynwent 'graveyard' is a borrowing from Latin *monumentum*, but it only occurs as a place-name element in modern times. Again, like *capel* it has been used by antiquarians to name ruined church sites such as *Mynwent Mwrog* in Llanfwrog, Anglesey, a site formerly known as *Capel Nett* (Llwyd 1833, 268).

Welsh Words

I come now to ecclesiastical place-name elements which are native Welsh words and I begin with one that, like *Basaleg*, occurs only once, namely *tŷ* 'house'. This element of course occurs in *Tyddewi* (St David's). The name however is only recorded from the mid-fifteenth century (Roberts 1914, 58). *tŷ* plus a saint's name does occur in the sense church in medieval Welsh poetry and prose but *Tyddewi* is the only example of an ecclesiastical place-name containing *tŷ*. In contrast the Irish cognate form of Welsh *tŷ*, *teg* or *tech*, does occur fairly commonly as an ecclesiastical place-name element in Ireland from early times. Whether *Tyddewi* shows Irish influence or whether it is a parallel development I cannot tell.

In North Wales *bod* 'home, abode' occurs quite commonly as a place-name element in the secular sense. It also occurs at least six times in parish or church names, namely *Bodedern, Bodewryd, Bodferin, Boduan, Bodwrog* and *Botwnnog*. In each case the second element is a saint's name. Names such as *Bodedern* may be a northern parallel to *Tyddewi. Bod* only occurs very rarely as a place-name element in south Wales.

I now come to the most common Welsh ecclesiastical place-name element of all — *llan*. A separate paper would be be needed to discuss fully the use and development of the element *llan* and its significance to archaeologists. However, I will attempt, quickly, to trace its semantic development, its development as a place-name element and to mention some second elements in *Llan-* names. The Celtic root word, which gave Welsh *llan*, meant 'land'. *Llan* is in fact cognate with English *land* (Richmond and Crawford 1949, 36). The word came to mean 'enclosed land' and *llan* has this meaning as a second element in compound Welsh nouns such as *perllan* 'orchard', *ydlan* 'rick-yard' and *corlan* 'sheep-fold'. Then *llan* came to mean, successively 'an enclosed cemetery', 'the church within an enclosed cemetery' and 'the area of land served by the church', ie the parish. Over centuries it developed further and came to mean 'the township surrounding a parish church', 'the farm next to the church' or even 'a sexton's cottage by a parish church'. It also became a common noun meaning 'church'. In time it also superseded other ecclesiastical place-name elements such as *betws* and *merthyr* whose rather technical meanings had been forgotten. It even superseded some secular place-name elements such as *nant* 'river, valley'. *Nanthoddni* became *Llanthony* and *Nantcarfan* became *Llancarfan* (Williams, I. 1945, 41).

The main elements that follow *llan* are personal names, topographical features, or river names. The personal name could be that of someone unknown, a Welsh saint, or a universal saint. In the case of a Welsh saint with a cult or a universal saint such as *Mair* (Mary), *Mihangel* (Michael), or *Pedr* (Peter), a township or river name was added as a qualifier. *Llan* has been used as a place-name element over and over again from the earliest times to the twentieth century. The name *Llandarcy*, for instance, commemorates the twentieth-century oil magnate William Knox D'Arcy (Jones, H.C. 1976, 46). *Llan* is therefore a complex element and any study of a *llan* site or a group of *llan* sites should include complete documentation of the name or names, all information about dedications and historical personages named, and any other historical information available. An attempt to reconstruct and compare patterns of *llan* enclosures could be interesting.

An English Loanword

The final element that I shall discuss is *betws*, a borrowing from Old English *bed-hus* 'an oratory'. *Betws* first occurs as a place-name element from the very beginning of the thirteenth century. It is not recorded as a common noun until the fifteenth century (Thomas, R.J., then Bevan, G.A. 1950–, i, 276). It is quite uncommon for a loanword of this kind to appear as a place-name element first and then as a common noun. *Betws* occurs commonly throughout Wales as a place-name element. It is often followed by a personal name and there is evidence to suggest that lay persons commemorated in some of the names were the founders of the oratories. One spectacular example, recorded about 1200, states that Gwerful Goch, daughter of Cynan ab Owain Gwynedd, built Betws Gwerful Goch (Bartrum 1963–4, 103).

Although the Old English *bed-hus* appears in *English Place-Name Elements* (Smith, A.H. 1956, 24) no examples of the place-name are given. I have also failed to trace any examples of the place-name in England.

Conclusion

Welsh ecclesiastical place-name elements can be of use to archaeology if treated carefully. Provided the concise meaning, usage, chronology, and distribution of the elements are known they can lead the archaeologist to important sites and help him or her avoid sites which are dubious or of no interest.

The Early Christian Latin Inscriptions of Britain and Gaul: Chronology and Context

Jeremy Knight

It is now 40 years since Victor Nash-Williams published his *Early Christian Monuments of Wales* (Nash-Williams 1950). It is also almost 140 since Edmond Le Blant, with the support of the Emperor Napoleon III, published the first volume of *Inscriptions Chrétiennes de la Gaule* (Le Blant 1856; 1865; hereafter I.C.G.; also 1892, hereafter N.R.), which, unlike other corpora of inscriptions — unlike the *Corpus Inscriptionum Latinarum* for example (Mommsen 1863 onwards, hereafter C.I.L.) — has small but accurate drawings of the inscriptions. Le Blant was a Parisian Catholic of liberal views (Leclerq in Cabrol and Leclerq 1913–53, viii, part 2, cols. 2143–218). Nash-Williams was a high Anglican and a Welshman. Both saw the inscriptions as evidence of the way in which their countries had developed from beginnings within the Roman Empire into literate Christian peoples. Le Blant wrote against the background of nineteenth-century French anticlericalism, which saw the Catholic church as an alien body hostile to the centralized state created by the Revolution. The Christian and Roman roots of French culture were a very relevant topic at such a time. I.C.G. no. 1 is the text on the placard carried before the martyr Attalus into the arena at Lyon in AD 177. Nash-Williams, who was of course a distinguished Roman archaeologist, was fond of remarking, *half* in jest, how the Welsh were already Christians when 'those English' were still a gang of pagans.

A key part of Nash-Williams's conclusions concerned the spread of the *Hic Iacet* formula, which appears on many of the French and Insular inscriptions:- 'The formula appears to have originated in Italy ... and passed thence to Gaul, where it had a restricted vogue covering the first half of the fifth century. Its use in Gaul was practically confined to two well-defined regions — (1) South Gaul, especially around Lyon and Vienne, the principal foci of Gallic Christianity and (2) the Rhineland ... Of these two areas, the latter is .... less likely to have transmitted the formula to Wales ... Lyon and Vienne on the other hand could possibly claim parentage of British Christianity, and from the early fifth century onwards, contact between Celtic Britain and South Gaul was close and continuous. From South Gaul, the formula must have reached Wales before 500.' (Nash-Williams 1950, 55).

The idea of a direct link between the churches of Lyon and of Britain had its origin in Victorian church history. For Victorian churchmen, if the British church did stem from that of the Lyon martyrs, many of whom were from Asia Minor, it need have no historical connection with Rome. I need hardly add that such prejudice would have been wholly alien to Nash-Williams and that his conclusions are based on a sequence of *Hic Iacet* inscriptions from Lyon and elsewhere with fifth-century consular dates.

This, or any other, explanation of the origin of the Insular series of Latin memorial stones immediately raises three basic questions. Firstly, what was the relationship, if any, between these post-Roman inscriptions and the Roman tombstones that we see at Caerleon, or along Hadrian's Wall? If Nash-Williams was right, there was none, and the post-Roman stones represent a fresh post-Roman introduction.

Secondly, if this was the case, how did the *Hic Iacet* formula, and all that went with it, reach western Britain from the very different urban society of southern Gaul? Was it by way of a fifth-century sub-Roman British church in what is now England? Was it a straightforward matter of contact between the fifth/sixth-century Insular church and that of contemporary Gaul? Or should we imagine Gallic missionaries sailing up the western seaways?

Thirdly, there is the problem of the physical change in the form of the memorial stones from a marble plaque set in a horizontal slab in the floor of a basilica or in an extra-mural cemetery to an erect monolith looking like a prehistoric standing stone or, as Radford has pointed out (1971, 8), a Roman milestone.

However we answer these questions, we have to start in fifth-century Gaul, in the 'Sunset at Avitacum' world of Sidonius Apollinaris and his friends (for the country-house life of the Wodehouse novels has, with a few carefully

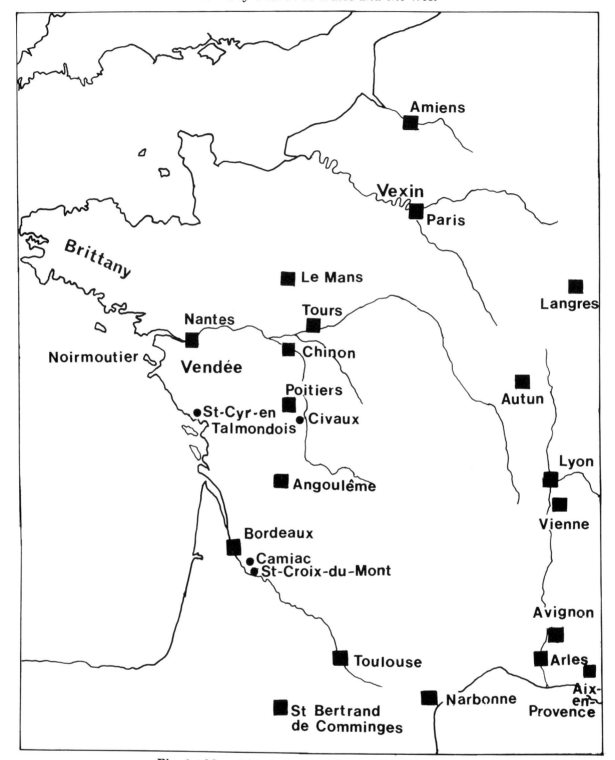

Fig. 6.1 Map of Gaul, showing sites mentioned in the text

preserved exceptions, disappeared from the English landscape as surely as the villas of Sidonius and his senatorial friends from that of Francia), or in those cities which, in Peter Brown's phrase 'collapsed inwards around their bishop'. Many aspects of these cities are familiar to us – the aristocratic bishop, often with family estates in the *civitas*, and now taking over various

secular as well as spiritual functions; the cathedral complex within the city walls with its atrium or piazza, where the people from the city and its territory gathered on the major feasts of the church, its baptistry and bishop's palace. At Aix-en-Provence recent excavations have shown how the cathedral directly replaced the Roman civic basilica, with the forum in front of it transformed into a great square or atrium dominated by the still suviving baptistry (Guild, Guyon and Rivet 1980; 1983; Kauffman 1983; Guyon in Gauthier and Picard 1986, 23–6; Gauthier 1986). With the bishop seated in his *cathedra* facing the congregation, just as a secular magistrate sat in his chair in the basilica, one could hardly ask for a clearei illustration of the shift of power within the *civitas*.

In the extra-mural cemeteries were the graves of martyrs and early bishops, the illustrious dead in sculptured sarcophagi within tomb chapels, and a host of humbler people under tombstones marked by simple Latin memorial inscriptions. This ecclesiastical geography is familiar to us from the town plans in Professor Charles Thomas's *Christianity in Roman Britain* (1981a) or from the French series *Topographie Chrétienne des Cités de la Gaule* (Gauthier and Picard 1986). Langres in Burgundy is a typical, but particularly interesting example (Fig. 6.2). The cathedral complex is within the late Roman walls, as usual. The medieval Spanish definition of a city – a *ciudad* or *civitas* – is relevant here, 'a city must have a bishop and walls' (cited Ortiz 1971, 130–1). At Langres however, the city and its cemeteries are 1,500m apart, for the city lies on a north-south ridge and the cemeteries (on the site of their Roman predecessors) lie at the other end of the early Roman town which has shrunk to a quarter of its early Roman size, like mercury going down in a thermometer (Picard in Gauthier and Picard 1986, iv; 11-4). Langres was on the road to Rome and it was in the Church of the Holy Brothers in the cemetery area south of the town that Ceolfrid, abbot of Jarrow and Monkwearmouth, was buried in 716 (*Bede Historia Abbatum* 21; Webb and Farmer 1983, 206–7).

The physical reality of such cemeteries can be seen in such excavated examples as Poundbury near Dorchester in England or St Irénée-St Just at Lyon in Gaul (Green 1979; Reynaud 1974; Reynaud *et al* 1982). St Irénée-St Just is the cemetery which produced the series of consular-dated stones central to Nash-Williams' chronology. We also have Sidonius' description of a hot autumn night there in October 469, on the feast of the bishop St Just (Sidonius *Letters* V, 17; Anderson, W.B. 1963–5, ii, 226–37). The crowds, with lights and candles, packed the hot airless basilica and Sidonius and his senatorial friends withdrew to the cool garden around the tomb of the praetorian prefect Syagrius and played ball while they waited for the bishop (the successor of St Just) and the dawn mass. The description can remind one of the distance

between this late classical world and that of our own Insular memorial stones.

Before considering how this distance might have been bridged, we shall need to consider the epigraphic sequence on which Nash-Williams'

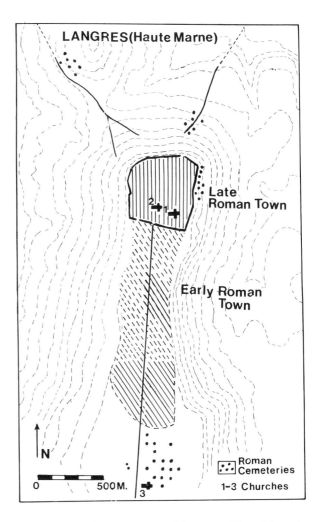

Fig. 6.2 The Roman town of Langres (Haut-Marne). The late Roman walled town, confined to the tip of the spur, was a fraction of the size of its early Roman predecessor (after Picard).

conclusions were based. By the mid-third century a distinctive form of Christian epitaph had emerged in Rome and a few other western cities. This included, in varying order, the name of the deceased, the date of his or her death (the 'heavenly birthday') and sometimes, but by no means always, the consuls of the year. There was a verb such as *Depositus* or *Decessit* and sometimes other words and phrases – *In Pace, Nomine, Memoria* ('the tombstone of') or *Hic Iacet*. Such stones are unknown in Gaul, save for one from Bordeaux, which commemorates a lady called Domitia, a native of Trier, buried in the pagan *Dis Manibus et Memoriae*, the other beginning *Hic Iacet* (C.I.L. xiii, 633; Etienne 1962, 266–8, Pl. XXI). It was known to Le Blant, though he and others have thought it a fake. If genuine, it shows that the prolific Rhineland *Hic Iacet* series may have begun earlier than thought and could in part be the origin of the much later Gallic series.

This stone might indeed seem to upset Nash-Williams' chronological applecart, but it should be put in perspective. Links between Rome and Trier were of course close under the late Empire and there is no doubt that the *Hic Iacet* formula was already current in Rome at this time. The Bordeaux stone however stands very much alone. There is a series of fourth-century Christian memorial stones from Gaul, many with consular dates between 334 and 405. They are distinctive in style, text and formula, using *Depositus* or *Decessit*. They continue the third-century Roman series, but are found throughout Gaul, not only in the Rhône Valley at Lyon, Vienne and Autun, but also in Aquitania, at Bordeaux, the western Pyrenees, the Gironde, the Vendée and the Charente. The series ends at the time of the great barbarian invasion of 406–7. From the Insular standpoint, the most important thing about these fourth-century stones is that there is nothing like them in Britain before or after 410. Even in Gaul they are a small minority among the far more common pagan series beginning *Dis Manibus et Memoriae*. The Insular series can hardly be derived from these fourth-century Christian stones and the former must be, as Nash-Williams thought, a fifth-century post-Roman introduction.

After the invasions, Aquitanian Gaul passed into eclipse under the Visigoths (Mathisen 1984). From now on, the great majority of Latin memorial inscriptions of all kinds come from the area of surviving *Romanitas* in Provence and the Rhône Valley. The new fifth-century series uses *Hic Iacet* or *Hic Requiescit* and it was from the St Irénée-St Just cemetery at Lyon that Nash-Williams derived his sequence of five *Hic Iacet* stones with dates between 422 and 449. The next dated stone, of 454, introduces a new fashion, of north Italian origin, for 'four-figure' formulae like *Hic Requiescit In Pace* or *Hic Requiescit Bon(a)e Memoriae*, which is incidentally also reflected in one or two Insular memorial stones (for example Macalister 1945, no. 479 from Hayle, Cornwall). The *Hic Iacet* series is not however confined to Provence and Burgundy, for there are inscriptions of this type from Bordeaux (C.I.L. xiii, 11,032); Fig. 6.3, Camiac, Gironde (Coupry 1967, 341-2); Gaillardon, Vendée (I.C.G, no. 575; C.I.L. xiii,

1185) and from Protet, Haute Garonne (N.R. no. 297A). These do away with the need, derived, as we have seen, in the last resort from Victorian church history, to trace our Insular series of inscriptions back to Lyon or Vienne (Fig. 6.4), which now seems inherently unlikely, if only on geographical grounds.

There is no need to rehearse here the other evidence for contacts with Gaul, particularly western Gaul, in this period. There is the transmission of works like the early (?pre 460) text of the *Vita Martini* in the Book of Armagh (Babut 1920), or the early sixth-century Burgundian *Passio Albani* used by Gildas (Levison 1941), or the pottery imports from western Gaul (Thomas, C. 1959; 1981b) — though on present showing the latter seem to begin later than the introduction of the memorial stones. The archaeology of western Gaul in this period is perhaps also a little closer to that of Britain and Ireland than is the late classical urban world of Lyon or Marseilles. The older archaeological literature of the period in western Gaul is dominated by the sarcophagus cemeteries, if only because it is difficult to overlook a six-foot (1.8m) stone sarcophagus, but where such cemeteries have been tested by modern excavation, as at Chinon, Civaux and elsewhere, or in the smaller rural cemeteries of areas like the Vendée, there is an early phase of long cists and earth graves almost without gravegoods and not unlike our Insular cemeteries of the period (for example, Fedière 1985, 302–3; Eygun, 1963, 453; 1967, 258–60).

The contexts of these western Gaulish cemeteries may be relevant to our Insular concerns, for they can be seen against a background of the extension of pastoral care from the *civitas* capital into the surrounding countryside. Church councils show that pastoral care rather than conversion was the main problem in much of fifth-century Gaul and Professor Wendy Davies has shown its relevance in an Insular context (see above). It was all very well for Martin of Tours to convert pagan rustics by miraculously felling a Jupiter column or demolishing a pagan temple, but someone had to instruct them in the faith afterwards and bring them to the city at Easter at the right time for baptism. Gregory of Tours lists the *ecclesiae diocesanae* (broadly, minsters) founded in Touraine by successive bishops from Martin (obit 397) to Volusianus (obit 498). There were 16 of them, often in Roman *vici* or market centres and forming a pattern over the diocese (*Historiae Francorum* X, 31; Thorpe 1974, 593–604; Arndt and Krusch 1885; Stancliffe 1979). Some are known to be the sites of important cemeteries of the type I have mentioned. Alongside these, an increasing number of landowners were founding *oratoria villaria* or estate churches on their land and *villa* here, as is well known, follows the semantic shift from Roman villa to medieval *vill* or estate. Two of the fourth-century Christian tombstones I have mentioned probably come from Roman villas (St Croix du Mont, Gironde – I.C.G. 59; C.I.L. xiii, 912 – Musée d'Aquitaine, Bordeaux; and St Cyr-en-Talmondois, Vendée – N.R. 256; C.I.L. xiii, 1182 – Ecomusée de la Vendée, château of Puy du Fou). These no doubt had chapels like Lullingstone, Kent, or some of the villas of Sidonius' friends. Monasteries form a third and quite separate strand, partly because of a different pattern of foundation, partly because monks should not of course have the cure of souls. Much of this pattern may be very relevant to our Insular concerns.

One contrast between Gaul and western Britain is the sharp break, like a geological fault, between the late Roman world and the early medieval world in the latter. We have evidence of late Roman Christianity at both Caerleon and Caerwent, the name of *Venta* survived as that of the post-Roman successor state of Gwent and there is now sub-Roman and early medieval metalwork from Caerwent (Knight forthcoming); but the memorial stones, as has often been noted, are most numerous in the least romanized areas of west and north Wales, and what there are in the south-east are late, as the compound formulae (*Hic Iacet/Filius*) and script show. Few, I think, would now claim that Christianity itself died out and had to be reintroduced, but this curious discontinuity is something that needs explaining.

The Irish ogam inscriptions probably represent the earliest phase of cultural borrowing (Harvey 1987, with a useful discussion of earlier views). They are a clear case of what the American anthropologist A.L. Kroeber (1948, 344–57) called 'stimulus diffusion'. This is a process of cultural borrowing where one society sees something it would like to copy from a neighbour, but cannot, since it lacks the knowledge or technology to digest the loan. It therefore mimics it, using something in its own cultural tool kit, and often produces something which appears quite novel. Thus the Dutch lacked the clays and kiln technology to copy Chinese porcelain, so used their existing technology of maiolica to copy it, and produced delftware. Kroeber cites a number of cases in west Africa and among American Indians where a member of

CAMIAC (Gironde)

Fig. 6.3 *A Fifth-century memorial stone from Camiac (Gironde), using the* Hic Iacet *formula (after Coupry 1967).*

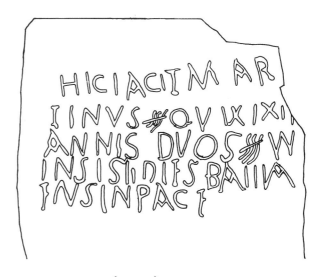

VIENNE (Isère)

Fig. 6.4 *A fifth-century memorial stone from Vienne (Isère), using the* Hic Iacet *formula (here* Hic Iacit, *as in the Insular stones) I.C.G. 422 A, C.I.L. XII, 2126.*

the native learned class devised an alphabet for their people and ogam is just one more example. If our only contact with writing was the Arabic graffiti that one sees on walls in parts of Cardiff, we could not begin to write Arabic because we would not know the sound values and some member of our native learned classes would have to invent an alphabet based on (say) the numbers on digital watches. Someone in the Irish world must have been familiar with Latin script from coins or inscriptions on looted silver plate before there were educated British slaves like Patrick around to teach him Latin, and so invented ogam.

My main concern however is not with ogam, but with the parallel cultural borrowing that gave us our Latin memorial stones. This must be seen, as I have tried to show, as part of a wider pattern of outside contacts, not least in church organization, some time after the inception of the Gallic *Hic Iacet* series in the second quarter of the fifth century. This particular way of commemorating the dead must have reached Britain as part of the normal traffic between the British and Gaulish churches, the sort of traffic that enabled Gildas to use the early sixth century *Passio Albani* or to parody a ruling of a series of Gallic church councils which presumably had British parallels which his readers would recognize (Knight 1984a, 340). Once again, the borrowing underwent a sea change, a form of stimulus diffusion. The new Insular inscriptions owed much, as Radford suggested (1971, 8), to Roman milestones, the only form of inscription, save for a few over fort gates, with which an untravelled tribesman or chieftain in western Britain is likely to have been familiar. Outside a few places like Caerleon, Chester or Hadrian's Wall, Roman tombstones are not all that common in Britain and the rather sparse series is dominated by soldiers, officials and foreigners and biased towards a first- and early second century date (Knight 1981, 57). A Welsh chieftain on the other hand might well be impressed by the way a Roman Emperor was able to record his name and titles on a milestone and might consider that his own name and lineage should be similarly marked, particularly if the stone recorded his ownership of a particular piece of territory and his own hereditary right to its ownership. In time, this borrowing came to be influenced by the norms of Insular society, with its emphasis on family, and by the new bookhands introduced by manuscript texts, which developed into Insular script in our larger monasteries during the sixth century (Bieler 1949).

To return finally to southern Gaul. The price that Provence and Burgundy paid for their sunset glow of *Romanitas* was isolation from what was happening in more active areas to the north. It became, in short, a backwater. In 559 the Merovingian king Lothar I offered the see of Avignon to the Parisian abbot Domnolus. Domnolus was appalled, regarding it as little better than a sentence of exile to a provincial backwater. One could hardly expect a plain man

like himself, he told Lothar, to be subjected to interminable learned discussions by members of old senatorial families, or to counts who wanted only to discuss the finer points of classical philosophy. Lothar sympathized, and gave him Le Mans instead (Gregory of Tours *Historiae Francorum* VI, 9; Thorpe 1974, 339–40; Arndt and Krusch 1885).

The public display of Latin inscriptions, and the assumption that lay people would be able to read them, was very much a part of the classical world. Michael Lapidge (1984) has charted the decline of secular public education in late Roman Britain and Gaul. In about the mid-seventh century the series of Latin memorial stones end, both in Britain and Gaul, though the end of the Insular series is of course much less clearly defined than in Gaul, with its post-consular dated sequence. Latin monumental inscriptions do not of course end thereafter but they are much rarer and more specifically ecclesiastical. Following generations chose to commemorate their dead differently and anonymously. The earlier cross-marked slabs of western Britain and Ireland can be matched in the Paris area, where some have been found *in situ* over seventh- or early eighth-century graves (Sirat 1966; 1970). Their similarity should cause no surprise, for this was after all the Gaul of Columbanus. But that is another and wholly medieval story.

We may conclude then that the Latin memorial formulae were introduced into western Britain from western France in the mid to late fifth century, and were grafted onto a separate tradition of Irish origin (whichever side of the Irish Sea it originated), using ogam script and the filiation so important in Insular society. Gildas Bernier (1982, 161–79) has drawn attention to a number of Breton inscriptions previously neglected by British archaeologists. One of these, from the church of St Budoc at Plourin-Ploudalmézau on the tip of Finistere north-west of Brest uses a *Hic Iacet* formula. Both this and the stone from Louannec on the coast north of Lannion (Côtes-du-Nord) with a vertical inscription in two lines reading *DISIDERI FILI BODGNOUS* would be quite at home in Wales or south-west England.[1] These inscriptions bring the origin of our Insular memorial stones within the orbit of the fifth-century British migrations, though routine contacts between the British and Gallic churches may be at least as important.

Note
1. I am deeply grateful to Professor Wendy Davies and to Paul Williams for drawing my attention to this important new evidence.

Epigraphic, Art-Historical, and Historical Approaches to the Chronology of Class I Inscribed Stones

Ken Dark

For dating the inscriptions the form of the letters gives little help, for they have been crudely fashioned with a pick.'

(Wright and Jackson 1968, 297)

Introduction

The corpus of Class I inscribed stone monuments (Macalister 1945; 1949; Nash-Williams 1950; Tomlin, R.S.O. 1975; Thomas, C. 1980; Wright and Jackson 1968; RCAHMW 1976; Tangye 1985) is one of the principal archaeological sources for fifth- to seventh-century AD western Britain. These have long been recognized as of interest to the archaeologist, historian, and philologist. In the nineteenth century they were the subject of antiquarian study and speculation, and in the first half of the twentieth century the two great studies by Macalister and Nash-Williams established the range and outlined a still almost universally accepted classification. Important work by Radford (1975), Jackson (1953), Bu'Lock (1956) and, more recently, Knight (1981), has contributed to forming a standard view and a chronology disputed in minor detail but generally accepted in outline. This sees the stones as fifth- to seventh-century memorials and asserts that they are usually capable of 'close dating' within centuries or even decades. No reconsideration of this outline chronology has ever proposed an essentially different scheme or varied from the historical, epigraphical and art-historical methods of classification. Thus, despite scepticism by Alcock (1971, 238–48) and more recently Knight (1981; see above), R.B. White (1983), and M.L. Jones (1984, 259–62), the classification and dating of stones has essentially remained unchanged since Nash-Williams' classic work, published in 1950.

This is surprising for many reasons – not least the importance of the stones for Celtic philology and as one of the few really sizable bodies of evidence for the early medieval period in general in Celtic Britain (eg. Jackson 1953, 149). The reasons for this conservatism are

unclear: perhaps the elegance and confidence of Nash-Williams' typology have been intimidating, perhaps few modern archaeologists have the necessary epigraphic knowledge, and perhaps it is indicative of the small number of archaeologists being trained in, and working in, early medieval Celtic archaeology as a whole. To suggest that few archaeologists seem to understand *how* Nash-Williams dated the stones may not be as frivolous as it at first sounds!

Previous criticisms of this chronology have centred on refuting the alleged 'internal dating' of specific memorials and on those inscriptions which can be linked to textual sources (Jones, M.L. 1984, 261–2), the stones sometimes being believed by archaeologists to be dated on philological grounds. The historical basis for dating the stones is, on the whole, hardly a surprising area of attack, for it should have been apparent to historians, since at least the late 1970s, that the historical associations so far adduced for dating lack acceptable textual support, except in relation to two stones, no. 138[1] from Castell Dwyran (Carms.) and no. 13 from Llangadwaladr (Anglesey), which would still seem to be datable to the sixth and seventh centuries respectively (see below).

Even the classification of the monuments has not been significantly changed since 1950. The only serious attempt to do so was in the Royal Commission's Glamorgan survey (RCAHMW 1976, 18–21). This proposed a simple 'ABC' equivalent of Nash-Williams' Classes I, II, and III (RCAHMW 1976, 18–9). A couple of 'new' classes were added on what might seem minor grounds, for example, dividing stones on the basis that some stood upright, while the remainder of that Class lay on the ground. This classification has neither come into general use, nor has it been seen as a very useful revision, although Myfanwy Lloyd Jones employed it in her recent study of the period (1984, 259–68).

Aside from my own work, little or no reclassification or drastic redating seems to be taking place, although the new edition of Nash-

Williams' corpus of the Welsh stones may involve some chronological adjustment. Jeremy Knight's (1981; see above) work has also clarified aspects of the chronology of these monuments and related work has been done in Scotland and Ireland, for example, by Okasha (1985, 43–69; and in progress), Hamlin (1982, 283–96) and Harvey (1987; 1990). Okasha has also been working on a *corpus* of the south-western British stones. However, it is no longer possible wholly to accept Nash-Williams' classification and chronology, even as modified by these later scholars.

It is first necessary to define Class I in explicit terms and to consider, in brief, the dating of Nash-Williams' Classes II – IV. Lastly, the dating and relationship to the Class I stones of ogam inscriptions will be discussed, as ogam occurs in addition to Latin inscriptions on Class I monuments in Britain.

Definition of Classes I, II, III, and IV

Nash-Williams divided the Early Christian Monuments of Wales into four types: I, II, III, and IV. Class I was defined as inscribed, unshaped, or roughly shaped, pillar-stones, and Class II as cross-marked stones (Nash-Williams 1950, 2–3, 17–8). Obviously these categories overlap when one observes stones which are cross-marked pillar-stones with inscriptions, such as no. 124 from Llanllyr (Cards.) and no. 287 from Towyn (Merioneth).

Nash-Williams seems to have arbitrarily divided these between Class I and Class II so that, Llanlleonfel (Brecs.) (no. 62) for instance, is a Class II stone, whereas the Catamanus stone from Llangadwaladr (no. 13) is a Class I stone, yet the former has only a small interlinear cross while the latter has a large and prominent cross. Obviously there is a 'fuzzy' division between the two classes as defined by Nash-Williams, and it seems best to clarify the division, and to place all the inscribed pillar-stones in Class I, and all the uninscribed, cross-marked, pillar-stones in Class II. It must be remembered, however, that these are modern classes, and need not have had any early medieval reality; people may not have perceived a division between these classes or, indeed, have perceived a different division between them.

Happily no problems of modern definition assail us with Classes III and IV, and we may accept Nash-Williams' attribution of stones to these groups (1950, 27–49). Class III includes both inscribed and uninscribed slab-crosses and freestanding crosses, and Class IV was defined by Nash-Williams (1950, 47) as 'a miscellaneous series of late monuments of early Romanesque types, found sporadically throughout Wales'. It seems logical to follow Nash-Williams' own, but later unused, division of Class III into two sub-groups: sub-group (a) (freestanding stone crosses) and sub-group (b) (slab-crosses) (Nash-Williams 1950, 32). Those slab-crosses that are inscribed, I shall call Class III (b.i), and those uninscribed Class III (b.ii). There is also a single 'hogback' tomb in Wales, no. 114 from Llanddewi-aber-Arth (Cards.), truly in a class by itself (Lang 1984)!

Lacking inscriptions, the Class II and Class III (b.ii) stones are hard to date. Some, such as no. 235 from Margam (Glamorgan) and no. 398 from St Lawrence (Pembs.), have features which we may assume to be seventh-century or later on the basis of comparison with Anglo-Saxon sculpture, and some may, for example, be assigned *terminus-post-quem* dates on the basis of comparison with Continental sculpture. It has been argued that, in Ireland, production of cross-marked slabs began in the seventh century, but recent work at Tintagel (Cornwall) suggests that cross-marked slabs were being produced in the sixth century in south-west Britain (Lionard 1961; Nowakowski and Thomas 1990, 18–22). Unless found in excavated contexts, however, only art-historical comparison with Irish, Anglo-Saxon, Scottish, or Continental sculpture is able to provide dating evidence for these uninscribed stones. Consequently, strictly speaking, only a *terminus-post-quem* date can be assigned to any of these monuments.

One way in which we might attempt to assign a date to the origin of Class II and Class III stones, failing dated excavated examples, is to employ John Lewis' argument (1976) that they do not usually occur on sites which also have Class I stones in Pembrokeshire. Lewis interpreted this in chronological terms, a conclusion recently supported by Heather James (1987, 66). Lewis argued that sites contemporary with the Class I stones were often disused prior to the currency of Class II stones. However, a cultural interpretation is also possible: Class I, Class II and Class III stones could have fulfilled different functions, or been pertinent to different groups, or to different types of site. Another possibility is that Class II and Class III stones may have been produced and distributed in a different way from that of Class I stones. Alternatively, we may see Class II stones as uninscribed Class I stones fulfilling the same function and of the same date. We are not at present able to answer these questions with confidence.

The cross-slabs of Class III(b) have external analogies for their decoration, indicative of a 700–1100 date for at least some of them; and there is no reason to assume that any belong to the preceding period (Nash-Williams 1950, 29–47). Their inscriptions all employ Half-uncial script, and some of the slab-crosses seem to relate to (and may precede?) the freestanding stone crosses, while others may be seen as elaborations of the cross-marked stones of Class II. While there may be problems in the detailed chronology of slab-crosses, an origin in the eighth century and, therefore, possibly prior to the freestanding stone crosses (which were being erected by the ninth century at latest) seems likely. Alternatively, however, both slab- and freestanding stone crosses may have originated in the same period. So, in outline at least, there are not necessarily chronological problems with Nash-Williams' classification and dating of the Class III monuments. In Ireland elaborate sculptured crosses, like those of Class III(a), began to be made in the eighth or possibly the ninth century (Edwards, N. 1983). In Anglo-Saxon England, freestanding stone crosses originated in the eighth century (Cramp 1978). However, although many of the motifs used, and the technique of stonecarving, were introduced as a result of contacts with the Continental Church, there are no freestanding stone crosses on the Continent, and their origins in Anglo-Saxon England are obscure (Edwards, N. 1990; and pers. comm. 1990). Wooden standing crosses may have been made in Anglo-Saxon England and Ireland (and Wales?) in the early seventh century or, in western Britain and Ireland, even in the sixth (Cramp 1978; Edwards, N. 1985).

Ogam and the Class I Inscriptions

Ogam is not capable, itself, of being dated epigraphically, and its chronology depends on philological or historical arguments; it has been conventionally philologically assumed to belong to the fifth to seventh centuries (Evans, D.S. 1979; Stevenson, J. 1989). A *terminus ante quem* for many ogam inscriptions is given by the formula *mucoi*, which was apparently obsolete by the eighth century (MacNeill 1907), but philological problems (Stevenson, J. 1989; Harvey 1987; 1990) and the later use of ogam (Thurneysen 1975, 10) complicate this simple chronology. Of especial importance is the growing consensus among specialists that ogam was in use in Ireland in the third, if not second, century AD (Harvey 1990). It may be, therefore, that ogam was in use, at least in Ireland, for a much longer period than has conventionally been supposed, although this clearly included the fifth to seventh centuries.

Ogam inscriptions are mainly found in the south-west of Ireland, and some in western Britain, but the British series are mainly bilingual in contrast to the monolingual inscriptions in Ireland. Recent work has demonstrated the close relationship between ogam and Latin literacy (Harvey 1990), and consequently it is unsurprising to find such bilingual inscriptions.

In Wales ogam occurs almost entirely in Pembrokeshire, Carmarthenshire, Cardiganshire, and Breconshire, and these are areas which historically may be thought of as the kingdoms of Dyfed and Brycheiniog. Both had Irish dynasties during the period 400–700. Ogam inscriptions also occur in south-western Britain and in north Wales, both areas apparently ruled by British kings. Bilingual ogam inscriptions presumably attest contact with, or settlement by, Irish speakers during the period of the Class I stones.

It cannot be established from the bilingual inscriptions themselves whether they were erected in order to be understood by Irish speakers, or by Irish speakers who wanted to be understood by those who read Latin but did not speak Irish, even if the individual commemorated had an Irish name. As D. Simon Evans has shown that Irish was a living language in western Britain in the fifth and sixth centuries, the British ogam inscriptions are potentially datable by philology based on Irish evidence (Evans, D.S. 1979). This might help us to date the western British Latin inscriptions if the relevant philological chronology was more certainly defined, but, as we have seen, this is at present controversial. In view of this controversy, the most reliable way of dating the ogam on bilingual Class I stones, is to attempt to date the Latin inscriptions, as the ogam can often be shown to be most probably contemporary with the Latin inscriptions, when it translates them into Irish.

Problems with Nash-Williams' Classification and Chronology of the Class I Stones

Nash-Williams based his chronology on historical links with textual sources, and on epigraphic and art-historical dating. The problems with the former have already been mentioned: most of the textual sources which he used are pseudo-historical, at best hagiographical. In any case, proving that, for instance, the 'Vendesetli' stone (no. 96), from Llannor (Caerns.) is related to the nearby church dedication (as Nash-Williams argued) would not be as easy as he assumed (Jones, M.L. 1984, 261). Even if the two were related, would it not, for example, be possible to argue that the dedication was derived from knowledge of the inscription itself rather than the person mentioned on it?

The problems with the epigraphic methods employed are equally severe. While Nash-Williams used the latest palaeographical techniques and data available to him, few if any modern scholars would accept his methods as still wholly valid. Notably, the estimation of date by percentage of Half-uncial forms is now seen as inadequate (Dumville, pers. comm. 1985, with reference to the still unpublished work on the subject by the late T. J. Brown). Problems of regional variability, external contacts, and the cultural and educational backgrounds of those who commissioned and made the inscriptions, may all further complicate this issue. Even if we knew who made an inscription we could not, on the available evidence, answer these larger questions. Indeed, all these may be just the sort of questions which we might hope to answer from the evidence of the stones.

Both Nash-Williams and subsequent researchers shared common preconceptions about the nature and function of these stones; these may also have influenced views of classification and even their dating. The basic premise upon which such researchers have worked is that (in sum) the stones were the tombstones of sub-Roman Christians. This was a common view in the academic world of the nineteenth century; and still dominates modern thought on the subject. Although not necessarily incorrect, such preconceptions have led scholars to assume a post-Roman dating for the corpus of stones, a view challenged only by Richard White (1983). This need not necessarily be true of specific stones considered individually. The assumption that the sequence of Class I stones ends with the Catamanus stone (no. 13) and, therefore, in the seventh century, has also played a major part in thinking about the monuments (eg. Jones, M.L. 1984, 259–62). One may note, for example, the relatively lengthy discussion of this monument's date (as the latest Class I stone) by Kenneth Jackson (1953, 160–2). It is not obvious at first

sight that this stone need be typologically the latest in the sequence.

Recent work has begun to move away from these preconceptions and to see the stones in new ways, for example, as boundary markers (Preston-Jones and Rose 1986, 157; Dark 1989, 386–7, 407; P. Williams and D. Walker, work in progress). However, no large-scale rigorous study of the hypothesis that the stones were boundary markers has yet been published, in contrast to a similar hypothesis in relation to pagan Anglo-Saxon burial sites (Charles-Edwards 1976, 84–5; Goodier 1984; Reilly 1988, 167–74, 184–6).

Some stones lack evidence of Christianity, and if the idea is valid that filiation was contrary to early medieval Christian practice on the Continent (Macalister 1945, x-xiii), many stones would have evidence militating against a Christian interpretation. As it is, filiation was almost certainly acceptable to early medieval western British Christians who employed genealogies and patronymics in their names, so there seems no reason why this should not have been expressed on stone monuments. Hamlin has proposed that, for early medieval Irish inscriptions, filiation merely expresses a clan-based society (1982, 285).

According to Nash-Williams' published dating (1950), the stones appear to range from the fifth to the twelfth centuries AD. Radford has pointed out (1975, 5) that this range does not necessarily preclude the late fourth century.

Individual minor errors have been recognized in Nash-Williams' work, as, for example, those pointed out by Myfanwy Lloyd Jones (1984, 259–62). But if there were major problems with Nash-Williams' chronology, that would obviously have implications for several areas of early medieval Celtic studies.

As Nash-Williams' chronology was based on history, art-history, and epigraphy, let us examine each of these methods in turn as a source for dating these monuments.

HISTORICAL DATING

We have already seen that two Class I inscriptions, Castell Dwyran and Llangadwaladr (nos. 138 and 13), may be historically dated. The former mentions Vortipor, whom we find in Gildas' *De Excidio* II.31 as an old man (Winterbottom 1978, 31). If we accept a generous date of 500 x 575 for Gildas' work, then Vortipor may be expected to have died between the outside limits of 500 and 600 (Dumville 1984a, 57). It is probable that we may accept a sixth-century date for the stone. Following the

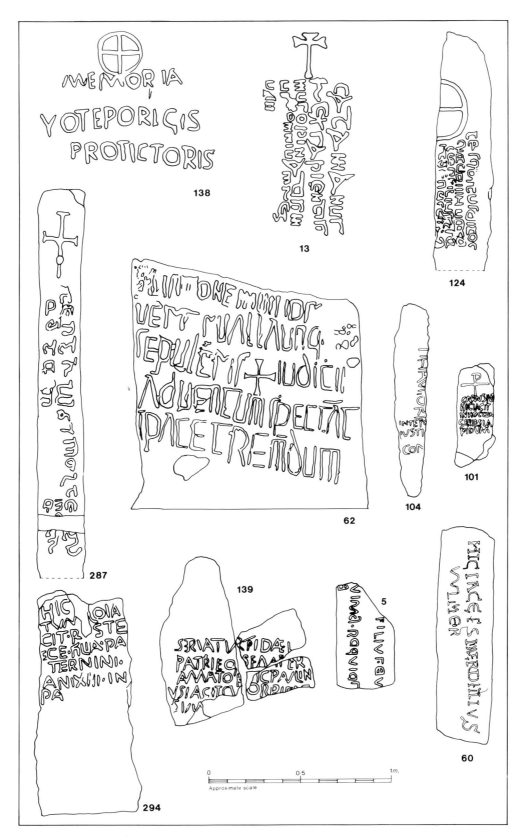

Fig. 7.1 *Class I Inscriptions from Wales used as examples in epigraphic and art-historical discussion in the text.*
(after Nash-Williams, 1950).

chronology for Gildas' work suggested by Dumville, I incline to see it as belonging to the middle or later part of that century (Dumville 1984b).

Unfortunately, neither of our two historically dated stones contains epigraphic forms found on other Class I stones, except in a very general sense. The Catamanus stone (no. 13) probably shows that Insular Half-uncial was being inscribed in western Britain by the mid-seventh century, if perhaps only at a royal court.

It has also been claimed that the Class I stone, no. 104, from Penmachno (Caerns.) is also historically dated, on the grounds that it contains a reference to the consulship of Justinus. Although this monument has both a vertical and horizontal element in its layout, perhaps suggesting two inscriptions, the technique of inscription is the same for both parts, perhaps suggesting contemporaneity. If we choose to follow Nash-Williams' reading, and assume that the 'Iustinus' mentioned is not a local British dignitary, then it would seem that this monument has a *terminus post quem* of 540. This seems the most reasonable interpretation, but even if so, 540 is a *terminus post quem*, not necessarily the date of the stone, for this formula could have been used by someone emulating a Continental convention, unaware of when the consulship of Justinus was. Consequently, the Penmachno stone, although provided with a *terminus post quem* by historical evidence, cannot be considered historically dated in the same sense as the Vortipor or Catamanus stones.

ART HISTORY

Very few different types of symbol occur on these monuments. The symbols used include the *alpha* and *omega*, the Constantinian and monogramatic *chi-rho*, and crosses (Nash-Williams 1950, 14–6). With the exception of the cross, all these symbols certainly occur in fourth-century contexts in Britain (Thomas, C. 1981a, 88 fig. 4, 89 fig. 5, 90 fig. 6, 105–16). Controversy surrounds the date at which the cross symbol was first employed, and it may well have been in use much earlier than the fifth-century date usually supposed. Watts has recently argued that the X cross was found on late Romano-British lead tanks (1988, 210–2, n. 12, 219), but, although these may well be Christian religious artefacts, this must be uncertain in the case of such a simple design (Thomas, C. 1981a, 122). A reference to an early fourth-century depiction of the Cross in Eusebius' *Vita Constantini* III.49 (Mango 1972, 11) seems to me to refute the argument that the cross was

first employed as a Christian symbol in the fifth century. This, however, refers to a Mediterranean, not British, situation.

In Britain the earliest certain depictions of the cross as a Christian symbol are on ceramics. If we accept the Tidworth lamp as a genuine find then this, as dated by Charles Thomas (1981a, 126) may indicate a *terminus post quem* for the cross-symbol of *c.* 425. Otherwise a *terminus post quem* for the equal-armed cross is provided by a Phocaean Red Slip Ware sherd from Tintagel dated *c.* 470, and the Latin cross is attested on an African Red Slip Ware sherd from Cadbury Congresbury, dated to the mid-sixth century (Thomas, C. 1981b, 9; Rahtz 1982, 103, fig. 10.5).

Thus all the main symbols in use on Class I stones were present in Britain by the mid-sixth century, and many may be found in Roman Britain. From this evidence we may argue that Britain was, perhaps, receiving all types of Christian symbolism (and other Christian ideas?), at the same time as, or, and possibly (but not necessarily) even earlier than, Gaul (Knight 1981, 55–7). This information, available to us today but not available in its entirety to Nash-Williams, must make us carefully reconsider our preconceptions about, not only the art-historical dating of these monuments, but also much broader issues in early Christian archaeology.

Returning to the specifics of these inscriptions it is interesting to find the ring-cross, which is found first in the Roman catacombs dated to c. 500 (De Rossi 1857–1861; Thomas, C. 1981a, 80), depicted on the Vortipor stone (no. 138) historically datable to the sixth century. Not only does this seem to indicate a spread of innovations into sixth-century western Britain shortly after their Mediterranean inception, but shows that even our most seemingly 'Celtic' or 'medieval' symbols may be found as early as the sixth century and be ultimately of continental, even Mediterranean, origin. This view is now supported by work at Tintagel, where compass-drawn designs, interpreted by Thomas as attempts at a cross of arcs, have been found on slates probably associated with early medieval (most likely sixth-century) burials (Nowakowski and Thomas 1990, 10 fig. 6, 11, and 18–22).

Clearly, as Thomas has shown, the artefactual evidence for long-range contacts forms a potential path of entry for such Mediterranean and Continental ideas, including symbolism, into both the material and organizational world of fifth- and sixth-century Britain (Thomas, C. 1987, 9–10; 1988a, 22). Fulford's recent demonstration that this contact might well include direct links with Constantinople is especially significant here (Fulford 1989).

The implication of this discussion for dating Class I stones is straightforward. As we saw for Class II stones, art-historical dating can only afford a *terminus post quem* for a monument. In the case of Class I stones, this *terminus post quem* is often going to lie in the fourth century, at the latest in the sixth century. Consequently, while art-historical dating may occasionally enable us to differentiate demonstrably sixth-century or later monuments from the remainder, it, for the most part, only demonstrates a fourth-century or later date for the monuments upon which it is found. An excellent example of how the dating provided by this evidence gives only a *terminus post quem* is the occurrence at Jarrow of a Constantinian *chi-rho* symbol in a late seventh-century context (Nash-Williams 1950, 16, 92; Cramp 1984, 113–4). Absence of symbols, or of any specific symbol, is of no chronological importance whatsoever.

EPIGRAPHY

Epigraphy is, of course, the obvious way to date inscribed stones, and was used thus by Macalister, Nash-Williams, and Radford. Epigraphy may not now seem, however, to constitute such an accurate dating method for these monuments as was once thought. On the one hand, a much narrower range of letter forms occurs on the stones than has usually been assumed, and the letter forms which do occur give only a broad date-range.

Nash-Williams argued (1950, 223–8) that there was a very wide range of letter forms on the monuments. This view was supported by taking each variant of a letter as constituting a separate letter form; such that, for example, the variants of the letter R shown in Fig. 7.2 would each be considered different letter forms. While such precision may be possible when considering letters written in ink on parchment, this approach ignores the technical aspects of the inscriptions. The technical problems may be divided into two parts: who made the inscriptions, and how did they make them? These are obvious and fundamental to any epigraphic study but have not been fully examined in the past. It has already been noted that we cannot, at present, assess whether the stones were inscribed by secular or ecclesiastical craftsmen, but the questions whether or not we are looking at the work of specialist stone-masons and to what cultural and technological tradition(s) the stones belong may nevertheless be approached.

There is little evidence of regional workshops, implying either local production or travelling craftsmen. Common features of the epigraphy, symbolism, and production of the inscriptions, such as the low setting of the symbols above the inscription on some Welsh stones, for example on the Vortipor stone (no. 138) and no. 101 from Penmachno (Caerns.), argue for the latter, and the inscriptions seem to represent a continuation of the latest Romano-British semi-formal stone-masonry, albeit blended with the sub-Roman, Continental and Mediterranean Christian traditions (Radford 1975, 4–5; Pearce 1978, 24; Thomas, C. 1986, 140, figs. 86–8). Yet, even on what may seem to us the most romanized stones, such as no. 294 from Llanerfyl (Montgomery) and no. 139 from Cynwyl Gaeo (Carms.), the standards of production, when compared with Romano-British formal inscriptions, are poor, and this is an important point to recall when considering the range and production of letter forms on these monuments.

We must also consider how these inscriptions were produced. Their style is necessarily imprecise, given that they are often cut or pocked onto unshaped and unsmoothed boulders. Pocking is a technique which hardly lends itself to precision. This may be seen in the depth of cutting, or pocking, which is not consistent and may partly be explained in this way, rather than by reference to different types of stone, or different craftsmen. As on Romano-British milestones, little attention was paid to correct 'Roman' layout (eg. Thomas, C. 1986, 140, figs 86–8); the lines straggle and are partly laid out according to the particular features of individual stones. It is hard to believe that mistakes would have been unknown, and that, once cut or pocked into a stone, they could have been easily corrected. Compressions, simplifications, and positioning of letters may have occurred in relation to the stone's shape and surface.

Many of the characteristics of the epigraphy of Class I monuments may be noticed on Romano-British inscriptions (Collingwood and Wright 1965), the recarving of letters, the failure to join the strokes making up letters, and the difficulty of carving and pocking curves. Thus, reversed, disjointed, and 'squared' letters do not represent separate forms, but merely poor reproductions of the standard types. If any, or all, of the people who made the Class I inscriptions were illiterate or semi-literate, simple copying of a written exemplar may have introduced even more errors.

Taking these problems into consideration, we thus reduce Nash-Williams' range of letter forms

Fig. 7.2 *The range of letter-forms on Class I Inscriptions in Wales proposed by Nash-Williams.*
Forms suggested as acceptably distinct are blacked-in, showing the possible extent of reduction in the
number of forms resulting from critical evaluation. Angular A is marked '1', R with horizontal arm '2'.

drastically. There are, for example, only six (or possibly even only four) basic forms of A, used on the stones, where he produced a range of 20! Likewise, of his 18 L's, only four seem distinctive letter forms. Previous considerations of these monuments have taken reversed, inverted, and tilted letters as constituting separate forms, and we must take this into consideration here. As we have seen, however, reversing is common in Romano-British inscriptions, and therefore may be discounted as a useful chronological indicator; and the same is true of inversion. Tilting may be of more significance, but is common only in the presence of the laterally tilted or horizontal I or |, which is epigraphically wholly Insular and found only on Class I inscriptions (Radford 1975, 5). Thus, considered as underlying paradigms of transformation, tilting, reversion, and inversion may be seen to have little chronological significance, and even the individual instances do not create new letter forms, but merely transform standard ones. The same is true of the use of serifs, and of the elongation of upward and downward strokes in letters such as B, but these may be of more chronological significance. The latter seems, in fact, to be a sixth-century Gallic feature (Nash-Williams 1950, 224, see B8 for example), whereas the former began to be used in the Roman world in the fourth century and continues later (Nash-Williams 1950, 223, see A 15–7). This brings us to a consideration of the epigraphic and palaeographical parallels for the letter forms on these monuments.

Two scripts were used on the Class I monuments, Capital and Half-uncial. The palaeographical parallels for almost all the letter forms on the Class I monuments are so wide that they are of no chronological value, especially in the case of the Capital script, of which the most to be said is that it resembles that of the latest extant Romano-British inscriptions, such as that at Ravenscar, and of the sub-Roman Christian inscriptions found in Gaul (Collingwood and Wright 1965, no. 721). The most widely distributed distinctive forms of Capital letters, the angular A and R with a horizontal arm (Fig. 7.2), are only very broadly datable. The angular A seems to have begun in the fifth century in the western Roman Empire and to have continued into the medieval period (Collingwood and Richmond 1969, 193–216, fig. 74e; Lowe 1972, 3 no. 124). This form of R occurs on a Romano-British cup from Boscence in Cornwall, and still occurs in eighth-century manuscripts (for the fifth to sixth centuries see Ireland 1983, 232, fig. 200; Lowe 1972, 29 no. 220). Moreover, the

difficulties of the situation become apparent if one seeks detailed analogies for the exact forms of R on the Class I stones, for the crucial angle of the horizontal arm of the letter is the sort of feature most vulnerable to variation produced only on technical grounds, so that a conceptual R in the stone-mason's mind may have been rendered, for technical reasons alone, in a wide variety of ways. While the overall similarities of the manuscript evidence and Continental epigraphic analogies indicate a broadly early medieval date for the letter forms, close dating seems impossible.

Nash-Williams himself produced very few examples of rarer letter forms assignable even to single centuries (1950, 223–4, 226–7), and, when these occur, they still offer only *termini post quos*, usually of the late fifth and sixth centuries. They thus coincide with the proposed outline chronology, and these *termini post quos* are, therefore, useful corroborative evidence, but they are hardly themselves sufficient dating evidence to assign any stone a date within a century.

The presence or absence of Half-uncial letter forms on any inscription was given great importance by Nash-Williams and others, and (without admitting his methods of dating by relative frequency of what he called 'Half-uncial' forms, or even his characterization in those terms of the non-Capital forms on the Class I stones) we may accept that this is a potentially useful datum (or perhaps data) through the material, assuming that we may see the introduction of non-Capital forms as representing a chronological horizon, however broad. The problems with this approach are obvious: we must be clear which non-Capital scripts were used on the stones, and at what date they originated. Rather than accepting Nash-Williams' division of the non-Capital scripts into 'Half-uncial' and 'rounded Half-uncial' (1950, 223–32), we may look at the non-Capital scripts of the stones in the light of modern palaeography.

Almost all the non-Capital letter forms of the Class I inscriptions fall within the canons of Insular Half-uncial and Insular minuscule. The chronology and place of origin of these scripts seem uncertain, although a sub-Roman British context for their emergence is at present preferred by palaeographers; it is clear that they had fully emerged by the mid-seventh century (Brown 1977; 1982). The most widely used of these scripts on the Class I stones is Insular Half-uncial, but minuscule a in particular is common; and in both scripts there is an admixture on the Class I stones of Uncial forms, some of which (notably G) had been in use in Roman Britain.

Exact manuscript parallels for the Insular letter forms found on Class I stones may then be found, but provide only a *floruit* for those stones on which they occur. That *floruit* is from the date at which we consider the Insular scripts to have emerged, to the date at which they ceased to be used. However, if the letter forms are taken to be more generally Half-uncial, and not peculiarly Insular, they might give a much earlier *terminus post quem*. The uncertainty surrounding the origin and chronology of Insular script is thus directly relevant to the chronology of the Class I stones.

The historically and art-historically dated Vortipor stone is of especial relevance here, as this royal memorial is not inscribed in Half-uncial letter forms of any kind. While this does not prove that Half-uncial had not been introduced anywhere in western Britain prior to the date of this stone, it is suggestive that the introduction of Insular Half-uncial may belong, in broad terms, to the mid-sixth to seventh centuries. On the evidence rehearsed so far, it is probably reasonable to see the presence of Half-uncial in inscriptions in western Britain as datable in the later sixth or seventh century, even perhaps (at broadest) in the period 550 to 650, although we cannot rule out, merely on the evidence of the Class I stones, the use of Half-uncial letter forms from an earlier sixth-century (or even fifth-century?) point.

Seven inscriptions of Class I type do not have either Capitals or the types of Half-uncial script already discussed, but what Nash-Williams called 'rounded Half-uncial', using the Half-uncial a and the sloping rounded form of *d* which we otherwise find first in a meaningful context in Insular script in the *Cathach* of St Columba in the early or mid-seventh century (Radford 1975, 5–7; Lowe 1972, 41 no. 266). This script seems to have had a long duration in western British epigraphy. On the basis of manuscript parallels Nash-Williams was probably correct in assigning these monuments to the seventh to ninth centuries, the greater correlation with manuscript evidence perhaps being a product of greater manuscript survival. Nor need we doubt, on the basis of modern palaeography, Nash-Williams' assignment of Class I stone no. 5 from Heneglwys (Anglesey), and no. 60 from Llangors (Brecs.), to the twelfth century; these monuments may indicate the survival of the tradition of erecting inscribed pillar-stones of Class I type into the late medieval period, albeit in a very reduced way. Obviously if

Class I stones were still being made in the twelfth century this has implications for the dating of other memorials in this class and refutes the widespread idea that the sequence of these monuments ended in the seventh century. An alternative view of these 'late' Class I stones is that they represent a conscious revival of the tradition of making Class I stones, a revival occasioned by wholly twelfth-century circumstances. On present evidence it is impossible to resolve this question with certainty, but the existence of Class I stones inscribed in 'rounded Half-uncial' cannot be dismissed, and may, in itself, serve to refute the idea of a seventh-century end for the sequence. Unless other evidence is forthcoming, it may be sensible to take the apparent evidence of twelfth-century epigraphic features at face value to indicate that Class I monuments were being erected up until this time.

To summarize, we may say that the epigraphy of the monuments does not in itself permit 'close dating' of many, if any, inscriptions. Despite this, epigraphy can inject some absolute chronology into a relative chronology constructed on other grounds by providing several *termini post quos* for monuments, in creating a 'dating horizon' of the introduction of Half-uncial letter forms, possibly in the late sixth or seventh century, and in the seventh and later centuries by direct parallels between the epigraphy of the monuments and surviving manuscript evidence.

Conclusion

Consequently, epigraphy may contribute, on the one hand, a broad *floruit* for many of these inscriptions and, on the other, a series of *terminus-post-quem* dates for individual monuments. It cannot, however, when used alone, enable the 'close dating' of any Class I stone, nor can it do so combined only with historical and art-historical dating.

Art history, epigraphy, and historical associations do not, then, enable us to construct a detailed chronology for these monuments, although they can assist us in this purpose. We may concur with Radford that on epigraphic grounds alone the inscriptions could have begun to be made in the fourth century (Radford 1975, 5), with Nash-Williams that some are epigraphically twelfth century, or later, and that the *floruit* of the majority of Class I monuments clearly lies in the intervening period, as is epigraphically and art-historically attested.

Such a realization has positive aspects. We

may, for example, now see that the series of Class I inscriptions almost certainly overlaps chronologically, not only with ogam, but with Classes II and III (which may themselves be, in part, contemporary) also. Negatively it must, for example, cast doubt on the use of the conventional dating of these monuments as a key chronological pointer in pre-Norman Celtic philology, and, therefore, on its absolute chronology. Consequently, the implications of this discussion extend far beyond the confines of the dating and classification of Class I inscribed stones, into many other aspects of early medieval archaeology, history, and even (via philology) literature.

If closer dating of the majority of Class I inscriptions is to be achieved it must clearly be on other grounds than epigraphy, art history, or historical dating. For this, I would argue, formula, direction, and technique of inscription, are our most promising sources of evidence.

Notes

1 'Stone number' in the above refers to catalogue number assigned in Nash-Williams 1950, unless otherwise stated. All dates given are A.D.

Air Photography of Ecclesiastical Sites in South Wales

Terrence A. James

Most church sites have been in use for many centuries. The successful ones today form urban nuclei or are prominent focal points at the centre of villages. But the less successful, serving scattered communities, are often found in remote locations surrounded by fields, whilst the unsuccessful have not only lost their congregations but have also become either abandoned ruins or have disappeared from view.

Air photography can be an invaluable tool in discovering otherwise buried information about a site's past. This cannot, however, be so useful in urban contexts where upstanding buildings mask earlier features. The fundamental questions posed by any features around churches are what date are they and what function? Are they earlier, later or contemporary with a church? Do the features represent a precursor to the church, or churchyard, or are they coeval with their evolution? Only in a very small number of cases will air photography alone be capable of answering any of these questions. Other evidence must be called into play. And what sort of features are we looking for? If we accept, as I think we must, the suggestion that early church 'foundations were settlements rather than isolated churches' (Davies, W. 1982a, 143), then it is evidence of settlement (either secular or ecclesiastical) that the aerial archaeologist seeks.

Evidence for settlement in the period under review is notoriously sparse. The paucity, or almost total lack, of surviving features has been blamed on the flimsy nature of structures, with much use of timber rather than stone, resulting in little substantive surviving archaeology — at least above ground. Yet settlements of anything other than a very short lifespan comprise more than just houses. The constant use of unmetalled roads and pathways, for example, would result in the formation of deep-rutted hollow ways. As Beresford (1954, 417) remarked in his survey of lost villages, 'sunken roadways are the most immediately visible features of [lost] village sites'.

The difficulty for us when trying to discover evidence for pre-conquest settlement around churches is that either subsequent activity has obliterated it, or that we are unable to date the visible features and thus establish what belongs to which period. One may cite, as an example, the fairly well-documented village once associated with Eglwys Cymyn, Carms. (SN231106). The church is enclosed by a near circular churchyard which both ground and aerial evidence suggests may have evolved from an earlier defensive site. It also contains the bilingual Latin and ogam Early Christian memorial stone commemorating Avitoria (Nash-Williams 1950, no. 142). There are good grounds, therefore, for believing that this church, or at least the churchyard, was founded before the Norman conquest (Fig. 8.2). Today the church has few habitations nearby, but earthwork evidence for a deserted village survives, albeit now very ploughed down. The villagers of Eglwys Cymyn worked demesne land to the north of the church in 1307 along with tenants of four adjoining bond hamlets (Thomas, W.S.G. 1969, 193–4). By 1609 however a survey of the Manor of Eglwys Cymyn (Thomas, W.S.G. 1969, 194) showed that the village had disappeared and the former bond hamlets were much reduced. In 1621 a Court of Exchequer heard of the disappearance of 'houses, barns, stables, cowhouses and suchlike' from the *town* of Eglwys Cymyn some 50 years previous. Moreover these were replaced by enclosures. The malefactors, it was alleged, had 'broken down and defaced the boundaries, meerstones and marks whereby the two tenements were distinguished' (Thomas, W.S.G. 1969, 194). We cannot here go into the reasons for the abandonment of the village, but Thomas concludes in his paper on lost villages in the area, that the illegal enclosure and destruction (which must have happened around 1570) had proceeded without opposition because there were by then no residents (Thomas, W.S.G. 1969, 194). All this is rehearsed to underline the following point. We know that a village existed at Eglwys Cymyn up to the early sixteenth century, and that there was physical destruction of some of the former tenements at this time. There *may* have been a settlement around the church before the conquest. But the only evidence for earthworks around the church today relates mainly to buildings still standing in the nineteenth century; the sixteenth-

Fig. 8.1 *Map of Dyfed showing places mentioned in the text*

century and earlier settlement has all but disappeared. The possibility of finding pre-conquest settlement evidence on the surface is thus very slim.

If we compare Eglwys Cymyn with, for example, St Edrin's, Pembs. (SM894283) (Fig. 8.3), a site with a curvilinear churchyard and well-endowed with Early Christian sculpture (Nash-Williams 1950, nos. 391–4), then the depressing fact is brought home: that the destructive processes of intensive modern farming have greatly diminished the possibility of discovering earthworks indicating settlement of any antiquity. Therefore, in this context, the best potential for air photography must lie with the discovery of cropmark evidence in occasional drought years such as 1976, 1984 and 1989.

Setting aside the evidence for settlement, I now wish to consider other features associated with early churches where air survey can certainly be of benefit. I think it is now generally accepted that *some* circular or curvilinear churchyards originated as *defensive* sites, possibly of the late prehistoric period. This is not a new idea, but recent archaeological excavation at, for example, Caer, Bayvil, Pembs., provides substantive evidence for the theory (James, H. 1987). In a paper on enclosed ecclesiastical sites, Leo Swan (1983, 269) has noted similar features in Wales, Scotland, and, more particularly Ireland. Ireland also has numerous examples of large outer enclosures of many acres in size encircling early ecclesiastical sites. In Wales, by contrast, we have few examples of such large outer enclosures, but it remains a moot point as to whether this is the result of the destruction of evidence in a more intensively farmed country, or the fact that few of these large outer enclosures

Fig. 8.2 *Eglwys Cymyn, Carms., photographed with a light dusting of snow, from the south-east, shows traces of ditches and banks to the east of the church. Earthworks of a settlement can be seen to the north, west and south-west of the church (mainly obscured by trees). The most prominent relate to buildings still extant in the 1830s (TAJ-AP83.4, January, 1979).*

Fig. 8.3 *St. Edrin's, Pembs. Today the curvilinear churchyard sits in a landscape of well-ploughed regular fields leaving no earthwork evidence for any settlement that might have existed around the church*

ever existed. Air survey since 1978, mainly in Dyfed, has begun to reveal evidence for church sites located immediately within defended enclosures (Llangan, Carms., Fig. 8.4) and large outer enclosures can also be postulated for a number of sites (Llanwinio, Carms. Fig. 8.8). A full understanding of the relationships between a church site and an associated defended enclosure has yet to be fully demonstrated.

Although air survey is capable, in some cases, of resolving questions of relative chronology, it remains for excavation to provide the detail and the absolute dating. Air survey's most productive role, therefore, will be in the discovery of new or additional features around church sites.

Methodology

There have been two basic approaches to the air survey of churches:

1. The photography of church sites with a known or suspected pre-conquest history, or sites with known archaeological potential. Here results have not proved as rewarding as might have been hoped. Nonetheless interesting results have been produced in terms of potential large outer enclosures around such sites as St Ishmael's and Rhoscrowdder (both are listed in the Seven Bishop Houses of Dyfed (Charles-Edwards 1971)); also Llanafan Fawr, Llandeilo Llwydarth and Llanwinio (see below).
2. The photography of all church sites irrespective of their assumed history or archaeology in an attempt to record their current morphology and analyse their development. These sites have been and will in future continue to be viewed in a variety of light and crop conditions, and eventually multiple photographic records of individual sites will be built up. Air photography has demonstrated the benefits of photographing other site types in a variety of conditions, thus enriching our understanding of particular examples. In practice this approach has paid interesting dividends.

Apart from small grants from the Board of Celtic Studies which Wyn Evans and I have used to examine sites with a known pre-conquest history, it has not been possible to pursue either of the above courses in a systematic way due to the lack of both time and money. However, in the process of air-survey work, largely connected with Cadw's air-monitoring programme of scheduled ancient monuments, I have attempted to photograph as many medieval church sites as possible *en passant*. As a by-product new chance discoveries have inevitably been made. On the basis of photography since 1978 it is evident that early churches (like some of their prehistoric progenitors) are sited at a diverse variety of locations and are enclosed by equally diverse sizes and shapes of enclosure. Because of this it is difficult to categorize sites. Indeed many churches fall into more than one of the headings under which I now propose to discuss some results and problems.

Defended sites with evidence for possible Christian use or burial, but without surviving churches

In addition to the partly excavated site at Caer, Bayvil, Pembs. (SN112417) (see below), a number of other sites have been examined. These include a multivallate hillfort called Caerau, Pembs. (SN124454), where the discovery of cist graves in areas between the ramparts was recorded in the nineteenth century (James, H. 1987, 72). The field names *Llain yr Eglwys* ('Church Strip') and *Yr Eglwys Ddiflodau* ('the church without flowers') suggest that a church was located somewhere within or close by and *Y Fynn Went* ('the cemetery') ties in nicely with the cist graves. On the face of it Caerau appears atypical of the type of site that seems to have been adopted for cemetery and/or subsequent church use. In contrast, Bayvil, for example, has no indications of being anything other than univallate. But recent analysis suggests that the enclosures around Eglwys Cymyn, Llangynog and Llangan were also once multivallate, with perhaps only the inner rampart surviving today as the churchyard wall. (Of course Llangan's churchyard (Fig. 8.4) may bear no relationship at all to the underlying cropmarks.) The innermost ramparts of prehistoric multivallate defended enclosures are usually the strongest, and this may help explain why the outer defences have disappeared leaving only the inner enclosure to become the churchyard wall on some church sites. What sort of prehistoric defended enclosure should we therefore see as a model for subsequent adoption as a cemetery/church site?

Air survey in the drought of 1984 (James, T.A. 1984) resulted in the discovery of very slight cropmarks indicating an outer 'palisade' trench (diameter 120m) around what is assumed to be a prehistoric concentric enclosure (diameter 50m) at Lan Farm, Llanboidy, Carms. (SN216205) (Fig. 8.6). This outer enclosure could never have

Fig. 8.4 *Near vertical photograph of Llangan, Carms., from the south-east showing cropmarks of ditches in parched grass. Note also the small circular cropmark at top centre of the photograph (DAT AP89-169.34, July 1989).*

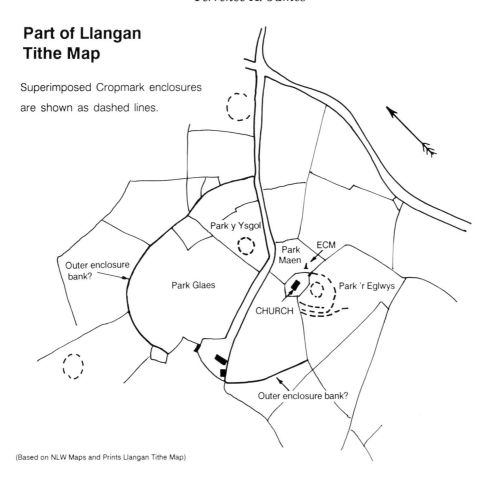

Part of Llangan Tithe Map

Superimposed Cropmark enclosures are shown as dashed lines.

Park y Ysgol

Outer enclosure bank?

Park Glaes

Park Maen

ECM

Park 'r Eglwys

CHURCH

Outer enclosure bank?

(Based on NLW Maps and Prints Llangan Tithe Map)

Fig. 8.5 *Interpretative drawing of Llangan cropmarks in relation to tithe-map names and field boundaries.*

been a strong defence, and should more properly be seen as a fence or stockade line. It is tempting to see such a fence as the precursor to, or in fact the *bangor* ('wattle enclosure'). Subsequent research has shown this site to be of considerable importance for the period under review. The farm name is recorded as *Llan* (rather than *Lan*) in the first one-inch edition of the Ordnance Survey map. Moreover the adjoining field to the north is called *Parc-y-Fynwent* ('Cemetery Field'). The morphology and size of the site are compatible with an Iron Age date. But it is likewise reminiscent of a circular churchyard enclosure, and may therefore also be (like Bayvil) an early abandoned burial ground. The present farmer's mother (whose family have worked this land since at least the eighteenth century) relates an interesting oral tradition that the first Llangan church stood on the site of this enclosure.

Not far distant is another apparently univallate defended enclosure, Cilsant, Carms. (SN268238) (Fig. 8.7). This important 'lost' site (surviving only as a place-name, Pen-y-Gaer Fawr) was photographed in 1984 when the ditch of the enclosure showed up as a cropmark in parched grass. Historically Cilsant was the residence of Cadifor Fawr (d. 1089–91) the 'supreme lord of Dyfed' (Jones, T. 1955, 33, 99), and father of Bledri Latimer the supposed purveyor of the Grail stories (Lloyd and Jenkins 1959, 41; Owen, H. 1906, 250–6). A possible inscribed stone once stood in or near the field in which the cropmark was observed, although it has since been lost and was never properly described (RCAHMW 1917, no. 590, 201) and a nearby field is called *Parc Ffynon Winio* ('St Gwinio's Well'). Lastly there is the significance of the name, Cilsant, which *could* be interpreted as 'Saint's cell'. Here, then, possibly, is an example of a defended enclosure with immediate pre-conquest historical associations, which could represent the 'failed' site that might otherwise have developed into a cemetery/church. If Cilsant had been an early medieval religious settlement, and subsequently became the caput of an eleventh-century local princely family, then this site may represent the opposite tradition in the development of early church sites. The prospect of excavation is indeed alluring.

Fig. 8.6 *Cropmarks of a circular enclosure at Lan, Llanboidy, Carms., with its outer 'palisade' trench and entrance on the south side, viewed from the NNE. The field in the foreground is called Parc-y-Fynwent (DAT AP84-65, July 1984).*

Fig. 8.7 *Cilsant, Carms. The circular enclosure, viewed from the east during drought conditions, shows as a cropmark in parched grass (DAT AP84-64.5, July 1984).*

Sites with surviving churches within presumed defended enclosures and/or within very large enclosed areas

There are a number of churches that fall into this category. An unusual example is Meidrim, Carms. (SN289209), a site, which appears to be located within an inland promontory fort. The more typical sites are similar to Eglwys Cymyn with circular or curvilinear churchyards which may form the surviving inner defences of multivallate sites (Fig. 8.2). (See Roberts above for the significance of the *eglwys* place-name element.) The evidence for multivallation, although not conclusive, is contained in photographs taken in winter where a light dusting of snow appears alternately to fill ditches or fail to cover very slight banks.

Llangan, Carms. (SN177186), is the most spectacular of the recent discoveries from the air (Figs 8.4 and 8.5). The church structure was late medieval but the probable Class I Early Christian monument, 'Canna's Chair' (Nash-Williams 1950, no. 322), located in the field to the north attests a much older history for the site. As can be seen from the photograph the graveyard sits within or partly astride a multivallate cropmark comprising at least three ditches. An entrance runs into the eastern side of the enclosure, south-east of the present church straight to a circular cropmark approximately 35m in diameter. There is possibly a second entrance on the west side. The difficulty is establishing the relationship between the present church and the cropmark, although there is little doubt that the church falls within the innermost defence line. A second circular cropmark, (*c.* 40m diam.) was visible about 150m NNW of the church and three others have been discovered not far distant (James, T.A. 1989, 34). The ubiquity of these cropmarks may indicate a focus for earlier (prehistoric?) burial activity (see Heather James below). At some distance north and north-west of the church is a curving hedgebank which might represent an outer enclosure (roughly 0.5 km in diam.) which takes in the principal cropmarks, including a field called Park Glaes (?Ditch Field), and interestingly follows part of the parish/county boundary. Aerial evidence alone cannot prove that there is any relationship between these features and the church/graveyard — they may be purely fortuitous. Only excavation has this potential.

Another church site with a Class I Early Christian memorial (Nash-Williams 1950, no. 169), Llanwinio, Carms. (SN261264), (Figs 8.8 and 8.9) may also lie within a defended enclosure or hillfort. In the early years of this century a small cottage which stood immediately south of

Fig. 8.8 *High-level vertical of Llanwinio, Carms., showing a possible very large outer enclosure defined by curving sunken lanes and hedge banks.*
North is at the top right-hand corner of the photograph (DAT CEGB/Merdian 1955).

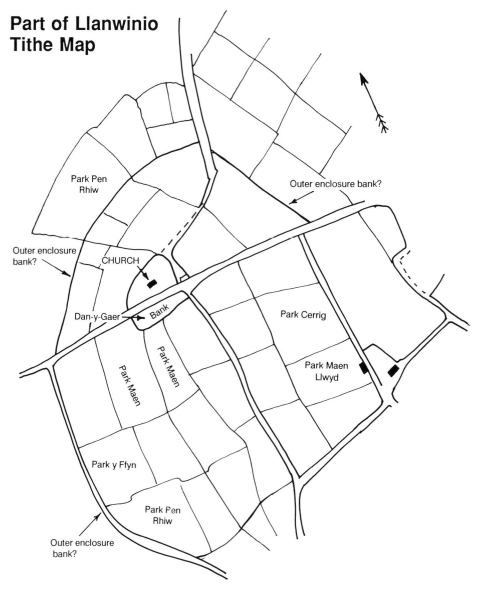

**Part of Llanwinio
Tithe Map**

Park Pen
Rhiw

Outer enclosure bank?

Outer enclosure
bank?

CHURCH

Dan-y-Gaer

Bank

Park Cerrig

Park Maen

Park Maen

Park Maen
Llwyd

Park y Ffyn

Park Pen
Rhiw

Outer enclosure
bank?

(Based on NLW Maps and Prints Llanwinio Tithe Map)

Fig. 8.9 *Interpretative drawing of Llanwinio tithe-map and field boundaries.*

the church was known as *Dan-y-Gaer* ('Below the Fort') (RCAHMW 1917, 200) the name which has now been adopted by an adjacent modern bungalow. Ground observation suggests there is a ditch or hollow way around the north-west and north sides immediately outside the churchyard wall. The field to the south on the opposite side of the road from the present churchyard is called 'Bank' in the tithe apportionment of 1848 (NLW Maps & Prints, Llanwinio Tithe and Apportionment), which may relate to the rampart on its south side. Llanwinio may additionally lie within a very much larger oval enclosure marked by a curving hedgebank that runs in an arc some

200–300m in radius around the east, north, and west sides of the church. The approximately north-south long axis measures about 1km in length. The continuation of the arc on the south-west side is marked by deeply-sunken lanes, which enclose fields called *Park Cerrig* ('Field of Stones'), *Parc Maen Llwyd* ('Field of the Grey [Standing?] Stone'), *Parc y Ffyn* ('Field of the Boundary') and two called *Parc Maen* ('[Standing?] Stone Field'). The present fields within this massive enclosed area may have been parcelled up from much larger units if not former unenclosed land, since many of them (some non-contiguous), bear the same names.

Church sites in close proximity to defended enclosures or hillforts

An adjunct to the search for church sites within defended enclosures has thrown up an interesting number of churches located close to, rather than within defended enclosures. Perhaps the best well-known example of this is Llanafan Fawr, Brecs. (SN969557). This classic site has a curvilinear churchyard, has good evidence for being within a large outer enclosure, and has the added distinction of a small defended ringwork about 300m to the west of the church (see Cambridge aerial photograph collection).

Air survey of Llangynog church, Carms. (SN337141), has resulted in an interesting discovery which in some ways might parallel the Llanafan situation. Llangynog has a near circular churchyard; yet photography on many occasions and in a variety of crop and light conditions suggests that the churchyard may sit within a less circular outer enclosure. In 1984 the cropmark of a second curvilinear enclosure was discovered some 150m west of the church (Fig. 8.10). This juxtaposition of church and adjacent enclosure was remarked upon by John Lewis (1976, 191) in his survey of Early Christian monuments west of the Taf, when he

drew attention to the closeness of Castell Henllys to St Fraid's chapel and Cribyn Gaer to St Silin's. Another site that may be considered is Llanstinan, Pembs. (SM953339), which lies 250m north of a small enclosure. Like Llangynog there is little evidence for any settlement around the church today apart from one small farm. The field pattern on the tithe map conforms closely to what survives today (NLW Maps and Prints, Llanstinan Tithe) but the adjacent defended enclosure appears to have lost the outer defences that are depicted on the tithe map and looks univallate and of comparable proportions to the size of the church enclosure. Further examples which can be cited are the church at Nevern, Pembs. (SN083400), with its adjacent earthwork castle *Castell Nanhyfer* and the church at Llanddowror, Carms. (SN256145), with its peculiar adjacent 'ringwork'. Both earthworks have a known or presumed post-conquest development, but their morphology is compatible with a pre-conquest or prehistoric origin. Equally the earthwork near Llanstinan could have been reused as a ringwork castle in the later Middle Ages. In terms of upstanding castle sites one inevitably thinks of the origins of Llawhaden, Pembs. (SN077188), a masonry castle based on a ringwork sited fairly close to a church that has a

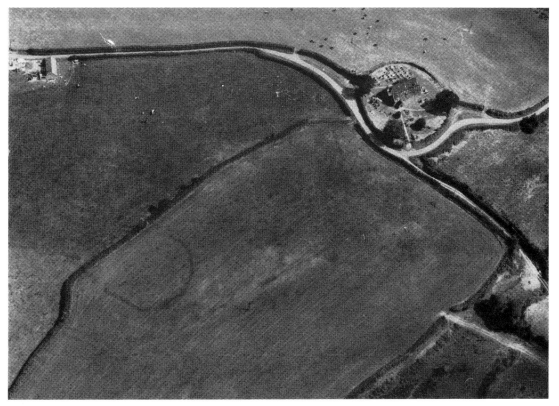

Fig. 8.10 *Llangynog, Carms. The near circular churchyard apparently sits within a larger irregular cropmark enclosure. To the west is a second enclosure which is part-overlaid by the present hedgebank. View from the south-west (DAT AP89-80.9, June 1989).*

number of Early Christian monuments (Nash-Williams 1950, nos. 342–3) and is listed as one of the Seven Bishop Houses of Dyfed (Charles-Edwards 1971).

In 1978 photography of the now ruinous site of Llandeilo Llwydarth church, Pembs. (SN099269), drew attention to a possible large oval enclosure about 250m to the west (Fig. 8.11). It now contains two adjacent farms, Temple Druid and Prisg. The name Temple Druid is a nineteenth-century coinage but the former name *Bwlch y Clawdd* ('Gateway/Breach in the Bank') (RCAHMW 1925, 207) is perhaps more interesting and may relate to the enclosure's banks. The enclosure also contains numerous standing stones and one chambered tomb. In addition the area has produced a number of Early Christian monuments. The church itself formerly had two fifth- or sixth-century inscribed stones (Nash-Williams 1950, nos. 314–5) and a third was located at Temple Druid Farm (RCAHMW 1925, 207; Nash-Williams 1950, no. 345).

Paired sites are not uncommon in the prehistoric period; indeed Dyfed Archaeological Trust has totally excavated an example of two adjacent small enclosures near Llawhaden. Both

of these sites have evidence — albeit rather scrappy — of possible Dark Age activity within them. One produced a radiocarbon date of cal. AD 896–1187 (CAR-673:1000±60bp) from one of a number of pits from the latest phase of activity within the site (Williams, Geo. 1985, 11; 1988, 51).

It is arguable in the case of some paired sites which started life as defended enclosures that one element continued in use during the early Christian period as a habitation site, whilst the second enclosure was adopted for use as a graveyard with or without a church. (We should bear in mind the possibility that Cilsant could fall into this category, as the present farm and a late medieval residence is located adjacent to and not within the cropmark enclosure.) On the basis of the observed occurrence of churches in close proximity to presumed prehistoric defended enclosures I have run a computer sort for further examples on the Dyfed Archaeological Trust's Sites and Monuments Record. The distribution of these (which also includes supposed medieval ringworks) shows a distinct Pembrokeshire and west Carmarthenshire bias. There are approximately 44 cases, which now need closer examination. Of the presumed Iron Age sites about 30% have *rath* or *castell* place-names.

Fig. 8.11 *Temple Druid and Prisg farms, Llandeilo Llwydarth, Carms. The church is located just off the photograph (left). The possible enclosure survives as a ditch in the foreground and two ditches beyond the farms (DAT AP88-51.2, February 1989).*

Segmented churchyard Enclosures

Much comparison is made between sites in Ireland and Wales in the period under discussion, and in terms of the area covered by this paper there are historical grounds for seeking parallels in view of the Irish influence manifest in Early Christian monuments and place-names (Lewis, J.M. 1976, 177–9). But the search for the type of subdivided curvilinear sites like that at Kiltiernan, Co Galway, and others depicted by Norman and St Joseph (1969, 90–121) has produced few if any conclusive parallels. The best possibility is the parish church of Llandyfaelog, Carms. (SN414118), (Fig. 8.12), which bears some comparison to Kiltiernan. The church appears to stand within a near-central sub-division with other units formed by the presence of numerous springs. The whole enclosure is large by local standards, and also contains ruins of the nineteenth-century vicarage on the north side. No other examples for Dyfed have been noted during air survey, although sites like Rhoscrowdder (SM903022), Llangyndeirn (SN456190) and Llanilar (SN623751) might have conformed in some way.

Rectilinear enclosures

A number of churches are sited within former Roman forts and towns, and Canon Wyn Evans' research has highlighted a number of churches possibly sited within less regular rectilinear enclosures. The most convincing site, St Ishmael's, Pembs. (SM830065), is located in a valley bottom. The church appears to be set to one side of a rectangular enclosure defined by substantial hedgebanks partly encircled by a trackway. Evidence for the enclosure on the north side is less convincing. Within the southern side, some 140m south-east of the church, ten slab-lined graves were exposed in a pipe trench in 1976, confirming observations of similar discoveries 60m from the church earlier this century (James, H. 1987, 74). The site is listed as one of the seven Bishop-Houses of Dyfed (Charles-Edwards 1971) and has two Early Christian memorials (Nash-Williams 1950, nos. 396–7).

Island sites

Many island sites have historic associations with the period. However few church sites have been

Fig. 8.12 *Llandyfaelog, Carms. A curvilinear graveyard divided internally into segments by springs, from the south (TAJ/AP-305.7, July 1983).*

recognized. Sites like Gateholm, Pembs. (SM769071), have been photographed in some detail, but no oriented structure that could represent a church has been highlighted. Should the thick mat of fescue grass that covers the islet ever be destroyed, then it is imperative that air survey be mounted immediately.

The enclosures on Cardigan Island (SN161515), which contain north-south aligned buildings, and features discovered on Ynys Meicel, Strumble (SM893403), need closer examination. In 1988 the latter was photographed for the first time when the outlines of buildings — one of which is oriented — were observed. Ground survey has shown these to have had a twentieth-century reuse; therefore their antiquity must for the moment remain questionable. The location of the presumed early church site on Caldey is obscure, but is believed to lie beneath the parish church of St David (SN143966), and that on Burry Holms, Glamorgan (SS401925), is covered by later medieval buildings, and has in any case been partly excavated (Hague 1973; RCAHMW 1976, 14–5).

Urban and village church sites

Many urban and village churches are now so surrounded by houses, streets and lanes that earlier earthwork evidence has been lost or obscured. Within the plans of many villages, however, there may be fossilized features which relate to earlier enclosures and internal divisions within these. The idea of a concentric 'monastic city' at Llandeilo Fawr, Carms. (SN629223), has been discussed by Lawrence Butler (1979, 460–2). When Llandeilo is viewed from the air (Fig. 8.13), the proposition seems most attractive. Unfortunately cartographic evidence conclusively demonstrates that the outer 'enclosure' formed by New and Crescent Roads is of no great antiquity. Indeed a map of 1822 (Carmarthen Record Office, Derwydd, CA52) shows that neither of the roads were then in existence, and that their lines do not follow earlier boundaries but actually cut across pre-existing hedges. However the validity of Butler's postulated inner enclosure line is not contested by this particular map. An interesting observation that can be made about Llandeilo is its position *vis-a-vis* the supposed Roman road over which the present main street runs. As can be seen in the photograph the road now cuts through the middle of the graveyard (a cut which dates from the late eighteenth century), but the churchyard itself can clearly be seen to straddle the line of the road which runs in a true line for a mile or two each side of the town.

Other urban sites which *could* have concentric curvilinear enclosures include St Dogmael's, Pembs. (SN164458), where the outer enclosure may be indicated by streets and property boundaries along three-quarters of its length, and Mathry, Pembs. (SM879320), a village on a hilltop with some streets and boundaries that could relate to an enclosure. (Mathry is a corruption of *merthyr*, equating to the English 'martyr', see Roberts above.) Both churches have Early Christian monuments associated with them (Nash-Williams 1950, nos. 346, 384–90), although we must consider a possibility that the church at St Dogmael's had shifted from an earlier location (Wyn Evans pers. comm.). But most village plans grouped around churches probably relate to Anglo-Norman development. Sites like Llansadwrnen, Carms. (SN281102), sited close to the supposed *leacht*, *Parc y Cerrig Sanctaidd* ('Field of the Sacred Stones') (RCAHMW 1917, no. 557; Nash-Williams 1950, no. 167), may fall into this category with its evidence of strip fields radiating from a pointed elliptical churchyard, a feature also to be found at Maenclochog, Pembs. (SN0827). Llansaint, Carms. (SN384080), may also be just a post-conquest nucleated plan, but who can say with any certainty from what origins the layout may stem?

At some villages with pre-conquest churches or graveyards there is evidence that the adjacent boundaries are probably post-conquest. Sites owned by the Bishops of St David's are noteworthy. A good example is Llanwnda, Pembs. (SM932295), a site rich in Early Christian monuments (Nash-Williams 1950, nos. 326–34). The church and now ragged village are surrounded by strip fields; the disparate, disconnected land ownership of these is displayed in a number of maps in the *Mapbook of the Estates of the Bishops of St Davids* (NLW, Maps and Prints). This presumably represents post-conquest reform and the imposition of open-field land management. Other examples, which I will not examine here, can be seen in the same mapbook. At Abergwili, Carms. (SN439209), a 'single street' planned town, the burgage plots are clear to see; the main street was realigned when Bishop Beck founded a collegiate church there in the 1280s, leaving the parish church set to one side of the village away from High Street (James, T.A. 1980, 20). But an earlier unsuccessful collegiate foundation at Llangadog, Carms. (SN706285), failed to wipe away evidence

Fig. 8.13 *Llandeilo Fawr, Carms., from the north-east. The suggestive enclosure framed by New and Crescent roads (foreground) results from nineteenth-century urban expanison, not an earlier enclosure. The line of the supposed Roman road bisects the churchyard and town, and continues south-westwards as intermittent trees and hedgebanks (DAT AP84-29.20, July 1984).*

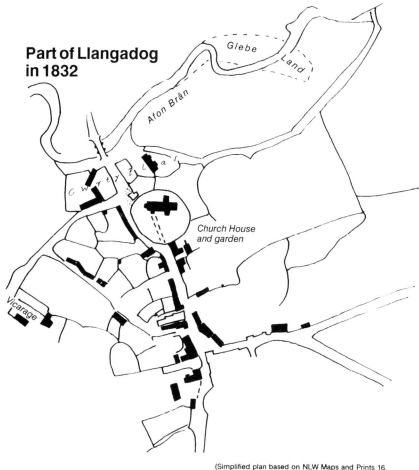

Part of Llangadog in 1832

Glebe Land

Afon Brân

Church House and garden

Vicarage

(Simplified plan based on NLW Maps and Prints 16,
Houses, Gardens and Lands in the town of Llangadock, Goode, 1832)

Fig. 8.14 *Simplified plan of Llangadog in 1832*

for the curvilinear churchyard there (Fig. 8.14). Both churches are mentioned as leading Dewi churches in the eleventh-century poetry of Gwynfardd Brycheiniog (Lewis, H. 1931, 42).

Conclusions

Air photography clearly has the potential for making major advances in our understanding of a subject where material archaeological evidence is scanty. There is considerable scope for further work throughout Wales. Three main areas have been highlighted by incidental survey work.

These are:

1. The identification of reused prehistoric enclosures that show no outward evidence for having had churches built within them, but which may have been used as cemeteries.
2. The survey and discovery of churches within defended enclosures.
3. Church sites with defended enclosures in close proximity.

Air photography can greatly increase both our understanding of existing sites and provide an increasing stock of new ones. The next stage must be excavation.

Acknowledgements

My thanks to the editors and Heather James for numerous suggestions and to Tomos Roberts and Muriel Bowen Evans for providing help on Welsh translations/interpretations.

The Early Christian Church
East and West of Offa's Dyke

Diane Brook

I intend in this paper to examine evidence for early British church sites on either side of Offa's Dyke. Two major features, curvilinear form and the large area of churchyards, were identified by Professor Thomas nearly 20 years ago (Thomas, C. 1971, 38, 50–1, 53) as important indicators of probable pre-Norman ecclesiastical sites in the Celtic West and I hope by studying a large sample of sites to see if these features show a significant correlation with other types of evidence. With this evidence we may then judge if these two aspects of ecclesiastical archaeology can usefully indicate British pre-English church sites in this area. In particular, this study will examine the possible continuity of early British church sites, founded in the fifth to seventh centuries, not only in Wales, but also in western England.

It is well known that Christianity was established in post-Roman western and northern Britain prior to the English mission of Augustine at the end of the sixth century. Churches, monasteries, and bishops are all mentioned in the few genuine early sources in what later became both Wales and England (Colgrave and Mynors 1969; Davies, W. 1979a; Winterbottom 1978). It seems fairly certain that post-Roman British Christianity was directly derived from that of late Roman Britain (Thomas, C. 1981a, 240–74).

The conquest and settlement of Britain by Germanic-speaking peoples took place largely from the east and south-east and it is generally agreed that the approximate political boundary between the English and the British in the mid-sixth century was roughly north-south down the centre of present-day England (Thomas, C. 1981a, 269, Fig. 49; Stenton 1971, 30–1, 40; Ordnance Survey 1971). The western fringes of England along the Welsh border were conquered or settled in the late sixth to the mid-eighth centuries (Stenton 1971, 28, 41, 46, 78). Offa's Dyke marks some sort of political frontier of the late eighth century, roughly equivalent to the modern boundary of England, though with some variations both to east and west (Fox, C. 1955, 290). Thus we can delineate the approximate boundaries of a zone in the western area of England which was once British in the sixth century and became English by the end of the eighth or earlier (Fig. 9.1).

Archaeological evidence for the first three centuries of the post-Roman period for southern Britain shows that pagan English burials are not found west of an irregular line to the east of the River Severn (Ordnance Survey 1971). Early Christian monuments of the earliest type, usually dated to the fifth to seventh centuries, are found only in the western and some southern parts of Wales and the West Country (Ordnance Survey 1971) with one outlier to the east at Wroxeter (Fig. 9.1). The area between these two distributions shows no signs of English or Irish incursions in this early period, and is thus the most likely area for the survival of post-Roman British traditions of Christianity.

If the British were largely Christian by the middle of the sixth century, and the evidence from Gildas suggests this is so (Winterbottom 1978, Ch. 4; Davies, W. 1982a, 169), then they must have had ecclesiastical sites in the once British areas of western England. There is evidence for a few such pre-English church sites in medieval Welsh place-names in western England (Renell 1963, 303, 305; Finberg 1961, 210).

Dating Pre-Norman Church Sites

In general, ecclesiastical sites show very great continuity of use. This can be easily demonstrated at very many sites from the twelfth century onwards in both England and Wales and there is substantial historical evidence and growing archaeological evidence that many such sites were founded in the pre-Norman period in both areas.

Several types of archaeological and historical evidence have been used to identify certain and probable pre-Norman ecclesiastical sites in Wales. Archaeology contributes evidence from excavations, all too sparse as yet, and there are also pre-Norman inscribed and sculptured stones. Some features, such as rounded churchyards, are thought to indicate pre-Norman church

N

0   10 Miles

– – – – – Eastern Limit of 5-7 Century Early Christian Monuments
— — — - Western Limit of Pagan Anglo-Saxon Burials
═══════ Offa's Dyke

Fig. 9.1 Map of early post-Roman Wales and the West Midlands showing the distribution limits of pagan Anglo-Saxon burials and Early Christian monuments.

foundations in the Celtic West, and large curved or occasionally rectangular enclosures have been taken to indicate early monastic sites (Thomas, C. 1971, 38, 50–1, 68). Historical evidence for early Welsh ecclesiastical sites is found in surviving early documents (Finberg 1961; Moore 1982; Thom and Thom 1982; 1983; 1986; Evans and Rhŷs 1893; Wade-Evans 1944; Dawson 1918), particular place-name elements (see Roberts above; Brook 1981, 129–44), dedications to pre-Norman Welsh saints, and special status in the Norman and later medieval period, such as prebendal churches and churches with dependent chapels (Brook 1981, 174–5, 179–84).

If these features also occur in western England, can they be taken to indicate that the English sites are of pre-English foundation, and date to the eighth century or earlier?

In this boundary zone, I have assembled all these types of evidence of pre-Norman date for the sites studied, although there are gaps in the evidence in each group. The distributions of the various groups of Early Christian monuments in Wales are very uneven with some areas lacking this class of evidence entirely at different dates within the pre-Norman period (Nash-Williams 1950, 1, 3–4, Table I, 17, Table II, 28, Table IV, 48, Table VII). Early charters survive only for south-east Wales (Davies, W. 1979a; see Pryce above) and England, with the English charters mentioning few churches (Finberg 1961, 31–150). Pre-Norman architectural evidence is confined to England (Taylor, H.M. and Taylor, J. 1965; 1978), but there is no study of pre-Norman English sculpture in the Welsh border areas comparable with the studies of Early Christian monuments in Wales (Nash-Williams 1950; RCAHMW 1976) or the corpus of Anglo-Saxon sculpture volumes for the north of England (Cramp 1984; Bailey and Cramp 1988).

Churchyards

In this paper, part of a larger research project on the early church in western Britain, the investigation has been confined to two archaeological indicators, churchyard form and churchyard area. The evidence used is modern, taken from churchyards which have survived until the present or to the period of modern mapping. In most cases, large-scale maps of individual sites rarely predate the nineteenth-century tithe maps, although there are a number of estate maps and a few early maps including urban churches and churchyards from the early seventeenth century. Comparison of estate, tithe and early Ordnance Survey maps for individual sites shows that two-thirds to three-quarters of sites retain the same or very nearly the same churchyard form throughout this series. This has been tested thoroughly for the 61 sites in the Vale of Glamorgan with surviving enclosures (Brook 1981, 169–70) and a sample of 28 sites in central Wales and western England shows exactly the same result (see also Preston-Jones below). Thus, it is likely that most sites have churchyard forms which date back to the early modern period at least. Certainly, each site needs individual study, but the overall pattern should be reliable.

Such modern evidence would be suspect if the aim were to demonstrate the reliability of curvilinear churchyard form as the sole indicator of pre-Norman date. At present, in the area studied we have only one excavated Welsh site, Capel Maelog, Radnorshire, with a curvilinear enclosure. This has produced evidence that the boundary was laid out in the pre-Norman period (Britnell 1986b, 58). However, the one excavation at a similar English site, at Abdon in south Shropshire, showed that the oval churchyard boundary overlay a thirteenth-century house site (Rowley 1972, 114–7). On the other hand, it is the coincidence of surviving curvilinear churchyards at sites with other certain or probable pre-Norman features that has prompted archaeologists to consider this recent evidence as significant.

Individual site histories from maps show that some sites have had their yard forms completely changed. If it is the case that early British Christians built curvilinear churchyards, it can also be shown that Capability Brown is responsible for some of them. The churchyard at Moccas, Herefordshire, very probably the site of an early Welsh monastery (Davies, W. 1978a, 135; Evans and Rhŷs 1893, 163b, 164), appears sub-oval on the early Ordnance Survey maps. A plan of Moccas park of the later eighteenth century made soon after Brown's landscaping shows the church within a ring of trees (Rowley 1986, 195). An earlier very detailed eighteenth-century estate map predating Brown's work shows a small rectangular yard on the south side of the church only (Hereford and Worcester Record Office C62/1). Thus churchyards with curved boundaries within parks may well not be of early date.

Large churchyard areas were suggested by Charles Thomas (1971, 30–2, 41) to indicate the sites of early major churches, as has been confirmed by my own work in the Vale of Glamorgan (Brook 1981, 42–3). If it can be shown to be a common feature of early major churches in general, large yards may help to identify other early sites which have lost their former high status and have not been recorded historically as important churches.

Churchyard area may change drastically if it is extended to accommodate a growing population, as, for example, at St John's Cardiff (Brook 1981, 464, Map SG 7) and Penarth, Glamorgan (Brook 1981, 505, Map SG 80). For this reason present churchyard evidence alone may be misleading. In the study area a few sites have probably had their yards extended in the modern period as a result of industrialization leading to a considerable increase in the local population density. Further work on early maps will mean revisions to the distributions in this study of both churchyard form and area, but the general conclusions will probably not be affected, as over a thousand sites have been analysed.

There is increasing aerial photographic evidence that Irish and some Welsh pre-Norman major churches had outlying boundaries forming very large enclosures around the churches and churchyards (Swan 1983; see T. A. James above). Such possible outer enclosures will not be considered in this study.

The area covered in this study is central eastern and south-eastern Wales south and west of the River Severn, and the area west of the Severn in England (Fig. 9.3). A portion of south-eastern Shropshire has not yet been researched. The area has been chosen deliberately to be arbitrary as the Severn was never a longstanding political boundary, nor a geographical barrier. The natural topography and known boundaries of political and ecclesiastical areas of the early and later medieval periods are cut by the Severn. Thus a variety of areas are included which are unified only by their lack of pagan Anglo-Saxon burials and their British political control before the early seventh century. Offa's Dyke crosses the study area from north to south, roughly down the centre. It must indicate some sort of approximate political boundary, although the exact boundary of Welsh and English language speakers has probably never coincided precisely with the line of the Dyke, and there is place-name evidence that English settlements had been made west of the line of the Dyke before its construction (Stenton 1971, 214). The Dyke is used here as a general guide to the political situation at the end of the eighth century. Where there are long gaps in the Dyke its approximate line or the river Wye has been taken as the boundary (Fox, C. 1955; Noble 1983).

Churchyard Form

To simplify the study of curved yards, a score has been given to each site. Clear overlays were made allowing a rectangle to be fitted to the edges of a churchyard plan on a large-scale map (Fig. 9.2). A further overlay was placed at the centre of the rectangle with vertical, horizontal and diagonal lines at 45° angles. These lines cut across the churchyard boundary dividing it into eight segments. These segments were then scored as curved or not. The total score indicated the degree to which the form was curved. A total of eight would indicate a perfect circle or oval, a score of more than four, a site with most of its boundary curved, and less than this, half or less of the boundary curved. All sites studied in central Wales and England have been scored in this way. Most of the sites previously studied in Gwent (Brook 1985–88) and Glamorgan (Brook 1981) have also been reassessed by this method. These scores have been simplified to largely curved, for scores of five or more; partly curved, scores of three or four curved segments; and non-curved for other forms, scores from zero to two. Although not entirely satisfactory, this method is

somewhat less arbitrary than deeming every yard with any portion of curved boundary a 'round churchyard'.

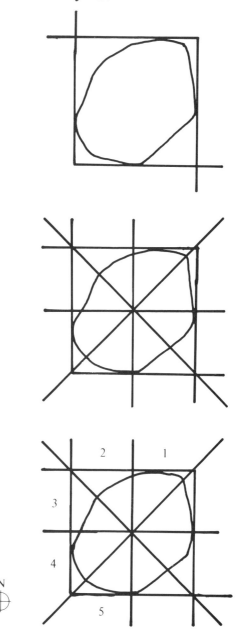

Fig. 9.2 Diagram showing the scoring system for calculating the curvilinearity of churchyards

If curved yards are significant, we need to know where they occur and in what numbers. Over 800 sites of the 1000 sites in the study area have surviving enclosures. About 500 are in Wales and the areas west of Offa's Dyke, and about 300 east of the Dyke. Those without enclosures are mostly abandoned, some even documented but unlocated, while a few are urban sites such as St Mary's, Brecon and All Saints,

Hereford. Abandoned sites include some early pre-Norman sites such as Doward, Herefordshire (Evans and Rhŷs 1893, 163b, 164). (Wales will be used interchangeably with the term 'west of the Dyke' and England with 'east of the Dyke' hereafter.)

The distribution of the largely curved yards is predominantly west of the Dyke (Fig. 9.3). There are only 12 in England but 45 in Wales. In proportion to the total number of sites on each side of the Dyke, the largely curved sites in England are about half as common. Even in Wales they form only about a tenth of the total.

This distribution is uneven. There appears to be only one strong concentration, in southern and central Radnorshire and north Breconshire. There are also scatters in Gwent, the Glamorgan uplands, and 'Welsh' Herefordshire, the part of that county south and west of the Wye. On the English side, there are three sites immediately east of the Dyke, in the south at Hewelsfield in Gloucestershire, and two in the north at Stow in Shropshire, and at Trelystan in Montgomeryshire (Martin 1986, 56). The three others in south Shropshire may form part of a group when work on this area is completed. The strongest grouping

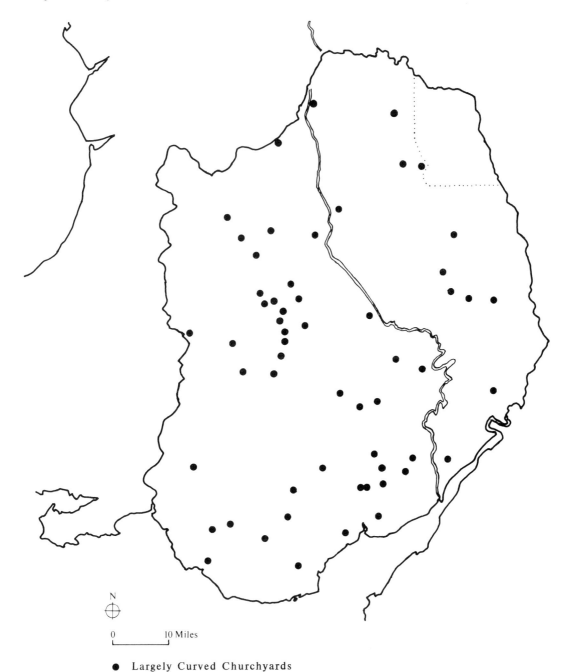

N

0   10 Miles

● Largely Curved Churchyards

Fig. 9.3 *Distribution of largely curved churchyards in the study area*

in the east is of five sites in north-east Herefordshire, at Stoke Bliss, Pencombe, Mathon, Much Cowarne, and Castle Frome.

With the addition of sites with partly curved yards to the distribution, the patterns are less clear (Fig. 9.4). Curved yards are still more common west of the Dyke, forming a third of all surviving enclosures. East of the Dyke, they are found at a quarter of the sites. The areas of greatest concentration remain the same, Radnorshire and north Breconshire, Gwent, and north-east Herefordshire, but there is much infilling in the pattern. Some of the gaps are

certainly of topographic and environmental origin, in the Brecon Beacons, for example, where there are very few sites at all. But, there are also apparently genuine blanks with a number of sites but no curved yards, in particular in northern Radnorshire and southern Montgomeryshire, in the extreme east of Worcestershire to the east of the Malvern Hills, and in north-central Herefordshire, in the Leominster area.

The distribution of sites with curved enclosures does suggest in part that curved yard boundaries may be of early British origin both

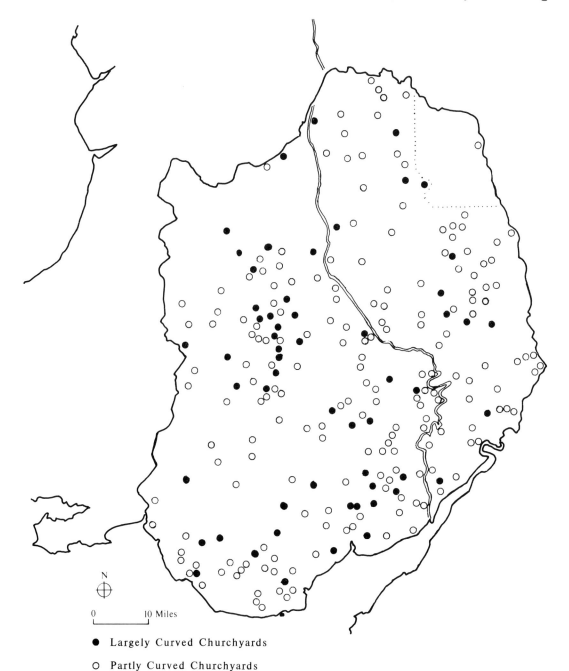

● Largely Curved Churchyards

○ Partly Curved Churchyards

Fig. 9.4 *Distribution of largely and partly curved churchyards in the study area*

east and west of the Dyke. Three of the largely curved yards east of the Dyke are very near the boundary, and are thus in the areas most likely to be settled last by the English or merely taken over politically rather than ethnically. The group in north-east Herefordshire lies in an area notable also for the survival of Celtic place-names and dispersed settlements, more typical of Wales than England (Sylvester 1969, 76–87, Fig.7, 202–6). The majority of the largely curved sites in England are also on uplands, perhaps indicating the survival of native British communities, although there are partly curved sites both in upland areas and on the lowlands near Gloucester and Tewkesbury.

To test further the date of curved enclosures, all sites have been analysed for evidence of foundation before AD 1100. This includes not only sites with excavation evidence, early inscribed or sculptured stones or early architecture, and certain pre-Norman documentary evidence from charters; but also churches listed in Domesday Book (Moore 1982; Thom and Thom 1982; 1983; 1986), late eleventh-century mentions of sites in other sources (Evans and Rhŷs 1893, 275–80) and the earliest hagiographical materials from Welsh sources such as Rhigyfarch's *Life of St David* (James, J.W. 1967; Wade-Evans 1944, 150–4), and *De Situ Brecheniauc* (Wade-Evans 1944, 313–5), the earliest list of the sainted Children of Brychan, thought to be copied from a document at least as early as the eleventh century (Wade-Evans 1944, xiii; Thornton 1988).

There are many certain pre-Norman sites, such as Llantwit Major, Glamorgan, which do not have curved enclosures (Brook 1981, 14, 180, 338, 497). The question remains as to how many of the sites with curved enclosures are certainly or probably pre-Norman, using only the types of evidence noted above. Evidence from Welsh dedications, typical Welsh ecclesiastical place-names, and later medieval status of churches has been excluded initially, as this is the type of evidence for early British churches mostly lost east of Offa's Dyke, if it did indeed exist. *Eccles*-place-names (Cameron 1968) have been ignored, as there are only three in the entire study area, Eccles Green, Eccles Alley and Eccleswall, all in Herefordshire, with only the latter a known ecclesiastical site and that without a surviving enclosure.

West of the Dyke, just under a third of the sites with curved enclosures can be shown to date from before 1100. In England just under a quarter of the curved sites are demonstrably early (Fig. 9.5). Pre-Norman curved sites are to be found in all areas which have curved enclosure sites. If additional factors, such as place-name elements, dedications, and later status are also examined, three-quarters of the largely curved sites in Wales are probably pre-Norman, and over a third of the partly curved sites. This type of evidence requires further work, especially on the English side of the Dyke.

To ask the question from the other direction, how many of the known pre-1100 sites have curved enclosures? This figure is quite high on either side of the Dyke, nearly 40% of early sites also having curved enclosures west of the Dyke, and over a quarter of the sites east of the Dyke. Thus it is a common feature of early sites in Wales and a fairly common feature of the early English sites. These demonstrations of apparent links do not constitute proof of the early date of other curved enclosures, but strongly suggest the possibility.

It is interesting and possibly significant that three of the five largely curved sites in north-east Herefordshire have churches which are listed in Domesday Book, a source not notable for its mentions of churches; Pencombe (Thom and Thom 1983, 186a, 19, 6, and note), Mathon (Thom and Thom 1983, E5, 6c, 175c), and Much Cowarne (Thom and Thom 1983, 19, 10, 186b), and a fourth, Castle Frome, has late Anglo-Saxon architectural remains (Taylor, H.M. and Taylor, J. 1965, Vol. 1, 152). Certainly these sites existed in the late eleventh century, with the strong possibility that they were founded long before that.

A dated list of all sites with surviving enclosures was made to test the earliest dates within the pre-Norman period at which sites with curved enclosures were known to exist (See Appendix 1). The early evidence is provided only by the first two classes of Early Christian monuments (Nash-Williams 1950) and the Llandaff charters (Evans and Rhŷs 1893; Davies, W. 1979a), and thus covers only sites west of Offa's Dyke, with the exception of Tidenham, Gloucestershire, also mentioned in the *Book of Llandaf* (Evans and Rhŷs 1893, 174b, 229b). All sites with Nash-Williams' Class I or Class II Early Christian monuments, normally dated to the fifth to seventh and seventh to ninth centuries respectively, were included, as were sites mentioned in the Llandaff charters before the ninth century.

Some 57 sites fulfilled these criteria. Nine can be allocated to the fifth or sixth century. None of the five sites with Class I monuments, Defynnog

(Nash-Williams 1950, 69, no. 44), Trallong (Nash-Williams 1950, 81, no. 70) and Ystradgynlais (Nash-Williams 1950, 82, nos 75–6) in Breconshire, and Capel Llanilterne (Nash-Williams 1950, 138, no. 214) and Merthyr Mawr (Nash-Williams 1950, 154, no. 238) in Glamorgan, had a surviving curved enclosure. Two of the four documented sites of this date did have such enclosures, at Llandinabo (Evans and Rhŷs 1893, 73a) and Dorstone (Evans and Rhŷs 1893, 72b), both in Herefordshire, while Llangoed, Breconshire (Evans and Rhŷs 1893, 166) and Welsh Bicknor, Herefordshire (Evans

and Rhŷs 1893, 72a) did not. The sites dated from the seventh to ninth centuries had curved enclosures in just under half the instances. About two-thirds of the seventh to ninth-century sites had evidence from Llandaff charters (Evans and Rhŷs 1893), the other third from Early Christian monuments of Nash-Williams' Class II (Nash-Williams 1950). A third of sites with charters and half the sites with Early Christian monuments had curved enclosures. This is evidence that there are a considerable number of sites with curved enclosures which may date back to the seventh to ninth centuries, but much

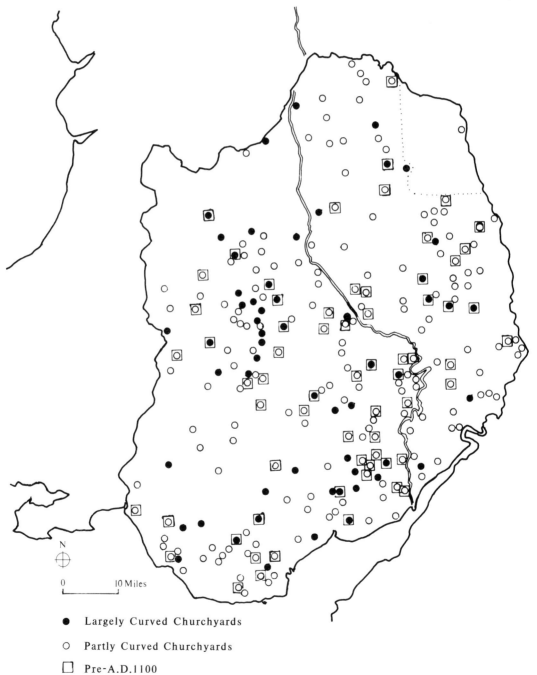

● Largely Curved Churchyards

○ Partly Curved Churchyards

□ Pre-A.D.1100

Fig. 9.5 *Distribution of largely and partly curved churchyards in relation to evidence of pre-Norman date*

less evidence that curvilinear yards date back to the fifth and sixth centuries.

Curvilinear churchyards have sometimes been assumed to indicate sites of early monastic status (Thomas, C. 1971, 38–43). References to 52 early major churches (monasteries, minsters and 'mother' churches) with surviving enclosures in the study area were analysed. Sites with dependent chapels in the later medieval period or with other late indicators of early high status were excluded and only those listed as certainly early from reliable sources were analysed (Knowles and Hadcock 1953; Ordnance Survey 1973; Hill, D. 1981; Davies, W. 1978a, 134–6). Known Norman foundations made just before AD 1100, such as Abergavenny, Monmouthshire, were excluded, but probable refoundations, such as Ewenny with its seven late pre-Norman stones (RCAHMW 1976, 66, nos 975–81) and two late stones (Nash-Williams 1950, 132, no. 196, RCAHMW 1976, 55, no. 924, 155, no. 244, 63, no. 955), and Margam (Brook 1981, 154–5), both in Glamorgan, were included.

Most of the major sites, 38 in all, lie west of the Dyke, with only 14 to the east. Exactly half of those in Wales have curved yards, but only one of the 14 sites in England has such an enclosure. Thus pre-Norman major churches in the British areas are very commonly found to have curved churchyards, but there are virtually no known early high-status churches in the area east of the Dyke with this feature. Either there were no curved high-status sites ever created east of the Dyke, or, sites with such status either lost their curved yards or lost their high status without historical record.

Churchyard Area

Large churchyard areas are quite independent of yard form. The writer's earlier studies of sites in Glamorgan and Gwent (Brook 1981; 1985–88) were not analysed for areas and so are not included in this section. Nearly 600 sites were analysed. A scaled grid was used on large-scale maps to calculate approximate areas for all sites with surviving enclosures in central Wales and western England. The average churchyard is between 0.5–1 acre (0.2ha-0.4ha) in area, with many more of less than 0.5acre (0.2ha), and a quarter of sites having yards of 1 acre (0.4ha) or more.

Yards of an acre or more were chosen arbitrarily as large. The distribution of large yards is fairly even between the western and eastern areas, but with somewhat over half in

the eastern, English area. Early major churches might be expected to have large yards on the basis of other studies (Thomas, C. 1971, 30–2; Brook 1981, 42–3). This is borne out here, with half the early major churches noted having large yards. This is predominantly an English feature, with a quarter of the early major churches with large yards lying west of the Dyke, and three-quarters to the east (Fig. 9.6). These proportions are maintained when looking at all pre-Norman sites also having large yards, the great majority being in England. This may merely indicate that English churchyards are usually larger, but the contrast when looking at early churches and early major churches east and west of the Dyke is much greater than the general difference in numbers of large yards in the two areas. Of the early major churches with surviving enclosures, a fifth of the Welsh sites had large yards. In the English area, nearly nine-tenths of the yards were over an acre in extent, including the former minster sites at Woolhope, Herefordshire (Thom and Thom 1983, 2,13), Lydbury North, Shropshire (Thom and Thom 1986, 2,1) and Stanton Lacy, Shropshire (Thom and Thom 1986, 7,4), as well the better known sites at Bromyard (Finberg 1961, 141, Ch. 415) and Leominster (Finberg 1961, 143, Ch. 418), both in Herefordshire, for example. It would therefore seem that some Welsh early major churches are notable for having large yards, and that it is an important feature of many English high-status sites.

Sites dated to the eighth century or before with large yards indicate further sites which may represent early high-status churches. Llanafan Fawr, Breconshire, is agreed to be a high-status site (Ordnance Survey 1973, 67). Large yards were also found at Defynnog, Breconshire, Llanelieu, Breconshire and Tidenham, Gloucestershire. Defynnog is very likely to be an early high-status site as it has several Early Christian monuments (Nash-Williams 1950, 70, 72, no. 44; Jones-Davies 1975, 6; Thomas, W.G. 1984), and had dependent chapels in the early thirteenth century (Davies, J.C. 1946–8, i 341, D. 406). Llanelieu has a partly curved yard and two Class II stones (Nash-Williams 1950, 74, No. 51–2). Tidenham has no other archaeological features of early type but was the subject of a royal Welsh grant in the eighth century (Evans and Rhŷs 1893, 174b), and of a royal English grant in the tenth (Finberg 1961, 54, no. 101). Ystradgynlais, Breconshire, with two Class I stones (Nash-Williams 1950, 82, nos 75–6) has probably had its yard extended in recent times and may not belong in this group.

Sites of early date with yards just under an acre in size are Llowes, Radnorshire, Llangors, Breconshire, Llanlleonfel, Breconshire and Clodock, Herefordshire. Llowes and Llangors are early major churches with curved yards. Llanlleonfel has a polygonal yard which may once have been curved. Clodock does not have a curved yard but was a *merthyr* church (Evans and Rhŷs 1893, 193, 195–6; see Roberts above) and had a short saint's Life written for its supposed 'martyr' (Evans and Rhŷs 1893, 193–5), suggesting that it was once a major church as well.

Large Curvilinear Churchyards

As large yards seem to be linked with early high-status sites and curvilinear yards are a feature of sites of early date, it is of interest to know which sites have both large and curved enclosures. Four sites with large curved yards are known high-status sites, Glascwm, Radnorshire, Llanafan Fawr, Merthyr Cynog, Breconshire and Stanton Lacy. The early high-status sites of Llangors and Llowes have curved yards and yard areas of just under one acre. Other sites with large curved yards are Nantmel,

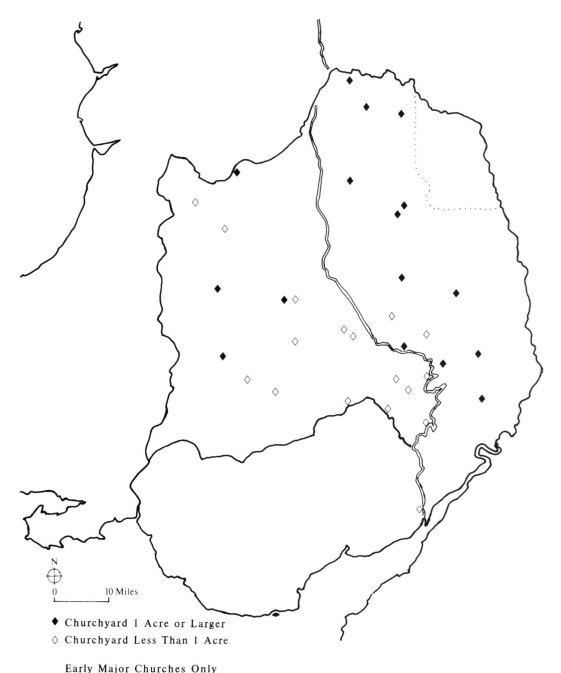

◆ Churchyard 1 Acre or Larger
◇ Churchyard Less Than 1 Acre

Early Major Churches Only

Fig. 9.6 *Distribution of early major churches showing churchyard size*

Cascob, and Boughrood, all in Radnorshire; Hewelsfield and Bulley in Gloucestershire, and Much Cowarne in north-east Herefordshire. Llanmerewig, Montgomeryshire, at the extreme north of the Welsh distribution, has a largely curved yard with an area of just under an acre. The Welsh sites with large curved enclosures have dedications to pre-Norman Welsh saints and may represent further early major churches.

The English sites with large curved yards *may* be lost high-status sites of British origin. Hewelsfield has had the same yard form, an oval, since the 1840 tithe plan (Gloucestershire Record Office GDR/T1/100), the earliest large-scale map of the site yet found. The church building may predate the Norman Conquest as the church guide suggests that the tall nave and square-headed south door are of Anglo-Saxon date (Anon. 1981). But the site is not listed as a definite or possible Anglo-Saxon building in the definitive study of the subject (Taylor, H.M. and Taylor, J. 1965, 1978) nor in the architectural guide to the county (Verey 1976, 268–9).

It is tempting to see Much Cowarne as a lost early major church in the north-east Herefordshire group, as it was in existence by 1086 (Thom and Thom 1983, 19, 10, 186b) and has a large curved yard.

Bulley, in eastern Gloucestershire, has an irregular largely curved yard, retaining the same form since the 1838 tithe plan (Gloucestershire Record Office GDR/T1/42/G4). It has a dedication to Michael which may indicate early British links (Fenn 1974; Brook 1981, 145, 147–8, 150).

Conclusions

It is still not possible to say for certain whether curvilinear churchyards are necessarily of pre-Norman date, but the evidence is quite strong that largely curved yards west of Offa's Dyke are overwhelmingly pre-Norman, based on archaeological and early historical evidence, with confirmation from dedications, place-names, and later status. The significance of partly curved yards is more uncertain and further work to classify these sites more precisely might be useful. Certainly many of the partly curved sites in Wales can be shown to be of pre-Norman origin. Half of the earliest sites west of the Dyke, those known to exist before the ninth century, have curvilinear churchyard boundaries, including the possible sixth-century monastery at Llandinabo, Herefordshire (Evans and Rhŷs 1893, 73a; Davies, W. 1978a, 134).

East of the Dyke, there is no dating evidence for any ecclesiastical site with a surviving enclosure before the ninth century except for Tidenham, as early English charters either do not survive or do not mention churches specifically and no architectural or sculptural remains of early date have been found at ecclesiastical sites. The English sites with largely curved enclosures can be shown to be in existence by AD 1100 and lie in areas known to have other indicators of the survival of British communities after the English takeover of the territories west of the Severn and east of the Dyke. There must be a strong possibility that these represent sites of British origin and date to the eighth century or earlier.

Large churchyards are a notable feature of early major churches in western England and of some early major churches in Wales. They may be an indicator of former high-status sites such as monasteries or episcopal churches for which no historical record survives.

Studies of the early church in Cornwall and Cumbria show that there are early sites with curvilinear churchyards in these areas, it being a common feature of early Cornish church sites and found at over a tenth of early sites in Cumbria (Preston-Jones and Rose 1986, 154–6; O'Sullivan 1980; see Preston-Jones below). The types of enclosure forms of known pre-Norman church sites should be studied further to investigate the dates and possible significance of different forms, whether curved, rectangular or any other form. Further detailed studies in all areas of Wales and England, especially eastern England, are needed to discover the distribution of curvilinear and large churchyards and to confirm their apparent early pre-Norman dates and significance as possible indicators of British church survival. We may then have more reliable information to examine the history of early Christianity in western Britain and the transition from British to English Christianity in the border counties.

APPENDIX 1

Sites with Surviving Enclosures and their Earliest Evidence before A.D.1100.

KEY

County Abbreviations:
Bre — Breconshire;
Gla — Glamorgan;
Gls — Gloucestershire;

Her — Herefordshire;
Mon — Monmouthshire;
Mtg — Montgomeryshire;
Rad — Radnorshire;
Shr — Shropshire;
Wor — Worcestershire.

Churchyard Curvature:
0 = uncurved;
1 = partly curved;
2 = largely curved

Location East or West of 'Offa's Dyke':
E = East;
W = West.

Site Name	County	Date by Century	Curved Score	Dyke
Defynnog	Bre	05–06	0	W
Trallong	Bre	05–06	0	W
Ystradgynlais	Bre	05–06	0	W
Capel Llanilterne	Gla	05–07	0	W
Merthyr Mawr	Gla	05–07	0	W
Llangoed	Bre	06	0	W
Dorstone	Her	06	1	W
Llandinabo	Her	06	2	W
Welsh Bicknor	Her	06	0	W
Llowes	Rad	07	2	W
Ballingham	Her	07	1	W
Garway	Her	07	0	W
Llancillo	Her	07	0	W
Lancaut	Gls	07	0	W
Llanarth	Mon	07	1	W
Llandogo	Mon	07	1	W
Llantilio Crossenny	Mon	07	0	W
Llantilio Pertholay	Mon	07	0	W
Llancarfan	Gla	07	1	W
Llandaff	Gla	07	1	W
Llandough by Cardiff	Gla	07	0	W
Llantwit Major	Gla	07	0	W
Much Dewchurch	Her	07	0	W
Moccas	Her	07	0	W
Mathern	Mon	07	0	W
St. Lythan's	Gla	07	1	W
Llanafan Fawr	Bre	07–09	1	W
Llanelieu	Bre	07–09	1	W
Llanfihangel Cwmdu	Bre	07–09	0	W
Llangammarch	Bre	07–09	1	W
Llanlleonfel	Bre	07–09	0	W
Llanspyddid	Bre	07–09	0	W
Bryngwyn	Rad	07–09	2	W
Baglan	Gla	07–09	1	W
Eglwysilan	Gla	07–09	2	W
Capel Brithdir	Gla	07–09	1	W
Capel Gwladys	Gla	07–09	0	W
Llantrisant	Gla	07–09	2	W
Llanwonno	Gla	07–09	0	W
Merthyr Tydfil	Gla	07–09	0	W
Llandeilo'r Fan	Bre	08	1	W
Llangors	Bre	08	1	W
Clodock	Her	08	0	W
Llangarren	Her	08	0	W
Llanwarne	Her	08	0	W
Llandegveth	Mon	08	2	W
Llandenny	Mon	08	1	W
Llangoven	Mon	08	1	W
Llansoy	Mon	08	1	W
Bishton	Mon	08	0	W
Dixton Newton	Mon	08	0	W
Llanvaches	Mon	08	0	W
Tidenham	Gls	08	0	E
Monmouth	Mon	08	0	W
Trelleck	Mon	08	0	W
Wonastow	Mon	08	0	W
Ewenny	Gla	08–10	0	W
Capel Maelog	Rad	09	2	W
Bromyard	Her	09	0	E
Little Dewchurch	Her	09	1	W
Foy	Her	09	0	W
Hereford Cathedral	Her	09	0	E
Kilpeck	Her	09	2	W
Acton Beauchamp	Wor	09	0	E
Dingestow	Mon	09	1	W
Llanvetherine	Mon	09	0	W
Llangwm Uchaf	Mon	09	1	W
Itton	Mon	09	0	W
Caldicot	Mon	09	0	W
Llangua	Mon	09	0	W
Llanvaply	Mon	09	0	W
Llampha	Gla	09	0	W
Newent	Gls	09	0	E
St. Maughan's	Mon	09	1	W
St. Bride's Netherwent	Mon	09	0	W
Llangan	Gla	09–10	0	W
Llandefaelog Fach	Bre	09–11	0	W
Coychurch	Gla	09–11	0	W
Leominster	Her	10	0	E
Llanishen	Mon	10	2	W
Llanwern	Mon	10	2	W
Kemeys Inferior	Mon	10	0	W
Caerwent	Mon	10	0	W
Llanfihangel near Roggiet	Mon	10	0	W
Llanfihangel Crucorney	Mon	10	0	W
Penterry	Mon	10	1	W
Rockfield	Mon	10	0	W
Trelleck Grange	Mon	10	0	W

Llanddetty	Bre	10–11	1	W	Astley	Wor	11	0	E
Llanhamlech	Bre	10–11	1	W	Clifton upon Teme	Wor	11	1	E
Caerleon	Mon	10–11	0	W	Eastham	Wor	11	0	E
Llangynwyd	Gla	10–11	1`	W	Great Malvern	Wor	11	0	E
Newchurch	Rad	10–11	0	W	Little Witley	Wor	11	0	E
Stanton Lacy	Shr	10–11	1	E	Longdon	Wor	11	1	E
St. Arvan's	Mon	10–11	1	W	Lower Sapey	Wor	11	0	E
Llangewydd	Gla	10–12	0	W	Bassaleg	Mon	11	0	W
Llantwit by Neath	Gla	10–12	0	W	Abergavenny	Mon	11	0	W
Margam	Gla	10–12	0	W	Chepstow	Mon	11	0	W
Tythegston	Gla	10–12	0	W	Merthyr Cynog	Bre	11	2	W
Llanbedr	Bre	11	0	W	Patrishow	Bre	11	2	W
Llangenny	Bre	11	1	W	Talgarth	Bre	11	0	W
Llanfaes	Bre	11	0	W	Much Cowarne	Her	11	2	E
Glascwm	Rad	11	2	W	Much Marcle	Her	11	0	E
Colva	Rad	11	0	W	Marstow	Her	11	1	W
Chirbury	Shr	11	0	E	Pencombe	Her	11	2	E
Llandinam	Mtg	11	0	W	Peterchurch	Her	11	0	W
Avenbury	Her	11	0	E	Preston-on-Wye	Her	11	1	W
Bishop's Frome	Her	11	0	E	Ross-on-Wye	Her	11	0	E
Bodenham	Her	11	0	E	St. Weonard's	Her	11	0	W
Bosbury	Her	11	0	E	Stoke Edith	Her	11	0	E
Brinsop	Her	11	1	E	Upton Bishop	Her	11	0	E
Burghill	Her	11	0	E	Wellington	Her	11	0	E
Canon Pyon	Her	11	0	E	Weobley	Her	11	1	E
Cradley	Her	11	0	E	Weston Beggard	Her	11	0	E
Dewsall	Her	11	0	W	Withington	Her	11	0	E
Eardisland	Her	11	0	E	Woolhope	Her	11	0	E
Fownhope	Her	11	0	E	Wormsley	Her	11	0	E
Hentland	Her	11	0	W	Onibury	Shr	11	0	E
Little Hereford	Her	11	0	E	Pontesbury	Shr	11	0	E
Holme Lacy	Her	11	0	W	Westbury	Shr	11	0	E
Kenderchurch	Her	11	1	W	Martley	Wor	11	0	E
Kentchurch	Her	11	0	W	Mathon	Wor	11	2	E
King's Pyon	Her	11	1	E	Pendock	Wor	11	0	E
Ledbury	Her	11	0	E	Powick	Wor	11	0	E
Letton	Her	11	0	W	Upton-on-Severn	Wor	11	0	E
Linton	Her	11	1	E	Michaelchurch				
Llanveynoe	Her	11	0	W	(with Tretire)	Her	11	0	W
Kyre Magna	Wor	11	1	E	St. Bride's-				
Awre	Gls	11	0	E	super-Ely	Gla	11	1	W
Churcham	Gls	11	0	E	Diddlebury	Shr	11	2	E
Dymock	Gls	11	0	E	Tenbury	Wor	11	0	E
Kempley	Gls	11	1	E	Bredwardine	Her	11–12	1	W
Berrington	Shr	11	1	E	Castle Frome	Her	11–12	2	E
Bromfield	Shr	11	0	E	Llysworney	Gla	11–12	0	W
Bucknell	Shr	11	1	E	Rhayader	Rad	11–12	0	W
Burford	Shr	11	0	E	St. Harmon	Rad	11–12	2	W
Cleobury Mortimer	Shr	11	1	E	Presteigne	Rad	11–12	0	E
Condover	Shr	11	0	E	Peterstow	Her	11–12	0	W
Lydbury North	Shr	11	0	E	Tedstone				
Lydham	Shr	11	0	E	Delamere	Her	11–12	1	E
Alberbury Priory	Shr	11	0	E	Wigmore	Her	11–12	0	E
Abberley	Wor	11	1	E	Rushbury	Shr	11–12	0	E

Early Medieval Cemeteries in Wales

Heather James

This paper will concentrate on new information, gained mainly through rescue excavations conducted over the past ten years or so by the four Welsh Archaeological Trusts. I am very conscious of presenting the work of my colleagues at second hand and perhaps in an over-simplified form and wish to thank them for allowing me to use their data so freely and for their comments on the published version of this paper. Few of the excavations to be discussed have yet been fully published, but most are in active preparation and may be expected within the next few years, with the definitive descriptions and interpretations of the sites.

Let us look first at the origins of early medieval cemeteries, both in terms of their location and their burial practices. There is now plenty of evidence for the reuse of Bronze Age ritual and funerary monuments for early medieval burial. But what we are increasingly aware of, from recent excavations, is the reuse, perhaps even continued use, of such monuments in the Iron Age and Romano-British periods, through into the early middle ages (Harding 1987; Williams, Geo. 1988). There is thus a conservatism in location of cemetery sites, together with change and innovation in burial practices.

In a Gazetteer of the admittedly limited data on Iron Age burials in Wales to be published with the excavation report on Plas Gogerddan by Dyfed Archaeological Trust (Murphy and Williams in Murphy forthcoming), two distinct locations are apparent. Firstly there are cremations and inhumations in Bronze Age ritual and funerary monuments, and secondly burials in or around defended enclosures. These traditions seem to extend into the early medieval period.

I would like now to consider the Plas Gogerddan excavation in the light of the first of these Iron Age burial traditions. The excavation at Plas Gogerddan in 1986 was a rescue excavation, one of a number along the route of a gas pipe-line between Machynlleth in Montgomeryshire and Aberystwyth in Ceredigion. As with most of the excavations to be described in this paper, there were no prior indications of the existence of an early medieval inhumation cemetery on the site. The reason for excavation was to investigate crop-marks visible along the pipe-line corridor north of a large barrow (James, T.A. 1984) and an area around a standing stone, again north of the barrow and adjacent to the pipe-line corridor. As suspected, excavation showed (Fig. 10.1) that the standing stone had been moved and erected in its present position to serve as a marker at one end of the known eighteenth- or early nineteenth-century race-course at Plas Gogerddan. A good case can be made out for it having been of prehistoric origin with its original socket being close by. The stone and indeed the barrows could thus have served as above-ground markers for the inhumation cemetery which was located mainly to the north and east of it.

The cropmarks observed in the air photographs were shown in excavation to be double and single ring-ditches — the ploughed-out remains of barrows — of late Bronze Age date. More interesting from the point of view of this paper was the demonstration of their reuse in the late Iron Age or early Romano-British period. A crouched burial was found in the ditch of the southernmost ring-ditch, with two bronze brooches accompanying it. Dr H. N. Savory gives these a date range of between the first century BC and the first century AD. Another brooch fragment from pits nearby may indicate further crouched burials of similar date (Savory in Murphy forthcoming).

To the north-east lay an inhumation cemetery. Bone did not survive the acid soils of the site but a single radiocarbon date derived from the fibrous remains of a coffin in grave 229 provided a date of cal. AD 263–636 (CAR-1045, 1580±60bp) (see Appendix 1 for full details of the radiocarbon dates). There were at least 22 graves identified in excavation though the cemetery's boundaries must lie outside the excavation on all but the western side. Coffin stains survived in nine graves and there were three special graves enclosed within rectangular timber structures. The best preserved of these — no. 373 — measured some 5.5 x 3.8m, with an entrance at the east end marked by two post-holes. The excavator is quite convinced that the dark stain down the centre of the trench represented decayed timbers. The slightly bowed sides and rounded corners further suggest walling of continuous planked uprights. An oriented grave was centrally placed within the structure, and in front of that, just inside the threshold, there was a small stone-lined pit with timber staining in its fill, suggesting to the excavator the former presence of a wooden box. There was a similar pit in the least well-preserved of the three special graves, no. 375. Of the remaining dug graves, some patterning in the form of rows is discernible, but grouping around and alignment

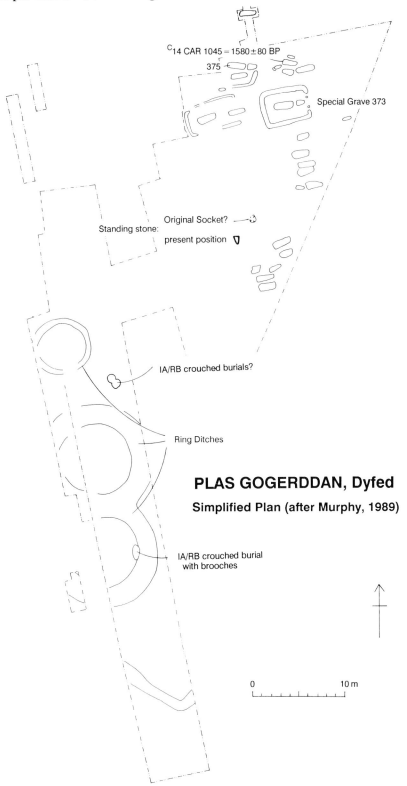

Fig. 10.1 Plas Gogerddan, Dyfed — simplified plan (after Murphy 1989)

on the enclosed graves seems to be a more dominant plan element.

There are no traditions of any lost chapel, no place-name indications, no holy well or Early Christian monument to suggest that the Gogerddan cemetery developed any further. The stone-lined pits suggest gravegoods, albeit perishable, accompanying the burial within the timber structures enclosing the special graves. But without knowing the overall size of the inhumation cemetery, we cannot be certain whether the types and organization of burials observed in excavation are the same throughout.

The size of the timber enclosures at Gogerddan and the presence within them of a single, oriented, centrally placed grave is reminiscent of the small rectangular structure built over the site of a levelled Neolithic cursus at Llandegai, near Bangor (Fig. 10.2) (Houlder 1968). An inhumation cemetery of oriented rows of graves was sited on the north side of the building, which measured 4.2 x 3.6m. It was quite reasonably interpreted at the time as a primitive chapel with a possible saint's grave showing signs of late disturbance, perhaps a translation when the church of St Tegai was built some 640m to the east. Twenty years later we might also consider an alternative interpretation of a timber structure around a special grave.

Though superficially similar it is now quite clear that the 'square-ditched graves' at Tandderwen in Clwyd (Fig. 10.3) recently excavated for Clwyd Powys Archaeological Trust, represent a different tradition (Brassil and Meredith 1986; Brassil and Owen 1987; Brassil 1988). The excavator is adamant that here we have square-ditched enclosures, not timber structures. This crop-mark site was identified from air photographs taken by C. R. Musson (CPAT APs: 84–MB-287–291) which show three possible ring-ditches and other square cropmarks. This is not the occasion to describe the prehistoric archaeology of the largest ring-ditch, but excavation showed that its circular ditched outline had been tightly enclosed within a square ditch with centrally placed gaps on all four sides. It is probable that this large barrow, unlike the smaller one to the north, was still a distinct feature in the landscape when the inhumation cemetery was marked out. Though perhaps a little fanciful, it is tempting to see the 'squaring', if we may term it that, of the barrow as absorbing, or in a sense claiming, the earlier mound for the new cemetery.

To the north of the large barrow there was a remarkable group of square-ditched enclosures surrounding graves with clusters of dug graves grouped around them. Bone did not survive, but well over half the graves produced coffin stains.

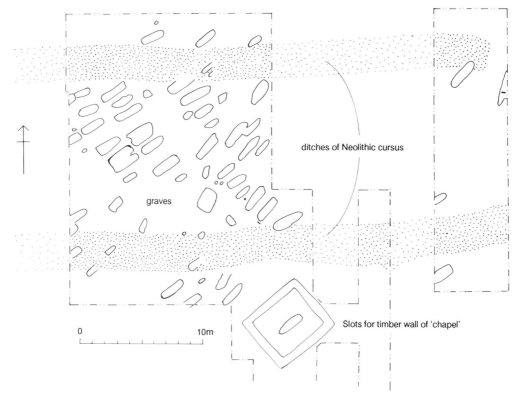

Fig. 10.2 Llandegai, Gwynedd – simplified plan (after Houlder 1968)

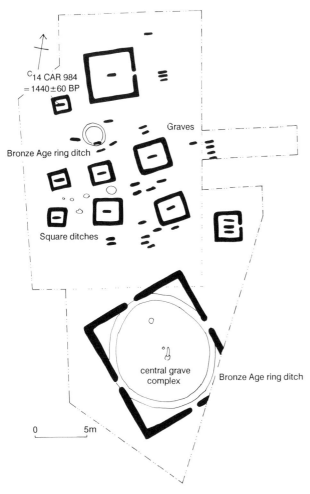

Fig. 10.3 *Tandderwen, Clwyd — simplified plan (after Brassil 1989)*

As at Gogerddan, it is from such exiguous remains that the single radiocarbon date of cal. AD 433–680 (CAR-984, 1440±60bp) was obtained. All but one of the square-ditched enclosures contained a single central grave, roughly oriented and the easternmost enclosure contained three symmetrically-placed burials. Only two square enclosures — the largest and the triple burial — had entrance gaps, both located on their eastern sides.

Very little stratigraphy survived in this intensely cultivated field, so it is uncertain whether the ditch spoil was wholly removed or piled up to form a square bank inside the ditch or a central mound over the grave. The excavator's preference is for the last interpretation which would result in a fairly prominent mound over the grave (its visibility enhanced by the wide, flat flood-plain setting) and an area around the grave, accessible, yet marked off from other burials by the ditch. The larger the square-ditched enclosure, the more

prominent the mound, which might explain differences in enclosure sizes and be a reflection of status.

Although the early medieval cemetery was not wholly contained within the area excavated, a sondage to the east indicated a possible boundary in that direction. The complex geology and pedology of the field make it unlikely that any indication of overall size would be gained from geophysical survey. The impression gained however is of a small cemetery, not in use over any extended period of time. This is an important point, because there is no denying the striking similarities between this site and square-ditched graves in eastern Scotland, and indeed with those of the La Tène Arras group in East Yorkshire (Cunliffe 1974, 289–91). The Tandderwen radiocarbon date thus extends the date range of square-ditched graves from the late Iron Age potentially to the seventh century AD. Also there is no denying that, at present, there are no other direct parallels for Tandderwen in Wales, so it is not surprising to find suggestions that this was the cemetery of an immigrant group (Keys 1988). The Scottish square-ditched graves are analysed by Elizabeth Alcock elsewhere in this volume (see below).

Full lists of the quite numerous instances of the reuse of Bronze Age burial mounds for later, oriented cist and dug graves, either as secondary inhumations in the mound itself, or in close proximity, have been published for Anglesey (Edwards, N. 1986) and Dyfed (James, H. 1987). Recent excavations of barrow cemeteries at Trelystan and Four Crosses, Powys, have provided more evidence of reuse (Britnell 1982; Warrilow, Owen and Britnell 1986). It is likely that, with modern techniques of excavation, more such instances will be revealed, not just of graves dug into barrows but also their location in the area around. I have suggested that one reason for such reuse might lie in a continuation of Iron Age/Romano-British burial practices. Where this is not evident, we can surely accept that, even after a millennium, Bronze Age burial mounds survived as recognizable, man-made, funerary monuments in the early medieval landscape.

As well as perhaps rather generalized notions about continued use of ancestral burial places, or staking claims to other peoples' ancestral burial places, we should also consider possibilities of burials on territorial boundaries, marked, *inter alia* by earlier mounds or stones. This has been demonstrated by Bonney in Anglo-Saxon Wiltshire (Bonney 1979; but also see Goodier 1984). Thomas Charles-Edwards, in a paper on

'Boundaries in Irish Law', has highlighted interesting parallels for the use of a grave mound, or mounds, as boundary markers, over which any claimant must drive his horses in a series of fairly elaborate entry rituals. He also draws attention to the legal phrase 'heir of a gravestone, which lies about the lands' — all suggesting that 'men may be buried upon the boundary of their land; their graves may be marked by ogam inscriptions on stone' (Charles-Edwards 1976, 84). The adoption of Christian burial practices in what became the churchyard might, he suggests, have erased such procedures from Welsh law.

There is of course the possibility that some barrows and cairns are of Romano-British or early medieval date. One strong candidate is the small cairn-like mound in Penbryn parish, Ceredigion, in which the inscribed stone commemorating *Corbalengus* is sited. Uniquely *Corbalengus* has the appellation *Ordous*, an Ordovician. Confused reports of opening the mound also refer to 'an urn full of ashes', actually an early Roman grey-ware jar, and an *aureus* of the Emperor Titus, both now in the National Museum of Wales (Nash-Williams 1950, no. 126).

J. Wyn Evans has suggested (pers. comm.) that the *Voteporix* stone (Nash-Williams 1950, no. 138) might originally have been sited on or near a large barrow, close to Castell Dwyran church, Carms. (SN 28905136, primary record number 2098 in Dyfed Archaeological Trust's Sites and Monuments Record, henceforth DAT prn). The field name recorded in the Tithe Schedule is *Parc Cerrig y Lluniau* — 'field of the stone with lines'. Such sites are perhaps more reminiscent of the graves of heroes celebrated in the surviving collections of *englynion* known as the *Stanzas of the Graves*, thought to be of ninth- or tenth-century date (Jones, T. 1967). Their purpose was to celebrate the lives and lament the deaths of warriors, not to provide the literal-minded archaeologist with a range of early medieval grave types and locations. But many of the burial practices for which we have archaeological evidence seem to be alluded to in the *Stanzas*. Of particular interest in the context of this paper, is the stanza referring to the grave of Gwryd ap Gwryd in some *caerau*, or 'fortified places' as Thomas Jones has it, located opposite a place called *Bryn Beddau* or 'Hill of the Graves' (Jones, T. 1967, 99). The use of the plural — *caerau* — which could be translated as 'fortifications' — instead of the commoner *caer* — 'camp' or 'fort' — might imply the idea of a multivallate site like the north Pembrokeshire site of that name discussed below.

The other preferred location for Iron Age burials in Wales, and indeed Britain in general, be they cremations or inhumations, is in or around hillforts and defended enclosures (Whimster 1981). There is further discussion of this from aerial-photographic evidence in T. A. James' paper in this volume, particularly the site at Caerau, north Pembrokeshire (SN 12464548, DAT prn 1054 see James above). Here most certainly are, or were, long-cist burials, presumably of early medieval date, set between the ramparts. Although the mid-nineteenth century report of the site is circumstantial and confusing, it does refer to 'hammers' and 'cutlasses' within graves (Vincent 1864), thereby suggesting the possibility of Iron Age burials as well.

In 1979 I conducted a trial excavation for Dyfed Archaeological Trust on the small defended enclosure of Caer, in Bayvil parish, only a few miles south of Caerau (James, H. 1987) (Fig. 10.4). A trench (I) was hand dug across the site to compare the well-preserved enclosure bank and the area interior to it on the north-west side with that on the more heavily plough-damaged south side. In addition a small area on the north side (Trench II) was part excavated to try and relocate the site of a cist-and-lintel grave cut into the bank which was found during ploughing in 1920. The section through the enclosure bank demonstrated two, perhaps three, phases of enclosure, which, together with pre-cemetery features across the interior, suggest that the site is of Iron Age origin. Cut into the ramparts at both the northern and southern ends of the trial trench were two cist-and-lintel graves. Fragmentary bone from the northern one yielded the single radiocarbon date of cal. AD 640–883 (CAR-291, 1290±60bp). The interior was filled by oriented graves, mainly simple dug graves but also some small cists, and part, even token, cists, interpreted as child or infant burials. Although it is impossible to be certain within the confines of a trench, the graves did appear to be set in rows. There was also quite a high degree of superimposition. If a similar density was present over the interior of the enclosure as a whole, it might have contained some 3,400 graves. It was not possible to say whether the cist-and-lintel graves, which were cut into the rampart, were the earliest, but these more elaborate burials do seem to be set radially around the bank. Although the stratigraphy across the trial trench had been damaged or removed by ploughing, there were indications that better preserved, stratified sequences still exist in other areas of the site, on the western side and around the entrance. A total area excavation might be able to throw light on the fundamental question of whether the site's final use as a cemetery came after a period of abandonment or was a change in function of a continuously occupied site.

The numbers of Iron Age enclosures which were used as early medieval cemeteries may be extended if we include those which contained Early Christian inscribed stones, if we can assume that these were grave-markers and/or foci for subsequent burials (for a list in Dyfed see Lewis, J.M. 1976). Recent work on both the typology of churchyards (see Brook above) and aerial survey of enclosures around them (see James above) should result in a better idea of how many churchyards developed from earlier enclosures. This is not to suggest that most defended enclosures ended up as early medieval

cemeteries or that all enclosures around churches are of Iron Age origin. But it is certain that the study of cemetery enclosures cannot be divorced from settlement archaeology in general; neither can it be based on anything other than detailed local landscape studies.

So we can see how the smaller defended enclosures might be used for early medieval burials, what we need to know is why. There is now a greater appreciation of the variety of Iron Age mortuary practices and ritual deposits within occupied defended enclosures and other settlements to add to the numerous instances of inhumation burials in ramparts, analysed at length by Wait (1985, 83–121). We do not at present wholly understand what changes there may have been in mortuary and ritual practices in the Roman period in those defended enclosures which continued to be occupied. But considerable advances have been made in Wales in the study of defended enclosures through large-scale rescue excavations, most notably

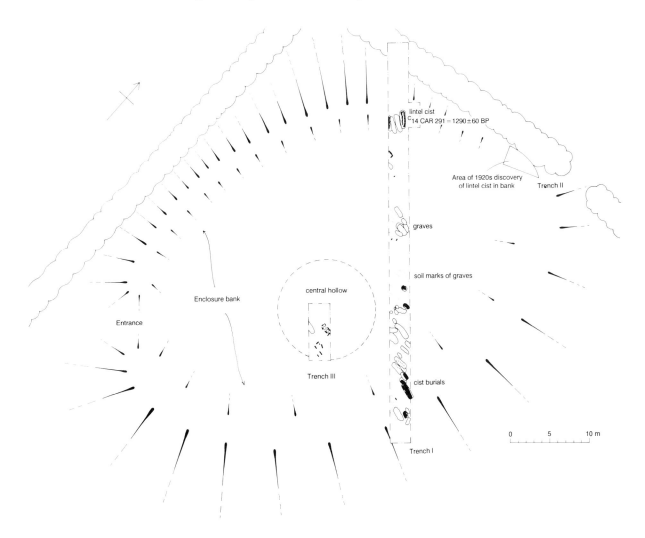

Fig. 10.4 *Caer, Bayvil, Dyfed — simplified plan (after James, H. 1987)*

those conducted by the Dyfed Archaeological Trust on a group of enclosures near Llawhaden (Williams, Geo. 1988). Not only were some of the Llawhaden sites occupied in the Roman, and possibly the post-Roman, periods but also it was possible to demonstrate changes in the status and function of such sites. In brief therefore Iron Age ritual and mortuary practices in defended settlements may have continued into the post-Roman period and when such settlements changed in function or were abandoned they may have been thought suitable for continued use by the dead rather than the living, perhaps through the mechanism of a founder's grave. These changes may have been particularly suitable for 'paired' enclosure sites, a possibility at present almost wholly evidenced by air photography and explored elsewhere in this volume (see James, T.A. above).

It seems likely that the cemetery site at Arfryn, Bodedern, Anglesey, may have originated within a defended enclosure (White, R.B. 1971–2). A cist burial, which had a Class I Early Christian memorial stone inscribed *Ercagni* reused as its lintel slab, was cut into the fill of a ditch encircling the hill top. In addition to oriented cist and dug graves, there were other dug graves broadly aligned north-south, two of which were cut by oriented graves. Until the full report is published it is impossible to say how the north-south graves relate to the enclosure itself. The most enigmatic structure in the cemetery at Arfryn was the so-called 'central feature'. This seemingly began as a levelled, surfaced circular area, surrounded by a fence, perhaps succeeded by a wooden cross, this being argued on the evidence of traces of timber emplacements, and then a timber chapel. The excavator draws attention in his interim report to the fact that the desire to be buried in close proximity to this central feature modified considerations both of the orientation of graves and their arrangement in rows. He uses the term 'quasi-radial'.

Although I have been stressing the early medieval inheritance of burial location and practice from the late Iron Age period, it would be quite misleading to ignore Roman traditions. Few now would doubt that British Christianity survived into post-Roman Wales, albeit to a limited extent. We should therefore look, in the first instance, to south-east Wales, as the most Romanized region, for evidence of survival and continuity. Rescue excavations in this area over the last decade have fleshed out our picture of a well-populated, prosperous and organized countryside (Robinson 1988a).

Only, as yet, for Caerwent (one of only two *civitas* capitals in Wales) do we have firm evidence for a Roman urban cemetery. It was characteristically sited outside the East Gate and continued to be used into the early medieval period, as radiocarbon dates between the fourth and eleventh centuries show (Edwards and Lane 1988, 137). Cist burials have also been recorded within the Roman town (Boon 1981–2). It is interesting to note that at the other *civitas* capital, Carmarthen, a comparable area immediately outside the eastern Roman town defences was part of the medieval Augustinian Priory enclosure. This house was on the site of a pre-Norman foundation, Llanteulyddog, one of the seven Bishop Houses of Dyfed (Charles-Edwards 1971). During excavations in 1979 by Dyfed Archaeological Trust, two ditches were found below the medieval cemetery to the east of the Priory Church, one of which yielded a radiocarbon date of cal AD 660–980 (CAR289, 1215±60bp) (James, T. A. 1985). There are nineteenth-century reports of lead coffins from the area, which could be medieval, or Roman. But the site surely has high potential as an urban Roman cemetery which continued into the post-Roman period and culminated in a pre-conquest church foundation.

We should probably see the Roman and post-Roman cemetery at the Atlantic Trading Estate, Barry (Fig. 10.5), recently excavated by the Glamorgan-Gwent Archaeological Trust, as a rural cemetery attached to an estate nucleus (Newman 1985; Newman and Parkin 1986; Price 1987; 1989). There is evidence to suggest the existence of such a Roman settlement to the east, towards Sully (Toft 1989). The date range of the cemetery itself, situated on the foreshore of a besanded inlet on the eastern side of Barry Island, could potentially extend from the second to the tenth centuries. A total of 44 burials were recorded, only ten completely undisturbed. Unusually for Wales, bone survival was excellent and a detailed pathological study has been carried out by Dr J. Wilkinson, of the Department of Anatomy, University of Wales College of Cardiff.

The cemetery was enclosed, indeed it is suggested that the landward boundary wall marked off the sanded foreshore from cultivable land; the seaward boundary has been eroded. Although the burials were all cut through sand dunes, a series of relict turf lines indicate periods of vegetational stability between sand-blows. Modern disturbance is severe and hampers the reconstruction of the Roman and post-Roman environment. The burials were all oriented, heads to the west and arranged in rows; there does not seem to have been any special or focal grave. There were a variety of burial methods: shrouds (as evidenced by a hunching and constriction of the shoulders), slab-lined graves and others with traces of wooden covers. Such variations do not however seem to relate to the

chronology of the burials, they are present both early and late in the dating sequence. So there is, at the Atlantic Trading Estate cemetery, a strong probability of continuity in burial practice from the Roman period perhaps to as late as the tenth century. Dr Wilkinson has identified genetic links between skeletons, and the impression is of an extended family group,

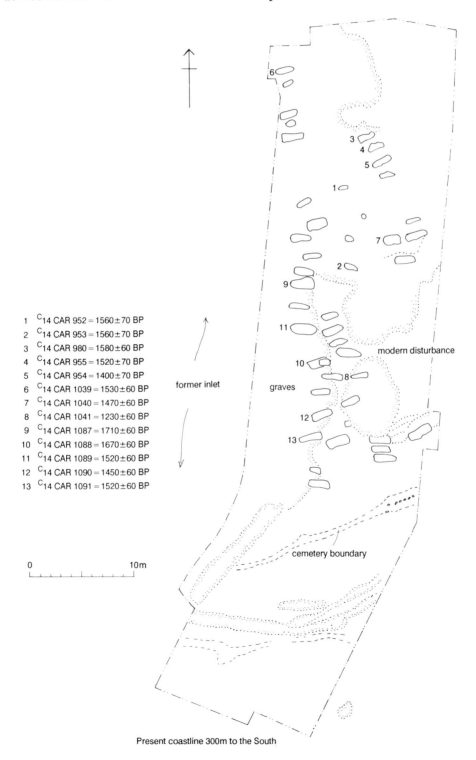

1	C_{14} CAR 952 = 1560±70 BP
2	C_{14} CAR 953 = 1560±70 BP
3	C_{14} CAR 980 = 1580±60 BP
4	C_{14} CAR 955 = 1520±70 BP
5	C_{14} CAR 954 = 1400±70 BP
6	C_{14} CAR 1039 = 1530±60 BP
7	C_{14} CAR 1040 = 1470±60 BP
8	C_{14} CAR 1041 = 1230±60 BP
9	C_{14} CAR 1087 = 1710±60 BP
10	C_{14} CAR 1088 = 1670±60 BP
11	C_{14} CAR 1089 = 1520±60 BP
12	C_{14} CAR 1090 = 1450±60 BP
13	C_{14} CAR 1091 = 1520±60 BP

former inlet

graves

modern disturbance

cemetery boundary

0   10m

Present coastline 300m to the South

Fig. 10.5 Atlantic Trading Estate, Barry, Glamorgan – simplified plan (after Price and Newman)

perhaps, as suggested already, from an estate centre rather than a larger nucleated settlement — it is after all a small cemetery.

At Llandough, south of Cardiff, close to the estuary of the Ely river, rescue excavations by the Glamorgan-Gwent Archaeological Trust recovered a large part of a Roman villa, occupied until the early fourth century (Owen-John 1988). During a subsequent watching brief north-west of the excavation area evidence for a cemetery was uncovered. Radiocarbon samples from two oriented graves provided dates of cal. AD 680–1000 (CAR-306, 1175±65bp) and 690–1016 (CAR-305, 1155±65bp). The medieval church and churchyard of St Dochdwy lie 75m north of the area of the partly explored cemetery. South of the church stands the cross shaft (Nash-Williams 1950, no. 206), dated to the late tenth or eleventh century, which has led to the identification of the churchyard area with a monastic enclosure referred to in early medieval documentary sources. Cemeteries which may have covered larger areas than those subsequently enclosed as the medieval churchyard are also known from west Wales, notably St Ishmael's, Pembrokeshire (see James, H. 1987, gazetteer no.33; and T.A. James above). There is no archaeological evidence for relationships between Roman villas and early monastic sites in Glamorgan but the survival of Roman estates into the post-Roman period (Davies, W. 1979b) might suggest that even if the villa was abandoned the monastery might be founded in another location within its estate.

We await the full report on the excavations by Siân White (White, S.I. 1981a; 1981b; 1982) for Gwynedd Archaeological Trust at Capel Eithin, Anglesey with great interest. Any statements made here can only be provisional. A small, square stone building of Roman date, variously interpreted as a temple or signal tower, was the only recognizable feature of this complex, multiperiod prehistoric site to survive in the early medieval landscape. A large inhumation cemetery, of which 97 graves were excavated, was located to the north of the Roman structure. The burials, mainly, though not all, oriented, fall into three main groups: those nearest to the Roman building consisted of three full-sized dug graves, and 13 smaller ones with full and part cists interpreted as child and infant burials. The second group, on a different alignment to the first, again had a preponderance of probable child and infant burials. The third group consisted of a large number of full-sized graves, the northern

boundaries of which must lie outside the excavated area. They were clearly focussed upon a small robbed-out stone building, 4.9m square, which contained a deep central grave, partially encisted, with the carbonized remains of a plank beneath the body. Two small (?child) graves were set alongside and finally a cist-and-lintel grave had been inserted across the threshold of the building. This structure, which probably had a timber precursor, was interpreted, very plausibly in view of the Roman associations of the site, as a *cella memoria*. This term is derived from continental examples of martyrial tombs and has been defined by Thomas as 'the accessible burial in an open-air surround' (Thomas, C. 1971, 140).

For the full sequence of evolution, or development, we now have the splendid example of Capel Maelog, Llandrindod Wells, Radnor, excavated by Clwyd-Powys Archaeological Trust (Britnell *et al* 1984; Britnell 1985; 1986a; 1990). Apart from a scatter of Neolithic and early Bronze Age flints, the earliest occupation on the modest hill-crest site was within a small sub-rectangular enclosure of late or sub-Roman date. No complete plan was recovered, but a length of ditch was found to underlie the east end of the medieval church, and some internal features survived between the later graves. Two radiocarbon dates of cal. AD 260–597 (CAR-1080, 1600±60bp) and 660–980 (CAR-938, 1220±60bp) were obtained from the ditch fills giving a wide date range for its occupation (Fig. 10.6).

Subsequently a small inhumation cemetery was set out both within the enclosure and over an area to the west of it. The cemetery became divided into eastern and western parts by a cross ditch, with a central causewayed gap across it. The cross ditch had cut at least one ditch of the pre-church cemetery. It seemed, in the excavator's words, to have had 'some enduring significance' in relation to a special grave and the later location of the church (Britnell 1990). An oriented special grave, which had pitched stone liners and contained a scattering of white quartz pebbles, was aligned on the causeway. There were other graves, more elaborate than the rest, seen elsewhere in the cemetery and it was stratigraphically clear that the special grave was not primary and should not therefore be termed a founder's grave.

The inhumation cemetery was enclosed in a bank which persisted as the medieval churchyard boundary. A radiocarbon date of cal. AD 776–1020 (CAR-936, 1100±60bp) gives a *terminus post quem* for its construction. A further *terminus post quem* for the first phase stone church is given by a radiocarbon date of cal. AD 1044–1280 (CAR-940, 790±60bp). Although the special grave was truncated, it seems to have been carefully incorporated into the chancel of the first stone church. Some time in the twelfth or early thirteenth century, the west wall of the nave and the whole chancel were demolished and replaced by curving apses, to produce what is to date a unique plan for a medieval parish church in Britain.

So we have in Capel Maelog a number of elements seen elsewhere: an inhumation cemetery relating to a small enclosure, and a special grave sited in relation to earlier features of cemetery organization and in turn influencing later church construction. It may be that the relatively late date of the cemetery allowed this direct progression to the by then well-established architectural form of stone nave and chancel, for there was no timber precursor. It is also important to note that the medieval church was not of any great importance. It was undoubtedly the *Landemaylon* or Llanfaelon of the 1291 *Taxatio Ecclesiastica* but appears to have fallen out of use by the early sixteenth century. The name Capel Maelog seems to be a fairly modern coinage.

We need far more excavations to date the appearance of stone churches within cemeteries in different parts of Wales; there is no evidence for them before the twelfth century (see Pryce

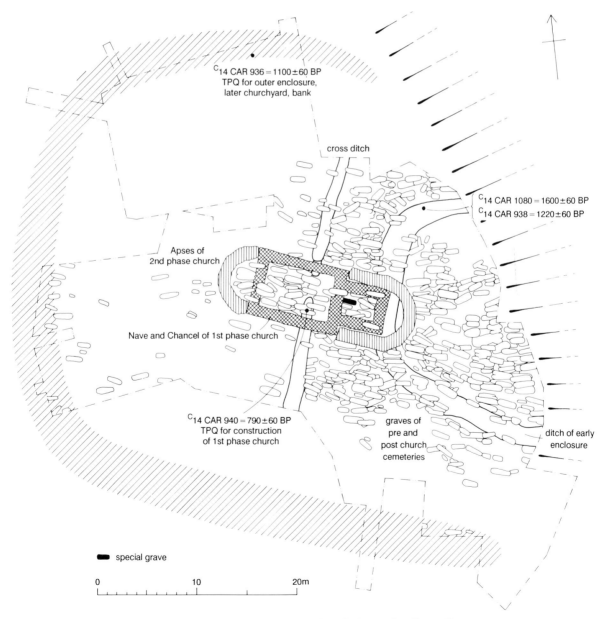

Fig. 10.6 Capel Maelog, Powys – simplified plan (after Britnell 1989)

above). At Llanychllwydog church in the Gwaun valley, Pembs. a radiocarbon date of cal. AD 747–1067 (CAR-918, 1060±60bp) came from a cist burial which was part of a group sealed below the medieval nave wall. Three at least of four Group II Early Christian monuments there (Nash-Williams 1950, nos 338–41) seem to have been original to the churchyard of this now redundant church. An unmarked stone has also been discovered which probably functioned as a grave marker (Murphy 1987).

The monastic sites of Wales, whose vicissitudes are chronicled in the Welsh Annals, whose fame was perpetuated in the Saints' Lives and whose architectural splendours may be guessed at from surviving Class III Early Christian monuments, have been reluctant to manifest themselves archaeologically. Possible topographical indications of such sites as Llandeilo Fawr are considered elsewhere in this volume (see T.A. James above). I cannot however leave a survey of recent work on early medieval cemetery sites in Wales without mentioning recent work by Gwynedd Archaeological Trust at Bangor.

Richard White has pointed out the existence of an oval enclosure to the east of the present cathedral on the south-east bank of the River Adda visible on John Speed's 1610 map of Bangor and suggested that this might be the location of Deiniol's monastery (in Longley forthcoming). The line of the present day High Street, south of the medieval Cathedral, also perpetuates the enclosure's boundaries (Edwards, N. pers. comm.). The area remained little changed in the seventeenth and eighteenth centuries, but the part called Berllan Fawr was built on in the nineteenth century. Some of these buildings have since been demolished allowing opportunities for excavation prior to redevelopment. A number of small areas were investigated, one of which established the existence of graves, and in 1984–5 a 450 sq.m area was excavated at Berllan Bach (Fig. 10.7). The earliest features on the site were 78 graves, variously aligned between north-east and south-west with a peak of alignment on the same line as the present cathedral and another close to true east. There was no indication within the excavated area of any boundary to this cemetery of simple inhumation graves. Some of the graves were cut by a rectilinear ditch, the lowest fills of which produced material radiocarbon dated to cal. AD 680–990 (CAR-950, 1180±60bp) and cal. AD 893–1160 (CAR-951, 1010±60bp) which gives a useful *terminus ante quem* for the cemetery.

The rectilinear ditch was partly cut by a cross ditch, with green-glazed medieval pottery in its fills. The rectilinear ditch is interpreted as marking a break and a change in this particular area of the site; it later contained a medieval chantry chapel, *Capel Gorfyw*, which was finally used as a Tithe Barn (Longley forthcoming).

It is at this point, and in drawing to a conclusion, that I would like to turn to the so-called 'long-cist cemeteries'. Ten or 15 years ago, without the excavated evidence I have been describing, they would have been the starting point in any discussion of early medieval cemeteries in Wales. By long-cist cemeteries I am thinking of Charles Thomas' 'undeveloped' sites, characterized by oriented burials, in stone cists, unaccompanied by gravegoods, and ascribed to the Early Christian period (Thomas, C. 1971, 48–90). They are widely distributed along the western seaboards of Britain, and indeed Brittany. In Wales the concentrations are most marked on the south-west and north-west coasts, particularly Pembrokeshire and Anglesey. Their essential characteristic is their lack of a church building and their failure to achieve full ecclesiastical status.

There has been considerable recent discussion of grave orientation, and it can certainly no longer be considered in itself as diagnostic of Christian beliefs (Black 1986). We have seen how cemetery management, the attraction of focal graves and later structures can modify strict orientation. In too few instances have variations in alignments been plotted – David Longley's diagram in the forthcoming Bangor report and W. Britnell's Capel Maelog report (1990) are exceptions. The origins of the practice of orienting burials were diverse, alignments dictated by the solar arc being one, and all have been recently examined by Kendall (1982). As a burial practice therefore orientation takes its place with a number of others inherited by Christianity from both Iron Age and Roman traditions.

Only when associated with other kinds of monuments or sites, either earlier, as we have seen with barrows and defended enclosures, or later chapels, or inscribed stones can we begin to suggest beliefs as well as burial practices. Most of our knowledge of cist-grave cemetery sites comes from essentially antiquarian sources and we still lack total excavation of a cemetery. However enough excavation has now been done to suspect that on the sites from which we have records of cist graves, further investigation might reveal a mixture of grave types, perhaps indicative of ranking, as well as the panoply of focal graves and structures, cemetery boundaries and organization. Put quite simply, on the basis of the scanty information we have behind those distribution dots on the maps of cist cemeteries, we just do not know what kind of cemetery site we are dealing with.

How in fact should we interpret these 'undeveloped' cemetery sites? Are they simply sites which failed to achieve ecclesiastical status or is their abandonment linked to changes which we sense happening in settlement as a whole in the seventh and eighth centuries? Were they kin burial grounds whose attraction waned against the more powerful pull of church cult sites and of

burial close to the relics of saints and martyrs? Elizabeth O'Brien has drawn attention (1984; see below) to interesting Irish evidence suggesting that there may have been some resistance to using the church-organized burial grounds. The eighth-century *Collectio Canonum Hibernensis* asserts that angels would not visit those Christians who were buried among evil men. The inference drawn by Elizabeth O'Brien is that such moral blackmail was necessary even as late as the eighth century to bring all burials into Christian (i.e. church) rather than pagan or mixed (i.e. kin/tribal) cemeteries.

Links between burial practices and religious beliefs can usually only be inferred, they are

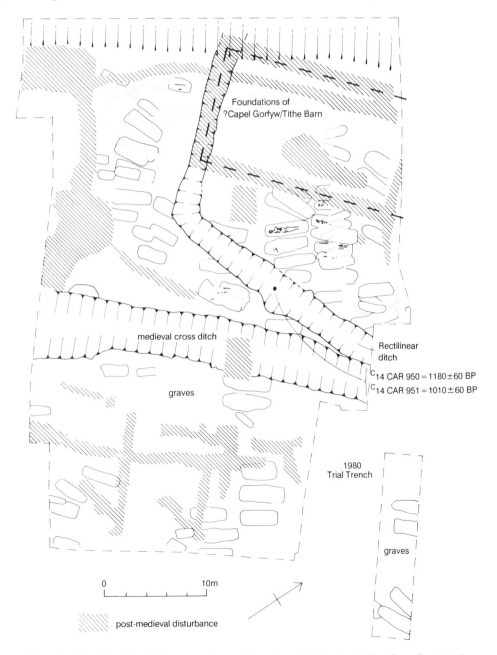

Fig. 10.7 Berllan Bach, Bangor, Gwynedd – simplified plan (after Longley 1989)

rarely explicit. However Professor Leslie Alcock was surely right, in conference discussion, to draw attention to the central importance of the Christian belief in bodily resurrection. We see this reflected in burial practice in protecting the corpse — by inhumation in stone cists, wooden coffins and shrouds — until the Day of Judgement. The cult of saints and relics, and the very literal understanding of the benefits of proximity to them in burial, can equally be seen reflected in burial practices like clustering around focal graves. In these instances we feel we are in a Christian world. Yet what this paper ventures to suggest, on the basis of the archaeological evidence, is that widespread acceptance of specifically Christian burial practices could not have succeeded so totally in the thinly populated, culturally conservative and politically fragmented region of dispersed settlement that was early medieval Wales, without developing from — indeed within — Iron Age/Romano-British traditions.

APPENDIX I

Site Name	Sample Ref.	Radio-Carbon Age Uncal.	1 Sigma Calibrated Range Cal. AD	2 Sigma Calibrated Range Cal. AD
Plas Gogerddan	CAR-1045	1580+60BP-370+60	410-542	263-636
Tandderwen	CAR-984	1440+60BP-510+60	556-650	433-680
Caer, Bayvil	CAR-291	1290+60BP-660+60	660-797	640-883
Caerwent	HAR-493	1090+70BP-860+70	886-1000	770-1148
	HAR-494	1410+70BP-540+70	576-666	435-768
	HAR-495	1540+80BP-410+70	419-601	263-650
	HAR-496	1250+80BP-700+80	668-875	640-980
	HAR-497	1460+80BP-490+80	536-649	410-690
Carmarthen Priory	CAR-289	1215+60BP-735+60	690-889	660-980
Atlantic Trading Estate, Barry	CAR-952	1560+70BP-390+70	413-571	263-640
	CAR-953	1560+70BP-390+70	413-571	263-640
	CAR-980	1580+60BP-370+60	410-542	263-636
	CAR-955	1520+70BP-430+70	429-637	365-650
	CAR-954	1400+70BP-550+70	582-670	530-771
	CAR-1039	1530+60BP-420+60	429-599	390-640
	CAR-1040	1470+60BP-480+60	538-642	430-660
	CAR-1041	1230+60BP-720+60	686-877	660-976
	CAR-1087	1710+60BP-240+60	241-409	133-527
	CAR-1088	1670+60BP-280+60	259-427	230-540
	CAR-1089	1520+60BP-430+60	430-635	410-640
	CAR-1090	1450+60BP-500+60	543-645	432-670
	CAR-1091	1520+60BP-430+60	430-635	410-640
Llandough	CAR-306	1175+65BP-775+65	773-976	680-1000
	CAR-305	1155+65BP-795+65	776-980	690-1016
Capel Maelog (selected dates)	CAR-936	1100+60BP-850+60	785-996	776-1020
	CAR-938	1220+60BP-730+60	689-887	660-980
	CAR-940	790+60BP-1160+60	1193-1278	1044-1280
	CAR-1080	1600+60BP-350+60	392-538	260-597
Llanychllwydog Church	CAR-918	1060+60BP-890+60	853-1004	747-1067
Bangor	CAR-950	1180+60BP-770+60	773-943	680-990
	CAR-951	1010+60BP-940+60	982-1148	893-1160

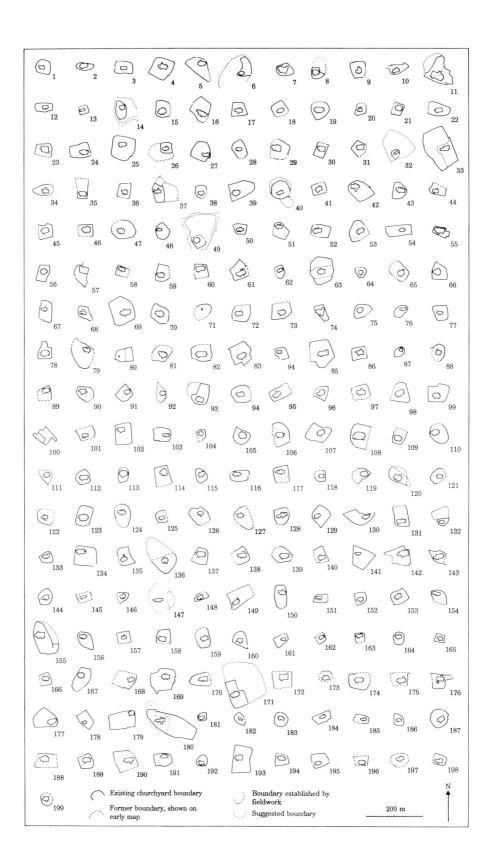

Decoding Cornish Churchyards

Ann Preston-Jones

In Cornwall, it is traditionally held that the typical church site was founded at the beginning of the Dark Ages, by a holy person who is often said to have travelled from Ireland, borne by some outlandish form of transport. A martyrdom or some miraculous event is frequently invoked to explain the often peculiar choice of site for the saint's foundation. That foundation is usually said to have been a small monastery containing initially a tiny wattle or wooden chapel and a few cells for the monks. Of course, nothing now remains of the monastery: the hoary, lichen-covered, ancient-looking churchyard cross is generally pointed out as the only tangible remnant of the Dark Age foundation. More recently, archaeology has added a new element to this tradition. A curving churchyard wall is now claimed to represent the boundary of the early monastic enclosure, or *lann*.

The purpose of this paper is to look in detail at the churchyards of Cornwall, to see exactly how many are curvilinear, and to see whether it is possible to substantiate the claim for a very early (ie. fifth to seventh century) origin which most church sites boast. It will be shown that there are indeed a large number of church sites which probably did begin as early, possibly monastic, enclosures, but there are also many which, although still pre-Norman in origin, did not. The fact that by no means all sites fit with the traditional view had already been indicated over 20 years ago by Charles Thomas' excavations at Merther Euny, the site of a chapel with a small oval yard (Thomas, C. 1968a; 1968b). This was shown to have been founded in about the tenth century, and therefore 500 years after the adoption of Christianity in Cornwall.

In the first part of this paper, churchyard plans will be examined and the evidence for their dating and nature in the early medieval period discussed. Then, by comparing churchyard shapes with other types of evidence, an attempt

---

Fig. 11.1 Plans of all Cornish churchyards: 1 Advent; 2 St Agnes; 3 St Allen; 4 Altarnun; 5 Anthony; 6 St Anthony in Meneage; 7 St Austell; 8 St Blazey; 9 Blisland; 10 Boconnoc; 11 Bodmin; 12 Botus Fleming; 13 Boyton; 14 Braddock; 15 Breage; 16 St Breock; 17 St Breward; 18 Budock; 19 St Buryan; 20 Caerhayes, St Michael; 21 Callington; 22 Calstock; 23 Camborne; 24 Cardinham; 25 St Cleer; 26 St Clement; 27 St Clether; 28 Colan; 29 St Columb Major; 31 Constantine; 32 Cornelly; 33 Crantock; 34 Creed; 35 Crowan; 36 Cubert; 37 Cuby; 38 Cury; 39 Davidstow; 40 St Dennis; 41 St Dominick; 42 Duloe; 43 Egloshayle; 44 Egloskerry; 45 St Endellion; 46 St Enoder; 47 St Erme; 48 St Erney; 49 St Erth; 50 St Ervan; 51 St Eval; 52 St Ewe; 53 Feock; 54 Forrabury; 55 Fowey; 56 St Gennys; 57 St Germans; 58 Germoe; 59 Gerrans; 60 St Gluvias; 61 Gorran; 62 Grade; 63 Gulval; 64 Gunwalloe; 65 Gwennap; 66 Gwinear; 67 Gwithian; 68 Helland; 69 Helston; 70 St Hilary; 71 Illogan; 72 St Issey; 73 St Ive; 74 St Ives; 75 Jacobstow; 76 St John; 77 St Juliot; 78 St Just in Penwith; 79 St Just in Roseland; 80 Old Kea; 81 Kenwyn; 82 St Keverne; 83 St Kew; 84 St Keyne; 85 Kilkhampton; 86 Ladock; 87 St John; 88 Landwednack; 89 Landrake; 90 Landulph; 91 Laneast; 92 Lanhydrock; 93 Lanivet; 94 Lanlivery; 95 Lanreath; 96 Lansallos; 97 Lanteglos by Camelford; 98 Lanteglos by Fowey; 99 Launcells; 100 Launceston, St Mary Magdalene; 101 Lawhitton; 102 Lelant; 103 Lesnewth; 104 St Leven; 105 Lewannick; 106 Lezant; 107 Linkinhorne; 108 Liskeard; 109 Ludgvan; 110 Luxulyan; 111 Mabe; 112 St Mabyn; 113 Madron; 114 Maker; 115 Manaccan; 116 Marhamchurch; 117 St Martin by Looe; 118 St Martin in Meneage; 119 St Mawgan in Meneage; 120 St Mawgan in Pydar; 121 Mawnan; 122 St Mellion; 123 Menheniot; 124 St Merryn; 125 Merther; 126 Mevagissey; 127 St Mewan; 128 St Michael Penkevil; 129 Michaelstow; 130 Minster; 131 St Minver; 132 Morvah; 133 Morval; 134 Morwenstow; 135 Mullion; 136 Mylor; 137 St Neot; 138 Newlyn; 139 North Hill; 140 North Tamerton; 141 Otterham; 142 Padstow; 143 Paul 144 Pelynt; 145 Perranarworthal; 146 Perranuthnoe; 147 Perranzabuloe; 148 Little Petherick; 149 Phillack; 150 Philleigh; 151 Pillaton; 152 St Pinnock; 153 Poughill; 154 Poundstock; 155 Probus; 156 Quethiock; 157 Rame; 158 Redruth; 159 Roche; 160 Ruan Lanihorne; 161 Ruan Major; 162 Ruan Minor; 163 St Samson Golant; 164 Sancreed; 165 Sennen; 166 Sheviock; 167 Sithney; 168 South Hill; 169 South Petherwin; 170 St Stephen in Brannell; 171 St Stephen by Launceston; 172 St Stephen by Saltash; 173 Stithians; 174 Stoke Climsland; 175 Stratton; 176 Talland; 177 St Teath; 178 Temple; 179 St Thomas by Launceston; 180 Tintagel; 181 Towednack; 182 Tremaine; 183 Treneglos; 184 Tresmeer; 185 Trevalga; 186 Trewen; 187 St Tudy; 188 Tywardreath; 189 St Veep; 190 Veryan; 191 Warbstow; 192 Warleggan; 193 Week St Mary; 194 Wendron; 195 St Wenn; 196 Whitstone; 197 St Winnow; 198 Withiel; 199 Zennor

will be made to distinguish the different types of
site. Those which may have originated as very
early enclosures or *lanns* will be discussed in
detail. Finally, the evidence will be drawn
together into an archaeological framework which
is in effect a model for the development of the
church in early medieval Cornwall.

Churchyard Shape

Churchyard plans are the primary source of
information, though they do not take the dating
of a churchyard boundary back very far. The
Ordnance Survey's 1:2500 maps provide a full
and comparable series and before this the Tithe
Award plans of *c.*1840 provide the only complete
coverage, though at scales varying from two to
eight chains per inch. A number of sites (45)
have plans at a useful scale for an earlier date,
the earliest known to me being a couple of plans
in Lord Burghley's maps of *c.*1580 (BL MS Royal
18 DIII) and estate surveys by Joel Gascoyne of
the late seventeenth century (The 'Lanhydrock
Atlas').

Thus, the cartographic evidence may,
exceptionally, take the dating of a churchyard
boundary back 400 years; 150 years is more
common. But this is only a small portion of the
life of any church site; so how can it be shown
whether the nineteenth-century boundary follows
the line of the later medieval, or even early
medieval graveyard? Firstly, there is the simple
probability that the consecrated area will have
been preserved, so long as it remained a living
part of the countryside, with an active graveyard.
Secondly, the cartographic evidence coupled with
fieldwork, shows that at least 50% of
churchyards have been altered or extended since
the mid-nineteenth century, whereas less than
10% appear to have been altered before then.
This suggests that the population dynamics and
sheer mechanical ability of the last 150 years
have wrought changes which would previously
have been unthought of, unnecessary, or
impossible. With hindsight, there is also the
evidence of the enclosures themselves. The fact
that they do fall into distinct groups and types
(as will be shown below) suggests that the plans
derived from maps do, to a large extent,
correspond to the form of the original enclosures.
In one instance excavation has demonstrated
that a modern churchyard wall follows an old
line (Preston-Jones 1987).

The resultant collection of over 200
churchyard plans is almost bewildering in its
variety (Fig. 11.1). Some churchyards are
unquestionably square or rectangular, others are
certainly round or oval, but the majority fall
somewhere in between, with sub-rectangular,
triangular, trapezoidal and parallelogram-like
shapes. The sizes vary too, the smallest being
0.05ha and the largest over 0.9ha. The average is
approximately 0.28ha.

Location

Location, like enclosure shape, is a variable
applicable to all churches, unlike many of the
other features to be discussed below. This makes
it very useful; but as with shape, there are as
many different locations as there are church
sites, and classification can therefore be difficult
and subjective. However, a few broad categories
which cover most options have been selected.
These are valley bottom, valley head, valley side,
plateau or hilltop, and spur.

Dating a Church Site

Before looking in more detail at the physical
characteristics of Cornish church sites, it is
useful to establish how many actually have some
form of dating evidence to support the tradition
of a pre-Norman origin. The dating evidence
takes many forms, including documentation,
sculpture, inscriptions, place-names and
dedications. The various types of evidence also
help to define groups against which churchyard
shape and location can be compared, to see
whether any significant correlations exist.

DOMESDAY BOOK

First, there is the retrospective evidence of
Domesday Book, which lists a number of small
Cornish religious houses as land-holders in 1086
(Thorn and Thorn 1979; Taylor, T. 1924). For
example, it states that *Canonici Sci Achebranni
tenent Lannachebran*, 'the canons of St Achebran
hold the lann of Achebran'. Canons of St Probus,
St Piran, St Carantoc, St Berion, St Niot, St
Constantine, St German, St Petroc, St Stephen
and St Michael are all referred to as land-holders
in the same way. In her recent book on *Early
Monasteries in Cornwall*, Olson (1989) has shown
that features in the entries for most of the
Cornish religious houses in Domesday Book
imply a pre-Norman Celtic origin. Altogether 13
religious houses are documented in this way:
they represent 7% of Cornish church sites.

Domesday Book also implies, but does not
actually mention, the existence of a church in the
names of secular manors such as *Hecglostudic*,
'the church of St Tudy', and *Heglosenuder*, 'the

church of St Enoder'. Other secular manorial names like *Scanct Mawan* (St Mawgan) and *Landelech* (Landulph) also suggest either estates of ecclesiastical origin or estates taking their names from nearby ecclesiastical sites. Eighteen manors have names of this sort.

PRE-NORMAN DOCUMENTATION

A handful of Cornish church sites are mentioned in pre-Norman documentary sources. With two important exceptions, these derive from an Anglo-Saxon background and consist mainly of charters. Two secular estates whose names betray an ecclesiastical origin (Lamorran and Lanlawren) are granted, and there are five charters known in which land is granted to pre-existing Cornish religious houses (St Buryan, St Kew, St Germans, ?St Michael's Mount, Lansallos: Birch 1885–93, 785, 1231; Finberg 1963, 42, 78, 84, 87, 99; 1969, 268–73; Kemble 1839–48, 914; Padel 1978). In addition, there are grants of eight estates, not apparently of ecclesiastical origin, which by at least the Norman period had a church at the manorial centre. A variety of other sources mention five other church sites: King Alfred prayed at the church of St Gueriir (Stevenson, W.H. 1904, Ch. 74); Bishop Kenstec issued a profession of obedience to the Archbishop of Canterbury from a monastery called *Dinuurrin* in 833 x 870 (Birch 1885–93, 527); St Petroc's Stow was ravaged by Vikings in 981 (Plummer 1892–9, I.124); there was a mint at Launceston, possibly from the reign of Edgar (Carlyon-Britton 1906; 1908; Dolley 1961, 146, 151); and manumissions were recorded in the Bodmin Gospels from 941 x 946 (Finberg 1963, 19; Jenner 1929–32).

One of the exceptions is a tenth-century list, in Old Cornish, of 48 names, of which 21 can confidently be recognized as the patron saints of Cornish parish churches. Apart from providing documentation for a number of sites which are not otherwise recorded until the eleventh or twelfth century, the List's importance is in its hint that in some parts of Cornwall the structure of the medieval parochial system was already in existence by the tenth century (Olson and Padel 1986). The earliest source is the Life of St Samson which refers to the *monasterium quod Docco vocatur* – that is, St Kew near Wadebridge – as a community which, when Samson was passing through Cornwall in the sixth century, had already been in existence long enough to have suffered a decline in standards of religious practice (Olson 1989, 14–5; arguments on the dating of the Life of Samson are summarized by Davies, W. 1982a, 215).

EARLY ARCHITECTURE

No Cornish parish church is certainly known to incorporate pre-Norman architectural remains, although this has been suggested for two sites: Tintagel (Canner 1982, 10; Cox 1912, 226) and St Germans (Cox 1912, 107; Miles Brown 1973, 86). Early buildings only survive where, as at Gwithian or Perranzabuloe, they have been abandoned to encroaching sand dunes (Thomas, C. 1964; Tomlin, E.W.F. 1982). But in these cases, the circumstances leading to their preservation have rendered them useless for present purposes, as the sand entirely masks the morphology of their associated enclosures. The dearth of early architecture, and the small size of the surviving examples perhaps reflects the insubstantial nature of early medieval Cornish churches.

PRE-NORMAN SCULPTURE

Although stone crosses are ubiquitous in Cornwall (there are over 500), only perhaps 13 church sites can claim early sculpture in support of a pre-Norman origin. It is impossible to be precise, as dating Cornish crosses is notoriously difficult and has only once been seriously attempted (Thomas, C. 1978). The reason is partly that very few have diagnostic, datable features. The range of dates which has been (soberly) suggested extends from the eighth century (Langdon 1896, 17–20) to the fifteenth (Thomas, C. 1967a, 98), but the earliest supportable date is the late ninth century for the St Neot and Doniert crosses (Langdon 1896, 377–9, 405–7). Tall ring-headed, interlace- and vinescroll-carved crosses, showing influences from Wales and Devon, seem to start the series (Preston-Jones and Rose 1986, 159) but it is clear that this style of cross was still being carved in Norman times (eg. Langdon 1896, 17–8, 387).

EARLY CHRISTIAN MEMORIALS

Some 32 Early Christian inscribed memorial stones are published for Cornwall. Half of these can be associated with a church site and altogether there are 14 church sites with inscribed stones (Macalister 1945; 1949; Tangye 1985; a new survey by Okasha (forthcoming) will almost certainly alter these figures). They are generally dated to between the fifth and seventh centuries (Jackson 1953, 160) and when they occur at a church site can probably be regarded as positive evidence for that site's early use. There is little evidence in Cornwall for the wholesale removal of these stones to the church from the surrounding countryside. (The stones at

St Clement and Southill were found outside, but very close to, the churchyards they now occupy and are therefore considered to have been associated with their respective church sites at an early date.) The idea of erecting these memorials is believed to have come to Cornwall from Wales (Thomas, C. 1957–8, 64); those with ogam or an Irish personal name reflect the presence in Cornwall of Irish settlers, in all probability from Wales, not direct from Ireland (Thomas, C. 1957–8, 64; 1972, 257–60; Olson 1989, 36–40, 48).

PLACE-NAMES
Numerically, place-name elements are the most important evidence for pre-Norman church sites. Four ecclesiastical elements are particularly relevant in Cornwall, namely *lann*, *eglos*, *merther* and Old English *stow*. Other elements which occur are *mynster*, 'endowed church', *plu*, 'parish', *meneghy*, 'sanctuary', **log*, 'chapel', and Old English *cirice* 'church'; but these are found in such small numbers that they are of little use for present purposes. All the place-name elements have been fully discussed by Padel (1974; 1976–7; 1985; 1989).

The precise meaning of *merther* in Cornwall is uncertain. Derived via Latin *martyrium* from Greek *martyrion* meaning 'place possessing a martyr's physical remains' (Thomas, C. 1971, 89), it has been explained for Cornwall as 'a place where the actual physical relics of a saint (originally a martyr, one who suffered for Christ) are preserved' (Thomas, C. 1967a, 47) or more economically 'saint's grave' (Padel 1985, 164). But this is despite the acknowledged fact that only one of the nine *merther*-named places in Cornwall is said to have possessed a shrine (Sithney, earlier *Merthersitheny*, while three other *merthers* are dedicated to saints whose relics were said to be elsewhere (for a complete list see Padel 1985, 164). A preferred explanation of the term will be described below.

The status of *eglos*, 'church', is uncertain. While it could be used to name a very early site, the word also remained current in Cornish until the language died out. When it ceased to be used as a name-forming element is not known. Even the precise meaning of *eglos* at any early date is uncertain. The term would seem to imply the presence of a significant building at a site, but exactly how a place called *eglos* differed from a *lann*, and whether or not it implied a monastic site, is unknown. At a later date one, St Buryan (*Eglosberrie*, 1086) had a religious community, but the evidence to be discussed below suggests

that on the whole *eglos* seems to have been used to name places of possibly later origin and of different type to *lann*.

Oliver Padel has shown that the use of *eglos* with a descriptive element to make a true place-name goes back to an early period. Egloshayle in Maker must have been named before the tenth century (Padel 1985, 91), and one of the two other Egloshayles (Phillack) has monumental evidence indicating a particularly early foundation (Thomas, C. 1963). Many of the instances recorded where *eglos* is combined with a saint's name are not considered to be place-names proper, but phrases in the Cornish language referring to a church site, which could be coined at any time (Padel 1976–7, 24). Amongst the latter, however, are a handful which can be regarded as true place-names since they are recorded as the names of estates or manors. The Domesday manors of *Hecglostudic* and *Heglosenuder* are examples which have already been referred to. These plus the descriptive *eglos* names give a total of 15 church sites which can be examined as a group.

On the other hand, *lann* is a demonstrably early element which may have gone out of use at a relatively early date (Padel 1976–7, 25). As the distribution map of the element (Fig. 11.8) shows, there are several examples in east Cornwall, which were probably formed before the English incursions over the Tamar and therefore probably before the eighth or ninth century. The development of this originally secular word from British *landa* is discussed elsewhere in this volume by Roberts (above, Chap. 5). When first used in a Christian context, *lann* probably meant simply 'enclosure'. Charles Thomas' (1971, 85–7) explanation of the term as 'enclosed cemetery' is, as Padel (1989, 191) has pointed out, probably too narrow, since it gives weight to what may have been only one aspect of a site. In Cornwall, the earliest written evidence for the meaning of *lann* appears in the possibly seventh-century Life of Samson, where the place known from later documents as *Landochou* is rendered in Latin as *monasterium quod Docco vocatur* (Olson 1989, 14); but it is easy to see how, if the early enclosure sometimes defined the precinct of a monastic community, the word might acquire the meaning of 'monastery'. In a rather later (early fourteenth century) source, which presumably reflects the medieval interpretation of a word which was by then obsolete in the Cornish language, *lann* is translated as *cimiterium* (Grosjean 1956, 153). *Lann* never acquired the meaning of 'church building' as it did in Wales.

The significance of *lann* in names referring to church sites is that it is liable to imply the existence of an early religious enclosure whose form, as Charles Thomas (1967a, 45–6) has suggested, may be reflected in the modern churchyard boundary. Approximately 25% of Cornish church sites have a name in *lann*.

Old English *stow*, 'church', is important because it is clear that in Cornwall, as in Wales, it could replace an earlier name in *lann*. For example, St Martin by Looe is attested as both *Lancoff* and *Martistowe* in early records (Padel 1989, 116; and information from W.M.M. Picken, via Oliver Padel). Gelling (1982, 189–90) suggests that *stow* could also be significant in denoting a church with a shrine, and this is certainly the case in some of the Cornish instances.

DEDICATIONS

Some 65% of Cornish church sites are dedicated to shadowy figures with Celtic names. The remainder, mainly in the east of Cornwall, where English influence was strongest and earliest, are dedicated to universal saints: the Archangel Michael, the patron saint of the whole county who is the most popular, the Virgin Mary, and the Evangelists.

The Celtic dedications need to be carefully evaluated, as not all are of very early origin; nor are they all undoubted saints. Firstly, it is clear that not all dedications go back to the earliest days of Christianity. Gerrans church, for example, is said to be dedicated to Gerent, an early eighth-century Cornish king (Doble 1938b). Secondly, not all dedications are derived from personal names. In a number of cases early forms of the name suggest that the 'saint' has been invented from a place-name. Saints Tallan, Kenwyn and Ludgvan are likely examples (Padel 1989, 23, 102, 160). At St Dennis, a universal saint has arisen from the place-name *dynas*, 'fort' (Henderson, C.G. 1925, 85). Finally, Pearce has suggested that many dedications to Celtic saints in Cornwall and the South West may be relatively late and based on English and Norman interest in the saints and their relics (Pearce 1973; 1978, 124–8). This is not the place to contest this hypothesis, which may have an element of truth in it, and may be applicable elsewhere. But it is difficult to accept, for example, that the dedication to Winwaloe at Landewednack is related to the acquisition by Exeter and Glastonbury of relics of Winwaloe in the tenth century since the site and name of Landewednack, which combines *lann* with the

pet-form of Winwaloe, *To-Winnoc (Padel 1976–7, 17–8), is probably of pre-tenth-century origin. With these qualifications in mind, I am generally prepared to take most Celtic dedications in Cornwall at face value — that is, as originating in a Cornish Christian context at some time in the pre-Norman period — though they need not all be particularly early. The tenth-century list of saints' names, mentioned earlier (Olson and Padel 1986), provides unique confirmation of the antiquity of a number of Cornish dedications which would otherwise rest only on tradition or a late record.

Celtic dedications in Cornwall may be divided into two types. The first are dedications to saints who are of some renown and found in more than one Celtic country. Samson, Winwaloe, Carantoc, Cuby and Mawgan are examples. For convenience, these will be referred to below as 'inter-Celtic' saints. In contrast, many Cornish churches are dedicated to completely obscure individuals associated with only one, or occasionally two, churches in Cornwall and nowhere else. In instances where a parallel dedication occurs at only one site abroad, it seems simplest to assume a coincidence of name, rather than a dedication to the same individual, unless there is good evidence to the contrary.

Analysis

The various forms of dating evidence described above combine to suggest that the majority of Cornish church sites are of early medieval origin. But pre-Norman Christianity spanned a period of over six centuries, during which time the religion and its institutions were not only born, but also grew, matured and no doubt changed. Therefore sites differing in function, date, status and complexity are to be expected and the variety in Cornish churchyards suggests that these differences may have a physical reflection.

In Fig. 11.2 the relationship between the topographical and other features of all church sites in Cornwall liable to be of early medieval origin is presented graphically. All the different types of evidence described above are listed along the two axes (apart from dedications, which will be dealt with separately) and the relationship between each group is then expressed as a percentage in the table. The purpose of this is to quantify any important correlations and to facilitate comparisons. For example, looking down the 'average size of enclosure' column, it is immediately apparent that mother churches generally have much larger enclosures than their

Fig. 11.2 *Table showing the occurrence of churchyards with various features and their locations*

	Number in group	% All churches	Average size of enclosures	% in valley bottom	% in valley head	% on valley side	% on spur	% on hilltop/plateau	% Domesday monasteries	% Direct Pre-Norman ref.	% Indirect Pre-Norman ref.	% Saxon period monument	% Inscribed stone	% LANN	% EGLOS	% MERTHER	% STOW	% Mother church	% Chapelry	% Rectangular	% Sub-rectangular	% Oval	% Round	% Sub-round
All churchyards	193	100	.66	22	15	25	19	19	7	7	6	7	7	24	15	3	4	14	18	14	16	27	9	12
Churchyards on valley bottom	43	22	.73	100	–	–	–	–	9	11	2	7	7	54	4	–	7	18	14	2	19	44	–	9
Churchyards in valley head	29	15	.54	–	100	–	–	–	7	10	3	7	7	31	14	0	7	14	24	7	17	38	7	17
Churchyards on valley side	47	25	.6	–	–	100	–	–	4	2	9	6	6	17	6	2	2	4	21	30	13	17	13	9
Churchyards on spur	36	19	.75	–	–	–	100	–	3	0	6	6	11	19	22	3	3	17	11	9	23	23	17	11
Churchyards on hilltop/plateau	36	19	.7	–	–	–	–	100	3	3	11	3	6	11	28	8	0	17	19	19	11	17	8	17
Domesday monasteries	13	7	1.1	39	15	15	15	8	100	54	8	31	8	77	8	0	15	31	0	9	27	36	9	0
Churches with Pre-Norman ref. (Direct)	14	7	.98	55	27	9	0	9	64	100	0	29	7	50	7	0	14	29	7	10	20	60	10	0
Churches with Pre-Norman ref.(Indirect)	12	6	.67	9	9	36	9	36	0	0	100	0	0	36	0	0	0	17	0	64	18	9	0	0
Churches with Saxon period monument	13	7	.80	23	15	39	15	8	31	23	8	100	39	46	23	0	15	39	8	15	23	15	15	0
Churches with inscribed stone	14	7	.75	21	14	21	36	–	7	7	0	36	100	50	29	7	0	14	0	7	36	14	7	21
LANN	47	24	.76	42	17	19	15	8	16	14	8	12	14	100	6	0	4	20	14	2	26	40	2	9
EGLOS	30	16	.65	7	17	17	27	33	3	3	0	10	13	10	100	7	0	20	3	17	17	17	20	10
MERTHER	6	3	.51	–	–	34	17	49	0	0	0	0	17	0	29	100	0	0	43	0	17	17	0	50
STOW	8	4	.77	38	25	25	12	–	25	25	0	13	0	25	0	0	100	13	13	13	13	13	13	13
Mother church	26	14	.91	31	15	8	23	23	23	15	8	19	8	38	23	0	4	100	0	12	19	27	15	4
Chapelry	34	18	.43	18	21	29	11	21	0	3	0	3	–	21	6	9	3	0	100	15	3	21	15	15
Rectangular enclosures	27	14	.62	4	7	52	11	26	4	4	26	7	4	4	19	0	4	11	19	100	–	–	–	–
Sub-rectangular enclosures	31	16	.84	26	16	19	26	13	10	3	7	10	16	39	16	3	3	16	3	–	100	–	–	–
Oval enclosures	52	27	.82	37	21	15	15	12	8	4	4	4	4	37	10	2	2	14	14	–	–	100	–	–
Round enclosures	17	9	.48	12	0	35	35	18	6	6	0	12	6	6	35	0	6	24	29	–	–	–	100	–
Sub-round enclosures	23	12	.51	17	22	17	17	27	0	0	0	0	13	17	13	4	13	4	22	–	–	–	–	100

chapelries, but the group with the largest enclosures of all are those for which communities are recorded in Domesday Book. Looking down the 'oval enclosures' column, we discover that altogether 27% of Cornish churchyards could be so-described, and that 37% of oval churchyards have a name in *lann*. Moreover, this stands out as one of the most significant features of oval churchyards, apart from a location in a valley bottom (also 37%). Looking at it in another way (ie. along the *lann* line), it appears that 40% of churchyards with a name in *lann* are oval, and, while only 14% of *lanns* have evidence of an early origin in the form of an early Christian inscription, these few actually account for half of the inscribed stones in churchyards. Already,

then, it appears that there may be some correlation between a place-name in *lann* and a curvilinear enclosure, and there is reason to believe that at least a few of the enclosures belong to the first centuries of Christianity in Cornwall.

But, as suggested above, it is probable that not all church sites in Cornwall originated as *lanns*. Those which are almost certainly not *lanns* will be examined first, before returning to describe the *lanns* in greater detail.

Post-Conquest Church Sites

Post-conquest sites include churches associated with towns and priories of Norman origin, a foundation of the Knights Templar (Temple, on Bodmin Moor) and Lelant and Gwithian, two early foundations rebuilt in new locations following the inundation of their original sites by blown sand (Thomas, C. 1963; 1964). As Fig. 11.3 shows, all of these have regular, rectilinear enclosures which suggest that, by Norman times at least, it was not the rule to construct a curvilinear churchyard.

Rectilinear Churchyards

Apart from the definitely post-Norman Conquest sites, there are 27 examples of rectilinear churchyards in Cornwall. The distribution map (Fig. 11.4a) shows that they fall into two distinct groups: one in east Cornwall, the other in the west. The two groups will be dealt with separately, taking those in east Cornwall first.

EAST CORNISH RECTILINEAR YARDS (Fig. 11.4b)
There are several factors which suggest that the church sites in this group may have a late Saxon origin. In the first place, their distribution shows marked concentrations in the north-east and south-east of the county — in areas where the

density of English place-names is believed to reflect extensive English settlement (Preston-Jones and Rose 1986, 140, Fig.3). Secondly, they are, with only one exception, dedicated to universal saints. Moreover none is associated with an inscribed stone or early sculpture and none have Cornish ecclesiastical names. Maker, Lawhitton (this name probably contains *nans*, not *lann*), Rame and Sheviock are all associated with important manors donated to English religious houses in Saxon charters (Finberg 1963, 42, 72, 76). Alfred left land at Stratton to his son in his will (Birch 1885–99, 553) and Whitstone, Boyton, Callington and North Tamerton churches are all named after Domesday manors. It is therefore not inconceivable that all these sites represent churches or chapels founded to serve pre-Norman manorial centres. This origin may explain the sites' physical characteristics, for the shape of their rectangular yards, which reflects the shape of the church within, suggests that they are primarily yards designed around a building, rather than enclosures which acquired a major building as a secondary consideration. Also, in common with most secular settlements in Cornwall, these churches are located on valley

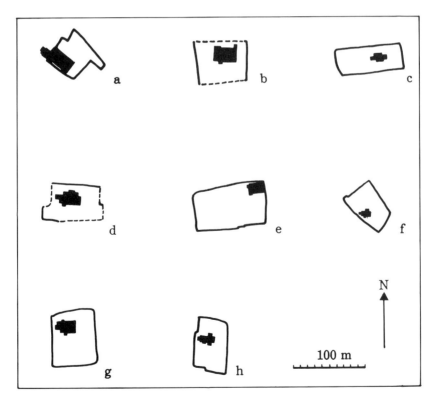

Fig. 11.3 *Churchyards of probable post-Norman Conquest origin.*
a. St Mary Magdalene, Launceston; b. St Stephen by Saltash; c. Forrabury Church, Boscastle
(church sites associated with Norman castles and towns); d. Tywardreath; e. St Thomas by Launceston;
f. Temple (church sites associated with post Conquest establishments); g. Lelant; h. Gwithian
(early Christian foundations on 'new' sites).

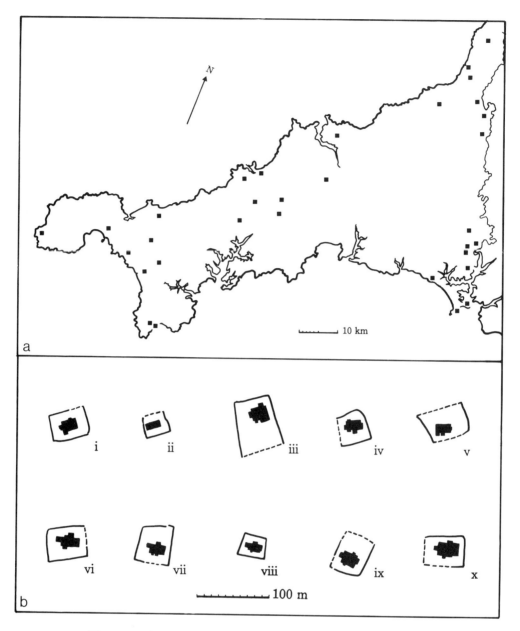

Fig. 11.4a *Distribution of rectilinear churchyards in Cornwall*
Fig. 11.4b *Plans of selected rectilinear churchyards: i St Dominick; ii Boyton; iii Maker;*
iv Sheviock; v Lawhitton; vi Ladock; vii Cubert; viii Sennen; ix Ludgvan; x St Enoder.

sides or hillslopes, and not in valley bottoms, in
contrast with the *lanns* discussed below.

WEST CORNISH RECTILINEAR YARDS
(Fig. 11.4b)
Comparison of the physical characteristics of the
east Cornish rectilinear yards with those of west
Cornwall suggests that the latter could also be of
relatively late, pre-Norman origin. The shapes of
the churchyards are very similar (for example,
compare Boyton with Sennen or St Dominick
with Ladock) and they generally occupy similar
valley side or upland locations. Their pre-

Norman date is supported by the fact that
Heglosenuder, 'the church of Enoder' is recorded
as a manor in Domesday Book (Thorn and Thorn
1979, 4, 12) and *Latoc* (Ladock) is mentioned in
the tenth-century List (Olson and Padel 1986,
52); but only one (Cubert) has an inscribed stone
and a name in *lann* and hence evidence of a
fifth- to seventh-century origin. Half of this
group can be associated with a manor but only
Ludgvan and Withiel churches are named after
the manor; and, whereas in east Cornwall the
manorial centre and church are usually close
together, in the west the two are generally

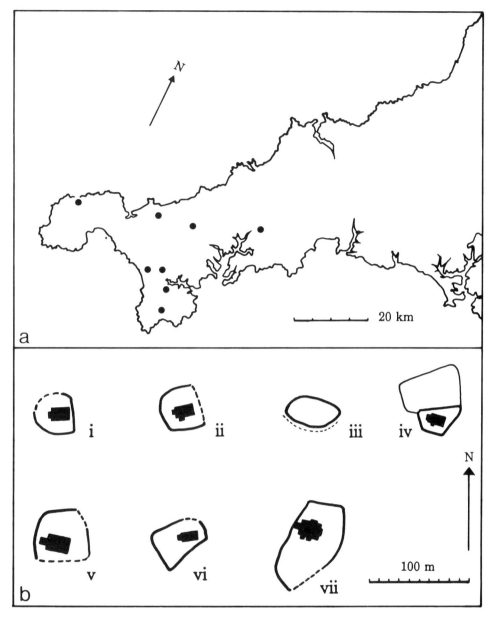

Fig. 11.5a *Distribution of church and chapel sites with a name in* merther.
Fig. 11.5b *Plans of the enclosures at church and chapel sites with a name in* merther. *i St Martin in Meneage* (Merther-anowe *(1407)* or Merther Mylor *(1328))*; *ii Merther; iii Merther Euny; iv Morvah* (Merthyr); *v Redruth* (Merther-euny *1301)*; *vi Ruan Major* (Merther *1329)*; *vii Sithney* (Merthersitheny *1230).*

between half a mile and a mile apart. The fact that a high proportion of the manors involved were owned in 1066 by St Petroc's church may suggest that this establishment – the most important ecclesiastical body in Cornwall in Domesday Book – was involved in their foundation. All of the churches in this group are dedicated to Celtic saints, and several have Cornish ecclesiastical place-names; but the place-names are (with the exception mentioned) always in *eglos* and the dedications are mostly to obscure Cornish saints.

In conclusion, comparison of these two groups

of rectilinear yards suggests that both could represent relatively late pre-Norman foundations of churches by either secular or lay authorities, but there appear to be differences, which may be cultural, in the way the foundations were made.

Merthers and Rounds

Another group of church sites may be singled out on the basis of their place-name and because one in the group, Merther Euny in Wendron, has been excavated. This small oval chapel yard, located on a spur above a deep valley, was dug in the 1960s by Charles Thomas (1968a; 1968b). His excavation showed, contrary to expectation, that the site was not a purpose-built Christian enclosure of early date. Instead, it originated as an Iron Age enclosed settlement or round, which was deserted in the second century AD and not reoccupied for Christian purposes until at least the tenth century.

There are indications that the eight other sites with a name in *merther* may likewise be relatively late; in addition, the form of their enclosures (Fig. 11.5b) and their invariably upland locations indicates that any of the *merthers* could in theory be on the site of an earlier round. As far as date is concerned, the fact that there are no instances of *merther* place-names in east Cornwall, where the English were well-established by the time Merther Euny was founded, may be relevant (although Charles Thomas' (1977) suggestion that the use of *merther* was simply a fashion restricted in time and space would also help to explain the westerly distribution). On the other hand, one (Redruth) is associated with a possible Early Christian memorial (Tangye 1985). In common with the west Cornish churches in rectilinear yards discussed above, the majority of *merthers* are dedicated to thoroughly local saints of whom four are traditionally said to have been martyrs, even though only one of these sites had a shrine. Thus an alternative meaning for *merther*, more in keeping with the evidence, might be 'chapel (with burial ground) in honour of a locally popular saint or martyr' (cf. Henderson, C.G. 1953–6; 1957–60, 350). The status implied in the use of the term chapel rather than church to describe these sites reflects the fact that of the nine Cornish *merthers* only three were full parish churches, whereas five were chapels. The site to which the ninth referred is lost.

Rounds and Churches

Rounds are the typical enclosed farming settlements of Cornwall in the Iron Age and Romano-British periods. These settlements of round or oval houses were enclosed by a substantial bank and ditch which is usually curvilinear but sometimes sub-rectangular. Hundreds are known in Cornwall, of all shapes and sizes (Johnson and Rose 1982, Figs 2 and 3). Rounds are typically located, like that at Merther Euny, on spurs or prominently on hillslopes. On excavation, some prove to have been occupied into the sixth or seventh centuries (Trethurgy: Miles, H. and Miles, T. 1973; and Grambla:

Saunders 1972), and rounds may still therefore have been the predominant settlement type when the earliest Christian sites were being established.

Because of Charles Thomas' discoveries at Merther Euny, it is necessary to consider the possibility that any curvilinear churchyard on a spur or high hillslope could be a reused round.

St Dennis is one example of a church which is almost certainly sitting within an earlier enclosure. It stands on a conical hilltop, within a perfectly circular churchyard, outside which excavation in the 1960s established the existence of a second concentric rampart (Thomas, C. 1965). All these features suggest an Iron Age hillfort, which is confirmed in the name of the site, Dennis being presumably derived from Cornish *dynas*, 'fort'. Charles Thomas' excavation, and another carried out more recently by Cornwall Archaeological Unit after the church had been gutted by fire, failed to locate any evidence for early medieval activity (Annual Report 1985–6, 19–20). It seems more probable that the church was established within the ramparts of the hillfort around the time of the Norman Conquest to serve the lords of the nearby Domesday manor of Domellick (C. Thomas, pers. comm.). The name of Domellick (*Dimelihoc*, 1086: Thorn and Thorn 1979, 5, 24, 11) presumably also refers to the fort.

The excavation at St Buryan, mentioned earlier, also provided the opportunity to test the theory that curvilinear churchyards in prominent upland locations may be reusing prehistoric settlement enclosures. The excavation was moderately successful in this respect. Behind the nineteenth-century wall were the remains of three earlier boundaries, of which the earliest was a stone-faced bank and ditch. A single sherd of Romano-British pottery was found in the ditch silts. Unfortunately, no evidence was found to suggest when the site was converted into a Christian enclosure (Preston-Jones 1987).

The possibility that many churches may be occupying pre-Christian earthworks is seen strikingly in Fig. 11.6, where a selection of rounds are compared with a number of curvilinear churchyards. The similarity of form between the two types of site emphasizes the fact that any church in Cornwall in a curvilinear enclosure on a spur, hillslope or hill top may have a round or hillfort as a churchyard. The example of Merther Euny, where the round was not reoccupied until about the tenth century, indicates that such churches are not necessarily very early foundations.

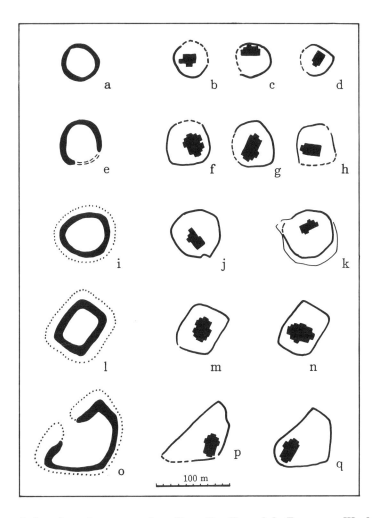

Fig. 11.6 *Rounds and churchyards compared: a. Tregullas Round; b. Zennor; c. Warbstow; d. St Martin in Meneage (Merther-anowe, 1407 or Merther Mylor, 1328); e. Trewannion Gate Round; f. Breage (Eglosbrek, 1181); g. St Buryan (Eglosberrie, 1086); h. Redruth (Merther-euny, 1301); i. Castle Fust; j. St Tudy (Ecglostudic, 1086); k. Bosence Round; l. St Hilary; m. Menheniot; n. Crenver Round; o. Antony; p. St Teath. Plans of rounds derived from Johnson and Rose 1982, fig 3.*

In fact, it is notable that very few of the churchyards which could be reused rounds have evidence of an early origin. Of about 40 potential reused rounds, only four have a name in *lann* and only two have Early Christian memorials — the two memorial stones being at two of the *lann*-named church sites (Lewannick and Madron/Landithy). On the other hand, like the rectilinear yards of west Cornwall, a relatively high proportion (approximately 25%) have a name in *eglos* and most are dedicated to obscure Cornish saints, though there is also a notable group with Breton connections (including Budock, Corentin, Melaine, Clether, Tudy). Two, or possibly three, of the dedications associated with upland churches in curvilinear yards are recorded in the tenth-century list of saints' names (*Gerent, Berion, Erbec*: Olson and Padel

1986, 45–9, 86), presumably indicating that the sites concerned were well-established by that date.

Lanns

Up to this point, a total of about 80 church sites have been discussed which, on the whole, need not be of very early Christian origin. It is now time to look more closely at those which may belong to the earlier phases of Christianity in Cornwall: that is, places with a name in *lann*.

We have seen that *lann* is found as the name of approximately 50 church sites in Cornwall (see Padel 1976–7, 17–9 for a list) and as the name of a similar number of secular settlements. The place-name is believed to have originally denoted an enclosure, although it later acquired the meanings of monastery and cemetery. It is possible that the shape of churchyards with a name in *lann* actually reflects the form of the original, purpose-built, Christian enclosure. Fig. 11.2 shows that the enclosures of church sites with a name in *lann* are overwhelmingly oval (40%) or sub-rectangular (26%) and hardly ever truly circular or rectilinear. A selection is illustrated in Fig. 11.7.

The table (Fig. 11.2) also shows that the locations of *lann* sites are generally very different from those of other groups discussed above, with 42% on a valley bottom and only 8% on a hilltop or plateau. Over 40% are close to creeks, estuaries or navigable waters and they are frequently at excellent natural harbours.

Landulph, for example, was formerly at the head of a small creek of the Tamar Estuary which, in the later medieval period, was a flourishing point of embarkation for pilgrims travelling to Compostella. The twelfth-century 'Life' of Ke describes Old Kea or *Landegei* as 'the port of Landegu' (Doble 1929, 11); and during the later medieval period, the ports at Padstow (*Languihenoc*) and Fowey (*Langorthou*) thrived to the extent that they became chartered boroughs. The distribution map (Fig. 11.8) emphasizes this. *Lann*-named churches are concentrated particularly around the harbours of the rivers Fal, Helford and Fowey on the south coast, and in the estuaries of the Hayle, Gannel, Camel and Bude rivers on the north.

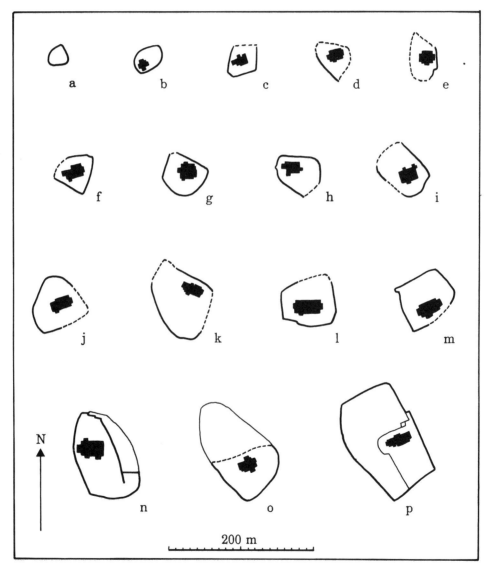

Fig. 11.7 *Plans of selected church sites with a name in* lann: *a. Helland, Mabe (*hen lann: non parochial); b. Lamorran; c. St Michael Caerhayes (Lanvyhaill, 1473–8); d. Mabe (Lavabe, 1640); e. Lanhydrock; f. Lansallos; g. Lewannick; h. Landulph; i. Gwennap (Lawenep, 1444); j. Feock (La Feock); k. St Just in Roseland (Lansioch, 1202); l. St Keverne (Lannachebran, 1086); m. St Kew (Landochou, C10); n. Probus (Lanbrebois, 1086); o. Mylor (Lawithick); p. Crantock (Langorroch, 1086).*

In fact the combination of an oval or sub-rectangular enclosure and a valley-bottom location, possibly near tidal waters, is such a distinctive characteristic of churches with a name in *lann* that for any church with similar attributes but no *lann* name, it seems reasonable to suggest that the *lann* name has been lost. It will be shown below that the postulated loss of a name in *lann* has been more frequent at the less important sites.

Some other features which do not appear to be significant of *lanns* as a whole, when looking along the *'lann*-line' of Fig. 11.2, acquire an enhanced significance when the question is not 'how many *lanns* possess feature x' but instead, 'how many sites with feature x are also *lanns*'? For example, only 16% of *lanns* are recorded in Domesday Book as the site of a religious community, yet altogether 27% of the Domesday communities have a name in *lann*. Similarly, it may be significant that 50% of Early Christian memorials and 46% of Saxon period monuments are at churches with a name in *lann*. Returning to features of location, it is notable that *lanns* are found more frequently in a valley head than any other group — apart from oval churchyards!

Where *lann* occurs in the name of a secular settlement it is generally assumed to denote the former existence of a Christian enclosure which went out of use at an early date, perhaps because the site was not of sufficient importance to acquire full parochial status. Despite the rather peculiar fact pointed out by Padel (1985, 144) that there is a lack of coincidence between non-parochial *lann* names and documented chapel sites, finds at two have helped to confirm the assumption. Building work at Lanvean in St Mawgan in Pydar uncovered a series of east-west oriented long-cist burials, remains of buildings, and the ditch of an enclosure (Wailes 1955–6). At Helland in Mabe (**hen-lann*, the 'old or disused *lann*'), a cross, a font, a stoup, and old building materials were found when digging a small, oval piece of raised ground known as the 'Graveyard' and said locally to be the site of an old Priory (Henderson, C.G. 1953–6; 1957–60, 316). Helland is the only non-parochial *lann* where the plan of the enclosure survives (Fig. 11.7a): with an area of only 0.05 ha, it is very small indeed.

As the term *lann* could be used to refer to a site like Helland which (at least officially) went out of use before Norman times, or to a community of sufficient importance to be recorded in Domesday Book, considerable variety is to be expected in the individual sites. Thus, although the average area of a *lann* is 0.31ha,

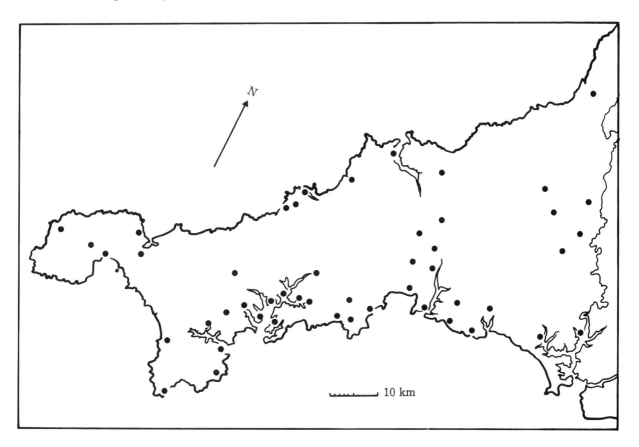

Fig. 11.8 Distribution of parish church sites with a place-name in lann

they range from only 0.05ha to over 0.9ha; and Figure 11.7 is also designed to show that on the whole, there is a close relationship between the size of a *lann* and its status. Helland, the non-parochial *lann* described above, has the smallest enclosure. Lanhydrock, Mabe (*Lavabe*) and St Michael Caerhayes (*Lanvyhaill*), *lanns* with smaller-than-average enclosures, are both chapelries. Lewannick is typical of most Cornish churches in that it is neither mother church nor chapelry, and its oval churchyard is very close in size to the average Cornish churchyard of 0.28 ha, though it is slightly smaller than the average *lann*. Like Lewannick, Lansallos (area 0.18 ha) is neither mother church nor chapelry, but it is uniquely documented as a land-owning church in a charter of the time of Athelstan (Padel 1978). The church must have been robbed of its lands soon after, for *Lansalhus* was a secular manor in Domesday Book (Thorn and Thorn 1979, 5, 3, 7). The churches with the largest enclosures are Mylor (*Lawithick*) and St Just-in-Roseland (*Lansioch*), both mother churches, and Probus (*Lanbrebois*) and Crantock (*Langorroch*), both of which had a land-owning religious community in 1086 (Thorn and Thorn 1979, 4, 24; 4, 25). Later traditions of seven churchyards, seven altars, and a chapel within the graveyard at Crantock suggest that this was a particularly complex site (Olson 1982). This relationship between size and status is perhaps not surprising, since *lanns* which are not on spurs or hilltops are likely to be purpose-built enclosures, designed to meet the requirements of their communities for space. The larger the community, the larger the enclosure needed.

It then follows that, if purpose-built and if not remodelled at some stage in their history, the large enclosures are likely to have been sites of importance from their foundation; and the fact that the enclosures of the Domesday communities are, on average, the largest of any group, must imply that only the most important sites retained their land-owning status until 1086. However, there are a few places with large enclosures but no documented significance. Might these also have once housed land-owning religious communities which lost an originally higher status at an early stage? St Anthony in Meneage (for which see Olson 1975), Veryan and Feock would be examples. Equally, might churches with enclosures of comparable size to Lansallos also once have been land-owning and capable of receiving, as an endowment, the estate of another *lann*, as happened at Lansallos?

A further aspect to the relationship between *lann* size and status involves location. Fig. 11.9

Fig. 11.9 Table showing the percentage occurrence of lann *sites in various locations*

	Valley Bottom No.(%) Size (ha)	Valley Head No.(%) Size (ha)	Valley side No.(%) Size (ha)	Nr navigable Water No.(%) Size (ha)
LANN	54% 0.36	20% 0.33	26% 0.31	64% 0.34
Poss. LANN	38% 0.25	31% 0.15	31% 0.22	42% 0.22

shows that slight differences exist in the average sizes of sites in different locations, the largest percentage of sites and the largest enclosures being on a valley bottom. In contrast, there are fewer *lanns*, and they tend to be slightly smaller, in more elevated locations, on a valley side or in a valley head. *Lanns* on spurs, hilltops or plateaus are omitted as they could include some reused prehistoric enclosures. The table also includes possible *lanns*, that is the curvilinear or sub-rectangular churchyards which are not in a location where they might be reused rounds. The average size of the whole group is smaller than that of the average *lann* (0.22ha as opposed to 0.31ha); but the relationship of size to location is similar in that the larger enclosures are again on a valley bottom and the smaller ones on a valley side or in a valley head.

A number of conclusions may be drawn from this. The first is that the sites which have possibly lost a name in *lann* are generally the smaller and less significant ones, in the more exposed topographical locations. Secondly, the choicest location for a *lann* appears to have been a valley bottom, for on the whole, the larger, more important enclosures, are found here. Moreover, the fact that 64% of the *lann*-named church sites considered in Fig. 11.9 with an average size of 0.34ha, are also close to navigable waters, suggests that this was also a favoured option. The relationship is exemplified by Mylor and Mabe churches. Mylor, originally *Lawithick*, the 'wooded *lann*', sits by the water's edge at an excellent natural harbour in the sheltered Fal Estuary, its large oval churchyard (0.93ha) now engulfed by the trappings of one of Cornwall's busiest marinas. Mylor is the mother church of Mabe, originally *Lavabe*, which stands 6km inland, on an open hillside at 122m OD, on the edge of a bleak granite upland. Mabe has a small enclosure of only 0.17ha. A temporal relationship may also be indicated. Both Mylor and Mabe are *lanns*, and therefore relatively early foundations. But probability suggests that the first to be founded was Mylor, with Mabe established somewhat later, perhaps as a daughter house to serve a remote rural area.

Dedications are also intertwined in these size/status relationships. It was mentioned earlier that Celtic dedications may be divided into two types, namely the purely local saints and the 'inter-Celtic' saints — ie. those found in other Celtic countries. It was also observed that the local saints are frequently associated, in west Cornwall, with churches in rectangular yards, or churches possibly in reused rounds, occasionally with a name in *eglos* or *merther*. A small proportion of the churches which may be in reused rounds are dedicated to Breton saints. But when looking at dedications associated with *lanns*, a rather different pattern emerges. In the first place, although dedications to Cornish saints are in the majority, there is nonetheless a substantial proportion (42%) with dedications to

inter-Celtic saints. In the second place, *lanns* dedicated to inter-Celtic saints have much larger enclosures (average 0.38ha) than those associated with purely local saints (average 0.3ha) and the implication of this, in view of the foregoing discussion, must be that the *lanns* dedicated to inter-Celtic saints are generally the more important, perhaps earlier, foundations. On looking in more detail at the inter-Celtic saints, further features of interest emerge. Two of these saints have parallels in Brittany (Mawseth, Melor) and four others have very tentative parallels (Moren, Dilic, Seoc, Livri); two are also found in England (Ke, Probus); two are saints of Welsh origin who achieved their greatest renown in Brittany (Winwaloe, Samson); but the remaining eight, who include Carantoc, Piran, Docco, Petroc and Mawgan, are all placed by tradition and parallel place-names in Wales. The majority of these are found along the north Cornish coast and three were at places of sufficient importance to survive as land-owning communities until 1086. Thus if, as Wendy

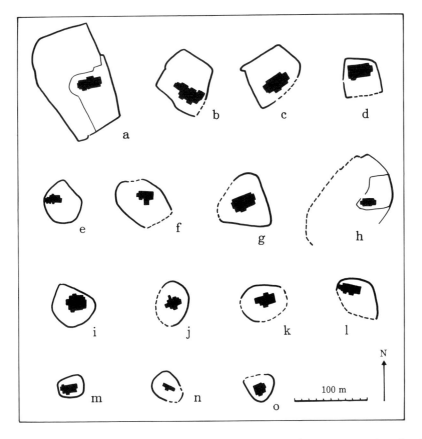

Fig. 11.10 *Correlations between enclosures and dedications. Enclosures associated with dedication to saints of Welsh origin: a. Crantock; b. St Breock; c. St Kew (*Landocco); d. St Gluvias. Enclosures associated with saints of Cornish origin: e. St Erney; f. Mevagissey; g. Lanteglos by Fowey (St Wyllow); h. St Anthony in Roseland (Entenin). Enclosures with dedication to Winwaloe: i. Lewannick; j. Landewednack; k. St Winnow; l. Poundstock; m. Towednack; n. Tremaine; o. Gunwalloe*

Davies suggests, dedications may be proprietorial and reflect the ownership of church-sites (Davies, W. 1978a, 142–6), this evidence may point to a strong and early presence from Wales in the establishment of Christianity in Cornwall. The fact that the distribution of dedications to saints of Welsh origin at both *lanns* and possible *lanns* agrees closely with the distribution of Early Christian memorials, which may also be of Welsh inspiration (with the notable exception of West Penwith), lends some support to this suggestion.

The enclosures associated with 'Welsh' *lanns* and possible *lanns* are markedly sub-rectangular, in contrast with the *lanns* of Cornish or other saints (Fig. 11.10). A number of very large oval enclosures with dedications to Cornish saints are found on or near the south coast, particularly around the Fal Estuary, perhaps suggesting that the impetus behind Christian foundations here was largely indigenous. With one exception, Breton saints do not seem to be significantly associated with foundations of *lanns* in Cornwall. The exception is in the dedications to Winwaloe, which are widely spread over Cornwall, yet present a uniform group comprising small and medium-sized oval enclosures. In fact, no other Celtic saint has more dedications in Cornwall — not even the county's most famous saints, Piran and Petroc. This perhaps reflects the claim made in the Life of Guenael, who succeeded Winwaloe as Abbot of Landévennec (Winwaloe's principal foundation in Brittany), that the former saint 'founded in Great Britain and Ireland, by miracles and apostolic labour, two famous monasteries, and afterwards others to the number of fifty' (Doble 1940, 47).

A final feature of *lanns* and possible *lanns* is that a number have evidence of an outer enclosure or enclosures. The clearest example is at St Mawgan in Meneage, a mother church (Fig. 11.11a). Here, an Early Christian memorial of possibly seventh-century date, which may be *in situ*, sits on the outer boundary, at the point where it is crossed by the main road to St Mawgan church (Macalister 1945, no. 447). The way the church is not centrally placed but lies on the edge of the outer enclosure compares with other examples in both Cornwall and Wales (Butler 1979). Documentary evidence suggests a similar feature at Padstow, the primary centre of St Petroc's cult, for his early fourteenth-century Life says that the saint 'surrounded the limits of his lands with very long ditches dug deep like valleys, the ruins of which remain to this day' (Doble 1938a, 14n). Around Padstow are several concentric boundaries, any or all of which may

have had a former significance in this context. They may alternatively have marked the limits of Padstow's privileged, extended sanctuary (Cox 1911, 220–4). Another Cornish church with a privileged sanctuary, said to date from a gift of Athelstan, was St Buryan (Cox 1911, 214–24). The extent of St Buryan's sanctuary is actually shown on a map of the reign of Elizabeth I; it evidently enclosed the entire village around St Buryan church, but is not easy to trace on the ground (Crofts 1955, 35–8). St Mawgan in Meneage, Padstow and St Buryan are important places, but this phenomenon is by no means confined to sites of higher status. Included with the examples illustrated in Fig. 11.11 is Mabe, the chapelry of Mylor which has already been referred to. Higher and Lower Spargo, the farms sitting on the outer boundary to the east and west of Mabe church, may hint at the nature of the boundary here, as their name is derived from Cornish *spern*, 'thorn', and *cor*, 'hedge' (Padel 1985, 65, 210).

The function of these outer boundaries is uncertain. They may, as at St Buryan and Padstow, be marking the limit of the ecclesiastical estate or the area over which a church's protection or sanctuary extended, or they may simply be defining the extent of enclosed agricultural land about the settlement. They presumably compare in some way with the indications of outer ecclesiastical boundaries on Welsh and Irish sites (Hughes, K. 1966, 148–9; Norman and St Joseph 1969, 98–119; Butler 1979).

Conclusion

Up to this point, the topographical, monumental and place-name evidence for church-sites in Cornwall has been explored. It has emerged that many of these, if not most, may be on sites of early medieval origin, and that the form of their present churchyards may reflect the shape of the original enclosure; but there are contrasts amongst the enclosures which may in part be explained as developments taking place during the six centuries (fifth to eleventh) over which the early medieval period extends.

In this concluding section, the material will be drawn together into a chronological sequence, and fleshed out by looking briefly at other, non-parochial sites. The result is a model for the development of Christian sites in Cornwall which is now in need of testing by excavation.

So far, there is no sign that Roman period

Lower Spargo

Higher Spargo

Inscribed stone

Camel Estuary

N

500 m

a

b

c

Fig. 11.11 *Early ecclesiastical sites with other boundaries: a. St Mawgan in Meneage; b. Mabe; c. Padstow*

Cornwall was Christian (Thomas, C. 1981a, Figs 14, 15, 16). The earliest evidence for Christianity in Cornwall is a small Chi-Rho incised stone of possible fifth-century date built into the porch of Phillack church (Thomas, C. 1963, 11). This stone suggests the direct influence of Continental ideas (Olson 1989, 41), which could have been transported to Cornwall with the imported Mediterranean pottery known from many sites in Western Britain and most notably Tintagel (see Thomas, C. 1988a and Fulford 1989 for the latest consideration of the nature of this contact), but other evidence indicates that the more influential source of Christianity in Cornwall lay to the north. There is evidence for Christianity at an earlier date in Wales, and Olson has suggested that Wales may have been the nursery for monasticism in western Britain (Olson 1989, 48–50). Dedications to Welsh saints along the north Cornish coast suggest that a number of Cornish church sites may have originated as daughter houses of Welsh monastic communities, and inscribed stones with ogam and Irish personal names indicate an actual migration to Cornwall of probably Christian people, originally of Irish descent, but from Wales (Thomas, C. 1957–8, 64). Two of the earliest Christian memorials in Cornwall commemorate people with Irish names using unambiguously Christian formulae, in both Latin and ogam. They are at Lewannick — a church with a name in *lann* and a raised oval churchyard. Enclosures called *lann* are a feature of early Christianity in Wales (see Roberts above), as in Cornwall, and it therefore appears that with Christianity came not merely the faith, but also the associated monuments, site types, place-names, and presumably also the method, so well-testified in Wales (eg. Davies, W. 1979b; 1978a, especially 161–3), by which parts of large estates could be alienated to provide support for the new communities. Evidence from Wales suggests that the new Christian foundations were settlements, rather than isolated churches (Davies, W. 1982a, 143), and they may therefore be expected to reflect the nature of contemporary settlement which in Cornwall and in parts of Wales (notably the south-west) was located in defensive enclosures (Johnson and Rose 1982; James and Williams 1982). Although the normal name for these sites was *lann*, some early Christian sites had or acquired a name in *eglos* (plus topographical element) whilst others, which may have once been called *lann*, appear to have lost their early place-name.

It is probable that the predominantly coastal and estuarine distribution of *lanns* reflects the fact that Christianity was first introduced from abroad, and then continued to spread and thrive by water-borne contact. But these foundations were not always at newly established sites. Occasional instances have evidence of a pre-Christian burial ground in the vicinity (Olson 1982, 179–81; Thomas, C. 1963, 10; 1971, 57). The number of place-names in *lann* in Cornwall, both parochial and non-parochial (about 100 in total), together with the church sites which may have lost a name in *lann*, suggests a rapid proliferation of sites. Along the north coast, many of the earliest foundations may have been due to Welsh influence, but the total distribution shows that the greatest multiplication of *lanns* was in the more fertile and heavily settled parts of south Cornwall. Here, church dedications suggest that some of the impetus came from Wales and Brittany, but was mostly indigenous.

Where the forms of the early Christian enclosures survive, in parish churchyard boundaries, a considerable variety in both size and shape is apparent, the different sizes seeming to reflect the status of the site and possibly the size of the original community. There is some evidence that the larger enclosures were amongst the earliest and most important foundations. Secondary foundations or daughter houses tended to be located further inland, away from the favoured estuaries. For the most part, their dedications are to obscure local individuals. There is no contemporary information about the nature of these sites.

It is possible that in the early days of Christianity, burial in a *lann* was a privilege reserved for clerics and important lay-persons only (Davies, W. 1982a, 185–7; see also H. James above). So how are the rest of the population to be accounted for, at least as far as their burial requirements are concerned? Again, it is necessary to fall back on the Welsh evidence, which suggests that burial in wild, isolated places or in the homestead was the preferred option (Davies, W. 1982a, 185–7) — a suggestion which finds reflection in the distribution of the Early Christian memorials in Cornwall. Approximately half of the Cornish memorials are associated with a church site, but the remainder are found by ridgeways or fords where they would be both isolated, yet in spots frequented by travellers. A number are on or close to boundaries where they may also have had a territorial significance (Charles-Edwards 1976, 84). The memorials at Lancarffe and Rialton are at settlements of undoubted early medieval origin (Preston-Jones and Rose 1986, 157). Around Endellion and Tintagel churches are extensive cemeteries of long-cists (Trudgian 1987; Thomas, C. 1988b), which by analogy with similar cemeteries elsewhere, may represent early Christian burial grounds for lay populations. At Tintagel, recent excavation has shown that the cemetery also included special graves, visible as low mounds (J. Nowakowski, pers. comm.). It is possible that these did not begin as early enclosures, but as cemeteries which acquired a church and parochial status later, because of their funerary tradition. Other such sites may well have existed but would have left no trace if stone cists were not used, as bone dissolves rapidly in the acid soils of Cornwall. The use of stone cists certainly appears to have had a limited distribution (Preston-Jones 1984, Fig. 8).

The pastoral care of the secular population may also have been catered for by places with a name in *eglos*, usually combined with a personal name. Like the small secondary *lanns*, these are generally located further inland; but unlike the majority of *lanns* they are found on well-drained valley sides, spurs or uplands. Those on valley sides generally have regular rectilinear yards while those in the more prominent upland locations have curvilinear enclosures. Excavations at St Buryan and Merther Euny suggest that some of the latter may be reused rounds and that some could be relatively late foundations. Thus, although a few have a name in *lann* or an Early Christian memorial stone, they may on the whole represent a later phase than *lanns*, designed to meet the needs of lay populations. Associated dedications suggest that this was mainly an internal development, but with some influence from Brittany.

The rectilinear yards may have been so-shaped because they reflect the shape of the building within. They would therefore be true churchyards, and if so, would represent a development whereby the church had superseded the enclosure as the most important aspect of a Christian site. Use of the term *eglos*, 'church', rather than *lann*, 'enclosure', may also suggest this. But at the same time, the fact that *Heglosenuder* was a manor in Domesday Book suggests that these churches might be land-owning, like the *lanns* (though not necessarily; *Heglosenuder* might simply have been a secular manor, named from the nearby church). The rectilinear churchyards of west Cornwall compare very closely with a group in east Cornwall which appear to reflect foundations of

churches or chapels at important English manors, perhaps from the eight or ninth century.

The limited evidence available from excavations suggests that during the latter part of the early medieval period other sites with sacred connotations such as holy wells were being elaborated with structures (Thomas, C. 1967a, 49, 81–2; 1967b; Pool and Russell 1968). Places with a name in *merther* may be part of this pre-Norman flowering of minor Christian sites. At Mawgan Porth, a cist-cemetery adjoined the tenth- to eleventh-century settlement (Bruce-Mitford 1956, 187–9), and other small local cemeteries may be indicated by the numerous examples of chapels with Celtic dedications or traditional, unlicensed burial grounds (Adams 1957, 49–50). In some places, there may eventually have been a very full provision of cemeteries (Preston-Jones and Rose 1986, 158, Fig. 4).

Beginning in the late ninth century, cross carving was also a late phenomenon. The earliest crosses compare very closely in concept with the inscribed stones, firstly in the fact that they are memorials, and secondly in that they are found not only in churchyards, but also out in the countryside, often by major routeways, and occasionally at manorial centres. A possibly eleventh-century memorial stone at Lanteglos by Camelford is a remarkable throw-back, for it commemorates people with English names, in the English language, but in thoroughly archaic Cornish style, with a vertically-written inscription (Okasha 1971, 90–1). Most pre-Norman crosses associated with churchyards are at sites with evidence of an early medieval origin, and the size of their enclosures indicates that it was generally the more important sites which were embellished in this way. The implication is that as Cornwall gradually came under English control, the Celtic Christian sites were not abolished but were taken over, and where appropriate, elaborated with new monuments.

But at the same time, it is clear that change was taking place. Whereas the place-name evidence alone suggests that there could have been over 100 land-owning religious communities in Cornwall in the early part of the early medieval period, by the time of Domesday Book, only a handful of the most important ones survived to be recorded. Most communities had disappeared, presumably as their estates were appropriated, first by the incoming English and then by the land-hungry Normans. Domesday Book actually bears witness to the despoliation of ecclesiastical lands when it records that the manor of St Neot, held in 1086 by the Count of Mortain, had formerly belonged to the clergy of St Neot. The Count left the clerics with a mere acre or two (Thorn and Thorn 1979, 4, 28) and not surprisingly, the community at St Neot is never heard of again. Gradually, therefore, the communities would have been replaced by a parish priest supported by payments of tithe, burial fees, and a small area of glebe. Inevitably, this process would have been linked with the closer definition of parochial boundaries and the demise of small local cemeteries.

By 1086, those communities which had survived had become more than simple religious settlements. At such sites, the need to furnish the wordly requirements of a non-agriculturally productive community may have encouraged a nucleation of settlement about the church (Preston-Jones and Rose 1986, 164). The lands of

St Petroc's Church were extensive and must have required a considerable team of estate managers (Thorn and Thorn 1979, 4, 3–4, 22). Of the five markets recorded in Cornwall in 1086, four were at ecclesiastical centres and two, St Stephen by Launceston and Bodmin, can be regarded as boroughs (Thorn and Thorn 1979, 4, 2; 4, 3). At St Stephens, which had been minting coins since 976 (Carlyon-Britton 1906; 1908), the ecclesiastical enclosure and the enclosure of the early town apparently lay side by side (Fig. 11.12). But in 1066, these urban and proto-urban places also became victims of Norman rapacity: Domesday Book records that the Count of Mortain took away St Stephen's market: he put it in his castle. St German's Sunday market had been reduced to nothing by the Count's market nearby, on the same day, in another of his new castles (Thorn and Thorn 1979, 2, 4).

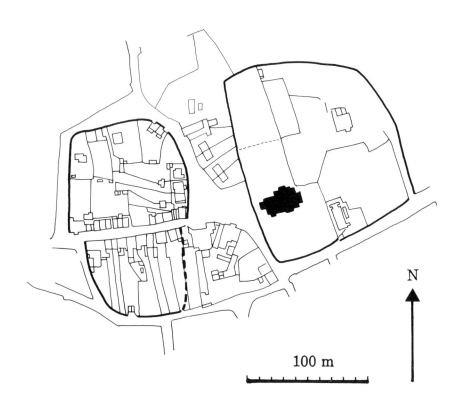

Fig. 11.12 *Ecclesiastical and early town enclosures at St Stephen by Launceston.*
The ecclesiastical enclosure is on the east, the town on the west; the south-eastern (dashed)
boundary of the town's enclosure is derived from 18th-century maps (see Sheppard 1980, 79–80).

Burials and Cemeteries in Scotland

Elizabeth Alcock

Varied is probably the most appropriate description of the grave rites of the period AD 400–1100 in Scotland. This paper concentrates on the earlier part of that span, and ignores the pagan graves of Anglo-Saxon Northumbria, and the Viking graves of the north and west. It should also be noted here that the term 'Scotland' is a misnomer at this date; the ethnic division, in so far as it existed, was between the Picts, mainly in eastern areas, north of the Forth-Clyde line, and the Britons to the south of it. To this basic division were added the Scots of Dalriada in Argyll, and the Angles of Northumbria, who extended Bernicia north to the Forth and west to the Irish Sea. In neither case is there any reason to assume large-scale folk settlement, and the imposition of a military hegemony seems more probable.

The ecclesiastical picture is confused. Ninian reputedly came to a sub-Roman Christian community at Whithorn and evangelized the southern Picts (*Hist. Ecc.* iii 4, Colgrave and Mynors 1969); but we do not know exactly what area Bede implies by this term. Nor do we know how widely or permanently he evangelized this and other areas. Similarly, Columba brought Christianity to Iona in the later sixth century (*Vita Columb.* 4a, Anderson, A.O. and Anderson, M.O. 1961), and evangelized the northern Picts (*Vita Columb.* 78a, Anderson, A.O. and Anderson, M.O. 1961), but again we do not know the full extent or permanence of his influence. Finally Northumbrian Christianity reached British areas south of the Forth by the later seventh century (*Hist. Ecc.* iv 26, Colgrave and Mynors 1969; Thomas, C. 1984), and eastern areas of Pictland between then and the early eighth century (*Hist. Ecc.* v 21, Colgrave and Mynors 1969). Its influence was ultimately paramount, and thereafter the multiplicity of burial- and cemetery-types dies out.

We may begin our survey in the south-west. Here, the main cemeteries are of simple inhumations in dug graves*.[1] They occur at places such as Whithorn, the enclosed chapel site on Ardwall Island (Thomas, C. 1967c) and the cemetery in the hill-fort at Trohoughton (Simpson and Scott-Elliot 1964). Coffins have not normally been recognized; but at Whithorn six tree-trunk coffins* were found (Hill, P. 1987, 3; Hill, P. 1988, 2, 6–8), and the unlikelihood of wood being preserved makes it probable that other coffins were originally present. Cemeteries of this type occur elsewhere; at Iona (RCAHMS 1982), at Yeavering (Hope-Taylor 1977), just across the modern border in Northumberland, and at Kirkhill, St Mary's of the Rock, St Andrews (Wordsworth 1982). It is also probably true that many graveyards have interments of this period beneath later burials.

The burial ground at Port nam Mairtir, Iona (RCAHMS 1982), had five long-cists* included among the inhumations. On the east coast, St Mary's of the Rock, St Andrews (Wordsworth 1982), where over 350 graves have been excavated, had three long-cists and one coffin among the simple dug-graves, but two radiocarbon age-estimates suggest a late date for this cemetery, of the ninth to the fourteenth centuries. It is tempting to see the long-cists as the earliest features here; but with the site not yet fully published and only two radiocarbon age-estimates available, such an inference would be premature.

Long-cists were common in Fife: at St Andrews alone, there were six cemeteries of this type. A long-cist was essentially a stone box. The sides were made of one or, more probably, several slabs of stone placed upright; it usually, but not invariably, had a stone base made of further slabs; if it had a lid made of slabs lying from side-to-side across the top, it is frequently known as a lintel-grave*. The cist was not of a pre-ordained length; this was adjusted according to whether the burial was that of a man, woman or child. Sometimes the sides are parallel, but they more often taper slightly towards the feet. These graves can occur singly throughout the area of modern Scotland. Cemeteries also occur from Cowal and the Rhinns of Galloway in the west to Berwickshire and Kincardine in the east. The area where they cluster most tightly is, however, south of the Forth in the Lothians and North Berwickshire. The south and east coasts of Fife also carry concentrations (Henshall 1956, fig. 6). The graves are arranged in rows (sometimes side-by-side, and less usually head-to-toe). The head is almost invariably to the west or south-west. This, combined with the fact that at one of the first cemeteries to be excavated, that at Kirkliston near Edinburgh (Hutchison 1866), the cemetery was associated with an Early Christian [inscribed] monument*, the Catstane, has led, in the past, to their frequent identification as Christian.

Indeed, three factors combine to indicate such an interpretation: first: the orientation of the graves; the head is almost always in the west or between the west and south-west; second: the association of the cemetery in one and perhaps two cases with an Early Christian monument (the Catstane and, less certainly, the Yarrow

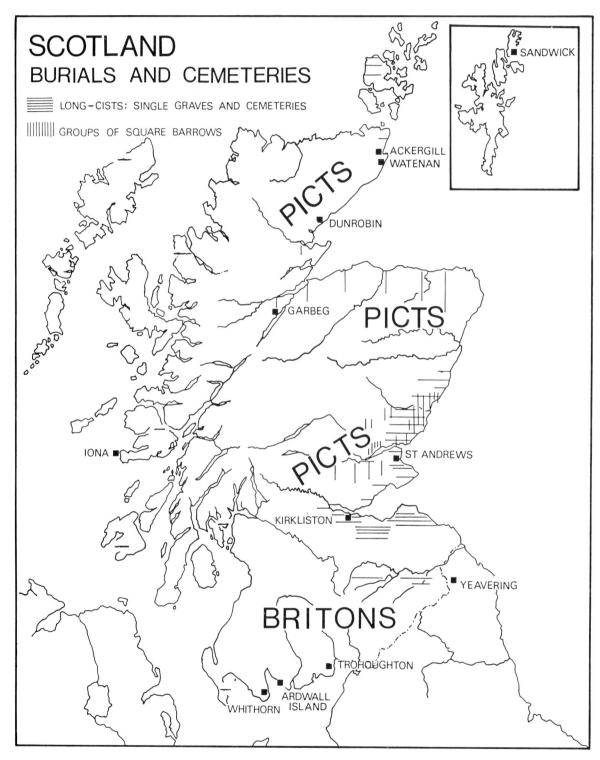

Fig. 12.1 Scotland: burials and cemeteries

stone (RCAHMS 1957)); and third: the absence of gravegoods. The last factor reinforces this interpretation; but, though the absence of gravegoods is a normal feature of Christian burial, it must also be remembered that other religions, for instance, that of the pre-Christian Picts, also buried without gravegoods. Their rarity may be more a reflection of the period than of Christianity.

The long-cist cemeteries are associated with one or two Early Christian monuments, and both individual long-cists and cemeteries are associated with Pictish incised slabs at, among other sites, Garbeg (Wedderburn and Grime 1984), Dairy Park, Dunrobin (Close-Brooks 1980), and Ackergill (Edwards, A.J.H. 1927). Long-cists may also be associated with low cairns, or they can also occur on ground which shows traces of either occupation or burial in the Bronze Age; for an accessible list see Henshall (1956 appendix). There may be stone-lined pits in the cemeteries or enclosing walls. All these features are so infrequent that it is difficult to see what, if any, importance was attached to them.

One absence from the list of associations must, however, be noted: no churches or chapels survive above ground in these cemeteries, nor have they been found in excavations. The only exceptions are where the main cemetery is late, eighth or ninth century. Indeed, have we been over-influenced by the Catstane? Relatively few cemeteries had been excavated by the early 1860s when it was first dug (Hutchison 1866). The excavation and publication of other cemeteries was frequently inadequate. The association of the Catstane with the adjacent graves was obvious and inevitable. From our greater knowledge, however, this interpretation needs reconsideration. The presence of the Catstane is certainly suggestive as proof of Christianity, but its presence may be coincidental, or it may have been erected by a descendant of the pagans originally buried in the cemetery to bring them the blessings of Christianity.

Two recent excavations may, however, give pointers worth noting. The latest work at the Catstane (Cowie 1978) has demonstrated a difference between the precise lines of graves lying side-by-side to the east of the stone and the more irregular arrangement of the graves around the stone itself, suggesting an almost circular lay-out. At Hallowhill, St Andrews (Proudfoot 1977), there are two graves which the recent excavator describes as pagan: one, a massive short cist, is accompanied by a bag with Roman bronzes, horse's teeth and quartz pebbles; the other, found in 1860, had 'a glass bowl, an iron knife and other items all now missing' and was also in a stone cist. At the Catstane, the differences in orientation have already been noted. Both at the Catstane and Hallowhill, the discrepant features may mean nothing, or they may be an indication that long-cist cemeteries began before the introduction of Christianity. Indeed, if the absence of churches, in contrast to their presence in the majority of dug-grave burial grounds, has any importance, then the main use of long-cist cemeteries was pre-Christian. The few examples of long-cists in dug-grave cemeteries may be merely the result of a clinging to old customs which would very shortly give way to new.

Some of these cemeteries, however, probably date from the third century onwards. The only method of dating is by radiocarbon age-estimates, but these are too imprecise to do more than confirm a mid-first millennium date. A large number of samples was collected at Hallowhill and indicate dates, uncalibrated, between the third and ninth centuries. At the Catstane, the cists were of both sandstone and mica-schist. Only bone in contact with mica-schist survived, so the dates given for five adjacent cists reflect the use of only one section of the cemetery. Three of the samples give uncalibrated dates for the period from the third to the sixth centuries, and the other two, from the late fourth to the ninth.

Long-cists are found both among the Britons and the Picts. Air photography over the last ten years has revealed another burial-type, which is, so far, confined to Pictland (Close-Brooks 1984). At the time of writing, this, the square-ditch barrow*, is most prominent in south-east Angus (Maxwell 1987, esp. fig. 3), with a handful in the area south of the Moray Firth. Further air photography might, however, alter the picture radically, particularly if it were allied to intensive field-work in areas unsuited to aerial survey. So far no square-ditch barrow found by air photography has been fully published.

The one excavation which has been adequately published is that at Garbeg in Inverness-shire (Wedderburn and Grime 1984), above the junction of Glen Urquhart and Loch Ness. This seems an atypical site because it is at a height of about 280m (925 feet) O.D., which is unusually high. Here, there was a cemetery containing square-ditch barrows which normally have causeways at the corners of the ditches, but, in one instance, small pillar stones. Round barrows, with both annular, and penannular ditches, lay among the square ones. An individual barrow may have part of its ditch in common with an adjacent one, whether round or square. The cairns are low, less than 0.45m in height, and they sometimes have a sizeable berm. The burial may be either in a long-cist or a simple dug-grave: both were present at Garbeg. Indeed, this site reveals very fully the variety of form of grave, cairn and encircling ditch which may be found on a single site.

Further north in Caithness, Sutherland, and the Northern Isles, there is what appears to be a variant of this type. There is the same mixture of low, square and round cairns but they are without ditches. There is even more variety in the construction of the grave itself, as is shown very clearly at Ackergill, Caithness (Edwards, A.J.H. 1927). Indeed, at Sandwick in Shetland (Bigelow 1984), one of a pair of cairns has no burial in it at all. The cairns themselves, in this northern group, have a kerb, and this is likely to have corner posts* and sometimes medial posts incorporated in it. What most clearly links these northern sites to the more southerly square-ditch barrows is the presence of Class I Pictish Stones. The sites where these have been recorded include Ackergill and Garbeg, as well as Watenan (Gourlay 1984) and Dairy Park, Dunrobin (Close-Brooks 1980). It cannot be proved that the stones were an integral part of the initial cairns rather than the result of subsequent field clearance, but the former seems likely. One feature which makes it more probable is that, further south, standing stones of Class I are increasingly being recorded in the centre of square-ditch barrows, with the remainder of the cemetery adjacent (Blackford, Perths.; Collessie, Fife; Edderton, Easter Ross). As yet air photographic cover is not sufficiently extensive to show whether this relationship is a normal Pictish custom but it seems probable.

The foregoing use of Pictish Class I stones may be related to the custom of using Class I slabs as either a side slab or cover slab in a cist. It seems very likely that such graves date from the period of currency of Class I Pictish stones, the fifth to seventh, or even eighth, centuries AD. The presence of the slabs proves that these graves cannot be earlier than this period. It is impossible to believe that people dug to depths approaching six feet (1.8m) in at least one instance, to attempt to insert a Pictish incised slab in an existing cist. Subsequent graves would have been Christian. The deliberate use of Pictish incised slabs in such Christian graves

seems unlikely. About a score of Class I Pictish stones are associated with graves, either those enclosed in square-ditch barrows or under cairns, or forming part of a cist. Another half dozen have turned up in old burial grounds. Deep ploughing and the escalating use of air-photography will doubtless increase this number.

The Pictish incised stones do indeed provide a link between all the varied graves of this period. The northern sites have both dug-graves and long-cists, which may either lie under cairns or be adjacent to them. Indeed, it is in the Pictish areas that the full variety of the grave-forms is most apparent. In all cases we have no immediate antecedents to those forms. Burials of any kind are notably rare in the period preceding the one considered here. By the Early Christian Period, almost two millennia had elapsed since any number or range of graves can be recognized. This makes the initial dates of the types considered here difficult to determine. It seems reasonable to assume that dug-grave cemeteries which are associated with churches are Christian. It could be argued that the churches were sited in places already devoted to religious purposes. But in these churchyard cemeteries, for instance Ardwall (Stewartry of Kirkcudbright) the graves are oriented parallel and close to the long walls of the chapel, suggesting a definite relationship. A more difficult case is that of Trohoughton (Simpson and Scott-Elliot 1964). Here, the graves were oriented either west-east or south/west-north/east. In the one example where skeletal material remained, teeth were found at the west end. The cemetery lay inside a hill-fort, but partly overlay a palisaded enclosure whose relation to the stone ramparts could not be determined. A first millennium AD date seems probable for the cemetery, though this does not necessarily imply that it was a Christian one.

It has already been noted that long-cist cemeteries may have pre- or non-Christian features. The presence of Bronze Age material on a number of sites suggests that there may be continuity of sanctity, though not of detectable use. At Hallowhill at least, the site would appear to have come into use at a date before the arrival of Christianity in Scotland. At Kirkliston too there are hints that the rigid orientation of the graves was not observed throughout the use of the site. Too much emphasis should not, perhaps, be laid on this: few early churches lie exactly east-west and, surely, we should not expect any greater precision in the lay-out of graves.

Another factor which may have affected the lay-out of a cemetery has to be remembered. This is the presence of a church or chapel. This would clearly provide a dominant orientation.

Only at St Mary's of the Rock, St Andrews (Wordsworth 1982) does the excavator give any estimate for the length of use of the site. He estimates that, during a period of 500 years, there were about 500 burials. Many long-cist cemeteries have interments numbered by the hundred. Whitekirk in Lothian has 500 plus. We do not know if this means one burial a year for 500 years (as St Mary's of the Rock averages) or 50 burials a year for ten years.

In the north, only one site has so far produced a published radiocarbon age-estimate: Dairy Park, Dunrobin (Close-Brooks 1980). Two samples were taken, giving an uncalibrated age-estimate of 515–715 ad. As with other examples, this is at two standard deviations. Dairy Park is an important site. Recent excavations have revealed a long-cist under a square cairn with a symbol stone lying on the cairn. In the mid-nineteenth century, another long-cist with a symbol stone for its capstone was found in the area (Kenworthy 1980), within 30m of the recent discovery. This was excavated but other graves of unrecorded form in the area were not disturbed. The juxtaposition of the two excavated graves suggests a link between the square cairns with symbol stones lying on them and the cists with symbol stones forming part of them. As in all other cases the symbol stones were of Class I.

Variety was mentioned in the opening sentence. It is peculiarly true of the northern cemeteries. Whereas in the Scottish and British areas, burials are either in simple dug-graves or stone-built long-cists, in the north, in Pictland, there are these two types, plus both square and round cairns; cairns which have kerbs, and may have both corner and medial posts; cairns which may have either square or round ditches; the square ditches having either causeways or corner posts, the round ones being either annular or penannular.

The burials discussed in this sketch include some that seem definitely Christian and others which are as certainly pagan. Lines have been drawn between these two types in the past. If this paper has a message, it is to suggest that the nature and attributes of the material rehearsed herein need to be looked at afresh. At the moment radiometric age-estimates tell us little that we did not already infer. It is to be hoped that scientists will devise a technique which can give reasonably precise dates in calendar years. For the time being the brackets are too wide to be of much help. When a satisfactory method of dating bone collagen or other bone material is found, then there will be a firmer basis for dating the graves and their contents discussed here. They may well be radically re-interpreted with more conviction.

Acknowledgements

I have to thank Mrs E.V.Proudfoot for providing a copy of the Hallowhill, St Andrews radiocarbon age-estimates in advance of publication. I must also thank Miss Loraine MacEwan for making a fair copy of the map, and finally my warmest thanks are due to my husband for constant help and encouragement.

GLOSSARY

corner post: a small pillar stone placed at the corner of a square barrow. It is sometimes placed in the ditch.

dug-grave: a grave dug directly into the soil and lined with neither stone nor wood. It may or may not contain a coffin.

Early Christian monument: a pillar or slab-like stone whose inscription shows Christian affinities.

lintel-grave: a grave with stone-lined walls and possibly also floor which is then roofed with slabs of stone.

long-cist: a grave which has its sides lined with stone slabs and in some instances its floor as well.

square-ditch barrow: a low barrow usually with a berm which is surrounded by a ditch. It frequently has causeways at the corners. It may have corner posts.

tree-trunk coffin: a coffin formed of a tree-trunk which has been halved and then hollowed out. This is then placed in a dug-grave.

Note
1 Because the terminology traditionally used in Northern Britain for types of burial differs in detail from that apparently current in England and Wales, a glossary is provided to the usage of asterisked forms in this paper.

Pagan and Christian Burial in Ireland during the first Millennium AD: Continuity and Change

Elizabeth O'Brien

In order to understand, or place in context, Early Christian burial rites and practices in Ireland, it is necessary to look back to the pre-Christian Iron Age. Burial rites established during the Iron Age did not change with the coming of Christianity in the fifth century. Indeed, it was not until the eighth or ninth century that burial in recognizably Christian ecclesiastical cemeteries became the norm. In Ireland a significant amount of information regarding death, burial, and associated phenomena such as the cult of relics, can be gleaned from datable early written sources,[1] and the value of such information is further enhanced when it is compared with the archaeological record.[2]

The Iron Age Background

The indigenous burial rite in Ireland in the Late Bronze Age was cremation, deposited either in an upright clay vessel or directly into a small pit, within, or at least associated with, a circular ring-ditched enclosure as exemplified by the Late Bronze Age burial at Rathgall, Co Wicklow (Raftery, B. 1976; 1981). A ring-ditched enclosure may be defined as a circular area, either flat or raised into a mound, surrounded by a fosse or ditch. This burial rite continued into the Iron Age with cremation deposits being placed either directly on the ground surface (and covered by a low mound), or in small pits within an enclosure and/or in the enclosing fosse. Variations on the ring-ditched enclosure are also found: the ring-barrow, a circular area, either flat or raised into a mound, surrounded by a fosse and outer bank, and the ring-cairn, a central cairn surrounded by an outer bank of stone.

A number of examples may be cited to illustrate the variations in monument type, burial rite and gravegoods. Site A, Carbury Hill, Co Kildare, and Grannagh and Oranbeg, Co Galway, are all examples of Iron Age ring-barrows. The ring-barrow at Site A, Carbury Hill enclosed a low central cairn containing a cremation deposit with a fused blue glass bead nearby, and further cremations in the fosse (Willmott 1938; Raftery, B. 1981; O'Brien 1990).

The ring-barrow (maximum diameter 15m) at Grannagh,[3] however, consisted of a low mound surrounded by a shallow fosse and low bank (Macalister 1916–7; Hawkes 1981; Raftery, B. 1981). It contained scattered cremations within the enclosure and four cremations in the fosse. Gravegoods accompanying the cremations included iron fragments, several types of bone and glass beads and fragments of bronze fibulae datable to the first centuries BC or AD (Hawkes 1981, 59–61). A similar though smaller (diameter 11m approx.) ring-barrow at Oranbeg[4] had one cremation in the enclosure and three in the fosse (Delaney 1970; Raftery, B. 1981). Gravegoods (all from the fosse) comprised five tiny blue glass beads, 77 tiny yellow glass beads, one tiny bronze knobbed rod or toggle, and three fragments of striated bronze armlet.

A number of sites include burials, not only of the Iron Age, but also of the Bronze Age or earlier. For example at Cush, Co Limerick, a complex of multi-period monuments included two ring- ditched enclosures datable to the Iron Age (Ó Ríordáin 1940; Caulfield 1981, 209; Raftery, B. 1981, 181). Tumulus II consisted of a low mound surrounded by a fosse (maximum diameter 13.7m). A pit beneath the mound contained a cremation and an ornamental bone plaque. Tumulus III was similar (maximum diameter 16.45m) and contained a spread of charcoal and cremated bone beneath the centre of the mound. On the other hand Carrowjames, Co Mayo, may be identified as a tumulus cemetery which contained six ring-barrows, three Bronze Age mounds and one ploughed-out monument (Raftery, J. 1938–9; 1940–1; Raftery B. 1981, 181). The ring-barrows all appear to be Iron Age and consist of low mounds (average diameter 7m) each surrounded by a shallow fosse. All contained cremations in pits beneath the mound and cremation deposits and charcoal in the fosse. Gravegoods consisted of corroded iron in a cremation deposit (Tumulus 7), four small solid bronze rods in a pit cremation (Tumulus 9), and Tumulus 8 had bronze rings, bronze studs and a collection of glass beads including dumb-bell-shaped examples, all from cremation pits.

Finally, at Kiltierney, Co Fermanagh, excavations have revealed that a Neolithic passage grave was adapted in the Iron Age for use as a ring-barrow by digging a shallow ditch around the main mound (Hawkes 1981; Raftery, B. 1981; Hamlin and Lynn 1988). Cremations placed in small pits in the main mound contained various glass beads and a bronze fibula with a trumpet motif datable to the first century BC or AD (Hawkes 1981, 63–4). Cremations were also placed on the old ground surface on the outside edge of the ditch, and were covered with small mounds of clay. An iron fibula from one of these is datable to the first century AD (Hamlin and Lynn 1988, 26).

By contrast, the rite of inhumation, initially crouched or flexed, appears to have been introduced into Ireland during the first century AD, probably due to influences spreading from Britain, where (apart from the atypical Aylesford Culture cremations) crouched or flexed inhumation was the 'native British burial tradition in the generations immediately before and after the Roman conquest' (Green 1982, 62; Whimster 1981). Evidence for direct contact in the first century AD with British people who practised the rite of crouched inhumation is provided by the burials discovered in 1927 on Lambay Island, Co Dublin (Macalister 1928–9; Bateson 1973; Warner 1976; Rynne 1976; Hawkes 1981; Raftery, B. 1981; O'Brien 1990). These burials, discovered above the high-water line, were crouched inhumations in unprotected dug graves accompanied by gravegoods which included an iron sword, an iron mirror, bronze rings, a beaded-bronze collar or torc and five bronze fibulae of Dolphin, Langton Down, and Thistle types. These artifacts can all be dated to the second half of the first century AD and are variously of Roman and British origin. The actual people involved have been described by Rynne as possibly Brigantian refugees fleeing from the Romans.

Evidence for the adoption of crouched inhumation burial alongside cremation, is provided by excavations at the Rath of the Synods, Tara, Co Meath (Ó Ríordáin, S.P. unpublished excavation).[5] Here, two areas of burial, sealed beneath the triple banked 'rath', have been identified. The first, an unenclosed area, contained two cremations (one in a pit and one deposited upon an earthfast boulder), four inhumations (three crouched and one extended, head west north-west), and one skull. One of the crouched burials (a child) was accompanied by an iron bolt, and another had possible gravegoods of iron, copper, bronze and bone. The extended inhumation had an object of bone on the ribs, an

animal jawbone and other bones. The grave-fills all contained charcoal and cremated bone. The second area of burial consisted of a cairn enclosed by a ring-ditch. The cairn contained five cremations, partially disturbed by the insertion of a crouched inhumation with animal bones. The fosse or ring-ditch contained four cremations. There is at present no scientific dating for any of these burials, but it is possible to suggest a date around the first or second centuries AD based on the contemporaneity of cremation and crouched inhumation burial rites.

Carrowbeg North, Co Galway (Willmot 1938–9, 121; Raftery, B. 1981, 187) provides a further example. Here two Bronze Age mounds were adapted to accommodate Iron Age burials. Tumulus I had a fosse dug around the mound; this fosse contained one crouched inhumation covered by stones, and three extended inhumations, one of which was also covered by stones. The crouched inhumation, which was female, was accompanied by a small bronze locket with a fragment of linen attached and 12 small bone beads at the left foot. Burial No. 3. which was male, had one piece of sharpened bone beside the head. Tumulus II also had a shallow fosse dug around the mound, and had a secondary, probably Iron Age, cremation deposited on top of the Bronze Age mound. Similarly the Iron Age phases at Knowth, Co Meath (Eogan 1968; 1974) produced nine crouched, four flexed, eight extended (heads south-west and west) and thirteen disturbed inhumations around the circumference of the main Neolithic passage grave. Four of the extended inhumations were in slab-lined graves (heads west) and were set slightly apart from the other burials. While there were no cremations found on this site, gravegoods, which were only found with the crouched and flexed inhumations, show close parallels with gravegoods datable to around the turn of the millennium from other cremation burials already mentioned. For example, the hundreds of tiny blue glass beads at Knowth are similar to those from Oranbeg and Grannagh. Other gravegoods from Knowth can be similarly paralleled; for example, the tiny amber-coloured beads at Oranbeg; the bone beads with off-centre perforations at Grannagh and Newgrange, Co Meath (Flanagan, L.N.W. 1960; Raftery, B. 1981); the unperforated bean-shaped glass toggle bead with greenish tint at Grannagh; the horntips, sawn off and smoothed, at Site A Carbury Hill, and the striated bronze rings are similar to fragments of striated bronze armlet from Oranbeg.

The burial rite of extended inhumation has already been referred to at Tara, where it is found accompanying cremation and crouched inhumation and at Knowth where it is found accompanying crouched inhumation. In the second century AD the Romans adopted the rite of inhumation and, as a result of the ritual attached to death, the body remained in an extended position (Toynbee 1971, 33–44). Extended inhumation was soon adopted in Roman Britain as evidenced in the Romano-British cemetery at Poundbury, Dorset. There, in the first century AD (cemetery 1) burials were crouched in the pre-Roman, British fashion; but in the second century (cemetery 2) they were extended (Green 1982). (Use of the rite of extended inhumation in the period immediately before the Roman invasion of Britain is only known from the later phases of the Arras Culture in Yorkshire (Stead 1979, 14) where it is invariably located in square-barrow cemeteries. Such square barrows have not as yet been identified in Ireland.)

Positive dating evidence for the presence of the Roman rite of extended inhumation in Ireland is provided by a group of unprotected extended inhumations (heads west) discovered by workmen in 1835 beside the beach at Bray, Co Wicklow (Lewis, S. 1837, 223; list of further refs. O'Brien 1984). These burials were laid side by side in unprotected dug graves with a stone at the head and feet. Coins of Trajan (97–117) and Hadrian (117–38) were recovered from the 'chest cavity', thus suggesting that they were originally placed in the mouth or on the chest as payment for the dead to cross on the Stygian ferry. The burials are Roman and date to the first half of the second century AD. The fact that they were buried in the 'correct' Roman fashion indicates that at least some of their companions survived their arrival on the Leinster coast.

Evidence for contacts between Ireland and Roman Britain during the first to fourth centuries AD has been documented by Bateson (1973; 1976), Warner (1976) and Thomas (Thomas, C. 1981a). The rite of extended inhumation was quickly adopted by the Irish but was used in conjunction with older rites and mainly within circular enclosures. This parallelism, already noted at Tara and Knowth, is also seen at Site B, Carbury Hill. Here the large ring-barrow initially contained four cremations set into a low cairn, one of which was accompanied by two small iron rings and an iron fragment. Fifteen extended inhumations (heads south-west), some of which disturbed the cremations, were added at a secondary level.

The biggest difference between Romano-British and Irish extended inhumations of the second to fourth centuries AD is in the provision of gravegoods. The majority of Romano-British burials of that period were encased in wooden coffins and provided with food offerings, coins, and hobnailed shoes for their journey to the otherworld (Green 1982, 62). But in Ireland the only instances of gravegoods accompanying extended inhumation are the deposition of food offerings with the extended inhumation at the Rath of the Synods, Tara, coins with the burials at Bray, and a pair of iron shears with one of the extended inhumations at Site B, Carbury Hill. This comparative lack of gravegoods with extended inhumations in Ireland would tend to suggest that the majority date from the fourth and subsequent centuries, but this does not necessarily mean that they are Christian (Thomas, C. 1981a, 234).

In Ireland the strict orientation of extended inhumations does not at first appear to have been an important factor, as is indicated at Tara, Knowth, Circle J Lough Gur, Co Limerick (Grogan and Eogan 1987), and Maddens Hill, Kiltale, Co Meath (Rynne 1974). However in Roman Britain excavations at Poundbury (Cemetery 3), where it was possible to date such phenomena, it is noticeable that by the early fourth century all burials were aligned roughly east/west, with heads to the west. This may also have been the case in Ireland.

It is difficult to be certain when the use of stone- or slab-lined graves was introduced. Green (1982, 67), commenting on the rite of cist burial with extended inhumations at Poundbury, states, 'as elsewhere in Western Britain its regular use for adults seems to have commenced in the fourth century'. In Ireland the term 'cist' has been applied to three related forms of extended inhumation burial: firstly, a stone-lined grave (a dug grave, lined or outlined with rough stones); secondly, a slab-lined grave (a dug grave lined with stone slabs; when covering slabs are present they often rest directly on the body); and thirdly, a lintel grave (a shallow, slab-lined grave with a series of covering lintel slabs resting on the side slabs). Lintel graves appear to have evolved from slab-lined graves in the Early Christian period.

Despite many major changes in burial practices during the early centuries AD, some sectors of the indigenous population may have continued to cling to ancient customs or rites into the fifth century, as evidenced at Furness, Co Kildare (Grogan 1983–4). Here excavation revealed a low mound covering a central stone core and kerb. Two cremations were discovered between the central core and the kerb and a further cremation in a pit was located outside the kerb. A stake hole located in a central position beneath the stone core contained charcoal which yielded a radiocarbon determination of cal. AD 430–580 (GrN-10472, 1540±30 bp. A fragment of a light blue glass bracelet was also recovered from beneath the central core.

Therefore the new rites of crouched and extended inhumation introduced into Ireland during the later Iron Age did not totally replace the older custom of cremation; rather they were absorbed and adapted. Indeed, one native burial custom which remained constant throughout the period was the use of circular ditches to enclose burial places.

Pagan and Christian Burial in the Seventh and Eighth Centuries AD

During the course of the sixth century the documentary sources suggest the gradual conversion of the Irish to Christianity but it was not until the seventh that the church was sufficiently strong to be fully integrated into early Irish society (Hughes, K. 1966, 44–56). It is also evident from the literature that in the late seventh and early eighth centuries in Ireland, burial in formal Christian cemeteries was not yet the norm, pagan burial practices were still in use and were even tolerated to some extent.

Tírechán, writing in the late seventh century, refers to the death of two newly converted daughters of a king, and comments 'the days of mourning for the king's daughters came to an end, and they buried them ... and they made a round ditch (*fossam rotundam*) after the manner of a *ferta*, because this is what the heathen Irish used to do, but we call it *relic*' (Bieler 1979, 145). The emphasis on the round ditch indicates that the type of monument being described is a ring-barrow or ring-ditched enclosure similar to those used in the Iron Age. In the late seventh century the practice of placing burials within such a circular ditched enclosure was accepted by Tírechán, but the name of this type of enclosure was in the process of being changed from *ferta* to *relic* as a method of christianizing a pagan burial practice. (*Relic* is a borrowing from the Latin *reliquiae* meaning 'the remains of the saints'. From this stems the Irish word *reilig* meaning a cemetery.) The reference to 'days of mourning' is an indication of the ritual attached to death. The bodies were laid out in the manner which had been in use from at least the second century AD

when extended inhumation burial was introduced into Ireland. A further indication of the Christianization of the burial place is included at the end of the passage quoted above, 'and the *ferta* was made over to Patrick with the bones of the holy virgins ... and he made an earthen church in that place' (Bieler 1979, 145). In the late seventh century this site, which was obviously known to Tírechán, was represented by a circular enclosure containing burials and possibly the remains of an earthen church.[6]

Some recently excavated examples of burials within circular enclosures include a cemetery of extended inhumations in unprotected dug graves, located approximately 200m south-east of the large ecclesiastical enclosure at Durrow, Co Offaly.[7] Limited excavation revealed that this cemetery, which had come to light during ploughing, was contained within an oval enclosure surrounded by a ditch 1.5–2m wide, enclosing an area 25–30m in overall diameter. In 1942 the site was reported to have been surrounded also by a bank 0.76–1.07m high.[8] It was not possible, due to disturbance, to be sure whether or not the enclosure was annular. Approximately 100m north-east of this site, on the eastern slope of a low hill, further burials were exposed. These were not excavated and the area was re-grassed. It is not possible at this stage to state whether or not these cemeteries are contemporary with the Columban monastery at Durrow which was founded in the sixth century.

Two of the cemeteries uncovered during recent work laying the gas pipeline north of Dublin are also of interest (Gowen forthcoming). The first is located at Colpe (*Inber Colpdi*) near the mouth of the River Boyne. This is an ancient area which is referred to in Irish mythology and is well-documented in the historic period (Gowen forthcoming). Limited excavation revealed part of a large enclosure surrounded by a deep ditch. In the south-east quadrant of this enclosure was a smaller, penannular enclosure (maximum diameter 14m) which contained extended inhumations in slab-lined and simple dug graves. The ditch surrounding this smaller enclosure measured 0.8–0.9m wide and 0.5–0.7m deep, and had an opening at the south-west. Continuous use for burial over an extended period of time was apparent from the fact that some of the later burials extended out over the edges of the silted-up ditch. Sherds of imported pottery (B and E ware) were recovered from the site. It is not possible on the present evidence to say whether or not the larger enclosure was ecclesiastical or secular in nature.

The second cemetery is located at Westreave (or Mount Ambrose) near Ballyboghil, Co Dublin (Gowen forthcoming). Here stone-lined graves overlaid and cut through the silted-up ditch of an enclosure approximately 9.5m in diameter. The ditch was 0.5m wide and 0.25–0.3m deep. Centrally located within this enclosure were three extended inhumations in unprotected dug graves. One of these burials was in an exceptionally large grave and the other two were in graves which were slightly larger than the norm. The suggestion is that at the earliest levels of this site, one, or perhaps three, burials were interred within a circular ditched enclosure or *fossam rotundam*. Later burials, in simple dug graves and stone-lined graves, were inserted throughout the site.

Burials in secular habitation sites (ring-forts, raths, cashels) are referred to in the literature and are known in the archaeological record. Tírechán refers to an incident involving Bishop Assicus, Patrick's coppersmith, who had sought refuge in *Rochuil* west of *Sliab Liacc* (Glencolumbkille, Co Donegal) 'his monks searched for him and ... took him forcibly with them, and he died in their company in the solitude of the mountains and they buried him in *Rath Cungi* in *Mag Sereth* [Racoon Hill, Co Donegal]' (Bieler 1979, 141). Tírechán also writes regarding a certain man called Hinu who had been baptized by Patrick as an infant, 'later [Hinu] gave hospitality to Assicus and his monks in *Ard Roissen*, that is in *Raith Congi* in *Mag Sereth*' (Bieler 1979, 161). This appears to be an instance where a rath was given over to a group of monks and was used by them for the burial of their bishop. There are references to the foundation of several churches in the general area around *Rath Congi* but none to the foundation of a church at that site, an indication that it may have been used for burial only. At Reask, Co Kerry (Fanning 1981), a radiocarbon date of cal. AD 260–650 (UB 2167, 1565±90 bp) derived from the hearth in a circular wooden structure may indicate that the primary occupation of that site was not ecclesiastical. Equally the cemeteries at Dooey, Co Donegal (Ó Ríordáin and Rynne 1961) and Millockstown, Co Louth (Manning 1986) are located in former enclosed habitation areas. At the Rath of Feerwore, Co Galway (Knox 1915–6, 190–3; Raftery, J. 1944, 23–52; other refs. see O'Brien 1984), the inhumation in a stone-lined grave was probably inserted after habitation of the site had ceased, and the same is the case for two burials in the ring-fort at Raheenamadra, Co Limerick,

where radiocarbon dates of cal. AD 340–870 (U-241, 1430±130bp), cal. AD 560–1000 (U-243, 1260±120bp), and cal. AD 540–990 (U-240, 1280±120bp) have been obtained from oak posts in the souterrain (Stenberger 1966). It is worth noting that these two burials were accompanied by iron knives and a rectangular belt buckle.

Isolated extended inhumations, usually in stone- or slab-lined graves are relatively common in the Irish archaeological record. References to this type of burial in the literature would seem to indicate that its practice did not seem unusual to seventh-century writers. For instance Muirchú, writing about the baptism by Patrick of the British maiden Monesan, says 'immediately afterwards she fell to the ground and gave up her spirit into the hands of the angels. She was buried on the spot where she died' (Bieler 1979, 101). Tírechán writing about Patrick's visit to *Mons Aigli* (Croagh Patrick) says 'and his charioteer died at *Muiresc Aigli* ... and there Patrick buried his charioteer Totmael and gathered stones for his burial place' (Bieler 1979, 153). A similar burial is mentioned by Adomnán when referring to Columba's baptism of a certain pagan old man and the man's subsequent death 'and after the rites of baptism had been performed, he presently died in that place ... and there his companions buried him, building a cairn of stones' (Anderson, A.O. and Anderson, M.O. 1961, 275). These extracts refer to isolated burials which took place away from a cemetery, and in two instances the suggestion is that cairns were erected over the graves.

These literary references find an echo in the archaeological evidence. For example, at Tumulus I, Carrowbeg North, two Iron Age burials in the fosse were covered with stones. Examples of isolated burials beneath mounds include an extended inhumation in a 'long stone cist' at Farganstown and Ballymacon, Co Meath (Kelly 1977), and two extended inhumations, one unprotected, the other in a stone-lined grave, at Ninch, Co Meath (Sweetman 1982–3b). A radiocarbon date from bone of the unprotected burial gave a reading of cal. AD 390–670 (GU 1453, 1490±85 BP).

Indications that in the late seventh and early eighth centuries Christians were still being buried in pagan (probably familial) cemeteries are noted in the Literature, with references to the burial of Christians among pagans, and exhortations from the clergy to Christians to bury their dead in Christian cemeteries. For example, Muirchú writes that Patrick and his charioteer passed a cross by the wayside 'he ...

prayed before the cross, and there he saw a tomb (*sepulcrum*) and he asked the dead man who had been buried there ... whether he had lived under the faith. The dead man answered "I was a pagan in life, and I was buried here. There was also a woman who lived in another province, and she had a son who died far away from her, and was buried in her absence, but after some days the mother came here in mourning, keening for the son she had lost, and in her distracted state of mind she mistook a pagan's tomb for the grave of her son and placed a cross beside a pagan ..." and Patrick transferred the cross to its proper place' (Bieler 1979, 115).

Tírechán also writes about the same episode: 'he [Patrick] came to Findmag in the territory of the Maine and found there the sign of the cross of Christ and two new graves, and from his chariot the holy man said "who is it that is buried here?" and a voice answered from the grave "I am a pagan". The holy man replied: "Why has the holy cross been placed beside you" and again he answered "because the mother of the man who is buried beside me asked that the sign of the cross be placed beside her son's grave. But a stupid and foolish man placed it beside me" and Patrick leaped from his chariot ... pulled the cross from the grave and placed it over the head of the baptized man' (Bieler 1979, 155–7).

There are several interesting inferences to be obtained from this story: first, at that time it was apparently normal practice for Christians and pagans to be buried together and in similar graves; secondly, the cemetery seems to have been by the wayside; and thirdly the cross was portable, and therefore probably made of wood.

In the *Collectio Canonum Hibernensis* (*De Martyribus*) (Wasserschleben 1885, 208–9) there are references to the effect that 'angels visit graves of martyrs in desert places, but do not visit graves among evil men ... and ... martyrs who are buried among evil people were visited by angels, but the angels returned sad'.[9] (In this context 'desert place' means *disert* or remote monastic site. 'Martyrs' simply means those who died as Christians, and 'evil men' are pagans.) The general inference is that Christians who were still using tribal or family burial grounds were now being threatened by the non-recognition of their graves.

An example of a non-ecclesiastical cemetery apparently in continuous use from the pre-Christian into the Christian period is provided by that excavated at Betaghstown (Bettystown) Co Meath.[10] Here 16 inhumations were found, two of which were crouched. One of these had

gravegoods comprising an oval bronze disk with traces of fine net adhering from the area of the head, two iron penannular brooches, one of which had a tiny textile fragment attached, an oval iron belt-buckle and a stone amulet. The brooches are of omega type (Fowler Type B) which emerged in Britain around the first century BC and continued in use into the Roman period (Fowler 1960). The other 14 inhumations were extended, ten were in unprotected dug graves and two were in stone-lined graves (heads west). At a later period two further burials were interred in slab-lined graves (heads south-west), one of which cut into one of the crouched inhumations.

A possibly similar situation existed at the cemetery located in a reused Neolithic enclosure (circle J) at Lough Gur, where 65 inhumation graves were excavated. Of these the majority of the undisturbed burials were extended, and six were flexed. Most of the burials were in unprotected dug graves, but four were in stone-lined graves and 14 were in slab-lined graves. Orientation, where observable, was east/west, but two burials were north/south. One north/south burial was accompanied by a stone bead and pottery sherd. Two of the stone-lined graves were located below slab-lined graves (Grogan and Eogan 1987). The four slab-lined graves at Knowth[11] are another example of the continuous use of a probable familial cemetery from the Iron Age into the Christian period. Similarly, the cemetery at Westreave (see above), which appears to have evolved from a small circular enclosure with one (or three) primary burials, has no known ecclesiastical associations.

Therefore the archaeological evidence, although extremely difficult to date with precision, points to the continued use, well into the Early Christian period, of pagan burial practices in the form of isolated burials, burial in circular enclosures, and the survival of kindred or familial cemeteries. This is also suggested by references in the source material, such as that by Tírechán to the burial of the newly baptized daughters of the king 'in the manner of the heathen Irish'; by Adomnán to Columba's baptism of a pagan old man, his subsequent death and burial beneath a cairn of stones; and by Tírechán to Patrick's method of burying his dead charioteer, all of which relate to burials purported to have taken place in the fifth and sixth centuries. However they also indicate that such practices were still known in the seventh. On the other hand, the references by both Muirchú and Tírechán to the cross which had mistakenly been placed beside a pagan instead of a Christian grave seem now to be stressing the dangers inherent in allowing Christian burial among pagans. The references in the *De Martyribus* section of the *Collectio Canonum Hibernensis* (early eighth century) about angels not wishing to visit Christians who were buried among evil men, are stressing the same point. The fact that such statements were deemed necessary to persuade Christians to bury in Christian places indicates that burial in non-Christian, family or tribal cemeteries was still commonplace. These inducements to bury in Christian cemeteries appear to be a result of the seventh-century expansion of the Irish church, and the growth of the cult of relics.

The Cult of Relics

In order to become strong and influential, churches needed to attract patronage, including burial, and to do this they had to possess important relics, preferably corporeal, either of their founder or of some other important saint. Prior to the seventh century, Roman law which had been adopted by the church in Rome, 'forbade interference with a *locus religiosus* except under exceptional circumstances' (Doherty 1984b, 90). Although it may have happened unofficially from time to time, the first official translation of relics took place in the mid-seventh century when Pope Theodore (642–8) transferred bodies into the Basilica of St Stephen in Rome (Doherty 1984b, 90). In the Irish context, pre-seventh century disinterest, and later seventh century interest in corporeal relics is evidenced by the fact that the burial places of saints who died in the fifth and sixth centuries appear to have been lost or forgotten by the time writers in the late seventh century had to justify the non-existence at their churches of the founder's corporeal relics. In the case of Patrick, Muirchú uses the device of an angel saying 'lest your body be removed from the ground, one cubit of earth shall be placed on your body' and he goes on to say that workmen who accidently dug up the ground (in recent times) saw fire burst forth from the tomb and retreated in fear (Bieler 1979, 121). A reference to the burial of Patrick in the *Notes Supplementary to Tírechán* states that 'Columb Cille, moved by the Holy Spirit, showed where Patrick's grave was' (Bieler 1979, 165), an obvious reference to the fact that, although the body was reputed to have been buried at Downpatrick, the actual site of the grave was unknown. Armagh makes up for its lack of Patrick's body by proclaiming (in the *Liber Angeli*) its possession of the important relics of

Peter, Paul, Stephen and Laurence, and by a special dispensation, the Blood of Christ on a linen cloth. Cogitosus, propagandizing on Kildare's behalf, describes the grandiose tombs containing the bodies of Brigit and Conlaed placed on either side of the altar. One must assume that either the Kildare church had been built over the site of the burials as was the custom in Rome, or that the 'tombs' were actually cenotaphs. A story cited by Tírechán regarding the bones of the holy priest Bruscus (Bieler 1979, 137) indicates that the device of a dream repeated three times was needed even in the late seventh century to justify the translation of relics.

The contents of seventh- and eighth-century hagiographical material suggests that, while in earlier times pagan burial practices were tolerated by the saints, the clergy was now seeking to establish burial in Christian cemeteries as the norm. In the late seventh century, possibly as a result of the recent series of plagues, Christian religious observances assumed added importance. One symptom of this is the emergence and growth of the cult of relics. The cult of relics and the associated veneration of certain saints, was then used as a device to attract patronage, including burial, to the relevant saint's church. In other words burial near the bones of the saint became a substitute for burial near the bones of the ancestors. Consequently, we would expect the old familial and tribal cemeteries to go gradually out of use and to be replaced by burial on consecrated ground.

Notes

1. The literary sources consulted for the purposes of this paper have all been reliably dated to the late seventh and early eighth centuries. These include *The Patrician Texts in the Book of Armagh* (Bieler 1979) (for dating see Bieler 1979; Kenney 1929/1966; Sharpe 1982b; 1984a; Doherty 1984b); the *Vita Brigitae* by Cogitosus (Connolly and Picard 1987) (for dating see Sharpe 1982a, 87; McCone 1982, 109); the *Life of Columba* by Adomnán (Anderson, A.O and Anderson, M.O. 1961) (for dating see Anderson, A.O. and Anderson, M.O. 1961; Kenney 1929/1966; Picard 1982); and the *Collectio Canonum Hibernensis* (Wasserschleben 1885) (for dating see Kenney 1929/1966, 249; Hughes, K. 1972, 68).

2. When using early written sources, especially hagiographical material, it must always be borne in mind that the temporal and spatial setting for the material is not that in which the saint reputedly lived (i.e. fifth/sixth century), but is that of the late seventh or early eighth century with which the writers were familiar.

3. Permission to refer to unpublished excavation granted by Professor E. Rynne, University College, Galway.
4. See note 3.
5. Permission to refer to unpublished excavation material granted by Dr S. Caulfield, University College, Dublin.
6. In Ireland, churches of earth/clay or wood were the norm in the seventh century. Tírechán also refers to the fact that Patrick made 'a square earthen church of clay, because no timber was near' (Bieler 1979, 159). The elaborate church described by Cogitosus at Kildare was made from wood (Connolly and Picard 1987). There is only one seventh-century reference to a stone church, i.e. Tírechán's reference to *'Dom Liacc*, that is, the house of stones of Ciannan, Duleek, Co Meath' (Bieler 1979, 147).
7. Permission to refer to unpublished excavation granted by Mr R. Ó Floinn, National Museum of Ireland, Dublin.
8. I.T.A. survey, Oliver Davies, 1942. National Museum of Ireland, Dublin.
9. The writer is grateful to Professor F. J. Byrne for originally drawing her attention to, and translating these passages.
10. Permission to refer to unpublished excavation granted by Mr E. P. Kelly, National Museum of Ireland, Dublin.
11. Publication pending. Permission to refer to material granted by Professor George Eogan, University College Dublin.

The Early Irish Church: Problems of Identification

Ann Hamlin

When I began to work on the early Irish church in the mid 1960s I was much concerned with site identification, clearly an essential starting-point in any enquiry. In the 25 years since then there have been all kinds of advances, historical and archaeological, which make it possible to treat the subject of identification more fully than in earlier years. In discussing this topic I shall be drawing on many other people's work as well as my own, and though the concentration is on Ireland (especially the north, because of my experience there) I hope that what I have to say will also have a bearing on work on the early church in Wales.

I suggest that identification can be looked at by discussing three questions. The first is to ask *which* were the early church sites? This is mainly approached through written sources, but there is also a contribution from archaeological fieldwork. Next we ask *where* were these sites? This question must be addressed mainly in the field, and it is not as straightforward as it may seem. Finally we enquire *what* were these churches? What was the nature of the ecclesiastical use of the site and can the surviving remains be interpreted in the light of our knowledge of the history of the early Irish church? This question can only be tackled by combining the historical and archaeological evidence.

The first task is to build up a roll-call of early churches, and it might seem tempting to reach for the Ordnance Survey's *Map of monastic Ireland* (1984) or Gwynn and Hadcock's *Medieval religious houses: Ireland* (1970). That is not the answer, of course, because these works draw on a limited range of sources of uneven quality, they take little account of the problems I am going to discuss, and unfortunately they perpetuate many mistakes and muddles.

The rich range of written sources which survive from the Early Christian period (Hughes, K. 1972) provides our main guide to which were the early churches, but these sources are chronologically and geographically uneven. The disastrous plagues of the mid sixth and mid seventh centuries disrupted what must have been a strongly oral tradition (Doherty 1980, 71),

with the result that we have only a very shadowy picture of the fifth and sixth centuries. Those plagues did, however, stimulate the writing down of learning and compiling of texts in the second half of the seventh and early eighth centuries. From the seventh-century lives of Patrick and Brigit (Bieler 1979; Connolly and Picard 1987) and Adomnán's *Life of Columba* (Anderson, A.O. and Anderson, M.O. 1961) a list of churches can be built up. Other church names occur in liturgical sources, such as litanies, in the annals, in genealogies, and from about 830 the two calendars of saints, the *Martyrology of Tallaght* and the *Martyrology of Oengus (Félire Óengusso)* (Best and Lawlor 1931; Stokes 1905). These are an underused source for the purpose of identification: Gwynn and Hadcock (1970), for example, did not use the calendars, and this results in many surprising omissions. For some northern churches the only pre-Norman reference I have found is in one of the calendars, for example 'Rathnat of *Cell Rathnaite*' (Kilraghts, Co Antrim) is listed at 9 August in the *Martyrology of Tallaght*.

In my regional study of the early church in the north (Hamlin 1976) I plotted documented ecclesiastical sites at two chronological horizons: in about 800, using the range of sources outlined above, and in the later twelfth century. For the later part of the Early Christian period the annals are an important contemporary source. There are many saints' Lives, including the *Tripartite Life* of Patrick of about 900 (Stokes 1887), and the twelfth-century Irish Life of Bairre of Cork, *Betha Bairre*, which Vincent Hurley used as a guide to sites in his regional study of Cork and Kerry (1982, 303 and *passim*). Glosses were added to the early calendars, and from the third quarter of the twelfth century we have the *Martyrology of Gorman*, which contributes to the roll-call of churches in existence by the end of the Early Christian period (Stokes 1895).

In using later sources, from the medieval period and the seventeenth century, the student is confronted by the problem of how much they can reliably tell about the *early* church. Many saints' Lives which survive in a medieval form do include early material. Kenney calls the Latin Life of Samthann 'late and brief', yet it clearly goes back to a good, early text (Kenney 1929, 465). Other medieval sources, like the registers of the Archibishops of Armagh (for example, Quigley and Roberts 1972), include ecclesiastical terms known to have originated in the early church — *coarb, erenagh, termon* — and it is likely that churches in which these terms were used in the middle ages had their origins in the Early Christian period. But these medieval sources, and seventeenth-century works like the *Annals of the Four Masters* (O'Donovan 1854) and the *Martyrology of Donegal* (Todd and Reeves 1864) must be used with great care as a source for the early church.

The geographical cover of written sources providing information about the early church is uneven. In general, the west of Ireland is poorly documented in the Early Christian period, while the midlands and east are better served. Written sources are sometimes imprecise as to location: a saint may be attributed to a region, such as 'Glunsalach of *Slíab Fuait*' (the mountains of south Armagh), rather than to a particular site.

There are sometimes problems over identifying documented churches. *Cell lomchon* is in Ulster, but where is it? The *Tripartite Life* describes how Patrick founded many groups of churches: seven at the river Faughan and seven among the Uí Thuirtri, for example. Many of these are identified but some are not.

Place-name studies are important, both for identifying churches in written sources and also because distinctively early ecclesiastical place-name elements can fill out the picture by pointing to otherwise undocumented sites. Deirdre Flanagan examined the occurrence and date-range of these elements (1969; 1984). To take the element *domnach*, for example, many of the northern *domnach* churches are documented, including the two Donaghmore sites (in Down and Tyrone), but other *domnach* sites do not occur in written sources, such as Donagreagh in north-east Armagh and Donaghanie in mid Tyrone (see Flanagan, D. 1984, 43–7 for maps of *domnach* names). Killinchy (Down) may be the *Cell Inse* mentioned in a twelfth-century calendar, but Killoan in west Tyrone is undocumented. Tyrella (Down) is identified in a

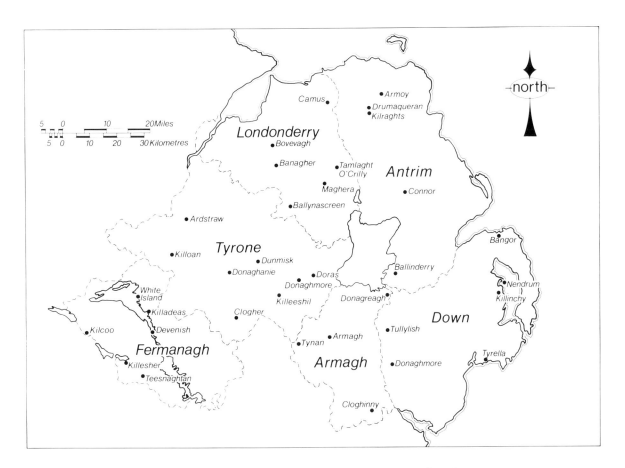

Fig. 14.1 *Map of sites in Northern Ireland mentioned in the text*

calendar gloss with *Tech Riagla*, but Teesnaghtan in Fermanagh (also including the element *tech*) has not been identified in any source, and there are many other examples of how place-names attest to otherwise undocumented churches.

In view of the chronological and geographical unevenness of the written sources, the unidentified sites and the impossibility of arguing from silence in documents, it should come as no surprise that archaeological evidence can contribute substantially to this 'roll-call' of early churches. In my 1976 study of Northern Ireland I mapped undocumented sites which have material evidence of early ecclesiastical activity: in 33 cases there was strong evidence and in 34 cases rather less secure evidence, from a total of 266 sites. A striking example in Fermanagh is the site on White Island where there is an important group of carved stone figures, yet the early name of the church is lost (Hickey 1985, 26–42). Two other Fermanagh sites have 'early' place-names but have not been identified in any early written source: Kilcoo, with a cross-shaft and inscribed grave-slabs, and Killadeas, with figure- and cross-carved stones.

Any attempt to identify *which* were the early churches will inevitably result in categories familiar to many researchers, of certain, probable, possible and doubtful early ecclesiastical sites. Some of the documented churches are, however, unidentified and unlocated in the landscape, and this leads to my second question: *where* were the early churches?

For a documented site this will involve establishing a link between the name in a source and a place on the ground, and sometimes there can be little doubt, but identification to a particular site is not always straightforward. There seem to have been two quite different pressures at work through history: towards continuity in the use of an ancient site, and towards a change of location. There has always been a strong preference for burial in a greatly revered cemetery, close to an honoured saint, and attachment to an ancient site has caused many to continue in use for burial, if not for worship. In other cases modern parish churches (for historical reasons usually Church of Ireland) still stand on early Christian period sites as at Armoy in north Antrim, where the nineteenth-century Church of Ireland church is close to the remains of a round tower.

There have also been pressures in the opposite direction. Written sources indicate that some early foundations did not flourish, because of plague, famine, warfare, or for dynastic reasons. It has been suggested that some foundations made by women were short-lived, because women had only a life-interest in property (Hughes, K. 1972, 234–5). In some areas there are strong traditions of a change in the site of a church: in mid and south-east Co Londonderry, for example, in the parishes of Ballynascreen, Banagher, Bovevagh and Tamlaght O'Crilly, at least. Banagher church is first documented in 1121, the surviving fabric is of the twelfth and thirteenth centuries, and there is a tradition that the founder, St Muiredhach O'Heney, was led to Banagher from his intended site in Templemoyle by a stag. There is a long-abandoned ecclesiastical site in nearby Templemoyle. It is impossible to be sure, but there could have been a resiting of the church in the eleventh or early twelfth century for family or political reasons (Waterman 1976, 40). What is certain is that at the period of the Plantation in the north in the early seventeenth century some early church sites were abandoned for new churches because the old ones were 'inconveniently' situated in relation to changing patterns of population, land exploitation and communications, and similar 'socio-economic' factors must have been at work in earlier centuries.

This identification on the ground of a site of early ecclesiastical activity — whether documented or not — is mainly an archaeological task, but it calls for an interdisciplinary approach. Reeves showed the way in 1844 when he established the link between Nendrum of the written sources and the site on Mahee Island in Co Down, by using local traditions, field survey and small-scale excavation to test his theory (Reeves 1902). In recent years workers have emphasized the importance of looking for several pointers from a range of possible indicators (for example, Swan 1983, 274–6). These will include documented ecclesiastical activity, an ecclesiastical place-name element, use of a site for burial, archaeological evidence (ruined churches, souterrains, crosses, cross-carved stones, bullaun stones), an enclosing element, a holy well, and pilgrimage and other traditions. I will look at some of these indicators and at examples of how they have contributed to the identification of sites in Northern Ireland.

In addition to the major place-names, already acknowledged as important, minor and local names can help in locating sites. The name *shankill* (old church), points to a church, while *relig* indicates burial, and there are also the

English forms, like Church Hill and Graveyard Field. In Cloghinny townland, for example, in south Armagh, a large boulder on the mountain-side is carved with two crosses, while the field downslope contains a souterrain and is called the Shankill Field (*Armagh*, forthcoming). At Killoan in west Tyrone the 'headstone' stands in the 'Graveyard Field'. The 'headstone' is a decorated cross-base, the place-name suggests a church connected with Eogan of Ardstraw, and there is a slight earthwork platform on the hillside, so again the evidence points to an otherwise undocumented church site (Hamlin 1971, 81–2). Tradition is one element of the cumulative picture at Ballinderry, close to Lough Neagh in south-west Co Antrim. Here there is a large, oval graveyard with a ruined church and two bullaun stones. The local name is 'La Loo', probably preserving the unusual *lann* church element, and traditionally the patron day was 4 August suggesting that the associated saint was Molua, listed in calendars at 4 August. The church does not appear in written sources until the early fourteenth century.

One of the most exciting developments in the archaeological study of the early Irish church in recent years has been the identification of hundreds of previously unrecognized ecclesiastical enclosures. Dr St Joseph pointed the way with his magnificent air photographs (Norman and St Joseph 1969, 90–121) and Leo Swan has advanced the study significantly, including much use of air photography (Swan 1983). In Northern Ireland we have recently been studying the Ordnance Survey air cover and as a result have identified at least 20 'new' enclosures at ecclesiastical sites. In addition to air photography there are clues in the line of townland boundaries, in hedges, banks, lanes and roads. The results have so far been most spectacular in the midlands, but Vincent Hurley has identified many enclosures in Cork and Kerry (1982), and as air photography and other research continue it is certain that more enclosures will be found throughout Ireland.

One small *caveat* must be entered here. A few quite modern churches are known to have been built in Early Christian period secular raths (ringforts). Examples in Northern Ireland include the Catholic churches at Camlough (Armagh), Craigavole (Londonderry) and Ballynagurragh (Tyrone). Earlier editions of Ordnance Survey maps will usually help in distinguishing these from Early Christian *ecclesiastical* enclosures, but for some enclosures with records of burials the situation may be less clear. Two cashels in Co Armagh are known as the *Relig*, indicating burials, but without excavation it is impossible to decide whether these are secular enclosures, later reused for burial, or ancient enclosed burial grounds (*Armagh*, forthcoming).

Finds of distinctively early archaeological material, whether derived from field survey or excavation, can help to confirm early activity at a site. Until recently it was thought *likely* that the circular graveyard with a ruined church in Killesher townland, overlooking Lough Macnean in Co Fermanagh, was '*Cill Lasrach* at the head of *Loch Mic nÉn*' mentioned in the Life of Lasair (Gwynn, L. 1911, 83), but the finding of an early cross-head there has confirmed the identification (Hamlin 1980, 53–5). The site of the Church of Ireland parish church at Killeeshil (Tyrone) was in the 'probable' category in my 1976 thesis, with its ecclesiastical place-name and early terminology in medieval sources, but the recent finding of a carved cross fragment and the identification of an enclosure have removed all doubt.

Archaeological material, however, is not always a clear guide. The occurrence of less diagnostically early material, like simple slabs, rough crosses and bullaun stones, is not alone enough to confirm early activity, though in conjunction with other evidence it may assume significance, as at Ballinderry (see above). Occasionally certainly early material may not be *in situ* and may not indicate an early ecclesiastical site. Crosses and other stones, in particular, were moved in the nineteenth century to embellish large estates. The three crosses in Tynan Abbey demesne, for example, come from nearby Tynan village (Armagh) and a site across the river Blackwater in Co Tyrone. I have suggested that the chi-rho-carved stone at Drumaqueran (Antrim) need not point to a church site. It could mark a route, a boundary, the site of an important event or have some other significance (Hamlin 1972).

Excavation can add substance to a possible identification, it can help to define the exact area of activity, and occasionally it can reveal a completely 'new', unsuspected, ecclesiastical site. Recent work at Doras, Newmills, Co Tyrone, has confirmed a tentative identification. Here the townland boundary seems to define a semicircular enclosure, there is a bullaun stone in the Church of Ireland church graveyard, and a bell from the site is in the National Museum in Dublin, but rescue excavation in 1983 and 1985 uncovered a circular, wattle-built house and radiocarbon evidence for eighth-century activity

(McDowell 1987). At Tullylish, Co Down, the circular hilltop graveyard was thought to be the site of the dramatic event recorded in the *Annals of Ulster* in 809: 'the killing of Dúnchú, abbot of *Telach-liss*, beside the shrine of Patrick, in the abbot's house of *Telach-liss*'. Excavation in 1983, however, showed that this was only part of a much bigger site defined by two deep ditches (Ivens 1987). It is clear from excavation and air photography that many of the distinctive circular and oval graveyards are simply the surviving 'core' of once much larger areas of activity.

It is less common for excavation to reveal 'new' sites, but three examples can be noted. At Knockea, Co Limerick, Professor O'Kelly excavated what was thought to be a squarish house site in an area of complex earthwork enclosures and found that it was full of apparently Christian burials, 66 in all (O'Kelly 1967, 74–83). The occurrence of a burial enclosure in this large settlement remains puzzling, but the other two examples are 'ecclesiastical' sites of some kind. Rescue excavation in 1980 of a newly-discovered settlement at Millockstown, Co Louth, showed that a secular site was superseded in the second half of the first millennium AD by a large ecclesiastical enclosure including a graveyard (Manning 1986). Recent rescue excavation of a hilltop 'fort' at Dunmisk, Co Tyrone, revealed that the site had been intensively used for burial (more than 400 graves). There were also two areas of metalworking and post-sockets for what may have been a wooden church (Hamlin and Lynn 1988, 27–9; Ivens forthcoming). Close dating was not possible, but the indications are that this was a very early ecclesiastical site which was abandoned long ago and totally forgotten. These examples add force to the earlier argument that church establishments waxed and waned and sometimes failed.

A general point which must be noted is that the survival of archaeological material varies greatly over Ireland. Broadly, survival is better in the west than the east, but there is also much material in the midlands. Ironically, this is the reverse of the situation for the survival of written sources, where the west is so poorly served. In the north, the area which I have studied most closely, there is a poor rate of survival of ecclesiastical material, though again there is more in the west (especially Fermanagh) than the east. The identification of enclosures from the air, and the gradual coming to light of new material through field survey and excavation, are therefore important in

supplementing the generally meagre archaeological evidence.

The third kind of identification, the question of the function of a site, is by far the most difficult. It is a task I hardly attempted in my northern regional study in the 1960s and early 1970s (Hamlin 1976). What was the nature of the activity at these 'ecclesiastical' sites? How are the surviving material remains to be interpreted in the light of our growing understanding of the historical development of the early church in Ireland? These questions can only be satisfactorily addressed by combining the historical and archaeological information, and this is potentially an exciting area for interdisciplinary study.

It has long been clear that the laws point to a wide range of church types. The *Córus Béscna*, for example, distinguishes carefully between the *annóit* church, the *dalta* church, the *compairche* church and the *cill* church, and elsewhere a 'noble church' is distinguished from a 'humble church' (*A.L.I.* 1865–1901, III, 65–79). The picture of church development which has been evolving in recent years embraces major episcopal centres, ancient missionary ('mother') churches, large and small monasteries, churches belonging to families and tribes, small 'proto-parish' churches (centres for pastoral work and burial), retreats and hermitages (Ó Corráin 1981a).

Very broadly, the archaeological material is consistent with this suggested pattern of diversity, but the fragmentary and uneven survival of that material creates great problems over offering confident interpretations. We are constantly faced with the problem of 'negative evidence': was a feature truly absent, or does it simply not survive? This is well illustrated by the survival of round towers (map in Barrow 1979, endpapers). How far is the distribution of surviving and documented towers a true reflection of their original distribution? Towers are found or recorded at important, well-documented sites like Armagh, Clonmacnois and Glendalough, but are absent from other important sites like Bangor, Durrow and Lismore. They are also found at some historically obscure sites, including Kilree (Kilkenny) and Dysert (Limerick). It is therefore difficult to suggest that a round tower characterized any particular kind of site.

Another problem arises over chronological definition. The historical framework, century by century, is gradually being refined, yet the chronology of the vast majority of early ecclesiastical sites is unknown. The close dating of most Early Christian period artifacts is notoriously difficult. A site like Devenish, Co Fermanagh, founded in the sixth century, was in ecclesiastical use until the seventeenth century, while the old church at Maghera (Londonderry) was used until 1819. Excavations at Nendrum (in the 1920s) and recently on Inishcaltra (Clare) illustrate the structural and chronological complexity of a long-lived site, and the majority of sites have not been excavated. In Cork and Kerry, the area studied by Vincent Hurley, ecclesiastical sites are thick on the ground, but without excavation we can rarely say with confidence when a church was established and how many were active at any particular time (Hurley 1982, 308–9).

Donnchadh Ó Corráin has considered the excavated sites on Church Island and Beginish, Co. Kerry, against the evolving picture of church development. He suggests the possibility that 'Church Island may have been a proprietory church which began as a remote hermit's cell', while 'Beginish may well have been the outfarm of the church, farmed on its behalf by church tenantry' (1981a, 339–40). I believe that this points the way to what needs to be done. Each site has to be subjected to scrutiny to see whether there are pointers, in written sources or archaeological material, to the nature of the activity on the particular site, bearing in mind always that its nature and role may have changed during a history extending often over many centuries. I will try to illustrate this approach by looking at a few examples from Northern Ireland.

Bishops are attested at about 12 northern sites in written sources of before *c.* 800. One of these is Clogher, Co Tyrone, where excavation suggests that the nearby hilltop enclosure was the royal headquarters of the Uí Chremthainn (Warner 1988, 55 and *passim*). This church was probably established in the fifth century as the seat of a bishop and a missionary centre under royal patronage. References to abbots in annals of the eighth, ninth, and tenth centuries suggest a monastic establishment by then, and the material evidence indicates a centre of craftsmanship and access to patronage in the later Early Christian period, with remains of three crosses and a sundial.

At Connor in Co Antrim the occurrence of at least five souterrains over a considerable area south of the present parish church points to a sizeable settlement, and we can note that the Life of Colmán Elo calls Connor a *civitas* (Plummer

1910, I, 259). Recent trial excavations on the site of a proposed new rectory north-east of the church have established the presence of a substantial, V-profiled ditch, of which there was no sign from the air, describing an arc of a large circle enclosing the church (Brannon forthcoming). Bishops of Connor are recorded in 659 and 726, whilst abbots occur from the late eighth century onwards. Was the settlement plundered by Vikings in 832 a bishop's establishment or a monastery in which a bishop could have resided, or did the two elements coexist?

There is no doubt that Bangor (Co Down) was a monastery, founded in the 550s, soon after the great plague. There is a wealth of written evidence including a hymn in praise of the rule of Bangor, another hymn listing the first 15 abbots, and a reference in a litany to 'four thousand monks with the grace of God under the yoke of Comgall of *Benchor*' (Plummer 1925, 61). Sadly there is very little archaeological material and the case rests on historical evidence. At Camus on the river Bann in Co Londonderry, perhaps a daughter-house of Bangor, both kinds of evidence point to a monastery. Adomnán's *Life of Columba* refers to Camus as a '*monasterium*' (Anderson, A.O. and Anderson, M.O. 1961, 318), there is excavated evidence of Early Christian period activity at the site, as well as a carved cross, a bullaun, and possible traces of an enclosure. Written sources indicate that Devenish in Co Fermanagh was certainly a monastery by the ninth century, and it may well have been monastic from its start in the mid sixth century, but there is no archaeological evidence for its very early history.

The case of Nendrum in Co Down is rather more complicated. There are indications in early tradition that a very early (fifth-century?) foundation did not flourish, but from the seventh century onwards there are frequent references to clergy in the annals, including both bishops and abbots in the seventh, eighth and ninth centuries. The archaeological evidence is plentiful, both the structures visible on the site and the material excavated in the 1920s, with enclosing walls, church, round tower, graveyard, cross-carved slabs, evidence for fine metalworking, trial-pieces, styli, a sundial and a bell (*Down* 1966, 292–5). I think, on balance, that the evidence points to monastic settlement from the seventh century onwards in which bishops were sometimes resident, rather than an episcopal establishment.

The place-name element *domnach* points to early ecclesiastical activity (Flanagan, D. 1984,

25–31), and it is likely that some of these *domnach* churches, especially the Donaghmore sites ('great church'), were early missionary bases or 'mother churches', centres for evangelizing an area. According to the *Tripartite Life* of Patrick, written in about 900, Patrick left the priest Columb at Donaghmore (Tyrone) with a service book and bell (Stokes 1887, 170–1), but otherwise the early history of the church is unknown. On the site is a fine carved cross, suggesting substantial patronage and artistic links with Armagh (perhaps in the tenth century). In 1195 the *Miscellaneous Irish Annals* record that the churches of Donaghmore and the refectory (*proinnteach*) of *Cruimthear Coluim* were burned (Ó hInnse 1947, 74–5), so in the late twelfth century there was more than one church and some kind of communal establishment. This was also the time when the O'Neills were establishing their chief seat or demesne in the parish of Donaghmore, their *Lucht Tighe*, which was still a distinctive unit in the early seventeenth century (Ó Doibhlin 1969, 10–62). There could be a parallel to be drawn here with a development traced by John Blair in late Saxon minster churches (Blair 1985). By the eleventh century some groups of clergy attached to English minsters seem to have served as royal or noble clerks, maintaining a degree of communal life but enjoying a good deal of freedom of action. My hypothetical sequence at Donaghmore would therefore include a fifth-century missionary church, perhaps (but not certainly) a monastic phase, and a community in the twelfth century serving not only the people but the local ruling family. Then, in the later middle ages, Donaghmore emerges like so many other early foundations as a parish church.

Excavated 'ecclesiastical' sites produce structural and artifactual evidence which is very similar to material from 'secular' settlements, but the presence of a church and graveyard sets them apart (Hamlin and Lynn 1989). A large enclosure, with evidence for a concentration of population and a variety of activities, economic, artistic and intellectual (like Nendrum), *could* be either a monastery or the seat of an important bishop. Written sources may allow a choice to be made, but doubt will often remain. It is likely that the majority of the hundreds of smaller ecclesiastical sites had a more modest, local, role as centres for pastoral work, with a church, burial-ground and priest's house. It is rarely possible to establish the nature of a settlement without extensive excavation, and most of our recent work on ecclesiastical sites in Northern Ireland has been in a rescue context and not on a large scale, but whatever the scale of the work it is important to bear in mind the range of possibilities which the written sources suggest.

This clearly leaves us with a far more complicated picture to untangle than any simple stereotype, like a totally 'monastic' church, but this approach will surely bring us closer to the (undoubtedly complicated) 'truth'. Despite the emphasis on problems in this paper, the work of identifying early ecclesiastical sites in Ireland is progressing in all the three ways I have been discussing. Active research on written sources and place-names is adding to the list of documented early churches. Archaeological field survey, air photography and excavation are continuing to locate sites on the ground, reveal their extent and elucidate their features. By bringing together the historical and archaeological evidence it is now at least possible to debate the nature of some of the sites and suggest how they fit into the evolving historical picture of the early Irish church.

Acknowledgements

This paper draws partly on my thesis (Hamlin 1976) in which detailed site bibliographies will be found, but also substantially on work by my colleagues in the Archaeological Survey, DOE(NI), both towards survey publications and excavations. My warm thanks go to them and to the editors of this volume.

The Early Church in Wales and the West: Concluding remarks

Charles Thomas

There are two moments in a man's life which are traumatic. One is when any of his children earn a larger income than he does; that has now happened to me, though of course on a professorial salary I can't say that that is very difficult to attain. The second is when an old synthesist like me sits there and hears all those expressions like 'dug grave' or 'E-ware' or 'special grave' or the concept of the primary cemetery and its development, and realizes with horror that I actually invented most of them. This is not a boast but a statement. If you go back over a series of youthful indiscretions, there they are. I am not sure that I meant them in the way in which they are used now but that does not matter. These are concepts which it is an archaeologist's duty to bring forward, and which should then go out and toddle round on their own and develop their own personality. We had a most interesting and well-planned assemblage of speeches. I shall mention them all though I am not actually going to go through them in detail.

To begin with Professor Wendy Davies issued a necessary counterblast to romanticism. It's a reminder, and a reminder that should be laid before you all from time to time, that there is no such thing as the 'Celtic Church'. There is merely 'the Christian church in Celtic-speaking lands', and the demonstration of lack of unity was the same sort of demonstration one could otherwise have in discussing any other district of the late Roman Empire. I don't know how we got into the Celtic Church fixation in the first place. I know how it was expanded and strengthened and popularized in the last 30 or 40 years, and this has been entirely due of course to some much-loved figures, none of whom were themselves Celts in the ethnic sense. Prominent among them was the late Nora Chadwick, who used this unhappy phrase on so many occasions, and really believed it, and to some extent wove a particular mythology all her own about it. This did not necessarily affect all her conclusions but it certainly affected a great many other people.

So, having cleared the ground, we were then able to deal in detail with Wales; and Canon Wyn Evans was right to start out of necessity with a retrospective argument. Drawing on detailed work in an area which will now forever be associated with him, he defined a *clas* as an association of interested persons. He gave us some significant instances which involved property and arguments about property which are necessarily only reflected in documents showing, I thought, (a) the capacity for the survival, and then the change, of spiritual overlordship, and (b) the likelihood that tenacity of custom is a dominant theme of Welsh society in the entire story of early medieval Welsh Christianity. This I think was the best possible demonstration. He did not actually talk about first millennium AD material at all, but merely inferred its presence with strong and persuasive examples and discussion.

He was followed in this by Huw Pryce, with an elegant discussion of the limits of inference. In the absence of finds, which he partly explained as due to the incursion of the Norsemen, we had references from early sources and from later ones, and questions about the later form of ecclesiastical estates; the question of free and bond tenants around religious towns; and this opened up a line of thinking which was followed by other speakers and which seems to me to have characterized the proceedings. I will return to this, when I try to draw a few conclusions at the end. There was a parallelism to Wyn Evans' talk in that Huw Pryce discussed the question of the physical reflections, and then of course passed over to archaeology and to the evidence of place-names.

And that takes me to Tomos Roberts. Tomos as always was able to dip into his own work and the late Melville Richards' extraordinary archive, the full publication of which we should now realize we shall never see. It's just too big. Tomos left us with one very valuable thought, one which was new to me; that there can be a distinction in Welsh place-names between those terms derived from the Latin language, which on the whole refer to burials and graves (in other words, the sacramental aspects of the disposal of the dead), and those *native* words which essentially seem to refer to buildings and constructions, that is to

the man-made features. But what he was saying
is that we are particularly fortunate in most
parts of the British Isles in possessing additional
languages which have left their mark in place-
names. Thus the linguistic stratification, and the
earliest strata (if I can use that analogy), are
important, because they will of course reflect
their usage at the time; not the usage we wish
retrospectively to force upon them, by looking
them up in the dictionary. We have the much
harder task of finding out what these words
meant in common usage at the time they were
applied. This is apposite to Wales; and it is
apposite to Ireland; it is also apposite to
Scotland, and to an area we haven't discussed
but which I can describe only as North Britain
(approximately Cumbria, Northumbria before the
Angles, and the extreme southern counties of
Scotland).

We went on then to what, to me, was a paper
of quite extraordinary interest. Jeremy Knight
alluded to Nash-Williams' background to start
with; and I cannot tell you how important it is to
have that on record. He then faced fairly the
need to explain the dichotomy, or discontinuity,
between a few aspects of Romano-British
Christianity (in particular the lack of stones in
the British Isles, the lack of those fourth-century
memorials that we have on the Continent), and
the appearance, surely in the second half of the
fifth century, of a variety of Insular forms of
these stones, particularly those inscribed with
the formula HIC IACIT. Now when Nash-
Williams wrote that footnote, about the origins of
the HIC IACIT formula in Britain (which has
been quoted as if it was the central part of the
whole book), the idea of Lyon, Vienne and the
upper Rhône Valley was, given the material of
the day, the one which could be most reasonably
put forward. It can now be expanded; it can only
be expanded by the kind of fieldwork, and the
informed visits, which Jeremy Knight and others
have been making, and by a search, always
prolonged and not always easy, through
Continental publications. I think one can say
that the general area of Gaul which could have
been seen, and in my view rightly *should* be
seen, as the principal source for the inscriptions
of post-Roman Britain moves nearer to the
Atlantic coast. It is then possible to envisage
models and contacts, of which perhaps we
possess the evidence, for between one and five
per cent of these precise links. In this instance,
I leave you with the thought that you don't need
to suppose a continuous string of introductions.
You merely need two or three introductions,

which are sufficiently influential to be adopted in
the areas in which the distribution map show us
these particular ideas are found. On a European
or Mediterranean scale, these are very small
areas indeed. We are not talking about the whole
of North Africa; we are talking about three or
four Welsh counties, or part of Cornwall and
Devon and the Isles of Scilly. So this is certainly
an explicable and acceptable model.

We moved then to the first of a series of
landscape papers. Terry James struck a
particular chord among your friends here from
Cornwall because his aerial survey is precisely
the sort of thing that, with the aid of the English
Royal Commission we have been doing, and
hoping to find the sort of evidence he showed.
And here one must acknowledge the lead and the
initial discoveries of a friend of many of us who
is not here today, Leo Swan; to whom the credit
goes for flying round in his Tiger Moth (held
together with electric flex and meccano bolts) and
spotting at Kildare and other places the
existence of the phenomenon of the enclosure and
the extent of the monastic or the ecclesiastical
nucleus, which appears to be much more widely
spread than we had originally realized. The
physical existence of outer enclosures is one of
the biggest challenges of Early Christian field
archaeology. One has these whole or part
additional earthworks; the enlarged
demarcations of concentric areas which may now
simply have become fields.

There are also from Wales accounts of paired
or twin enclosures. Ann Preston-Jones would not
have had time to prepare a riposte from the deep
south-west to this. But my immediate reaction is,
'Yes', similar native earthworks in the south-west
also occur in pairs. I don't know what the
interpretation is; the common pattern of two of
these sites fairly close together in Cornwall is
either that they are contemporary, or one is a
replacement of the other, or perhaps it
represents 'familial doubling', i.e. a family had
spread to the point where an additional enclosure
was added. It seems to me that if one of them is
then selected for use as a Christian enclosure,
this in itself is interesting. Are we looking at
something no earlier than the seventh century,
perhaps in the eighth century? This may be the
point at which, in much of Atlantic Britain, the
enclosed farmstead or enclosed homestead is
giving way to the open homestead. This is a very
imprecise but perceptible pattern, and one
reflected in place-names; and if so, this adds yet
another element of value to the tremendously
interesting and attractively presented work

which is coming out of Dyfed Archaeological Trust.

There was a break between the papers by Terry and Heather James, and we had Diane Brook's meticulous paper, which gave *me* particular pleasure because her first map was a very clear and persuasive definition of what I tried to show some years ago is 'Sub-Roman' in the sense of being later than the Roman period but earlier than the English settlement. She showed us all this area, a great slice coming down the western half of the British Isles, which she rightly mapped on either side of the Severn and Offa's Dyke (Fig. 9.1). Then she proceeded to give a persuasive and cogent analysis of curvilinear churchyards, and the churchyards with large areas. We had the value of standardized criteria, and the application of these to isolate percentages and fractions. The importance of her demonstration is the strong reminder that the 'Celtic' area of Christianity does not stop at Offa's Dyke, any more than it stops at the Tamar Bridge or the River Tweed.

There are also areas of Northumberland where precisely this sort of treatment could be done. I suspect there are areas of the West Midlands (I won't define that more closely) and the whole of Cumbria. Of course counties like Hereford and Shropshire are also places where a great deal more work needs to be done. We look forward immensely to the elaboration of Diane Brook's fieldwork, and the conclusions which will come from this, because on such a structure which is raised from first-hand observation and analysis we can impose historical interpretations.

From Heather James we had a presentation which made me long to interrupt her and say 'Where is that published?' or 'Where is that going to be published?' We flashed through more and more remarkable examples of what is being dug up in Wales, raising questions of the location and the reuse of prehistoric ritual and funerary monuments of a very early stage, and then of the reuse of some that should belong to the pre-Roman Iron Age, or to what elsewhere would be within the full Roman period. Conservatism in the choice of sites, and innovation in practice, was another extremely useful and valuable observation, and one brilliantly developed in the presentation of that evidence.

I believe that the best line towards clarification of the reuse of these monuments lies in what Thomas Charles-Edwards pointed out about boundaries; but I would expand that, as a fieldworker, to point out that the boundary is a mark of marginal land, and that the precise location and distribution of many of these ritual sites are on those areas not required for prime agrarian use. This is probably a sorry reflection on the human race! We are quite prepared to sacrifice the things we don't want to spiritual need, like the man who gives a halfpenny or a trouser button in the collection plate. To that extent, the land you require to set aside permanently for burial is almost certainly the land you don't want for anything else. I suspect that so mundane and secular a wish probably overrides ideas of sacrifice.

This is something that can be tested in maps, and obviously has been tested; and that takes me to Ann Preston-Jones. Ann has come as an ambassadress, representing some 20 or 30 years of work in Cornwall. Let me give an idea of the extraordinary richness and the potential of what we have, in a small area, a small peninsula whose bounds for about six-sevenths of its perimeter are fixed by the sea. At least we know when we can stop! We have a fossilized landscape, and one which is changing very rapidly. By the time that I am 6 feet down, the Cornwall which I knew as a boy will no longer exist. It barely exists now, because it is being carved up at such an alarming rate. We have at the moment only a few potential redundant churches in the Diocese of Truro. This does not mean that there are now some 200 flourishing churches; in other areas about 30 would have been declared redundant some time ago, and many of them with their graveyards cannot be kept up. I am not suggesting this is an open licence for the archaeologist to go and excavate churchyards although there are one or two cases where this would, I think, be justified. What it means is that analysis of the first millennium AD landscape must proceed at a faster rate. You have seen sketched out for you an extraordinary range of examples; with a partial rehabilitation of geographical determinism. You also got the message that the kind of place-name work Tomos Roberts has done, and that Oliver Padel has been doing in Cornwall, is principally of value to the archaeologist. Of course it is of interest to the historical linguist, the lexicographer and to the place-name student; but if you take this out in the field, it does add a complete dimension to fieldwork, to the identification of sites and to their interpretation. Exciting news from Cornwall should be expected during the next lustrum.

We ended with what can be described as 'a broadening of the horizons'. Elizabeth Alcock brought you the news, which will not be familiar to everyone, that there is a completely new look in the concept of early burial types in north and north-east Scotland, which has only emerged in comparatively recent years as the result of chance discoveries, air photography and some excavations. I have never wavered in the view, which I put forward some 30 years ago, that given all the alternatives the least improbable explanation of the Pictish Class I stones is that they mark burials. In the interval I have seen some very peculiar books, none of which have convinced me because they have failed to address questions which are legitimate questions arising from the material. I do not believe we need look to south-east Asia for anthropological explanations. In my view, there is all the reason in the world to suppose that Picts were interring or inhuming or cremating or otherwise getting rid of their dead, in a pagan fashion, as late as the sixth and seventh centuries. I think this entirely possible. Bear in mind the size of Scotland, the difficulty of field work in those enormous areas, the absence, for historical and explicable reasons, of Royal Commission Inventories for Perthshire and Aberdeen, which are the crucial areas, which, alas, can never now be inventoried in the old style, and the relatively few people on the ground. I say nothing about the shortage of funds; and it is wonderful that results come out at all. We should be grateful for everything, and we are very grateful to Elizabeth for drawing this to our attention.

What is striking about the collection of papers we have heard this weekend and, indeed, about the entire conference is the difference between it and the kind of similar meeting we had or could have had or, indeed, used to have 15 or 25 years ago. The entire tenor has changed. I can recall, and Leslie and Elizabeth Alcock will also recall, events of this nature which were carried out almost entirely in terms of art-history; going round in those art-historical circles which seem to have no release, no beginning and no ending; or else matters were discussed entirely in terms of epigraphy, and proceedings would end with the linguists almost having fisticuffs at the back. We had very little of the *field* evidence.

What is new is the explosion of fieldwork, the information that has come out of field survey, particularly by professional units, which is why we must be so delighted the Dyfed Archeological Trust made a contribution here. Inevitably, this is producing a meaningful collection of data which can be interpreted and analysed to some extent as the work goes along, and at least half of which is going to refer to the remains in the

landscape of the last few millennia, and therefore by definition to Christian archaeology in the field. If this is so, and you must agree that it has been demonstrated to be amply so in the papers given here, then this indicates the next stage; and I now confine my remarks to Wales.

In the past one of the problems in Wales has been the country's own geography. We have this near-saucer, with all the intellectual riches concentrated round the rim; modern communications, to which I need hardly refer; and the difficulties of keeping in touch, and of having to spread a limited number of people around the landscape. It's always been extremely difficult to see how a coherent policy of fieldwork or excavation could ever emerge. I don't think this is crucial. What *is* necessary is contact between people; the intercommunication of those working in the field, and the insemination of ideas as between one group and another. Don't misunderstand me when I say that I don't think more excavation is necessarily at the top of the list. Excavation in many cases will give the answer; in many cases it is forced upon us by the circumstances of rescue, or development. But I would have thought that, if money is available, target number one would be a greatly-increased programme of air photography. I was alarmed to learn how very poorly this is funded in Wales. It seems to me that pressure should be placed heavily, not only on the Commission, but on other agencies that should be making grants, at least to bring funding to the level at which the English Royal Commission funds flying in England, because proportionately the rewards here in Wales seem enormous. That is point one. The next should be the encouragement by any means of deeper analysis of the landscape, along the various lines which have been laid down over this weekend. There are so many things to do. One does not have to bite off the whole of Dyfed at one go. You can see the kind of thing that goes on in a place like Cornwall, which is really quite small. Anglesey is a prime instance and work there can hardly fail to give you a series of alternatives for, say, that half-millennium between AD 600 and 1100, for which conclusions are certain to emerge which might be tested by excavation. The results so far, which in a sense have arisen haphazardly because individuals are pursuing lines of research which overlap one with the other, have given a picture of work and progress and understanding in Wales of the development of the Christian landscape and society, which I think would have been impossible ten years ago. It might even have been difficult to present it all in this form five years ago. I am immensely heartened to see this. I have found this an instructive and exciting weekend and I hope that this work will continue. Don't bother so much about the minutiae for the time-being. It is the broad canvas that is necessary.

One wants to know what is happening in the landscape; what these sites and early divisions *mean*. You have, in Wales, the advantages of two languages, Latin and Welsh, of all the place-names. You have both the oral tradition and that entire historical advantage the moment that either language is committed to writing. One has the documentation and the continuity which has been explained to us. I know that Wales has suffered for many years under the whips and lashes of Whitehall, but let us all be thankful for the Tithe Apportionment Commissioners and Finsbury Square. Without the Tithe Maps, there are many parts of the British Isles where it would be almost impossible to start working backwards. I trust that this extended summary gives not only my reactions, which aren't important, but an indication of the fact that work in Wales is clearly on the right lines and should proceed very much in these directions. It's all landscape archaeology now, and quite rightly so.

Bibliography

Acta Sanctorum 1887. *Acta Sanctorum, Novembris, Tome 1*, Paris.

Adams, J.H. 1957. The mediaeval chapels of Cornwall, *J. Roy. Inst. Cornwall*, new series 3(1), 48–65.

A.E. 1846. A few words to church repairers and restorers, *Archaeol. Cambrensis*, 1, 364–8.

Alcock, L. 1971. *Arthur's Britain: history and archaeology A.D. 367–634*, London.

A.L.I. 1865–1901. *Ancient Laws of Ireland*, 6 vols, Dublin.

Allen, J.R. 1899. Early Christian art in Wales, *Archaeol. Cambrensis*, 5th ser. 16, 1–69.

Allen, J.R. 1989. *Celtic Crosses of Wales*, (reprint of Allen 1899) Felinfach.

Allen, J.R. and Anderson, J. 1903. *The Early Christian monuments of Scotland*, Edinburgh.

Anderson, A.O. and M. O. (ed. and trans.) 1961. *Adomnan's Life of Columba*, London/ Edinburgh.

Anderson, W.B. (ed.) 1963–5. *Sidonius Apollinaris: Letters*, 2 vols, London.

Anon., 1819–20. Miscellaneous intelligence, *The Cambro-Briton*, 1, 359–60.

Anon., 1981. *The parish church of St. Mary Magdalene, Hewelsfield*, no publication details, available at the church.

Anwyl, E. (ed.) 1909. *The poetry of the Gogynfeirdd from the Myvyrian Archaeology of Wales*, Denbigh.

Armagh, forthcoming. *An archaeological survey of County Armagh*.

Arndt, W. and Krusch, B. (eds) 1885. *Historiae Francorum. Monumenta Germaniae Historica, Scriptores rerum Merovingicarum*, Vol.1, Hanover.

Babut, C. 1920. *Saint Martin de Tours*, Paris.

Bailey, R.N. and Cramp, R. 1988. *Corpus of Anglo-Saxon stone sculpture. Vol. 2: Cumberland, Westmorland and Lancashire North-of-the Sands*, Oxford.

Baring-Gould, S. and Fisher, J. 1907–13. *The Lives of the British Saints*, 4 vols, London.

Barley, M.W. and Hanson, R.P.C. (eds) 1968 *Christianity in Britain, 300–700*, Leicester.

Baron Hill Mss. at Univ. Coll. N. Wales Library, Bangor.

Barrow, G.L. 1979. *The round towers of Ireland: a study and gazetteer*, Dublin.

Bartrum, P.C. 1963–4. The pedigrees of the Welsh tribal patriarchs, *Nat. Lib. Wales J.*, 13, 93–146.

Bartrum, P.C. (ed.) 1966. *Early Welsh genealogical tracts*, Cardiff.

Bartrum, P.C. 1974. *Welsh genealogies AD 300–1400*, Cardiff.

Bateson, J.D. 1973. Roman material from Ireland: a re-consideration, *Proc. Roy. Ir. Acad.*, 73C, 21–97.

Bateson, J.D. 1976. Further finds of Roman material from Ireland, *Proc. Roy. Ir. Acad.*, 76C, 171-80.

Baynes, E.N. 1920. The old monasteries, abbeys, and chapels of Anglesey, *Trans. Anglesey Antiq. Soc.*, 33–43.

Baynes, E.N. 1935. Some stone-lined graves at Llanrhyddlad, *Trans. Anglesey Antiq. Soc.*, 189–91.

Beresford, M.W. 1954. *The lost villages of England*, London.

Bernier, G. 1982. *Les Chrétientes Bretonnes Continentales depuis les origines jusqu'au IXe siècle*, Dossiers du centre regional archéologique d'Alet, Rennes.

Best, R.I. and Lawlor, H.J. (eds) 1931. *The Martyrology of Tallaght*, London.

Biddle, M. and Kjolbe-Biddle, B. forthcoming. *The Anglo-Saxon Minsters at Winchester*, Winchester Studies 4.i.

Bieler, L. 1949. Insular palaeography, present state and problems, *Scriptorium*, 3, 267–94.

Bieler, L. (ed.) 1963. *The Irish penitentials*, Dublin.

Bieler, L. (ed.) 1979. *The Patrician texts in the Book of Armagh*, Dublin.

Bigelow, G.F. 1984. Two kerbed cairns from Sandwick, Unst, Shetland, in eds J.G.P. Friell and W.G.Watson, 115–30.

Birch, W. de G. (ed.) 1885–93. *Cartularium Saxonicum: a collection of charters relating to Anglo-Saxon history*, 3 vols, London.

Black, E.W. 1986. Romano-British burial customs and religious beliefs in south-east England, *Archaeol. J.*, 143, 201–39.

Blair, J. 1985. Secular minister churches in Domesday Book, in (ed. P.H. Sawyer) *Domesday Book: a reassessment*, 104–42, London.

Blair, J. (ed.) 1988. *Minsters and parish churches. The local church in transition 950–1200*, Oxford.

Bliss, W.H. and Twemlow, J.A. (eds) 1904. *Calendar of entries in the papal registers relating to Great Britain and Ireland, papal letters, Vol. V, A.D. 1396–1404*, London.

Boake, E.J. 1926. Report on the excavations of the Chapel of St Justinian, St Davids, *Archaeol. Cambrensis*, 81, 381–94.

Bonney, D. 1979. Early boundaries and estates in southern England, in (ed. P.H. Sawyer) *Medieval settlement: continuity and change*, 41–51, London.

Boon, G.C. 1962. A Christian monogram at Caerwent, *Bull. Board Celtic Stud.*, 19, 338–44.

Boon, G.C. 1981–2. Three bones of S. Tatheus or Duw yn anghyfiawn ni rann, *Monmouthshire Ant.*,4 (3–4), 2–5.

Bourke, C. 1980. Early Irish hand-bells, *J. Roy. Soc. Antiq. Ir.*, 110, 52–66.

Bowen, E.G. 1954. *The settlements of the Celtic saints in Wales*, Cardiff.

Bowen, E.G. 1977. *Saints, seaways and settlements in the Celtic lands*, Cardiff.

Bowen, E.G. 1979. *A history of Llanbadarn Fawr*, Llandysul.

Bradley, R. 1987. Time regained: the creation of continuity, *J. Brit. Archaeol. Ass.*, 140, 1–17.

Brannon, N.F. forthcoming. Report on Connor excavation, *Ulster J. Archaeol.*

Brassil, K.S. 1988. Tandderwen, *Archaeol. Wales*, 28, 51.

Brassil, K.S. and Meredith, P.J., 1986. Square-plan ditches: Dark Age graves at Tandderwen, Denbigh, Clwyd, *Archaeol. Wales*, 26, 21–2.

Brassil, K.S. and Owen, W.G., 1987. Tandderwen, Denbigh, *Archaeol. Wales*, 27, 58.

Brett, M. 1975. *The English church under Henry I*, Oxford.

Brewer, J.S., Dimock, J.F. and Warner, G.F. (eds) 1861–91. *Giraldi Cambrensis Opera*, Rolls series, 8 vols, London (NB *De Jure* = Vol. 3).

Britnell, W. 1982. The excavation of two round barrows at Trelystan, Powys, *Proc. Prehist. Soc.*, 48, 133–201.

Britnell, W. 1985. Capel Maelog, *Archaeol. Wales*, 25, 44–6.

Britnell, W. 1986a. Capel Maelog rediscovered, *Trans. Radnorshire Soc.*, 56, 14–9.

Britnell, W. 1986b. Capel Maelog, *Archaeol. Wales*, 26, 58–9.

Britnell, W. 1990. Capel Maelog, Llandrindod Wells, Powys: excavations 1984–87, *Medieval Archaeol.* 34, 27–96.

Britnell, W., Arnold, C. and Dorling, P. 1984. Capel Maelog Llandrindod Wells, *Archaeol. Wales*, 24, 74–5.

Britnell, W. and Jones, N. 1989. Pennant Melangell, Llangynog, *Archl. Wales*, 29, 63–4.

Bromwich, R. (ed.) 1972. *The beginnings of Welsh poetry: studies by Sir Ifor Williams*, Cardiff.

Brook, D.L. 1981. Early ecclesiastical sites in south-east Wales, unpublished M.A. thesis, Cardiff, Univ. of Wales.

Brook, D.L. 1985–88. The Early Christian church in Gwent, *Monmouthshire Antiq.*, 5 (3), 67–84.

Brooke, C.N.L. 1986. *The church and the Welsh border in the central middle ages*, Woodbridge.

Brown, T.J. 1977. The Insular system of scripts, *c.* 600– *c.*850, *The James P. R. Lyell Lectures in Bibliography*, unpublished lectures series, Univ. Oxford.

Brown, T.J. 1982. The Irish element in the Insular system of scripts to circa A.D. 850, in (ed. Löwe, H.) *Die Iren und Europa im früheren Mittelalter*, 101–19, Stuttgart.

Brown, T. J. 1984. The oldest Irish manuscripts and their late antique background, in eds P. Ní Chatháin and M. Richter, 311–27.

Brownbill, J. (ed.) 1914. The ledger-book of Vale Royal Abbey, *Lancs. Chesh. Record Soc.*, 68.

Bruce-Mitford, R.L.S. 1956. A Dark Age settlement at Mawgan Porth, Cornwall, in (ed. R.L.S. Bruce-Mitford) *Recent archaeological excavations in Britain*, 167–96, London.

Bu'Lock, J.D. 1956. Early Christian memorial formulae, *Archaeol. Cambrensis*, 105, 133–41.

Bullough, D. 1983. Burial, community and belief in the early medieval West, in (ed. P. Wormald) *Ideal and reality in Frankish and Anglo-Saxon society: studies presented to J M Wallace-Hadrill*, 177–201, Oxford.

Butler, L.A.S. 1979. The 'monastic city' in Wales: myth or reality?, *Bull. Board. Celtic Stud.*, 28 (3), 458–67.

Cabrol, F. and Leclerq, H. 1913–53. *Dictionnaire d'archéologie Chrétienne et de liturgie*, 15 vols, Paris.

Cambridge, E. 1989. Why did the community of St Cuthbert settle at Chester-le-Street?, in (eds G. Bonner, D. Rollason and C. Stancliffe) *St Cuthbert, his cult and his community to AD 1200*, 367–86, Woodbridge.

Camden, W. 1722. *Camden's Wales*, reprinted Carmarthen 1984.

Cameron, K. 1968. *Eccles* in English place-names, in eds M.W. Barley and R.P.C. Hanson, 87–92.

Campbell, A. (ed.) 1967. *Aethelwulf, De Abbatibus*, Oxford.

Campbell, J. 1986. *Essays in Anglo-Saxon history*, London/Ronceverte.

Canner, A.C. 1982. *The parish of Tintagel: some historical notes*, Camelford.

Carlyon-Britton, P.W.P. 1906. Cornish numismatics, *J. Roy. Inst. Cornwall*, 17, 52–62.

Carlyon-Britton, P.W.P. 1908. Cornish numismatics, *Brit. Numis. J.*, 3, 107.

Caulfield, S. 1981. Celtic problems in the Irish Iron Age, in ed. D.Ó Corráin, 205–15.

Chadwick, N.K. 1958. Intellectual life in west Wales in the last days of the Celtic church, in (eds N.K. Chadwick *et al*) *Studies in the early British church*, 121–82, Cambridge.

Charles-Edwards, T. 1971. The seven bishop houses of Dyfed, *Bull. Board Celtic Stud.*, 24, 247–62.

Charles-Edwards, T. 1976. Boundaries in Irish law, in (ed. Sawyer, P.H.) *Medieval settlement: continuity and change*, 83–7, London.

Charles-Edwards, T. 1983. Bede, the Irish and the Britons, *Studia Celtica*, 15, 42–52.

Charles-Edwards, T. 1984. The church and settlement, in eds P. Ní Chatháin and M. Richter, 167–75.

Clark, G.L. (ed.) 1910. *Cartae et Aliae Munimenta quae ad Dominium de Glamorgancia pertinent*, 6 vols, Talygarn.

Clarke, H.B. and Sims, A. (eds) 1985 *The comparative history of urban origins in non-Roman Europe*, 2 vols, Brit. Archaeol. Rep. S255, Oxford.

Clarke, J. 1981. Welsh sculptured crosses and cross-slabs of the pre-Norman period, unpublished Ph.D. thesis, Univ. Coll. London.

Clercq, C. de (ed.) 1963. *Concilia Galliae, A.511–A.695* Corpus Christianorum Series Latina 148a, Turnhout.

Close-Brooks, J. 1980. Excavations in the Dairy Park, Dunrobin, Sutherland, 1977, *Proc. Soc. Antiq. Scot.*, 110, 328–45.

Close-Brooks, J. 1984. Pictish and other burials, in eds J.G.P. Friell and W.G. Watson, 87–114.

Colgrave, B. (ed.) 1927. *Eddius, Life of Wilfrid*, Cambridge.

Colgrave, B. and Mynors, R.A.B. (eds) 1969. *Bede's*

Ecclesiastical History of the English People, Oxford.

Collingwood, R.G. and Richmond, I. 1969. *The archaeology of Roman Britain*, London.

Collingwood, R.G. and Wright, R.P. 1965. *Roman inscriptions of Britain*, Oxford.

The Commissioners of the Public Records of the Kingdom 1810–34. *Valor Ecclesiasticus Temp. Henr. VIII Auctoritate Regia Institutus*, 6 vols, London.

Connolly, S. and Picard, J.M. 1987. Cogitosus: Life of Saint Brigit, *J. Roy. Soc. Antiq. Ir.*, 117, 5–27.

Contreni, J.J. 1986. The Irish contribution to the European classroom, in eds D. E. Evans, J. G. Griffith and E. M. Jope, 79–90.

Coupry, M.J. 1967. Circonscription d'Aquitaine, *Gallia*, 25, 327–72.

Cowie, T. 1978. Excavations at the Catstane, Midlothian, 1977, *Proc. Soc. Antiq. Scot.*, 109, 166–201.

Cowley, F.G. 1971. The church in Glamorgan from the Norman Conquest to the beginning of the fourteenth century, in (ed. T.B. Pugh) *Glamorgan County History*, Vol. 3, 87–135, Cardiff.

Cowley, F.G. 1977. *The monastic order in south Wales 1066–1349*, Cardiff.

Cox, J.C. 1911. *The sanctuaries and sanctuary seekers of mediaeval England*, London.

Cox, J C. 1912. *The churches of Cornwall*, London.

Coxe, W. 1904. *An historical tour through Monmouthshire*, Brecon.

Cramp, R.J. 1969. Excavation at the Anglo-Saxon monastic sites of Wearmouth and Jarrow, *Medieval Archaeol.*, 13, 21–66.

Cramp, R.J. 1976. Monastic sites, in (ed. D.M. Wilson) *The archaeology of Anglo-Saxon England*, 201–52, London.

Cramp, R.J. 1978. The Anglo-Saxon tradition in the ninth century, in ed. J. Lang, 1–32.

Cramp, R.J. 1984. *Corpus of Anglo-Saxon stone sculpture., Vol. 1: County Durham and Northumberland*, Oxford.

Crofts, C.B. 1955. *A short history of St Buryan*, Camborne.

Crouch, D. 1989. Urban: first bishop of Llandaff, 1107–34, *J. Welsh Eccles. Hist.*, 6, 1–15.

Cunliffe, B. 1974. *Iron Age communities in Britain*, London.

Daniels, R. 1988. The Anglo-Saxon monastery at Church Close, Hartlepool, Cleveland, *Archaeol. J.*, 145, 158–210.

Dark, K. R. 1989. High status sites, kingship and state formation in post-Roman Western Britain A.D. 400–700, unpublished Ph.D. thesis, Univ. Cambridge.

Davidson, A.F. and J.E., Owen-John, H.S. and Toft, L.A. 1987. Excavations at the sand covered medieval settlement at Rhossili, West Glamorgan, *Bull. Board Celtic Stud.*, 34, 244–69.

Davies, J.C. 1943–4. A grant by David ap Gruffydd, *Nat. Lib. Wales J.*, 3, 29–32.

Davies, J.C. (ed.) 1946–8. *Episcopal acts and cognate documents relating to Welsh dioceses, 1066–1272*, 2 vols, Cardiff.

Davies, R.R. 1987. *Conquest, coexistence and change: Wales 1063–1415*, Oxford.

Davies, W. 1973. Liber Landavensis: its construction and credibility, *Eng. Hist. Rev.*, 88, 335–51.

Davies, W. 1974–5. The Celtic Church, *J. Religious Stud.*, 8, 406–11.

Davies, W. 1978a. *An early Welsh microcosm: studies in the Llandaff Charters*, London.

Davies, W. 1978b. Land and power in early medieval Wales, *Past and Present*, 81, 3–23.

Davies, W. 1979a. *The Llandaff Charters*, Aberystwyth.

Davies, W. 1979b. Roman settlements and post-Roman estates in south-east Wales, in (ed. P.J. Casey) *The end of Roman Britain*, 155–173, Brit. Archaeol. Rep. 71, Oxford.

Davies, W. 1981. Property rights and property claims in Welsh *Vitae* of the eleventh century, in (eds E. Patlagean and P. Riché) *Hagiographie, cultures et sociétés IVe-XIIe siècles*, 515–33, Paris.

Davies, W. 1982a. *Wales in the early middle ages*, Leicester.

Davies, W. 1982b. The Latin charter-tradition in western Britain, Brittany and Ireland in the early mediaeval period, in (eds D. Whitelock, R. McKitterick and D. Dumville) *Ireland in early mediaeval Europe*, 258–80, Cambridge.

Davies, W. 1982c. Clerics as rulers: some implications of the terminology of ecclesiastical authority in early medieval Ireland, in (ed. N. Brooks) *Latin and the vernacular languages in early medieval Britain*, 81–97, Leicester.

Davies, W. 1983. Priests and rural communities in east Brittany in the ninth century, *Études Celtiques*, 20, 177–97.

Davies, W. 1988. *Small worlds. The village community in early medieval Brittany*, London.

Davies, W. and Wormald, P. 1980. *The Celtic Church*, Audio-Learning Tape.

Davies, W.H. 1968. The church in Wales, in eds M.W. Barley and R.P.C. Hanson, 131–50.

Dawson, M.L. 1918. Notes on the history of Glasbury, *Archaeol. Cambrensis*, 18, 6th ser., 6–34, 279–319.

Delaney, T. (ed.) 1970–6. *Excavations, summary accounts of archaeological work in Ireland*, Belfast.

The Deputy Keeper of the Records (superintendent) 1891. *Calendar of the Patent Rolls preserved in the Public Record Office, Edward III, 1327–30*, London.

De Rossi, J. (ed.) 1857–61. *Inscriptiones Christianae Urbis Romae septimo saeculo antiquiores*, 2 vols, Rome.

Dimock, J.F. (ed.) 1868. *Giraldi Cambrensis Itinerarium Kambriae et Descriptio Kambriae*, in (eds J.S. Brewer, J.F. Dimock and G.F. Warner) *Giraldi Cambrensis Opera*, 8 vols., Rolls Series, 1861–91), Vol. 6, London.

Doble, G.H. 1929. *Four saints of the Fal: St Gluvias, St Kea, St Fili, St Rumon*, Cornish saints series 20.

Doble, G.H. 1938a. *Saint Petrock, abbot and confessor*, Cornish saints series 11 (3rd ed.).

Doble, G.H. 1938b. *Saint Gerent*, Cornish saints series 41.

Doble, G.H. 1940. *Saint Winwaloe*, Cornish saints series 4 (2nd ed.).

Dodwell, C.R. 1982. *Anglo-Saxon art: a new perspective*, Manchester.

Doherty, C. 1980. Exchange and trade in medieval Ireland, *J. Roy. Soc. Antiq. Ir.*, 110, 67–89.

Doherty, C. 1984a. The basilica in early Ireland, *Peritia*, 3, 303–15.

Doherty, C. l984b. The use of relics in early Ireland, in eds P. Ní Chatháin and M. Richter, 89–101.

Doherty, C. 1985. The monastic town in early medieval Ireland, in eds H.B. Clarke and A. Simms, Vol. 1, 45–75.

Dolley, M. and Knight, J.K. 1970. Some single finds of tenth- and eleventh-century English coins from Wales, *Archaeol. Cambrensis*, 119, 75–82.

Dolley, R.H.M. (ed.) 1961. *Anglo-Saxon coins*, London.

Donaldson, G. 1952–3. Scottish bishops' sees before the reign of David I, *Proc. Soc. Antiq. Scot.*, 87, 106–17.

Down 1966. An archaeological survey of County Down, Belfast.

Dumville, D.N. 1974. Some aspects of the chronology of the *Historia Brittonum*, *Bull. Board Celtic Stud.*, 25, 439–45.

Dumville, D.N. 1984a. Gildas and Maelgwn, in eds M. Lapidge and D. Dumville, 51–9.

Dumville, D.N. 1984b. The chronology of De Excidio Britanniae, Book I, in eds M. Lapidge and D. Dumville, 61–84.

Dumville, D.N. 1984c. Gildas and Uinniau, in eds M. Lapidge and D. Dumville, 207–14.

Dumville, D.N. 1984d. Some British aspects of the earliest Irish Christianity, in eds P. Ní Chatháin and M. Richter, 16–24.

Dumville, D.N. 1985a. On editing and translating medieval Irish chronicles, *Cambridge Medieval Celtic Stud.*, 10, 67–86.

Dumville, D.N. 1985b. Late seventh- or eighth-century evidence for the British transmission of Pelagius, *Cambridge Medieval Celtic Stud.*, 10, 39–52.

Duncan, A.A.M. 1975. *Scotland: the making of the kingdom*, Edinburgh.

Edwards, A.J.H. 1927. Excavation of graves at Ackergill, *Proc. Soc. Antiq. Scot.*, 61, 196–200.

Edwards, N. 1983. An early group of crosses from the kingdom of Ossory, *J. Roy. Soc. Antiq. Ir.*, 113, 5–46.

Edwards, N. 1985. The origins of the free-standing cross in Ireland: imitation or innovation?, *Bull. Board Celtic Stud.*, 32, 393–410.

Edwards, N. 1986. Anglesey in the early middle ages: the archaeological evidence, *Trans. Anglesey Antiq. Soc.*, 19–41.

Edwards, N. 1990. *The archaeology of early medieval Ireland*, London.

Edwards, N. forthcoming. Dark Age Clwyd, in *The archaeology of Clwyd* .

Edwards, N. and Lane, A. (eds) 1988. *Early medieval settlements in Wales AD 400–1100*, Bangor/Cardiff.

Ellis, H. (ed.) 1838. *Registrum vulgariter nuncupatum "The Record of Caernarvon" e codice MS. Harleiano 696 descriptum*, Record Commission, London.

Emanuel, H.D. (ed.) 1967. *The Latin texts of the Welsh laws*, Cardiff.

Enright, M.J. 1985. Royal succession and abbatial prerogative in Adomnán's *Vita Columbae*, *Peritia*, 4, 83–103.

Eogan, G. 1968. Excavations at Knowth, Co. Meath. 1962–5, *Proc. Roy. Ir. Acad.*, 66C, 299–400.

Eogan, G. 1974. Report on the excavations of some passage-graves, unprotected inhumation burials and a settlement site at Knowth, Co. Meath, *Proc. Roy. Ir. Acad.*, 74C, 11-112.

Etienne, R. 1962. *Bordeaux Antique*, Bordeaux.

Evans, D.E. Griffith, J.C. and Jope, E.M. (eds) 1986. *Proceedings of the seventh international congress of Celtic studies, Oxford 1983*, Oxford.

Evans, D.S. (ed.) 1977. *Historia Gruffud vab Kenan*, Cardiff.

Evans, D.S. 1979. Irish and the languages of post-Roman Wales, *Studies* 68, 19–32.

Evans, E. 1949–50. Arwystli and Cyfeiliog in the sixteenth century. An Elizabethan inquisition, *Montgomery Collections*, 51, 23–37.

Evans, J.G. (ed.) 1888. *Facsimile edition of the Black Book of Carmarthen*, Oxford.

Evans, J.G. (ed.) 1898. *Reports on manuscripts in the Welsh language*, Vol. 1, London.

Evans, J.G. and Rhys, J. (eds) 1893. *The text of the Book of Llan Dav*, Oxford (repr. Aberystwyth, 1979).

Evans, J.W. 1986. The early church in Denbighshire, *Trans. Denbighs. Hist. Soc.*, 35, 61–81.

Eygun, M.F. 1963. Circonscription de Poitiers, *Gallia*, 21, 433–84.

Eygun, M.F. 1967. Circonscription de Poitou-Charentes, *Gallia*, 25, 239–70.

Fanning, T. 1981. Excavation of an Early Christian cemetery and settlement at Reask, Co. Kerry, *Proc. Roy. Ir. Acad.*, 81C, 67–172.

Fawtier, R. (ed.) 1912. *La Vie de Saint Samson*, Paris.

Fedière, A. 1985. Circonscription du Centre, *Gallia*, 43, 297–356.

Fenn, R.W.D. 1974. Isolation or involvement? in (eds O.W. Jones and D. Walker) *Links with the past, Swansea and Brecon historical essays*, 21–35, Llandybie.

Fenton, R. 1810. *A historical tour through Pembrokeshire*, London, (reprinted 1903, Hereford).

Finberg, H.P.R. 1961. *The early charters of the West Midlands*, Leicester.

Finberg, H.P.R. 1963. *Early charters of Devon and Cornwall* (2nd ed.), Leicester.

Fisher, J. 1926. The Welsh Celtic bells, *Archaeol. Cambrensis*, 81, 324–34.

Flanagan, D. 1969. Ecclesiastical nomenclature in Irish texts and place-names: a comparison, *Proc. 10th international congress of onomastic sciences*, 2, 379–88.

Flanagan, D. 1984. The Christian impact on early Ireland: place-names evidence, in eds P. Ní Chatháin and M. Richter, 25–51.

Flanagan, L.N.W. 1960. Bone beads and ring from Newgrange Co. Meath, *Ulster J. Archaeol*, 23, 61-2.

Ford, P.J. 1970. Llywarch, ancestor of Welsh Princes, *Speculum*, 45, 442–50.

Fournier, P. 1909. Le Liber ex lege Moysi et les tendances bibliques du droit canonique irlandais, *Revue Celtique*, 30, 221–34.

Fowler, E. 1960. The origin and development of the penannular brooch in Europe, *Proc. Prehist. Soc.*, 26, 149–77.

Fox, A. 1939. The siting of some inscribed stones of the Dark Ages in Glamorgan and Breconshire, *Archaeol. Cambrensis*, 94, 30–41.

Fox, A. 1946. Early Christian period. I. Settlement sites and other remains, in (ed. V.E. Nash-Williams) *A hundred years of Welsh archaeology. Centenary volume, 1846–1946*, 105–22, Cambrian Archaeol. Assoc.

Fox, C. 1940a. The re-erection of the Maen Madoc, Ystradfellte, Breconshire, *Archaeol. Cambrensis*, 95, 210–6.

Fox, C. 1940b. An Irish bronze pin from Anglesey, *Archaeol. Cambrensis*, 95, 248.

Fox, C. 1955. *Offa's Dyke*, Oxford.

Friell, J.G.P. and Watson, W.G. (eds) 1984. *Pictish studies: settlement, burial and art in Dark Age Northern Britain*, Brit. Archaeol. Rep. 125, Oxford.

Fulford, M.J. 1989. Byzantium and Britain: a Mediterranean perspective on post-Roman Mediterranean imports in western Britain and Ireland, *Medieval Archaeol.* 33, 1–6.

Gauthier, M. 1986. Aix-en-Provence, *Gallia*, 44, 379–83.

Gauthier, M. and Picard, J.C. 1986. *Topographie Chrétienne des Cités de la Gaule des origines au milieu du VIIIe siècle, Vol. 1, Province Ecclésiastique de Trier (Belgica Prima), Vol. 2, Provinces Ecclésiastique d'Aix et d'Embrun (Narbonensis Secunda et Alpes Maritimae et Corsisca), Vol. 3, Provinces Ecclésiastiques de Vienne et d'Arles (Viennensis et Alpes Graiae et Poenincae), Vol. 4, Province Ecclésiastique de Lyon (Lugdunensis Prima)*, Paris.

Gelling, M. 1982. Some meanings of stow, in ed. S M Pearce, 187–96.

Gem, R. 1988. The English parish church in the 11th and early 12th centuries: a great rebuilding?, in ed. J. Blair, 21–30.

Goodier, A. 1984. The formation of boundaries in Anglo-Saxon England: a statistical study, *Medieval Archaeol.* 28, 1–21.

Gougaud, L. 1922. La question des abbayes-évêchés bretonnes, *Revue Mabillon*, 12, 90–104.

Gourlay, R. 1984. A symbol stone and cairn at Watenan, Caithness, in eds Friell, J.G.P. and Watson, W.G., 131–4.

Gowen, M. forthcoming. *Report of archaeological excavations on north-east gas pipeline, phase 2.*

Gratwick, A.S. 1982. *Latinitas Britannica*: was British Latin archaic?, in (ed. N. Brooks) *Latin and the vernacular languages in early medieval Britain*, 1–79, Leicester.

Green, C.J.S. 1979. *Poundbury — a summary of recent excavations at Poundbury, Dorchester*, Dorchester.

Green, C.J.S. 1982. The cemetery of a Romano-British Christian community at Poundbury, Dorchester, Dorset, in ed. S.M. Pearce, 61-76.

Gresham, C.A. 1968. *Medieval stone carving in north Wales*, Cardiff.

Griffiths, M. 1988–9. Native society on the Anglo-Norman frontier: the evidence of the Margam charters, *Welsh Hist. Rev.*, 14, 179–216.

Griffiths, R.A. 1977. The three castles at Aberystwyth, *Archaeol. Cambrensis*, 126, 74–87.

Grogan, E. and Eogan, G. 1987. Lough Gur excavations by Séan P. Ó Ríordáin: further Neolithic and Beaker habitations on Knockadoon, *Proc. Roy. Ir. Acad.*, 87C, 299–506.

Grogan, E. 1983–4. Excavation of an Iron Age burial mound at Furness, *J. Co. Kildare Archaeol. Soc.*, 16 (4), 298–316.

Grosjean, P. 1956. Vies et Miracles de S Petroc, *Analecta Bollandiana*, 74, 131–88.

Gruffydd, G. and Owen, H.P. 1956–8. The earliest mention of St. David?, *Bull. Board Celtic Stud.*, 17, 185–93.

Guild, R., Guyon, J. and Rivet, L. 1980. Recherches archéologiques dans le cloître Saint-Sauveur d'Aix en Provence, *Revue Archéol. du Narbonnaise*, 13, 115–64.

Guild, R., Guyon, J. and Rivet, L. 1983. Les origines du baptistère de la cathédrale Saint-Sauveur — étude de topographie aixoise, *Revue Archéol. du Narbonnaise*, 16, 171–232.

Guillotel, H. 1977. Les origines du ressort de l'évêché de Dol, *Mémoires de la Soc. d'Hist. et d'Archéol. de Bretagne*, 54, 31–68.

Guillotel, H. 1979. Les évêques d'Alet du ixe au milieu du xiie siècle, *Annales de la Soc. d'Hist. et d'Archéol. de l'arrondissement de St-Malo*, 251–66.

Guillotel, H. 1985. Recherches sur l'activité des scriptoria bretons IXe siècle, *Mémoires de la Soc. d'Hist. et d'Archéol. de Bretagne*, 62, 9–36.

Gwynn, A. and Hadcock, R.N. 1970. *Medieval religious houses: Ireland*, London.

Gwynn, L. (ed.) 1911. The Life of Saint Lasair, *Ériu*, 5, 73–109.

Haddan, A.W. and Stubbs, W. (eds) 1869–71. *Councils and ecclesiastical documents relating to Great Britain and Ireland*, 3 vols, Oxford.

Hague, D.B. 1973. Some Welsh evidence, *Scot. Archaeol. Forum*, 5, 17–35.

Hamlin, A. 1971. Church sites in Langfield parish, Co. Tyrone, *Ulster J. Archaeol.*, 34, 79–83.

Hamlin, A. 1972. A *chi-rho*-carved stone at Drumaqueran, Co. Antrim, *Ulster J. Archaeol.*, 35, 22–8.

Hamlin, A. 1976. The archaeology of early Christianity in the north of Ireland, unpublished Ph.D thesis, Queen's Univ., Belfast.

Hamlin, A. 1980. Two cross-heads from County Fermanagh: Killesher and Galloon, *Ulster J. Archaeol.*, 43, 53–8.

Hamlin, A. 1982. Early Irish stone carving: content and context, in ed. S.M. Pearce, 283–96.

Hamlin, A. 1984. The study of early Irish churches, in eds P. Ní Chatháin and M. Richter, 117–26.

Hamlin, A. and Lynn, C. (eds) 1988. *Pieces of the past: archaeological excavations by the Department of the Environment for Northern Ireland, 1970–1986*, Belfast.

Hamlin, A. and Lynn, C. 1989. Zur Archäologie früher kirchlicher und profaner Siedlungen in Irland, in (ed. J. Erichsen) *Kilian: Mönch aus Irland aller Franken Patron*, 57–73, Munich.

Harding, A.E. with Lee, G.E. 1987. *Henge monuments and related sites of Great Britain*, Brit. Archaeol. Rep. 175, Oxford.

Hardinge, L. 1972. *The Celtic Church in Britain*, London.

Hare, M. with Hamlin, A. 1986. The study of early church architecture in Ireland: an Anglo-Saxon viewpoint, with an appendix on documentary evidence for round towers, in (eds L.A.S. Butler and R.K. Morris) *The Anglo-Saxon church. Papers on history, architecture, and archaeology in honour of Dr H.M. Taylor*, 131–45, Council Brit. Archaeol., Research Rep. 60, London.

Harrison, K. 1977–8. Epacts in Irish chronicles, *Studia Celtica*, 12–3, 17–32.

Harrison, K. 1982. Episodes in the history of Easter cycles in Ireland, in eds D. Whitelock, R. McKitterick and D. Dumville, 307–19.

Harrison, K. 1984. A letter from Rome to the Irish clergy, AD 640, *Peritia*, 3, 222–9.

Hart, W. (ed.) 1863. *Historia et cartularium monasterii S. Petri Gloucestrie*, London.

Harvey, A. 1987. Early literacy in Ireland: the evidence from ogam, *Cambridge Medieval Celtic Stud.*, 14, 1–15.

Harvey, A. 1989. Some significant points of early Celtic Insular orthography, in (eds D. Ó Corráin, L. Breatnach and K. McKone) *Sages, Saints and Storytellers*, 56–66, Maynooth.

Harvey, A. 1990. The ogham inscriptions and the Roman alphabet: two traditions or one?, *Archaeol. Ir.*, 4 (1), 13–4.

Hase, P.H. 1988. The mother churches of Hampshire, in ed. J. Blair, 45–66.

Hawkes, C.F.C. 1981. The wearing of the brooch: Early Iron Age dress among the Irish in (ed. B.G. Scott) *Studies on early Ireland*, 51–73, Belfast.

Hay, M.V. 1927. *A chain of error in Scottish history*, London.

Henderson, C.G. 1925. *Cornish church guide*, Truro.

Henderson, C.G. 1953–6, 1957–60. Ecclesiastical antiquities (ed. J.H. Adams), *J. Roy. Inst. Cornwall*, new ser. 2–3.

Henderson, G. 1987. *From Durrow to Kells. The Insular gospel-books 650–800*, London.

Henshall, A.S. 1956. The long cist cemetery at Lasswade, Midlothian, *Proc. Soc. Antiq. Scot.*, 89, 252–83.

Hickey, H. 1985. *Images of stone: figure sculpture of the Lough Erne basin*, Fermanagh.

Hill, D. 1981. *An Atlas of Anglo-Saxon England*, Oxford.

Hill, P. 1987. *Whithorn 1: Excavations 1984 1986: interim report.*

Hill, P. 1988. *Whithorn 2: Excavations 1984 1987: interim report.*

Hope-Taylor, B. 1977. *Yeavering: an Anglo-British centre of early Northumbria*, London.

Horstmann, C. (ed.) 1901. *Nova legenda Anglie*, Vol. 1, Oxford.

Houlder, C.H. 1968. The henge monuments at Llandegai, *Antiquity*, 42, 216–21.

Hubbard, E. 1986. *Clwyd*, Harmondsworth.

Hughes, H. 1901. Ynys Seiriol, *Archaeol. Cambrensis*, 90–108.

Hughes, H. 1923. Early Christian decorative art in Anglesey, *Archaeol. Cambrensis* 78, 53–69.

Hughes, K. 1966. *The church in early Irish society*, London.

Hughes, K. 1970. Some aspects of Irish influence on early English private prayer, *Studia Celtica*, 5, 48–61.

Hughes, K. 1972. *Early Christian Ireland: introduction to the sources*, London.

Hughes, K. 1980. Where are the writings of Erly Scotland?, in (ed. D. Dumville) *Celtic Britain in the early middle ages*, 1–21 Woodbridge.

Hughes, K. 1981. The Celtic Church: is this a valid concept?, *Cambridge Medieval Celtic Stud.*, 1, 1–20.

Hughes, K. and Hamlin, A. 1977. *The modern traveller to the early Irish church*, London.

Hurley, V. 1982. The early church in the south-west of Ireland: settlement and organisation, in ed. S.M. Pearce, 297–332.

Hutchison, R. 1866. Notice of stone cists discovered near the 'Catstane', Kirkliston, *Proc. Soc. Antiq. Scot.*, 6, 184–98.

Huws, D. 1986. The manuscripts, in (eds T.M. Charles-Edwards, M.E. Owen and D.B. Walters) *Lawyers and laymen. Studies in the history of law presented to Professor Dafydd Jenkins on his seventy-fifth birthday*, 119–36, Cardiff.

Ireland, R. 1983. Epigraphy, in (ed. M. Hennig) *A handbook of Roman art: a survey of the visual arts of the Roman world*, 220–233, Oxford.

Ivens, R.J. 1987. The Early Christian monastic enclosure at Tullylish, Co. Down, *Ulster J. Archaeol.*, 50, 55–121.

Ivens, R.J. forthcoming. Report on Dunmisk, *Ulster J. Archaeol.*

Jackson, K. 1953. *Language and history in early Britain*, Edinburgh.

Jackson, K. (ed.) 1969. *The Gododdin*, Edinburgh.

James, E. 1982. Ireland and western Gaul in the Merovingian period, in eds D. Whitelock, R. McKitterick and D. Dumville, 362–86.

James, E. 1984. Bede and the tonsure question, *Peritia*, 3, 85–98.

James, H. 1987. Excavations at Caer Bayvil 1979, *Archaeol. Cambrensis*, 136, 51–76.

James, H. and Williams, G. 1982. Rural settlement in Roman Dyfed, in ed. D. Miles, 289–312.

James, J.W. (ed.) 1967. *Rhigyfarch's Life of St. David*, Cardiff.

James, T.A. 1980. The Bishop's Palace and collegiate

church, Abergwili, *Carmarthenshire Antiq.*, 16, 19–44.

James, T.A. 1984. Aerial reconnaissance in Dyfed, 1984, *Archaeol. Wales*, 24, 12–24.

James, T.A. 1985. Excavations at the Augustinian Priory of St. John and St. Teulyddog, Carmarthen 1979, *Archaeol. Cambrensis*, 134, 120–161.

James, T.A. 1989. Aerial photography by the Dyfed Archaeological Trust 1989, *Archaeol. Wales*, 29, 31–4.

Jenkins, D. (ed.) 1973. *Damweiniau Colan*, Aberystwyth.

Jenkins, D. and Owen, M.E. 1983. The Welsh marginalia in the Lichfield Gospels. Part 1, *Cambridge Medieval Celtic Stud.*, 5, 37–66.

Jenner, H. 1929–32. The manumissions in the Bodmin Gospels, *J. Roy. Inst. Cornwall*, 21, 235–60.

Johns, C.N. 1960. The Celtic monasteries of North Wales, *Trans. Caenarvonshire Hist. Soc.*, 21, 14–43.

Johnson, N.D. and Rose, P.G. 1982. Defended settlement in Cornwall: an illustrated discussion, in ed. D. Miles, 151–208.

Jones, B.L. 1973. Dafydd ap Huw, Berach, Llaneilian (M. 1696) Huw Davies, Llundain a Threcastell (m. 1771) *Trans. Anglesey Antiq. Soc.*, 182–7.

Jones, C.W. (ed.) 1943. *Bedae Opera de Temporibus*, Cambridge Mass.

Jones, F. 1954. *The holy wells of Wales*, Cardiff.

Jones, G.R.J. 1960–3. The tribal system in Wales: a re-assessment in the light of settlement studies, *Welsh Hist. Rev.*, 1, 111–32.

Jones, G.R.J. 1972. Post-Roman Wales, in (ed. H.P.R. Finberg) *The agrarian history of England and Wales*, Vol. 1 (2), 283–382, Cambridge.

Jones, G.R.J. 1979. Early historic settlement in border territory. A case-study of Archenfield and its environs in Herefordshire, in (ed. C. Christians) *Recherches de géographie rurale. Hommage au Professeur Frans Dussart*, 117–32, Liège.

Jones, G.R.J. 1984. The multiple estate: a model for tracing the inter-relationships of society, economy, and habitat, in (ed. K. Biddick) *Archaeological approaches to medieval Europe*, 9–41, Studies in Medieval Culture, 18, Kalamazoo.

Jones, H.C. 1976. *Placenames in Glamorgan*, Risca.

Jones, M.L. 1984. *Society and settlement in Wales and the Marches 500 B.C. – A.D. 1100*, 2 vols, Brit. Archaeol. Rep. 121, Oxford.

Jones, T. (ed.) 1941. *Brut y Tywysogyon, Peniarth MS. 20*, Cardiff.

Jones, T. (ed.) 1952. *Brut y Tywysogyon or the Chronicle of the Princes, Peniarth MS. 20 version*, Cardiff.

Jones, T. (ed. and trans.) 1955, 1973. *Brut y Tywysogyon or the Chronicle of the Princes, Red Book of Hergest version*, 2nd ed. 1973, Cardiff.

Jones, T. 1967. The Black Book of Carmarthen 'Stanzas of the Graves', *Proc. Brit. Acad.*, 53, 97–136.

Jones-Davies, J. 1975. Presidential address, *Archaeol. Cambrensis*, 124, 1–14.

Kauffman, A. 1983. Cardo et place dallée à Aix-en-Provence, *Revue Archéol. du Narbonnaise*, 16, 233–46.

Kelly, E.P. 1977. A burial at Farganstown and Ballymacon, Co. Meath, *Ríocht na Midhe*, 6, 65–7.

Kemble, J.M. (ed.) 1839–48. *Codex Diplomaticus Aevi Saxonici*, 6 vols, London.

Kendall, G. 1982. A study of grave orientation in several Roman and post-Roman cemeteries from southern Britain, *Archaeol. J.*, 139, 101–23.

Kenney, J.F. 1929, 1966. *Sources for the early history of Ireland: Vol. 1. Ecclesiastical*, Columbia 1929, reprint New York 1966.

Kenworthy, J.B. 1980. Appendix to Close-Brooks, *J. 1980*, 343–4.

Keynes, S. and Lapidge, M. (trans.) 1983. *Alfred the Great. Asser's 'Life of Alfred' and other contemporary sources*, Harmondsworth.

Keys, D. 1988. *The Independent*, 10th Feb.

Knight, J.K 1970–1. St. Tatheus of Caerwent: an analysis of the Vespasian Life, *Monmouthshire Antiq.*, 3 (1), 29–35.

Knight, J.K. 1981. In Tempore Iustini Consularis: contacts between the British and Gaulish church before Augustine, in (ed. A. Detsicas) *Collectanea historica: essays in memory of Stuart Rigold*, 54–62, Maidstone.

Knight, J.K. 1984a. Glamorgan A.D. 400–1100: archaeology and history, in ed. H.N. Savory, 315–64.

Knight, J.K. 1984b. Sources for the early history of Morgannwg, in ed. H.N. Savory, 365–409.

Knight, J.K. forthcoming. *Post-Roman evidence from Caerwent.*

Knowles, D. and Hadcock, R.N. 1953, 1971. *Medieval religious houses, England and Wales*, 2nd ed. 1971, London.

Knox, H.T. 1915–6. The Turoe Stone and the Rath of Feerwore, Co. Galway, *J. Galway Archaeol. Hist. Soc.*, 9, 190–3.

Kroeber, A.L. 1948. *Anthropology*, New York.

La Borderie, A. le Moyne de (ed.) 1888. Vita Winwaloei, in *Cartulaire de Landévennec*, 1–135, Rennes.

La Borderie, A. le Moyne de 1898. *Histoire de Bretagne*, Vol. 2, Rennes.

Lang, J. (ed.) 1978. *Anglo-Saxon and Viking Age Sculpture*, Brit. Archaeol. Rep. 49, Oxford.

Lang, J. 1984. The hogback. A Viking colonial monument, *Anglo-Saxon Stud. Archaeol. Hist. 3*, 83–176.

Langdon, A.G. 1896. *Old Cornish crosses*, Truro.

Lapidge, M. 1973–4. The Welsh-Latin poetry of Sulien's family, *Studia Celtica*, 8–9, 68–106.

Lapidge, M. 1984. Gildas's education and the Latin culture of sub-Roman Britain, in eds M. Lapidge and D. Dumville, 27–50.

Lapidge, M. 1986. Latin learning in Dark Age Wales: some prolegomena, in eds D.E. Evans, J.G. Griffith and E.M. Jope, 91–107.

Lapidge, M. and Dumville, D. (eds) 1984. *Gildas: new approaches*, Woodbridge.

Lapidge, M. and Sharpe, R. 1985. *A bibliography of Celtic-Latin literature 400–1200*, Dublin.

Lawlor, H.J. (ed.) 1914. *The Psalter and Martyrology of Ricemarch*, 2 vols, Henry Bradshaw Soc. 47–8, London.

Lawlor, H.J. (ed.) 1920. *St Bernard of Clairvaux's Life of St Malachy of Armagh*, London.

Le Blant, E. 1856. *Inscriptions Chrétiennes de la Gaule antérieures au VIIIe siècle. Vol.1, Provinces Gallicanes*, Paris.

Le Blant, E. 1865. *Inscriptions Chrétiennes de la Gaule antérieures au VIIIe siècle. Vol.2, Les sept provinces*, Paris.

Le Blant, E. 1892. *Nouveau Receuil des Inscriptions Chrétiennes de la Gaule antérieures au VIIIe siècle*, Paris.

Lemarignier, J.F. 1982. Encadrement religieux des campagnes et conjonctiure politique, in *Cristianizzazione ed organizzazione ecclesiastica delle campagne, Settimane di Studio del Centro Italiano di studi sull'alto medioevo 1980*, 28 (2), 765–800.

Lennard, R.V. 1959. *Rural England 1086–1135, a study of social and agrarian conditions*, Oxford.

Levison, W. 1941. St. Alban and St. Albans, *Antiquity*, 16, 337–59.

Lewis, F.R. 1938. The history of Llanbadarn Fawr, Cardiganshire, in the later middle ages, *Cardiganshire Antiq. Soc. Trans.*, 13, 16–41.

Lewis, H. 1931. *Canu y Dewi. Gwynnuart Brycheinyawc a'e cant' yn Hen Gerddi Crefyddol.*

Lewis, J.M. 1976. A survey of early Christian monuments of Dyfed, west of the Taf, in (eds G.C. Boon and J.M. Lewis) *Welsh antiquity*, 177–92, Cardiff.

Lewis, S. 1837. *A topographical dictionary of Ireland*, 2 vols, London.

Leyser, K. 1982. *Medieval Germany and its neighbours 900–1250*, London.

Lhwyd, A. 1833. *A history of the island of Mona*, Ruthin.

Lindsay, W.M. 1912. *Early Welsh script*, Oxford.

Lionard, R. 1961. Early Irish grave slabs, *Proc. Roy. Ir. Acad.*, 61C, 95–169.

Lloyd, J.E. 1911. *A history of Wales from the earliest times to the Edwardian Conquest*, 1st ed., London.

Lloyd, J.E. 1928. The Welsh chronicles, *Proc. Brit. Acad.*, 14, 369–91.

Lloyd, J.E. 1937. *The story of Ceredigion*, Cardiff.

Lloyd, J.E. and Jenkins, R.T. (eds) 1959. *Dictionary of Welsh biography down to 1940*, London.

Llwyd, A. 1833. *History of the Island of Mona*, Ruthin.

Longley, D. forthcoming. *Excavations at Bangor, Gwynedd 1981–4.*

Lowe, E. A. 1972. *Codices Latini antiquiores*, Vol. 2, 2nd ed., Oxford.

Lunt, W.E. 1926. *The Valuation of Norwich*, Oxford.

Macalister, R.A.S. 1916–7. A report on some excavations recently conducted in Co. Galway, *Proc. Roy. Ir. Acad.*, 33C, 505–10.

Macalister, R.A.S. 1928–9. On some antiquities discovered upon Lambay, *Proc. Roy. Ir. Acad.*, 38C, 240–6.

Macalister, R.A.S. 1945, 1949. *Corpus Inscriptionum Insularum Celticarum*, 2 vols, Dublin.

MacNeill, E. 1907. Mocu, Maccu, *Ériu*, 3, 42–9.

Maddicott, J.R. 1989. Trade, industry and the wealth of King Alfred, *Past and Present*, 123, 3–51.

Mango C. 1972. *The art of the Byzantine Empire 312–1453*, Englewood Cliffs.

Manning, C. 1986. Archaeological excavation of a succession of enclosures at Millockstown, Co. Louth, *Proc. Roy. Ir. Acad.*, 86C, 135–81.

Martin, C.H.R. 1986. Trelystan churchyard, *Archaeol. Wales*, 26, 56.

Mathison, R.W. 1984. Emigrants, exiles and survivors: aristocratic options in Visigothic Aquitaine, *Phoenix*, 38, 159–170.

Maxwell, G.S. 1987. Settlement in southern Pictland — a new overview, in ed. A. Small, 31–44.

Mayr-Harting, H. 1972. *The coming of Christianity to Anglo-Saxon England*, London.

McCone, K. 1982. Brigid in the 7th Century — a saint with three Lives, *Peritia*, 1, 107–45.

McDowell, J.A. 1987. Excavation in an ecclesiastical enclosure at Doras, Co. Tyrone, *Ulster J. Archaeol.*, 50, 137–54.

McGurk, P. 1987. The Gospel Book in Celtic lands before AD 850: contents and arrangement, in eds P. Ní Chatháin and M. Richter, 165–89.

McKitterick, R. 1975. see Pierce 1975.

McKitterick, R. 1977. *The Frankish church and the Carolingian reforms, 789–895*, London.

McNeill, J.T. 1974. *The Celtic Churches*, Chicago and London.

Miket, R. and Burgess, C. (eds) 1984. *Between and beyond the Walls*, Edinburgh.

Miles, D. (ed.) 1982. *The Romano-British countryside: studies in rural settlement and economy*, Brit. Archaeol. Rep. 103, Oxford.

Miles, H. and Miles, T. 1973. Excavations at Trethurgy, St Austell: interim report, *Cornish Archaeol.*, 12, 25–9.

Miles Brown, H. 1973. *What to look for in Cornish churches*, Newton Abbot.

Mommsen, T. 1863–. *Corpus Inscriptionum Latinarum*, 15 vols, Berlin.

Moore, J.S. (ed.) 1982. *Domesday Book, Gloucestershire*, Chichester.

Morris, L. 1878. *Celtic remains*, London.

Morris, R.K. 1988. Churches in York and its hinterland: building patterns and stone sources in the 11th and 12th centuries, in ed. J. Blair, 191–9.

Murphy, K. 1987. Excavations at Llanychlwydog Church, Dyfed, *Archaeol. Cambrensis*, 136, 77–93.

Murphy, K. forthcoming. *Plas Gogerddan, Dyfed: a multi-period ritual and burial site.*

Murphy, K. and Williams, Geo. forthcoming. Appendix 6: a gazetteer of 73 Iron Age burials in Wales, in Murphy forthcoming.

Nash-Williams, V.E. 1950. *The Early Christian monuments of Wales*, Cardiff.

Newman, R. 1985. Atlantic Trading Estate, Barry, *Archaeol. Wales*, 25, 37–8.

Newman, R. and Parkin, L. 1986. Atlantic Trading Estate, Barry, *Archaeol. Wales*, 26, 55.

Ní Chatháin, P. and Richter, M. (eds) 1984. Irland und Europa, Ireland and Europe, Stuttgart.

Ní Chatháin, P. and Richter, M. (eds) 1987. Irland und die Christenheit, Ireland and Christendom, Stuttgart.

Nicolaisen, W.F.H. (ed.) 1970. *The names of towns and cities in Britain*, London.

Noble, F. 1983. *Offa's Dyke Reviewed*, Brit. Archaeol. Rep. 114, Oxford.

Norman, E.R. and St. Joseph, J.K.S. 1969. *The early development of Irish society: the evidence of aerial photography*, Cambridge.

Nowakowski, J. and Thomas, C. 1990. *Excavations at Tintagel parish churchyard, Cornwall, Spring 1990*, Truro.

O'Brien, E. 1984. *Late Prehistoric — Early Historic Ireland: the burial evidence reviewed*, unpublished M. Phil. thesis, Nat. Univ. Ir., Univ. Coll. Dublin.

O'Brien, E. 1990. Iron Age burial practices in Leinster: continuity and change, *Emania*, 7, 37–42.

Ó Corráin, D. 1981a. The early Irish churches: some aspects of organisation, in ed. D. Ó Corráin, 327–41.

Ó Corráin, D. (ed.) 1981b. *Irish Antiquity*, Cork.

Ó Corráin, D., Breatnach, L. and Breen, A. 1984. The laws of the Irish, *Peritia*, 3, 382–438.

Ó Cróinín, D. 1982. Mo-Sinnu moccu Min and the computus of Bangor, *Peritia*, 1, 281–95.

Ó Doibhlin, E. 1969. *Domhnach Mór: an outline of parish history*, Omagh.

O'Donovan, J. (ed.) 1854. *Annals of the kingdom of Ireland, by the Four Masters, from the earliest period to the year 1616*, 7 vols, Dublin.

Ó hInnse, S. (ed.) 1947. *Miscellaneous Irish annals (A.D. 1114–1437)*, Dublin.

O'Kelly, M.J. 1967. Knockea, Co. Limerick, in (ed. E. Rynne) *North Munster studies*, 72–101, Limerick.

Ó Riain, P. 1981. The Irish element in Welsh hagiographical tradition, in ed. D. Ó Corráin, 291–303.

Ó Ríordáin, A.B. and Rynne, E. 1961. A settlement in the sandhills at Dooey, Co. Donegal, *J. Roy. Soc. Antiq. Ir.*, 91, 58–64.

Ó Ríordáin, S.P. 1940. Excavations at Cush. Co. Limerick, *Proc. Roy. Ir. Acad.*, 45C, 83–181.

O'Sullivan, D. 1980. Curvilinear churchyards in Cumbria, *Bull. Council Brit. Archaeol. Churches Committee*, 13, 3–5.

Okasha, E. 1971. *Hand-list of Anglo-Saxon non-runic inscriptions*, Cambridge.

Okasha, E. 1985. The non-ogam inscriptions of Pictland, *Cambridge Medieval Celtic Stud.*, 9, 43–69.

Olson, B.L. 1975. Saint Entenyn, *Cornish Stud.*, 3, 25–8.

Olson, B.L. 1982. Crantock, Cornwall, as an early monastic site, in ed. S.M. Pearce, 177–86.

Olson, B.L. 1989. *Early monasteries in Cornwall*, Woodbridge.

Olson, B.L. and Padel, O.J. 1986. A tenth-century list of Cornish parochial saints, *Cambridge Medieval Celtic Stud.* 12, 33–71.

Ordnance Survey 1971. *Britain in the Dark Ages*, 2nd ed., Southampton.

Ordnance Survey 1973. *Britain before the Norman Conquest*, Southampton.

Ordnance Survey 1984. *Map of monastic Ireland*, Dublin.

Ortiz, A.D. 1971. *The Golden Age of Spain, 1516–1659*, London.

Owen, A. (ed.) 1841. *The ancient laws and institutes of Wales*, 2 vols, Record Commission, London.

Owen, H. (ed.) 1906. *The description of Pembrokeshire by George Owen of Henllys*, parts 3 and 4, London.

Owen, M.E. 1974. Y cyfreithiau (I) Natur y testunau, in (ed. G. Bowen) *Y traddodiad rhyddiaith yn yr oesau canol*, 196–219, Llandysul.

Owen-John, H. 1988. Llandough: the rescue excavation of a multi-period site near Cardiff, South Glamorgan in ed. D.M. Robinson, 123–77.

Padel, O.J. 1974. Cornish language notes: 2. Cornish plu, "parish", *Cornish Stud.*, 2, 75–7.

Padel, O.J. 1976–7. Cornish names of parish churches, *Cornish Stud.*, 4–5, 15–27.

Padel, O.J. 1978. Two new pre-Conquest charters for Cornwall, *Cornish Stud.*, 6, 20–6.

Padel, O.J. 1985. Cornish place-name elements, *Eng. Place-Name Soc.*, 56–7, Nottingham.

Padel, O.J. 1989. *A popular dictionary of Cornish place-names*, Penzance.

Palmer, A.N. 1886. The portionary churches of mediaeval north Wales, *Archaeol. Cambrensis*, 5th ser., 3, 175–209.

Pearce, S.M. 1973. The dating of some Celtic dedications and hagiographical traditions in south-western Britain, *Trans. Devon Ass.*, 105, 95–120.

Pearce, S.M. 1978. *The Kingdom of Dumnonia*, Padstow.

Pearce, S.M. (ed.) 1982. *The early church in western Britain and Ireland*, Brit. Archaeol. Rep. 102, Oxford.

Peden, A. 1981. Science and philosophy in Wales at the time of the Norman Conquest: a Macrobus manuscript from Llanbadarn, *Cambridge Medieval Celtic Stud.* 2, 21–45.

Picard, J.M. 1982. The purpose of Adomnán's Vita Columbae, *Peritia*, 1, 160–77.

Pierce, G.O. 1968. *The place-names of the Dinas Powys Hundred*, Cardiff.

Pierce, R. 1975. The 'Frankish' Penitentials, in (ed. D. Baker) *The materials sources and methods of ecclesiastical history*, Studies in Church History 11, 31–9.

Plummer, C. (ed.) 1892–9. *Two of the Saxon Chronicles parallel, with supplementary extracts from the others. A revised text on the basis of an edition by John Earle*, 2 vols, Oxford, revised impression by D. Whitelock, 1952.

Plummer, C. (ed.) 1896. *Venerabilis Baedae opera historica*, 2 vols, Oxford.

Plummer, C. (ed.) 1910. *Vitae sanctorum Hiberniae*, 2 vols, Oxford.

Plummer, C. (ed.) 1925. *Irish litanies*, London.

Pool, P.A.S. and Russell, V.M. 1968. The excavation of Chapel Jane, Zennor, *Cornish Archaeol.*, 7, 43–60.

Porter, H.M. 1971. *The Celtic Church in Somerset*, Bath.

Preston-Jones, A. 1984. The excavation of a long-cist cemetery at Carnanton, St Mawgan, 1943, *Cornish Archaeol.*, 23, 157–78.

Preston-Jones, A. 1987. Road widening at St Buryan and Pelynt churchyards, *Cornish Archaeol.*, 26, 153–60.

Preston-Jones, A. and Rose, P.G. 1986. Medieval Cornwall, *Cornish Archaeol.*, 25, 135–85.

Price, C. 1987. Atlantic Trading Estate, Barry, *Archaeol. Wales*, 27, 60–1.

Price, C. 1989. New data from old bones, *Siluria*, 2, 19.

Prichard, H. 1898. Old Llangaffo Church and cross, *Archaeol. Cambrensis*, 288–90.

Proudfoot, E.V. 1977. Hallowhill, St Andrews, Fife, in eds Webster, L.E. and Cherry, J., 217.

Pryce, H. 1984. Ecclesiastical sanctuary in thirteenth-century Welsh law, *J. Legal Hist.*, 5, 1–13.

Pryce, H. 1986. Early Irish canons and medieval Welsh law, *Peritia*, 5, 107–27.

Pryce, H. 1986-7. In search of a medieval society: Deheubarth in the writings of Gerald of Wales, *Welsh Hist. Rev.*, 13, 265–81.

Pryce, H. 1988. Church and society in Wales, 1150–1250: an Irish perspective, in (ed. R.R. Davies) *The British Isles 1100–1500. Comparisons, contrasts and connections*, 27–47, Edinburgh.

Pryce, H. forthcoming. Pastoral care in early medieval Wales, in (eds J. Blair and R. Sharpe) *Pastoral care before the parish*, London.

Quigley, W.G.H. and Roberts, E.F.D. (eds.) 1972. *Registrum Iohannis Mey: the register of John Mey, Archbishop of Armagh, 1443–1456*, Belfast.

Radford, C.A.R. 1971. Christian origins in Britain, *Medieval Archaeol.*, 15, 1–12.

Radford, C.A.R. 1975. *The Early Christian inscriptions of Dumnonia*, Redruth.

Radford, C.A.R. and Hemp, W.J. 1959. *Pennant Melangell: the church and the shrine, Archaeol. Cambrensis*, 108, 81–113.

Raftery, B. 1976. Dowris, Hallstatt and La Tène in Ireland and problems of the transition from Bronze to Iron, in (ed. J. de Laet) *Acculturation and continuity in Atlantic Europe*, 189–97, Brugge.

Raftery, B. 1981. Iron Age Burials in Ireland, in ed. D. Ó Corráin, 173–204.

Raftery, J. 1938-9. The tumulus cemetery of Carrowjames, Co. Mayo, Part 1, *J. Galway Archaeol. Hist. Soc.*, 18, 157–67.

Raftery, J. 1940-1. The tumulus cemetery of Carrowjames, Co. Mayo, Part 2, *J. Galway Archaeol. Hist. Soc.*, 19, 16–88.

Raftery, J. 1944. The Turoe Stone and the Rath of Feerwore, *J. Roy. Soc. Antiq. Ir.*, 74, 23–62.

Rahtz, P.A. 1976. *Excavations at St Mary's Church, Deerhurst, 1971–73*, Council Brit. Archaeol. research. rep. 15, London.

Rahtz, P.A. 1978 Grave orientation, *Archaeol. J.*, 135, 1–14.

Rahtz, P.A. 1982. The Dark Ages 400–700 A.D., in (eds M. Aston and I. Burrow) *The archaeology of Somerset*, 99–107, Taunton.

RCAHMS 1957. *An inventory of the ancient monuments of Selkirkshire*, Edinburgh.

RCAHMS 1982. *An inventory of the ancient monuments of Argyll*, Vol. 4, Iona, Edinburgh.

RCAHMW 1917. *An inventory of the ancient monuments, 5, County of Carmarthenshire*, London.

RCAHMW 1925. *An inventory of the ancient monuments, 7, County of Pembroke*, London.

RCAHMW 1937. *An inventory of the ancient monuments in Anglesey*, London.

RCAHMW 1956. *An inventory of the ancient monuments in Caernarvonshire Vol.1: East*, London.

RCAHMW 1960. *An inventory of the ancient monuments in Caernarvonshire Vol.2: Central*, London.

RCAHMW 1976. *An inventory of the ancient monuments in Glamorgan Vol 1: pre-Norman, Part 3, The Early Christian period*, Cardiff.

Record Commission 1802. *Taxatio ecclesiastica Angliae et Walliae auctoritate P. Nicolai circa A.D. 1291*, London.

Record Commission 1818. *Placita de quo warranto*, London.

Reece, R. 1981. *Excavations in Iona 1964 to 1974*, Institute of Archaeology, Occasional Publication no. 5, London.

Rees, A.D. 1935. Notes on the significance of white stones in Celtic archaeology and folk-lore with reference to recent excavations at Ffynnon Degla, Denbighshire, *Bull. Board Celtic Stud.*, 8–9, 87–90.

Rees, W. (ed.) 1975. *Calendar of ancient petitions relating to Wales*, Cardiff.

Reeves, W. 1902. A description of Nendrum, commonly called Mahee Island, embracing its present condition and past history, *Ulster J. Archaeol.*, 8, 13–22, 58–68.

Reilly, P. 1988. *Computer analysis of an archaeological landscape. Medieval land divisions in the Isle of Man*, Brit. Archaeol. Rep. 190, Oxford.

Renell of Rodd, Lord 1963. The Land of Lene, in (eds I. Ll. Foster and L. Alcock) *Culture and Environment*, 303–26, London.

Reynaud, J.F. 1974. La nécropole de Saint-Just, *Revue Archéol. d'Est et du Centre Est*, 25 (1), 111–23.

Reynaud, J.F. with Helly, B. and le Glay, M. 1982. Nouvelles inscriptions de Lyon, *Gallia*, 40, 123–48.

Rhys, J. 1877a. *Lectures on Welsh philology*, London.

Rhys, J. 1877b. On some of our early inscribed stones, *Archaeol. Cambrensis*, 8 (4th series), 135–44.

Richards, M. 1968. Ecclesiastical and secular in Welsh medieval settlement, *Studia Celtica*, 3, 9–18.

Richards, M. 1971. Places and persons of the early Welsh Church, *Welsh Hist. Rev.*, 5, 333–49.

Richmond, I.A. and Crawford O.G.S. 1949. The British section of the Ravenna Cosmography, *Archaeologia*, 93, 1–50.

Richter, M. (ed.) 1974. *Giraldus Cambrensis: Speculum Duorum or A mirror of two men*, Cardiff.

Roberts, T. 1914. *Gwaith Dafydd ab Edmwnd*, Bangor.

Robinson, D.M. 1988a. Notes on Romano-British rural settlement in south-east Wales, in ed. D.M. Robinson, vii-xxiv.

Robinson, D.M. (ed.) 1988b. *Biglis, Caldicot and Llandough: three late Iron Age and Romano-British sites in south-east Wales. Excavations 1977–79*, Brit. Archaeol. Rep. 188, Oxford.

Rodwell, W. 1981 The Lady Chapel by the cloister at Wells and the site of the Anglo-Saxon Cathedral, in (eds N. Coldstream and P. Draper) *Medieval art and architecture at Wells and Glastonbury* , 1–9, Brit. Archaeol. Ass. conference transactions for the year 1978.

Rowley, T. 1972. *The Shropshire landscape*, London.

Rowley, T. 1986. *The landscape of the Welsh Marches*, London.

Russell, P. 1985. Recent work in British Latin, *Cambridge Medieval Celtic Stud.*, 9, 19–29.

Rynne, E. 1974. Excavations at Maddens Hill, Kiltale, Co. Meath, *Proc. Roy. Ir. Acad.*, 74C, 267–75.

Rynne, E. 1976. The La Tène and Roman finds from Lambay, Co. Dublin. A re-assessment, *Proc. Roy. Ir. Acad.*, 76C, 231-44.

Saunders, C. 1972. The excavations at Grambla, Wendron, 1972: interim report, *Cornish Archaeol.*, 11, 50–2.

Savory, H.N. (ed.) 1984. *Glamorgan county history, Vol. 2, Early Glamorgan. Pre-history and early history*, Cardiff.

Sharpe, R. 1982a. Vitae S. Brigitae; the oldest texts, *Peritia*, 1, 81-106.

Sharpe, R. 1982b. Palaeographical considerations in the study of the Patrician documents in the Book of Armagh, *Scriptorium*, 36, 3–28.

Sharpe, R. 1984a. Armagh and Rome in the seventh century, in eds P. Ní Chatháin and M. Richter, 58–72.

Sharpe, R. 1984b. Some problems concerning the organisation of the church in early medieval Ireland, *Peritia*, 3, 230–70.

Sharpe, R. 1984c. Gildas as a father of the church, in eds M. Lapidge and D. Dumville, 193–205.

Sheppard, P.A. 1980. *The historic towns of Cornwall: an archaeological survey*, Truro.

Simpson, D.D.A. and Scott-Elliot, J. 1964. Excavations at Camp Hill, Trohoughton, Dumfries, *Trans. Dumfries Galloway Nat. Hist. Antiq. Soc.*, 41, 125–34.

Sims-Williams, P. 1982. Review of Evans and Rhys 1893, Davies, W. 1978a and Davies, W. 1979a, *J. Eccles. Hist.*, 33, 124–9.

Sims-Williams, P. 1986. The Visionary Celt: the construction of an ethnic preconception, *Cambridge Medieval Celtic Stud.*, 11, 71–96.

Sirat, J. 1966. Les stèles mérovingiennes du Vexin francais, *Bull. Archéol. du Vexin Francais*, 2, 73–83.

Sirat, J. 1970. Les stèles mérovingiennes du Vexin francais – inventaire complémentaire, *Bull. Archaeol. du Vexin Francais*, 6, 95–103.

Small, A. (ed.) 1987. *The Picts: a new look at old problems*, Dundee.

Smith, A.H. 1956. *English place-name elements*, Vol.1, Cambridge.

Smith J.B. (ed.) 1972. *Medieval Welsh society: selected essays by T. Jones Pierce*, Cardiff.

Smith, J.M.H. 1982. The 'archbishopric' of Dol and the ecclesiastical politics of ninth-century Brittany, in (ed. S Mews) *Religion and national identity*, Studies in Church History 18, 59–70.

Smith, L.T. 1906. *The itinerary in Wales of John Leland*, London.

Sotheby Mss at the Nat. Lib. of Wales, Aberystwyth.

Stallybrass, B. 1914. Recent discoveries at Clynnogfawr, *Archaeol. Cambrensis*, 6th ser., 14, 271–96.

Stancliffe, C.E. 1979. From town to country: the Christianization of the Touraine 370–600, *Studies in Church History* 16, 43–59.

Stanley, W.O. 1846. Towyn-y-Capel, *Archaeol. J.*, 3, 223–8.

Stead, I.M. 1979. *The Arras Culture*, York.

Stenberger, M. 1966. A ringfort at Raheennamadra, Knocklong, Co. Limerick, *Proc. Roy. Ir. Acad.*, 65C, 37–64.

Stenton, F.M. 1971. *Anglo-Saxon England*, 3rd ed., Oxford.

Stevenson, J. 1987. Introduction to the second edition of Warren 1881, ix-cxxviii.

Stevenson, J. 1989. The beginnings of literacy in Ireland, *Proc. Roy. Ir. Acad.*, 89C, 127–65.

Stevenson, W.H. (ed.) 1904. *Asser's Life of King Alfred*, Oxford.

Stevenson, W.H. (ed.) 1929. *Early scholastic colloquies*, Oxford.

Stokes, W. (ed.) 1887. *The Tripartite Life of Patrick*, 2 vols, London.

Stokes, W. (ed.) 1895. *The Martyrology of Gorman*, London.

Stokes, W. (ed.) 1905. *The Martyrology of Oengus*, London.

Stokes, W. and Meyer, K. (eds) 1900. *Archiv für celtische lexikographie*, Halle.

Swan, L. 1983. Enclosed ecclesiastical sites and their relevance to settlement patterns of the first millennium A.D., in (eds T. Reeves-Smith and F. Hammond) *Landscape archaeology in Ireland*, 269–94, Brit. Archaeol. Rep. 116, Oxford.

Swan, L. 1985. Monastic proto-towns in early medieval Ireland: the evidence of aerial photography, in eds H.B. Clarke and A. Simms, 77–102.

Sweetman P.D. 1982–3a. Souterrain and burials at Boolies Little, Co. Meath, *Riocht na Midhe*, 7, 42–57.

Sweetman P.D. 1982–3b. Reconstruction and partial excavation of a burial mound at Ninch, Co. Meath, *Riocht na Midhe*, 7, 58–60.

Sylvester, D. 1969. *The rural landscape of the Welsh borderland*, London.

Tangye, M. 1985. A new inscribed stone and churchyard cross, St Euny's Church, Redruth, *Cornish Archaeol.*, 24, 171–2.

Taylor, H.M. and Taylor, J. 1965, 1978. *Anglo-Saxon Architecture*, 3 vols, Cambridge.

Taylor, T. 1924. The Domesday Survey for Cornwall – translation of the text, in (ed. W. Page) *The Victoria History of the County of Cornwall*, Part 8, London.

Thacker, A.T. 1987. Anglo-Saxon Cheshire, in (ed. B.E. Harris assisted by A.T. Thacker) *A history of the County of Chester, Vol. 1*, 237–92, Victoria History of the Counties of England, Oxford.

Thom, F. and Thom, C. (eds) 1982. *Domesday Book, Worcestershire*, Chichester.

Thom, F. and Thom, C. (eds) 1983. *Domesday Book, Herefordshire*, Chichester.

Thom, F. and Thom, C. (eds) 1986. *Domesday Book, Shropshire*, Chichester.

Thomas, C. 1957–8. Cornwall in the Dark Ages, *Proc. West Cornwall Field Club*, 2(1), 59–72.

Thomas, C. 1959. Imported pottery in Dark-Age western Britain, *Medieval Archaeol.*, 3, 89–111.

Thomas, C. 1963. *Phillack Church: an illustrated history of the Celtic, Norman and Medieval foundations*, Phillack and Gwithian.

Thomas, C. 1964. *Gwithian: notes on the church, parish and St Gothian's Chapel*, Gwithian.

Thomas, C. 1965. The hillfort at St Dennis, *Cornish Archaeol.*, 4, 31–5.

Thomas, C. 1967a. *Christian antiquities of Camborne*, Camborne.

Thomas, C 1967b. Fenton-la Chapel, Troon, *Cornish Archaeol.*, 6, 77.

Thomas, C. 1967c. An early Christian cemetery and chapel on Ardwall Island, Kirkcudbright, *Medieval Archaeol.*, 11, 127–86.

Thomas, C. 1968a. Merther Uny Wendron, *Cornwall Archaeol. Soc. Field Guide*, 11.

Thomas, C. 1968b. Merther Uny, Wendron, *Cornish Archaeol.*, 6, 78–9.

Thomas, C. 1971. *The Early Christian archaeology of North Britain*, Oxford.

Thomas, C. 1972. The Irish settlements in post-Roman western Britain: a survey of the evidence, *J. Roy. Inst. Cornwall*, 4 (4), 251–74.

Thomas, C. 1977. *The earliest Christian place-names of Cornwall*, Henry Lewis Memorial Lecture, Univ. Coll. Cardiff.

Thomas, C. 1978. Ninth-century sculpture in Cornwall: a note, in ed. J. Lang, 75–84.

Thomas, C. 1980. An Early Christian inscribed stone from Boskenna, St. Buryon, *Cornish Archaeol.*, 19, 107–8.

Thomas, C. 1981a. *Christianity in Roman Britain to AD 500*, London.

Thomas, C. 1981b. *A provisional list of imported pottery in post-Roman western Britain and Ireland*, Institute of Cornish Studies, Special Report no. 7, Redruth.

Thomas, C. 1984. Abercorn and the Provincia Pictorum, in eds R. Miket and C. Burgess, 324–37.

Thomas, C. 1986. *Celtic Britain*, London.

Thomas, C. 1987. The earliest Christian art in Ireland and Britain, in (ed. M. Ryan) *Ireland and Insular art A.D. 500–1200*, 7–11, Dublin.

Thomas, C. 1988a. The context of Tintagel: a new model for the diffusion of post-Roman Mediterranean imports, *Cornish Archaeol.*, 27, 7–25 .

Thomas, C. 1988b. The archaeology of Tintagel parish churchyard, *Cornish Stud.*, 16, 79–91.

Thomas, H.J. 1983. Michaelston Super Ely, *Morgannwg*, 27, 73.

Thomas, L. 1930. *The reformation in the old diocese of Llandaff*, Cardiff.

Thomas, R.J. then Bevan, G.A. (eds) 1950–. *Geiriadur Prifysgol Cymru*, Caerdydd.

Thomas, W.G. 1984. A cross-slab at Defynnog (Brecs.), *Archaeol. Cambrensis*, 133, 152–3.

Thomas, W.S.G. 1969. Lost villages in south-west Carmarthenshire, *Inst. Brit. Geographers' Trans.*, 47, 191–203.

Thorn, C. and F. (eds) 1979. *Domesday Book, 10, Cornwall* (from a draft translation by O. Padel), Chichester.

Thornton, D.E. 1988. Brychan and Welsh Genealogy, unpublished M.A. thesis, Univ. Coll. North Wales, Bangor.

Thorpe, L. (ed. and trans.) 1974. *Gregory of Tours: The history of the Franks*, Harmondsworth.

Thorpe, L. (trans.) 1978. *Gerald of Wales: The Journey through Wales and the Description of Wales*, Harmondsworth.

Thurneysen, R. 1975. *A grammar of Old Irish*, rev. ed., Dublin.

Todd, J.H. and Reeves, W. (eds) 1864. *The Martyrology of Donegal: a calendar of the saints of Ireland*, Dublin.

Toft, L. 1989. The Sully coin hoard, *Siluria*, 2, 19–22.

Tomlin, E.W.F. 1982. *In search of St Piran*, Padstow.

Tomlin, R.S.O. 1975. A sub-Roman gravestone from Aberhydfer near Trecastle, Breconshire, *Archaeol. Cambrensis*, 124, 68–72.

Toynbee, J.M.C. 1971. *Death and burial in the Roman world*, London.

Trudgian, P. 1987. Excavation of a burial ground at St Endellion, Cornwall, *Cornish Archaeol.*, 26, 145–52.

Verey, D. 1976. *Gloucestershire, Vol. 2, The Vale and the Forest of Dean*, Buildings of England Series, Harmondsworth.

Victory, S. 1977. *The Celtic Church in Wales*, London.

Vincent, H.J. 1864. (Caerau), *Archaeol. Cambrensis*, 10, 299–301.

Vinogradoff, P. and Morgan, F. (eds) 1914. *The Survey of the Honour of Denbigh*, London.

Wade-Evans, A.W. 1910. Parochiale Wallicanum, *Y Cymmrodor*, 22, 22–113.

Wade-Evans, A.W. (ed.) 1944. *Vitae Sanctorum Britanniae et Genealogiae*, Cardiff.

Wailes, B. 1955–6. A late Dark Ages/Early Mediaeval site at Lanvean, St Mawgan-in-Pydar, *Proc. West Cornwall Field Club*, 1 (4), 141–4.

Wait, G.A. 1985. *Ritual and religion in Iron Age Britain*, 2 vols, Brit. Archaeol. Rep. 149, Oxford.

Walker, G.S.M. (ed.) 1957. *Sancti Columbani Opera*, Dublin.

Walls, C. 1984. *Interim report on excavations at Llanelen in 1983*, Pendragon Society information sheet.

Warner, R.B. 1976. Some observations on the context and importation of exotic material in Ireland, from the first century B.C. to the second century A.D., *Proc. Roy. Ir. Acad.*, 76C, 267–89.

Warner, R.B. 1988. The archaeology of early historic Irish kingship, in (eds S.T. Driscoll and M.R. Nieke) *Power and politics in early medieval Britain and Ireland*, 47–68, Edinburgh.

Warren, F.E. 1881. *The liturgy and ritual of the Celtic Church*, Oxford, (2nd ed. 1987).

Warrilow, W., Owen, G. and Britnell, W. 1986. Eight ring-ditches at Four Crosses, Llantysilio, Powys 1981–5, *Proc. Prehist. Soc.*, 52, 53–89.

Wasserschleben, H. 1885. *Die irische Kanonensammlung*, Leipzig.

Waterman, D.M. 1976. Banagher Church, County Derry, *Ulster J. Archaeol.*, 39, 25–41.

Watt, D.E.R. 1969. *Fasti Ecclesiae Scoticanae Medii Aevi Ad Annum 1638*, Second Draft, Scot. Record Soc., n.s.l., Edinburgh.

Watt, D.E.R. 1975. Ecclesiastical organisation c.1274, in (eds P. McNeill and R. Nicholson) *An historical atlas of Scotland, c.400–c.1600*, 35–6, 136, St Andrews.

Watts, D.J. 1988. Circular lead tanks and their significance for Romano-British Christianity, *Antiq. J.*, 68, 210–22.

Webb, J.F. (trans.) and Farmer, D.H. (ed.) 1983. *The age of Bede*, Harmondsworth.

Webster, L.E. and Cherry, J. 1977. Medieval Britain in 1976, *Medieval Archaeol.* 21, 204–62.

Wedderburn, L.M.M. and Grime, D. 1984. The cairn cemetery at Garbeg, Drumnadrochit, in eds J.G.P. Friell and W.G. Watson, 151–68.

Westwood, T.J. 1876–9. *Lapidarium Walliae*, Oxford.

Whimster, R. 1981. *Burial practices in Iron Age Britain c.700 B.C.-A.D.43*, Brit. Archaeol. Rep. 90, Oxford.

White, R.B. 1971–2. Excavations at Arfryn, Bodedern, long-cist cemeteries and the origins of Christianity in Britain, *Trans. Anglesey Antiq. Soc.*, 19–51.

White, R.B. 1983. In Tempore Justini Consulis? A minimal view of the date and purpose of Early Christian monuments in Wales, unpublished conference paper given at The archaeology of early medieval Wales conference, Gregynog.

White, S.I. 1981a. Excavations at Capel Eithin, Gaerwen, Anglesey, 1980: first interim report, *Trans. Anglesey Antiq. Soc.*, 15–27.

White, S.I. 1981b. Capel Eithin in eds S.M. Youngs and J. Clark, 186.

White, S.I. 1982. Capel Eithin, in eds S.M. Youngs and J. Clark, 226–7.

Whitelock, D. (ed.) 1955. *English historical documents, Vol. 1, c.500–1042*, London.

Whitelock, D., McKitterick, R. and Dumville, D. (eds) 1982. *Ireland in early mediaeval Europe*, Cambridge.

Wickham, C. 1985. Pastoralism and underdevelopment in the early middle ages, *Settimane di Studio del Centro Italiano di Studi sull'Alto Medioevo* (Spoleto), 31, 401–51.

William, A.R. (ed.) 1960. *Llyfr Iorwerth*, Cardiff.

Williams, Geo. 1985. *Fighting and farming in Iron Age west Wales: excavations at Llawhaden 1980–1984*, Dyfed Archaeological Trust.

Williams, Geo. 1988. Recent work on rural settlement in later prehistoric and early historic Dyfed, *Antiq. J.*, 68, 30–54.

Williams, Gl. 1962. *The Welsh Church, from Conquest to Reformation*, Cardiff.

Williams, H. (ed.) 1899–1901. *Gildas*, 2 vols, London.

Williams, I. 1927. Llyfr Ffortun Bangor, *Bull. Board Celtic Stud.*, 3, 90–119.

Williams, I. 1933–5. Maesaleg, Basaleg, *Bull. Board Celtic Stud.* 7, 277.

Williams, I. 1935. *Canu Llywarch Hen*, Cardiff.

Williams, I. 1945. *Enwau Lleoedd*, Liverpool.

Williams, I. 1980. Two poems from the Book of Taliesin, in (ed. R. Bromwich) *The beginnings of Welsh poetry. Studies by Sir Ifor Williams*, 155–80, 2nd ed., Cardiff.

Williams ab Ithel, J. (ed.) 1860. *Annales Cambriae*, Rolls Series, London.

Williams, R. (ed.) 1848. Pennant Melangell, Montgomeryshire, *Archaeol. Cambrensis* 3, 137–42.

Williams, R.T. 1877 *Nodion o Caergybi*, Conwy.

Williams, S.J. and Powell, J.E. (eds) 1961. *Cyfreithiau Hywel Dda yn ôl Llyfr Blegywryd*, Cardiff.

Williams, S.W. 1889. The Cistercian Abbey of Strata Florida, London.

Willis Bund, J.W. 1897. *The Celtic Church in Wales*, London.

Willmot, G.F. 1938. Three burial sites at Carbury, Co. Kildare, *J. Roy. Soc. Antiq. Ir.*, 68, 130–42.

Willmot, G.F. 1938–9. Two Bronze Age burials at Carrowbeg North, Belclare, Co. Galway, *J. Galway. Archaeol. Hist. Soc.*, 18, 121-40.

Winterbottom, M. (ed. and trans.) 1978. *Gildas, the Ruin of Britain and other works*, London and Chichester.

Wood, I.N. 1984. The end of Roman Britain: continental evidence and parallels, in eds M. Lapidge and D. Dumville, 1–25.

Wood, I.N. 1988. Forgery in Merovingian hagiography, in *Fälschungen im Mittelalter, Internationaler Kongress der Monumenta Germaniae Historica, München, 16–19 September 1986*, 5 vols, Vol. 5, 369–84, Hannover (=MGH Schriften, 33. v).

Wordsworth, J. 1982. St Mary's of the Rock, St Andrews, Fife, in eds S.M. Youngs and J. Clark, 219.

Wormald, P. 1978. Review of Victory 1977, *Medieval Archaeol.*, 22, 198–200.

Wright, R.P. and Jackson, K.H. 1968. A late inscription from Wroxeter, *Antiq. J.*, 148, 296–300.

Yates, W.N. 1973 The distribution and proportion of Celtic and non-Celtic church dedications in Wales, *J. Hist. Soc. Church Wales* 28, 5–17.

Youngs, S.M. and Clark, J. (eds) 1981. Medieval Britain in 1980, *Medieval Archaeol.* 25, 166–228.

Youngs, S.M. and Clark, J. (eds) 1982. Medieval Britain in 1981, *Medieval Archaeol.* 26, 164–227.

Index